ASSESSING

CHILDREN'S LANGUAGE

IN

NATURALISTIC CONTEXTS

third edition

NANCY J. LUND
State University College at Buffalo

JUDITH F. DUCHAN
State University of New York/Buffalo

Prentice Hall, Englewood Cliffs, New Jersey 07632

Library of Congress Cataloging-in-Publication Data

Lund, Nancy J.
    Assessing children's language in naturalistic contexts / Nancy J.
Lund, Judith F. Duchan.—3rd ed.
        p.   cm.
    Includes bibliographical references and index.
    ISBN 0-13-051905-7
    1. Language acquisition.   2. Language and languages—Ability
testing.   3. Communicative competence in children.   I. Duchan,
Judith F.   II. Title.
P118.L86   1992
401'.93—dc20   92-4411
                                                                    CIP

Acquisitions editor: Carol Wada
Editorial/production supervision and interior design: Serena Hoffman
Prepress buyer: Kelly Behr
Manufacturing buyer: Mary Ann Gloriande
Copy editor: Nancy Savio-Marcello
Cover design: Patricia Kelly
Cover art: Brian Bellow, age 4

Printed in the United States of America
10   9   8   7   6   5   4   3   2   1

ISBN 0-13-051905-7

PRENTICE-HALL INTERNATIONAL (UK) LIMITED, *London*
PRENTICE-HALL OF AUSTRALIA PTY. LIMITED, *Sydney*
PRENTICE-HALL CANADA INC., *Toronto*
PRENTICE-HALL HISPANOAMERICANA, S.A., *Mexico*
PRENTICE HALL OF INDIA PRIVATE LIMITED, *New Delhi*
PRENTICE-HALL OF JAPAN, INC., *Tokyo*
SIMON & SCHUSTER ASIA PTE. LTD., *Singapore*
EDITORA PRENTICE-HALL DO BRASIL, LTDA., *Rio de Janeiro*

We dedicate this book to our intellectual mothers,
those women scholars whose shoulders we stand on,
and to our biological mothers,
whose shoulders we have leaned on

Contents

Preface

This is the third edition of *Assessing Children's Language in Naturalistic Contexts*. It is not just an updated rendition of earlier versions but differs from them in two ways. First, it is expanded to include general procedures for assessing children from diverse cultures—those who are bilingual, bidialectical, bicultural. Second, this edition adopts a cognitive science perspective in which language users are seen as engaging in a creative process of constructing meanings beyond those offered by the words and sentences of the language. This mental models view is especially present in our treatment of discourse, where we develop an alternative to the popular text-based view, such as that proffered by Halliday and Hasan.

The aim of this edition, as in the earlier editions, is to aid the beginning student as well as the practicing clinician in evaluating the communication competence of young children. The assessment method is that of *structural analysis*, which involves finding patterns in children's behaviors. The method is also *naturalistic* in that it involves observing and collecting information from children as they engage in everyday events. Finally, in keeping with the *pragmatic* tradition in child language, we view language as being part and parcel of communication in situated contexts.

The approach differs from a diagnostic approach, whose aim is to determine whether a child is abnormal, and if so, to assign the child a diagnostic category. Our method does not focus on the differences between children with language disorders and their normal learning peers, but rather on what children know and how they perform in everyday contexts. For this reason we do not review the prolific literature on the group performance characteristics of children with language disorders.

We are close to celebrating the book's tenth birthday. We have seen radical changes in the field through those years, especially in the area of pragmatics and multicultural assessment procedures. The most recent changes are reflected in Chapter 8 on discourse, which includes sections on discourse coherence and discourse cohesion, and the infusion throughout the book of information about dialect speakers and bilingual children whose second language is English.

There are several ways to teach and learn from this book. The book's primary objective is to serve as a text in first- or second-level language courses that introduce students to normal language and language assessment in children. It is written as a guide for assessing communication between children and their conversational partners. For this purpose we recommend the book be read in the sequence presented. For those who are interested primarily in language acquisition for normal children, we recommend the following order for reading the chapters: Begin with Chapter 3, which covers fine tuning between mothers and their beginning language learners and event learning and intentionality as precursors to first words. This could be followed by the chapters on phonology (Chapter 4), morphology (Chapter 5), syntax (Chapter 6), and semantics (Chapter 7), which describe these facets of language and the acquisition of these linguistic structures. Chapter 8 on discourse would finish the sequence. The portions of each of these chapters dealing specifically with assessment procedures could be skipped over, if the focus is on understanding what children come to know about communication, rather than on how to assess their knowledge.

The book can also serve the experienced clinician as a reference for conducting detailed analyses of severely involved children. For that reason, we have included extensive information about each area of language, more than might be needed for someone new to language. For example, Chapter 6 on syntax includes subordinate predicate clauses, a structure which need not be covered in a beginning course on language assessment.

We hope this new edition will continue to be useful for both clinicians and students in training, as they engage in the exciting endeavor of determining what children from their own and from different cultures know about their language and how those children use that knowledge in their daily communication.

Nancy J. Lund
Judith F. Duchan

Overview
of Assessment Approaches

HISTORICAL REVIEW

Speech pathologists have been involved in the assessment of children's language since the 1950s. The intervening years have seen great diversity in the theory and practice of language assessment as changing views of the nature of language have spawned new procedures for sampling and describing language and for categorizing deviations from normal language.

The Decade of the 1950s   Two approaches to language assessment were developing at this time. The first, which we could call *normative*, was the approach taken by Johnson, Darley, and Spriestersbach in the first widely used book on diagnostic methods in "speech correction." Their book (1952) had no section on language disorders but rather had a brief discussion of measures such as mean sentence length in words, parts of speech used, sentence structure, and ratings of verbal output. Their emphasis was on how normal children at different ages performed on these measures. Normative research for these indices were referred to (e.g., McCarthy, 1930), but no data were presented. In a later text (1963), Johnson, Darley, and Spriestersbach included a whole chapter on language development and language disorders, reflecting the growth in the study of these topics. Normative data were included from the extensive study by Templin (1957), among others, thus making available to the diagnostician information on what is "normal" for children at different ages with regard to measures such as median number of one-word responses; percentage of responses classified as simple, compound, and complex sentences; mean percentage of parts of speech used; size of vocabulary; and mean structural complexity score, which was computed according to sentence completeness and complexity. The clinician was given no direction for using this information in assessing an individual child's language.

The contrasting approach to language assessment that emerged in the 1950s we will call a *pathology* approach. Based on a medical model, the goal of assessment was to identify the "disease" or underlying cause of the presenting symptoms. Disordered language was viewed as one of a cluster of symptoms that could lead the clinician to diagnosing the problem—that is, determining the etiology or cause. The presumption was that the condition thus identified explained the speech or language problem, and treatment efforts would be directed toward alleviating the condition rather than further examining the symptoms. The best example of, and most influential force behind, this approach was Myklebust's *Auditory Disorders in Children* (1954). In this work, Myklebust presented symptom clusters which are manifested in the conditions of deafness, mental retardation, brain damage or "aphasia," and emotional disturbance. Originally intended as a manual for differential diagnosis of nonverbal children for pediatricians, psychologists, and audiologists, this approach was readily adopted by speech pathologists, and along with it Myklebust's model of expressive, inner, and receptive language function. While Myklebust emphasized the importance of understanding complex language functioning in order to diagnose the type of disorder, he gave little direction to the clinician for identifying or understanding receptive, inner, or expressive language disorders.

The Decade of the 1960s This period brought new trends in language assessment for speech pathologists. The impact of an older, behavioristic movement in American psychology became apparent when the emphasis shifted from deviant language behavior as a symptom of an underlying disorder to a view that the disordered language itself was the problem. In this framework, language behavior, like all behavior, was seen as developing out of the interaction between the current behavior of the organism and the environmental antecedents and consequences of that behavior (Sloane and MacAulay, 1968). That is, language response was viewed as under the control of both stimulus and reinforcement. The discriminative stimulus, which is the situational condition under which a response will be followed by reinforcement, and the reinforcement, which can be any event that changes the frequency of the response it follows, thus became the focus of the *behavioral* approach to assessment (Schiefelbusch, 1963).

Changing the stimuli or reinforcement in the environment became the means for remediating language disorders. Growing out of B. F. Skinner's orientation, as presented in *Verbal Behavior* (1957), language behaviors, or responses, were often classified according to the conditions that prompted them. Responses that function as demands and requests were called *mands,* those that are controlled by a discriminative stimulus (naming, referring) were called *tacts,* and others were classified as being under the control of verbal stimuli (echoing, verbal associations, answering questions). With this approach, the actual response was generally not described, except insofar as necessary to classify it.

Osgood (1957) elaborated the stimulus-response-reinforcement framework of the radical behaviorists. Osgood's behavioristic model included mental associations which an organism can make to a stimulus. According to Osgood, internal associations, or *mediators,* are also in the form of stimuli and responses. He called them *response mediators* (r_m) and *stimulus mediators* (s_m). These internal associations sometimes led to overt responses and sometimes not. They accounted for some of the jumps in associations people made in their errors on verbal learning experiments. For example, Osgood's model accounted for subjects who answered "joy" instead of the correct word "glee" in an experiment by saying that the stimulus led to an internal, already-learned association between "joy" and "glee."

Kirk and McCarthy (1961) borrowed heavily from Osgood's conceptualization and used Osgood's model to design parts of their test, the *Illinois Test of Psycholinguistic Abilities* (*ITPA*). The test reflects a behavioristic orientation by virtue of its focus on the stimulus in some subtests (e.g., visual reception, auditory reception), its mediational subtests (visual association, auditory association), and its response subtests (verbal expression, manual expression).

The ITPA had a profound effect on the speech pathologist's view of language disorders. It became available at a time when clinicians were becoming aware of language disorders and frustrated by the lack of direction and assessment tools provided by the normative and pathology approaches. The test thus became widely used, and in the late 1960s and early 1970s it became an operational definition of language for many speech pathologists.

In addition to borrowing from Osgood's theory, Kirk and McCarthy have subtests of the ITPA which involve memory and closure. These tests reflect another historical trend, the *auditory processing* framework, which combines behaviorism and information processing theory. Auditory processing models began to emerge in the 1960s and are still prevalent (Lasky and Katz, 1983; Levinson and Sloan, 1980).

The auditory processing framework grew out of the behaviorism of the 1950s and 1960s. It presents the view that language processing begins with the stimulus and proceeds through various steps until it is stored in memory. While rooted in behavioristic sensibilities, it is more elaborate than the Skinner or Osgood formulations—it involves more than chainlike associations because it takes into account factors such as various memories, perceptual processes, and temporal ordering. The tendency toward more mentalistic, psychological constructs of auditory processing shows the influence of computer models of information processing over the last two decades (Fodor, Bever, and Garrett, 1974).

The general format for auditory processing conceptualizations is that information contained in the auditory stimulus proceeds through several encoding steps—it is first received, then perceived, then categorized into meanings, and then stored; and later it is retrieved for future processing. Thus the test batteries or specific tests have been designed to test children's auditory processing abilities—such as speech-sound discrimination, auditory memory, sequencing, figure-ground discrimination, and auditory closure (Goldman, Fristoe, and Woodcock, 1974).

There are at least two varieties of auditory processing models. One leans more toward a behavioristic framework and treats auditory processing as a set of processing skills which are applied similarly to all types of auditory information (Eisenson, 1972). Another has a more mentalistic focus and regards speech perception as something different from other types of processing, something requiring special innate mechanisms (Sanders, 1977). Both frameworks emphasize processing over rule knowledge or content, both see reception of the language as primary and fundamental to language learning, and both emphasize modalities or channels as significant in learning. They are what might be characterized as "getting-information-in-and-out" models and differ from models such as those developed by linguists that focus on information content rather than on the transmission of information from one person to another.

We can trace our history of linguistic approaches to assessment as also originating during the early 1960s when several important studies were done by psychologists examining children's acquisition of syntax. Using analytic techniques and terminology of descriptive linguists, researchers in child language began to formulate grammars or rules that both described and attempted to explain child language. From around the country came reports of investigations of normal children, all confirming that child language is not merely an inaccurate or incomplete version of adult language, but a unique system governed by its own rules (Ferguson and Slobin, 1973). The rules are characterized as making up the child's competence in the various levels of language: phonology, morphology, syntax, and semantics.

Late in the 1960s A new sense of the importance of studying child language was felt because of issues that were being debated in linguistics and philosophy (Steinberg and Jakobovits, 1971). Noam Chomsky, a linguist, had forwarded a theory of language that differentiated a surface from an underlying structure. His theory of syntax (Chomsky, 1957) proposed that the phrase structure that makes up the sentences we hear can be derived from a more abstract underlying structure through a series of changes governed by algebra-like rules. These rules, or transformations, convert underlying abstract phrase structures to their surface manifestations.

If Chomsky's theory of syntax worked to account for such linguistic phenomena as ambiguous sentences and paraphrases, maybe it is a process speakers and listeners actually go through when they speak and understand sentences. This debate about whether Chomsky's linguistic theory is psychologically real was one that created much activity and literature during the late 1960s and produced a new branch of psychology—psycholinguistics. Of most apparent concern was the problem of how people come to know the abstract structure of sentences, since it is not obvious in the sentences they hear; and listeners, according to the theory, cannot understand those sentences without already knowing the abstract structure.

Chomsky's resolution to the paradox was a radical one. He proposed that children are born with knowledge of the underlying structure and that they learn how the deep structures apply to particular surface structures in the course of their exposure to language. Chomsky's nativist theory contrasted sharply with the empiricist and behaviorist notions that language is learned only through experience.

Those who subscribed to the nativistic or innate position looked for evidence from children's language development to support their view. They took as evidence children's common stages of language learning found across cultures and the structures children had in common within each of those stages (Lenneberg, 1967). That is to say, if children in China go through similar stages in learning to speak Chinese as children in England do to speak English, it would follow that they do so from their biologically inherited knowledge of deep structure. If common stages exist in the development of the embryo, why not for the same organism after birth? Empiricists, on the other hand, pointed to differences in children's language learning in different cultures to support the importance of environmental influences and looked for more simple ways to account for Chomsky's abstract structure (Braine, 1976).

The result of the debate and of the linguistic approach for speech and language pathologists has been to look at children's abnormal language in terms of its syntactic structure. Under this *syntax approach,* we confine our explorations to surface structure patterns, not following Chomsky's emphasis on searching for more abstract origins of surface patterns (Duchan, 1983a). Linguistic analyses of children's phonology, morphology, and syntax have led us away from the behavioristic way of thinking about children's language to a more mentalistic approach. That is, we are no longer talking about language as made up of responses pulled from a response repertoire. We now talk about linguistic rules which children and adults use to understand and produce language.

The 1970s This brings us to the next period in the emergence of language assessment procedures which has come to be called the *semantic emphasis* and which emerged in the 1970s. It resulted again from a shift in emphasis in linguistics, but this time generative semanticists formed a renegade group within Chomsky's generative theory camp and argued that Chomsky's emphasis was too much on syntax and not enough on semantics (Lakoff, 1971; McCawley, 1971). The semantic emphasis had its predecessors (Fillmore, 1968), but the focus did not develop a following or have an influence in psychology until around 1975 (Palermo, 1978).

The generative semanticists tried to derive a model for the meanings of words, phrases, and sentences and understandably became heavily involved in philosophical issues and in the differences between language meaning and meanings for things in the world in general. For those studying child language, the emphasis on meaning led to questions about the conceptual bases of first words and two-word combinations (Clark, 1977; Nelson, 1974; Rosch, 1973). Whereas Chomsky's syntactic emphasis led to postulation that words and word phrases derived from deep structure phrases (Bloom, 1970), the semantic emphasis allowed a deep structure that was meaning based, such as having semantic cases (Antinucci and Parisi, 1973), semantic relations (Brown, 1973), semantic features (Clark, 1977), or conceptual prototypes (Rosch, 1973). Thus we find new assessment approaches in language pathology emerging from the cognitive approaches in linguistics which examine children's language for its semantic content and its cognitive base (MacDonald, 1978; McLean and Snyder-McLean, 1978).

In this same time period, in part as a result of the focus on semantics, there was a renewed interest in Piaget's cognitive theory, leading to a *cognitive emphasis* in assessment. Attempts were made to tie the stages which Piaget discovered in cognitive development to those in language development. The sensorimotor period of development, from birth to two years, drew the most attention, and researchers and clinicians attempted to identify which sensori-motor understandings were precursors to language learning during this early period of life in normal children (e.g., Miller and others, 1980; Bates, 1979). The assessment focus became one which asked whether the language-impaired child had the necessary prerequisite cognitive knowledge for language learning.

This type of assessment can be used with nonverbal children who cannot be assessed by procedures built on linguistic structural models. Those models work only if the child is already using language.

In sum, we find new approaches in assessment emerging in the 1970s that focus on examining children's language for its semantic content and its cognitive base. Assessment approaches with semantic emphases focus on the meaning expressed as utterances are produced. The cognitive approach to assessment stresses the experiences and concepts that are presumed to be prerequisite to the emergence of language.

This concern in the 1970s about meanings of words, phrases, and sentences led to the realization that sentences derive their meanings from the contexts in which they occur. The same word or sentence means something different on different occasions. This realization then led to a move away from thinking about language knowledge as a fixed set of meanings as listed in a dictionary to an examination of how context influences meaning and how language functions differently for speakers at different times. This contextual influence is the study of language from a *pragmatics perspective* and has come to be the most recent movement in linguistics and psychology, and one that has resulted in a radical change in how speech-language pathologists carry out language assessment. In short it has created what has been referred to as the "pragmatics revolution" (Duchan, 1983b).

The assessment approach in the early stages of the pragmatics revolution was borrowed from philosophers of "speech acts" (Searle, 1969; Austin, 1962). The focus of speech act theorists was on the speaker's use of the utterance for purposes of achieving an intent. The 1970s saw the first of many studies where psychologists and linguists discovered the intents expressed by normal language learners and the stages through which normal children progress as they become better at expressing intents (Dore, 1979; Ervin-Tripp, 1977; Bates, 1976; Halliday, 1975). Language pathologists reasoned that if normal children expressed a given set of intents at different stages in their development, we need to find out whether language-impaired children also express them (Chapman, 1981; Bloom and Lahey, 1978). Language-impaired children were evaluated to determine whether or not they expressed intents such as requests for actions, greetings, or acknowledgments. Assessment procedures involved imputing intentions to children by looking at the form of the act as well as its result. So, if the language pathologist sees the child reach toward an object and an adult hand it over, the act is said to function as a request for an object. Assessment of intents might be called the *speech act approach*.

The 1980s This period brought with it another contextual perspective which was to be placed under the pragmatics umbrella—the context of the interaction. Assessment approaches which had been focused on children and their language performance were widened in the 1980s to include various aspects of the interaction: the ways interactants cooperated in conversation, especially with regard to turn taking; the ways they performed activities together; and the effect of the language style of the interactants on children's language learning. Our approaches to interaction assessment have been borrowed from our sister disciplines in the social sciences. The conversational analysts in sociology gave us insights into how to analyze conversations (Sacks, Schegloff, and Jefferson, 1974), the psychologists studying early mother–child routines brought us to procedures for analyzing interactions during everyday events (Bruner, 1975), and the psycholinguists studying the effects of language input on normal children's language acquisition offered us an approach to assessing adult input to language-impaired children (Ferguson and Snow, 1977). We identify this as the *interactional approach.*

A second perspective to emerge in the 1980s was one which examined language in terms of its event context. Bruner's work (1975) on routine events during the child's first year of life was extended by Nelson (1981) to the study of children's acquisition of event knowledge at three years. She dubbed this form of knowledge "scripts," a term first used by Schank and Abelson (1977) in relation to adult knowledge needed to carry out common everyday events. Nelson and Gruendel (1981) have argued that knowledge of scripts is needed for children to develop from single-sentence discourse to discourse involving longer stretches of language such as that needed for event descriptions (Duchan, 1986, 1991). We will be calling this focus in pragmatics the *event focus approach.*

The 1990s The pragmatics focus has continued into the 1990s with an expansion of methods for assessing children's knowledge of different types of discourse. The most emphasized areas of *discourse analyses* have been conversations and stories (e.g., Brinton and Fujiki, 1989; Roth and Spekman, 1986; Liles, 1985); a third, less emphasized area has been event descriptions (Duchan, 1991); and a fourth area just coming to the fore is expository (Westby, 1989).

The 1990s have also brought the realization of how assessment methods developed over the last forty years have been embedded in the language and culture of white, middle-class, standard-English-speaking America. Attempts to eliminate the cultural bias of our earlier assessment approaches has led to new approaches that are more culturally sensitive to children from different cultural groups who speak nonstandard dialects of English or who are bilingual. The most exciting of these new approaches is one that borrows the *ethnographic methods* developed by anthropologists studying exotic cultures and uses them to develop assessment approaches compatible with the child's understanding of his or her home culture and language (Westby and Erickson, in press; Kovarsky and Crago, 1991; Crago and Cole, 1991; Damico, Maxwell, and Kovarsky, 1990).

It can be seen from this historical account that divergent views of language and language pathology have evolved from a variety of sources. Trying to assimilate all of these orientations into a cohesive model from which to view assessment and intervention is at best difficult for at least two reasons. First, these orientations reflect different theoretical conceptions of language and use categories of observations that are relevant only within a particular theoretical orientation. The second difficulty is that when we attempt to make comparisons about the efficacy of the various theoretical views, we find that they direct us to different diagnostic questions. The normative approach asks questions about normalcy; the pathology approach about etiology; whereas the behavioral, ITPA, syntax, semantic, cognitive, pragmatics, discourse, and ethnographic approaches direct us toward a description or explanation of the problem.

It is important to realize that the clinical observations we make reflect someone's view of language—that is, the categories we use in our observation are deemed relevant because they derive from a theoretical conception of language. Assessment tools and techniques that are available have evolved out of the different approaches we have discussed and thus reflect the diverse views of language. Clinicians should be aware of these differences and realize that using a test or therapy kit also involves adopting the author's view of language.

In sum, we have briefly traced some stages in the history of language pathology. The main point we have been making is that language assessment occurs in a theoretical and practical context, and it is the context that determines our approaches. The periods and dates in our development, like stages and ages in children's development, are somewhat arbitrarily drawn but are roughly as follows:

1950s	The normative approach
	The pathology approach
1960s	The behaviorist approach
	The auditory processing approach
	The ITPA approach
	The syntax approach
1970s	The semantic approach
	The cognitive approach
	The speech act approach
1980s	The interactional approach
	The event focus approach
1990s	The discourse approach
	The ethnographic approach

ASSESSMENT QUESTIONS

Selection of language assessment instruments should be guided by the assessment questions we are asking. Different questions call for the selection of different tools. All too often this process is reversed—a test is administered because it is available, and then the clinician finds that the test has revealed no new or useful information because it was designed to answer questions other than those of interest. Let us turn to the questions typically asked in language assessment, which we can now recognize as related to our outline of historical development.

Does This Child Have a Language Problem?

This question is generally answered with reference to deviation from average performance of a group so it is best handled with the normative approach. In some cases our initial observation of a child leads us to make the judgment of language disorder because the language displayed is below or different from our impression of what is "normal" for a child of this age. Our knowledge of normal development and our interactions with normally developing children lead us to certain expectations that serve as our standard of normal, against which we compare the particular child.

For more "objective" bases for comparison, there are numerous scales of normal development available, along with data collected by McCarthy (1930), Templin (1957), and many others on normal children. With these data, it is possible for the clinician to compare a child to others of the same age or to obtain an age-equivalence for a particular child. It remains the clinician's judgment how much deviation from the average is considered allowable. If, for example, the clinician finds that the mean length of response (MLR) (in words) for three-year-olds is 4.1 and the three-year-old in question has an MLR of 3.5, should the child be considered deviant? The answer is largely a matter of clinical judgment, although there are some guidelines which can be followed (see Chapter 9, Tools of Assessment).

There are now many language tests available that have been "standardized" on normal children, so the performance of a particular child can be compared to that of normally developing children taking the same test. Again, the child can be compared to other children of the same chronological age, or an age-equivalency can be determined for his or her language skill. Some tests have "cutoff" scores, or guidelines for the amount of deviation from the average that would indicate a language disorder. Others simply present the data on normal children and leave it to the clinician to decide what constitutes a disorder. Thus, most tests or norm-referenced measures do not lead to a simple yes or no in answer to the question of normalcy but rather lead to descriptions such as the following: below the 10th percentile; 18 months delay; below average; age-equivalent of $4\frac{1}{2}$ years.

What Is Causing the Problem?

Attempts to answer this question can take several forms. We may attempt to diagnose an underlying physical or psychological problem through assessment of nonlanguage functions, such as hearing acuity, neurological functions, motor performance, or intelligence. We may rely on the reports of other professionals to give us some of this information. The case history is another tool that is used in identifying possible causes of a language problem. Following the pathology approach, attempts are made to identify clusters of symptoms that are associated with various underlying conditions. For example, a history of a difficult birth, high fevers, or convulsions would lead one to suspect the presence of brain damage. Likewise, a history of uniformly delayed motor and social development along with language development would point to mental retardation.

Children often come to the speech-language pathologist with a diagnostic label such as aphasic, autistic, or mentally retarded already assigned them. Occasionally the language evaluation may be part of the assessment procedure designed to arrive at such a label. However, there has been a trend in speech pathology away from engaging in this type of categorical diagnosis, since some of the etiological categories are questionable (e.g., minimal brain damage) and because such diagnostic labels often negatively affect the child. There has also been increased professional specialization since the early publication of Myklebust (1954), and it is often regarded as inappropriate for a speech-language pathologist to make a diagnosis such as autism or emotional disturbance (see

Sanders, 1972). This professional territoriality has been a matter with no general agreement, and some authors argue for the speech-language pathologist as diagnostician (e.g., Darley, 1978; Nation and Aram, 1977).

In addition to the classic differential diagnostic labels, there are a variety of comments, such as "forceps delivery," "single-parent family," "tension in the home," and "maternal overprotection" in diagnostic reports, which carry the implication that there is, in fact, some sort of causal relationship between these conditions and the child's language. In some cases, terms originally used to describe an aspect of the child's behavior or environment have come to be used as diagnostic labels; so we find it has become increasingly common to see a diagnosis of "hyperactivity" or "cultural deprivation" with the implication that these are etiological categories.

Any inference about the cause of a language disorder must be made with caution. If a mentally retarded child has a language problem, we cannot assume that the retardation is causing the problem, since there are retarded children who do not have such problems. We must be even more careful not to imply a causal relationship between the language problem and some behavioral or social description of the child, unless we have appropriate supporting evidence. Most of the time we do not know the cause of a child's language learning problem. Further, knowing the cause is often not very helpful in planning remediation, unless it is a condition that can be changed, since therapy techniques generally do not vary significantly depending on underlying etiology. We must often be prepared to acknowledge that we do not know what is causing the problem and proceed with more productive aspects of assessment.

What Are the Areas of Deficit?

This question is directed to a description of the language problem. The behaviorist model, the ITPA model, the auditory processing model, and the various linguistic models can all be used to answer this question, but the description arrived at by each will be different because each defines the areas of language differently. Using a behavioristic model, categories of behaviors, such as mands and tacts or questions, statements, and commands, could be described according to the rate or frequency of occurrence. Deviations from adult language might be explained by constructs such as "stimulus overselectivity" or "response overgeneralization." Generally, with a behaviorist orientation, the primary focus is on changes that occur over time or under different conditions, with behaviors being quantified to make these comparisons.

Using the ITPA model, problems would be categorized in terms of the subtests, such as "visual association problem" or "auditory closure problem." It is not always clear whether some of the deficits identified by the ITPA are meant as descriptions or causes of language problems. For example, the auditory sequential memory subtest consists of strings of unrelated digits. If an individual is found to have a poor memory for digits, do we consider this to be a language problem, or do we instead infer that the poor memory is causing an independently identified language problem? Some of the ITPA subtests seem to be directed more to identifying the cause than to describing the language problem, but this distinction is not made by the test. It is left to the individual clinician to decide how to interpret these areas of deficit once they have been identified.

Auditory processing models would cast areas of deficit into the various processes through which the listener is seen as progressing on the way to decoding information contained in the auditory signal. Separate areas would be evaluated, such as auditory discrimination, auditory memory span, auditory closure, and auditory sequencing.

The linguistic model would lead to the identification of problems within the various linguistic levels, such as "phonological problems" (which might include "articulation disorder") or "morphological problems." As with the ITPA model, distinctions between "receptive" and "expressive" deficits might be identified.

It is more difficult to identify areas of semantic deficit, since there is not a comprehensive framework which covers various areas of semantics. Descriptions of semantic problems within each model do not relate to each other as parts of the same whole as the elements in phonology, morphology, and syntax do. There are several semantic models that would lead us to identify different areas of deficit. If we work from a model of lexical meaning, we could identify deficits within conceptual areas or word classes, such as confusion on nouns; or alternatively classify types of deviations, such as word deficits or overextensions. If we work from a model of relational meaning, there are several classification systems that would lead to identification of deficit areas consistent with the relational taxonomy. For example, a model built around semantic relations would identify the absence of particular relations, such as possession or attribution (Bloom and Lahey, 1978); whereas a model which views semantic cases as the deep structure of language would identify categories, such as agent or experiencer (Miller, 1981).

Language clinicians have used Piaget's rendition of cognitive areas during the sensorimotor period to examine cognitive performance, and thus they test for children's sensorimotor knowledge of object permanence, means–ends distinctions, causality, relation of objects in space, imitation, and development of schemes in relation to objects (e.g., Miller and others, 1980). These cognitive assessments are used to compare children's cognitive performance to that of normal children and thereby identify cognitive deficits. They are also used to see if children have the cognitive competence to learn language.

Finally, the influence of pragmatics on language assessment has just begun to be recognized. Pragmatics, like the other areas of assessment, is influenced by the discoveries in the developmental literature. The areas of pragmatic deficit are even less well defined than those in semantics because the theoretical framework for pragmatics is not cohesive. Thus, deficits are studied and described separately. Children, for example, are said to have problems in areas of turn taking, functions, or use of deictic terms.

•　•　•

After addressing these three assessment questions, clinicians are confronted with a question that is really uppermost in their minds: What should I do in therapy? Knowing that a child is mentally retarded, below the 10th percentile on a standardized test, and has morphology problems is of little use when it is time to begin therapy. We suggest that none of the approaches to assessment discussed thus far will bring the clinician to the point of describing the child's language problem in sufficient detail to plan individual remediation.

This planning requires careful observation to determine what the child is attempting and the specific problems the child is having. Such observation leads to recognition of patterns that may appear to be "inconsistencies" until we find that the child performs differently in differing contexts.

This awareness of contextual influences is very important to planning and assessing therapy for a number of reasons. First, we cannot assume that knowledge of any language structure is all or nothing—that is, we cannot assume that if children display the structure in one instance (such as on a test), they "know" it in all contexts; or conversely that if they do not display it appropriately in our sample, they do not know it at all. More typically a child will be correct in some contexts and incorrect in others.

Second, to establish meaningful goals for the child, we need to know the discrepancies between what the child is intending to communicate and what is actually being communicated. Also, we need to know the favorable and unfavorable circumstances for expressing intended messages. Recognizing these patterns, we can plan therapy to provide facilitating contexts. Third, in judging the efficacy of our therapy, we must be aware that varying language behaviors are displayed in different contexts. Children's language is often different in the therapy interaction, and we should not unduly emphasize performance only in this narrow framework. Before we can decide on a direction in therapy, we need to answer our fourth assessment question, which addresses the quest for patterns.

What Are the Regularities in the Child's Language Performance?

Inasmuch as the previously discussed approaches to language assessment cannot answer this question, we propose that assessment be done through the technique of *structural analysis*. Structural analysis involves examining the patterns exhibited by the child and the interactant, determining areas of strength and deficit, and looking for contextual factors that account for the child showing more proficiency in some situations than in others. For example, a child who seems to use the *-ed* suffix inconsistently might be seen to incorrectly omit it when an ongoing action is interrupted and use it correctly when an event is finished. The child appears to interpret past tense as an indication of completed activity and is perfectly consistent from this point of view. Using the structural approach, the clinician can design therapy to fit the way the child thinks about language and the world and focus on the elements that will help the child understand the concepts behind different kinds of expressions.

The techniques of structural analysis, when first devised, treated structures as fixed entities which were invariant and highly predictable. Thus the regularities that were discovered tended to be those which occurred across all contexts, such as a /w/ for /r/ substitution in phonology. Structural analysts have found, however, that many language structures are influenced by context, and the technique now includes looking across contexts to determine the influencing factors. Such factors include the event or activity, the familiarity of the interactive partners, the purpose of the interaction, the length of the utterances, or the child's role within the event.

The structural analyst typically examines contexts for sampling and subsequent analysis that entail features of the child's life situations outside of the clinical setting. That is, sampling occurs while the child is engaged in commonly occurring events such as conversations or play, and with those people that the child most frequently communicates with, such as parents or teachers. The sampling may be done in situations outside of the therapy room or may be part of a more traditional assessment by creating or recreating naturally occurring events within the context of the clinic. The child's performance in these events can be contrasted with results obtained on tests or other measures to determine contextual influences.

When doing structural analysis, we attempt to take the child's point of view and ask ourselves why the child does or says the things that deviate from adult standards. We try to determine how the behavior in question fits with the child's language knowledge system or sense of the world and how the behavior might function for the child on the occasions under analysis. For example, through structural analysis we might find that a child always answers yes–no questions with an affirmative nod in an apparent attempt to be interactive rather than as an indication of affirmation.

What Is Recommended for This Child?

Through structural analysis we can identify what is being attempted by the child, what is being accomplished, and what conditions promote or impede success. Results of the analyses offer many suggested directions for therapy. Efforts may be made to help the child achieve his or her communicative goals by improving on the means used for attaining the goals (e.g., improving pronunciation or sentence structure), as well as by helping the interactant better respond to the child's communicative attempts (e.g., working on a teacher's fine tuning). Clinicians might also focus on creating contexts which facilitate the child's success as well as enhance the child's learning (e.g., structured versus unstructured events). The intervention goals and the intervention approaches can and should be designed on the basis of the findings from the structural analysis.

Structural analysis is an ongoing assessment approach. It does not stop when therapy begins. Rather it is a way of observing and thinking that leaves the observer always searching for new patterns and ready to change hypotheses and approaches when the child's performance so indicates. It makes every interaction with a child a part of the ongoing assessment of language and communication.

• • •

Of the five questions presented, those concerning regularities and recommendations are generally the most relevant for practicing clinicians who are involved in intervention. The body of this book discusses how to find the regularities that help us help children become better communicators. We begin in Chapter 2 by describing in greater detail the goals and techniques of structural analysis.

REFERENCES

ANTINUCCI F., AND D. PARISI. Early Language Acquisition: A Model and Some Data, in *Studies of Child Language Development*, eds. C. Ferguson and D. Slobin. New York: Holt, Rinehart & Winston, 1973.

AUSTIN, J. *How to Do Things with Words*. Oxford, England: Oxford University Press, 1962.

BATES, E. *Language and Context: The Acquisition of Pragmatics*. New York: Academic Press, 1976.

BATES, E. *The Emergence of Symbols*. New York: Academic Press, 1979.

BLOOM, L. *Language Development: Form and Function in Emerging Grammars*. Cambridge, Mass.: M.I.T. Press, 1970.

BLOOM, L., AND M. LAHEY. *Language Development and Language Disorders*. New York: John Wiley, 1978.

BRAINE, M. D. S. Children's First Word Combinations, *Monographs of the Society for Research in Child Development*, 41, 1976 (serial no. 164).

BRINTON, B., AND M. FUJIKI. *Conversational Management with Language-Impaired Children*. Rockville, Md.: Aspen Publishers, 1989.

BROWN, R. *A First Language*. Cambridge, Mass.: Harvard University Press, 1973.

BRUNER, J. The Ontogenesis of Speech Acts, *Journal of Child Language*, 2, 1975, 1–19.

CHAPMAN, R. Mother–Child Interaction in the Second Year of Life: Its Role in Language Development, in *Early Language: Acquisition and Intervention*, eds. R. Schiefelbusch and D. Bricker. Baltimore: University Park Press, 1981.

CHOMSKY, N. *Syntactic Structures*. The Hague: Mouton, 1957.

CLARK, E. Strategies and the Mapping Problem in First Language Acquisition, in *Language Learning and Thought*, ed. J. Macnamara. New York: Academic Press, 1977, 147–68.

CRAGO, M., AND E. COLE. Using Ethnography to Bring Children's Communicative and Cultural Worlds into Focus, in *Pragmatics of Language: Clinical Practice Issues*, ed. T. Gallagher. San Diego, Calif.: Singular Publishing, 1991, pp. 99–131.

DAMICO, J., M. MAXWELL, AND D. KOVARSKY, eds. Ethonographic Inquiries into Communication Sciences and Disorders. *Journal of Childhood Communication Disorders*, Vol. 13, 1990.

DARLEY, F. A Philosophy of Appraisal and Diagnosis, in *Diagnostic Methods in Speech Pathology*, 2nd ed., eds. F. Darley and D. C. Spriestersbach, New York: Harper & Row, 1978.

DORE, J. Conversational and Preschool Language Development, in *Language Acquisition*, eds. P. Fletcher and M. Garman. Cambridge, England: Cambridge University Press, 1979, p. 337–62.

DUCHAN, J. Elephants Are Soft and Mushy: Problems in Assessing Children's Language, in *Speech Language and Hearing*, eds. N. Lass, L. McReynolds, J. Northern, and D. Yoder. Philadelphia: Saunders, 1983a.

DUCHAN, J. Recent Advances in Language Assessment: The Pragmatics Revolution, in *Recent Advances in Language Sciences*, ed. R. Naremore. San Diego, Calif.: College Hill Press, 1983b, 147–180.

DUCHAN, J. Language Intervention Through Sensemaking and Fine Tuning, In *Language Competence: Assessment and Intervention*, ed. R. Schiefelbusch. San Diego, Calif.: College Hill Press, 1986, pp. 187–212.

DUCHAN, J. Everyday Events: Their Role in Language Assessment and Intervention, in *Pragmatics of Language: Clinical Practice Issues*, ed. T. Gallagher. San Diego, Calif.: Singular Publishing, 1991, pp. 43–98.

EISENSON, J. *Aphasia in Children*. New York: Harper & Row, 1972.

ERVIN-TRIPP, S. Wait for Me Roller-Skate, in *Child Discourse*, eds. S. Ervin-Tripp and C. Mitchel-Kernan. New York: Academic Press, 1977.

FERGUSON, C., AND D. SLOBIN, eds. *Studies of Child Language Development*. New York: Holt, Rinehart & Winston, 1973.

FERGUSON, C., AND C. SNOW, eds. *Talking to Children*. Cambridge, England: Cambridge University Press, 1977.

FILLMORE, C. The Case for Case, in *Universals in Linguistic Theory*, eds. E. Bach and R. Harms, New York: Holt, Rinehart & Winston, 1968.

FODOR, J., T. BEVER, AND M. GARRETT. *The Psychology of Language*. New York: McGraw-Hill, 1974.

GOLDMAN, R., M. FRISTOE, AND R. WOODCOCK. *Goldman, Fristoe, Woodcock Auditory Skills Battery*. Circle Pines, Minn.: American Guidance Service, 1974.

HALLIDAY, M. A. K. *Learning How to Mean: Explorations in the Development of Language*. London: Edward Arnold, 1975.

JOHNSON, W., F. DARLEY, AND D. C. SPRIESTERSBACH. *Diagnostic Manual in Speech Correction*. New York: Harper & Row, 1952.

JOHNSON, W., F. DARLEY, AND D. C. SPRIESTERSBACH. *Diagnostic Methods in Speech Pathology*. New York: Harper & Row, 1963.

KIRK, S., AND J. MCCARTHY. *Illinois Test of Psycholinguistic Abilities*. Urbana, Ill.: University of Illinois Press, 1961.

KIRK, S., J. MCCARTHY, AND W. KIRK. *Illinois Test of Psycholinguistic Abilities*. Urbana, Ill.: University of Illinois Press, 1968.

KOVARSKY, D., AND M. CRAGO. Toward an Ethnography of Communication Disorders, *Journal of the National Students of Speech-Language and Hearing Association*, 1991, 44–55.

LAKOFF, G. On Generative Semantics, in *Semantics: An Interdisciplinary Reader in Philosophy, Linguistics and Psychology*, eds. D. Steinberg and L. Jakobovits. London: Cambridge University Press, 1971.

LASKY, E., AND J. KATZ, eds. *Central Auditory Disorders: Problems of Speech Language and Learning*. Baltimore: University Park Press, 1983.

LENNEBERG, E. *Biological Foundations of Language*. New York: John Wiley, 1967.

LEVINSON, P., AND C. SLOAN, eds. *Auditory Processing and Language*. New York: Grune & Stratton, 1980.

LILES, B. Production and Comprehension of Narrative Discourse in Normal and Language-Disordered Children, *Journal of Communication Disorders*, 18, 1985, 409–27.

MACDONALD, J. *Environmental Language Inventory*. Columbus, Ohio: Chas. E. Merrill, 1978.

MCCARTHY, D. *The Language Development of the Pre-School Child*. Minneapolis: University of Minnesota Press, 1930.

MCCAWLEY, J. Where Do Noun Phrases Come From? in *Semantics: An Interdisciplinary Reader in Philosophy, Linguistics and Psychology*, eds. S. Steinberg and L. Jakobovits. London: Cambridge University Press, 1971.

MCLEAN, J., AND L. SNYDER-MCLEAN. *A Transactional Approach to Early Language Training*. Columbus, Ohio: Chas. E. Merrill, 1978.

MILLER, J. *Assessing Language Production in Children*. Baltimore: University Park Press, 1981.

MILLER, J., R. CHAPMAN, M. BRANSTON, AND J. REICHLE. Language Comprehension in Sensorimotor States V and VI, *Journal of Speech and Hearing Research*, 23: 1980, 284–311.

MYKLEBUST, H. R. *Auditory Disorders in Children: A Manual for Differential Diagnosis*. New York: Grune & Stratton, 1954.

NATION, J., AND D. ARAM. *Diagnosis of Speech and Language Disorders*. St. Louis, Mo.: C. V. Mosby, 1977.

NELSON, K. Concept, Word and Sentence: Interrelations in Acquisition and Development, *Psychological Review*, 81:1974, 267–85.

NELSON, K. Social Cognition in a Script Framework, in *Social Cognitive Development: Frontier and Possible Futures*, eds. J. Flavell and L. Ross. New York: Cambridge University Press, 1981.

NELSON, K., AND J. GRUENDEL. Generalized Event Representations: Basic Building Blocks of Cognitive Development, in *Advances in Developmental Psychology*, eds. M. Lamb and A. Brown. Hillsdale, N.J.: Lawrence Erlbaum, 1981.

OSGOOD, C. A Behavioristic Analysis of Perception and Language as Cognitive Phenomena, in *Contemporary Approaches to Cognition*. Cambridge, Mass.: Harvard University Press, 1957.

PALERMO, D. *Psychology of Language*. Glenview, Ill.: Scott, Foresman, 1978.

ROSCH, E. On the Internal Structure of Perceptual and Semantic Categories, in *Cognitive Development and the Acquisition of Language*, ed. T. Moore. New York: Academic Press, 1973.

ROTH, F., AND N. SPEKMAN. Narrative Discourse: Spontaneously Generated Stories of Learning-Disabled and Normally Achieving Students, *Journal of Speech and Hearing Disorders*, 51, 1986, 8–23.

SACKS, H., E. SHEGLOFF, AND G. JEFFERSON. A Simplest Systematics for the Organization of Turn-Taking for Conversation, *Language*, 50, 1974, 696–735.

SANDERS, D. *Auditory Perception of Speech*, Englewood Cliffs, N. J.: Prentice-Hall, 1977.

SANDERS, L. *Evaluation of Speech and Language Disorders in Children*. Danville, Ill.: Interstate Printers and Publishers, 1972.

SCHANK, R., AND R. ABELSON. *Scripts, Plans, Goals, and Understanding*. Hillsdale, N.J.: Lawrence Erlbaum, 1977.

SCHIEFELBUSCH, R. Language Studies of Mentally Retarded Children, *Journal of Speech and Hearing Disorders*, Monograph Supplement, 10, 1963, 4.

SEARLE, J. *Speech Acts*. Cambridge, England: Cambridge University Press, 1969.

SKINNER, B. F. *Verbal Behavior*. Englewood Cliffs, N.J.: Prentice-Hall, 1957.

SLOANE, H. N., AND B. MACAULAY. *Operant Procedures in Remedial Speech and Language Training*. Boston: Houghton Mifflin, 1968.

STEINBERG, S., AND L. JAKOBOVITS, eds. *Semantics: An Interdisciplinary Reader in Philosophy, Linguistics and Psychology*. New York: Cambridge University Press, 1971.

TEMPLIN, M. C. Certain Language Skills in Children: Their Development and Interrelationships, *Child Welfare Monographs*, no. 26. Minneapolis: University of Minnesota Press, 1957.

WESTBY, C. Assessing and Remediating Text Comprehension Problems, in *Reading Disabilities: A Developmental Language Perspective*, eds. A. Kamhi and H. Catts. Boston, Mass.: Little, Brown, 1989.

WESTBY, C. AND J. ERICKSON. *Topics in Language Disorders*. (in press).

2

A Framework
for Assessment

During the normative period of assessment a framework for thinking about children's language competence was established. The framework presumed that children's knowledge was testable and quantifiable. The testing contexts for measuring language performance were highly controlled to make assessment comparable for different test takers on different occasions. Thus the standardized test emerged. It was called the formal test, perhaps because of its prescribed testing procedures, perhaps because of the formal, serious stance which was assumed by the test giver.

The formality of the normative period changed during the linguistic period. It was replaced by informal sampling procedures. The linguistic approach involved taking a sample of the child's language in conversational or play contexts and later analyzing it for linguistic patterns in the areas of phonology, morphology, syntax, and semantics. Under this version of the linguistic approach, clinicians analyzed for patterns in the samples and compared them to the language patterns exhibited by normal children or adults.

Both formal tests and informal language sampling procedures involve a priori decisions about what is to be analyzed. In the case of the test, the decisions are made by the testmaker who chooses the items. For the informal procedures, the analyst typically is looking for the presence or absence of a predetermined set of structures (e.g., Miller, 1981; Lee, 1974). With both approaches there is essentially a checklist of structures to consider that guides the assessment.

The checklist approach has met with some problems in recent years because of the proliferation of new areas of assessment that have made their way into the clinician's assessment consciousness. New areas to evaluate in pragmatics, for example, have included domains of intentionality, mutuality, event structure, perspective taking, and more (Gallagher, 1991; Duchan, 1984; Gallagher and Prutting, 1983; Irwin, 1982). Not only have the areas to assess become too numerous, but clinicians frequently find that a given child's performance does not quite fit into the categories on the list, or that by concentrating on listed structures, they overlook some critical dimensions that are not on the list. An attempt to list ahead of time all structures or domains to assess is likely to fail not only because it is unwieldy but also because it is impossible to make a workable list of all aspects of communication that are important to evaluate in each instance.

THE CHILD-CENTERED PRAGMATICS FRAMEWORK

The framework we propose is one of informal assessment, where the clinician does not decide beforehand what will be assessed but rather waits to see what is relevant for the child being evaluated. We call the approach the *child-centered pragmatics framework.* We will be assuming the child's viewpoint in three ways: (1) in terms of how the child makes sense of what is going on—or the child's *sensemaking,* (2) in terms of what the child wants to achieve by what he or she does—the *function* of the utterance or act, and (3) in terms of how well the child and the co-interactant understand and respond to one another's sensemaking and wants—the *fine tuning* of the participants. We will describe and elaborate on each in turn.

Sensemaking

"What are you doing?" is a question that gets answers such as "Washing dishes" or "Eating dinner." The answers may refer to particular acts ("I'm picking the lint off your shoulder") or to entire events ("I'm putting away the clothes") or to beginnings of events ("I'm getting ready for bed") or to the end of events ("I'm finishing the book"). Such answers are labels for the participants' sense of what they are doing, which we are calling *sensemaking* (Duchan, 1986).

Children engage in sensemaking even though they may not have the language to answer questions about what they think is going on. Sensemaking for both children and adults tends to be grounded in events in that a particular act takes on its meaning from the ongoing event. This is especially true for younger or naive children who are just learning how events get carried out (Nelson and Gruendel, 1981). Sometimes, however, the performer's sense of what is happening may be unrelated to the structure of the ongoing event, such as when a pencil breaks in the course of playing tic-tac-toe, or when a child is trying to figure out how to ask for something during mealtime. We are distinguishing between the child's overall construction of the event and the child's momentary focus as he or she proceeds through the event. We are calling the construction of the entire event the *sense of the event,* whereas the specific part of the event to which the child is paying attention will be called the *sensemaking focus.*

Assessment guided by the child's sensemaking addresses both the child's sense of the event and the sensemaking focus. Such an approach, rather than asking what the child knows about language in the abstract, asks how the child understands events which are commonly experienced, how the child regards or highlights elements of these events, and how well the child is able to maintain participation in the events. This view regards the child's performance as "sensible" from the child's perception of the event and obligates the observer to figure out what is going on for the child that makes the observed performance make sense.

Functionalism

Functionalism adds a particular angle to the assessment of sensemaking in that it asks what the communicators want to achieve by doing what they do. Assessment of the function of communicative acts when couched in events requires not only that individual acts be scrutinized for their intent but also that the acts be grouped together as a single event and that they be examined in light of the overall organization of the event. Thus a child who says "peek-a-boo" when the blanket is lowered, says it as part of the whole peek-a-boo event, and the scope of meaning spans the whole event. Likewise, the child who is trying to persuade his teacher to bend the rules uses several communicative acts to that end.

Assessment of various linguistic structures from this perspective involves looking not only at which structures are used by children to express their ideas but also at how language structures work to carry out agendas and how they work in behalf of the ongoing event. On the deficit side, interactions are assessed to determine when the child fails to achieve an intent or an agenda or points at which the event breaks down because of linguistic misuse or naïveté.

At the heart of the sensemaking perspective is the question of how well children function in ordinary everyday events, and whether their language serves them well in meeting their agendas. If it does not, the assessor needs to determine what sorts of things can be done to improve functionality. This may involve probing the child's sense of various everyday events to find out what they are like, what purpose they serve, and how they are similar to or different from other events. We cannot, for example, expect a child to ask for help getting dressed if the child has no sense of "time to get dressed" or dislikes the dressing event.

Fine Tuning

Our pragmatic approach to assessment looks not only at the language of the child who is identified as communicatively impaired but also at the responsiveness of those who interact with the child. Some interactive partners seem to fit the communicative needs and style of the child better than do others. Being able to interact in a manner that gives the child neither too much nor too little responsibility for the interaction, that is, to formulate realistic expectations for the child's performance or recognize signs of confusion, involves having both background knowledge about the child and sensitivity to the immediate moment. We are calling this sensitivity "fine tuning," a term we borrow from Cross (1977), who uses it to describe interactions between young children and their mothers. She found that mothers change their linguistic input as their child's language comprehension increases, presumably because of the mother's sensitivity to subtle changes in the child's behavior. We are using the term not only to apply to mothers' responsiveness but also to that of children, and see fine tuning affecting all aspects of the communicative interaction rather than just linguistic form. It appears that fine tuning depends on having a model of one's interactive partner that includes assumptions about what the other person knows, wants, feels, and can do. This model, which is the basis of knowing how to act with that person, is continually being revised to be consistent with observed performance.

Some events depend much more on fine tuning for their success than do others. Routines in which two people have engaged together numerous times require little fine tuning; the past history with the event is a good predictor of how each will perform with little need to question each other's motivation or new knowledge. Jointly engaging in a novel activity, however, involves each participant "guessing" about his or her partner's sense of what the event is, what role each will want to play, what the goals will be, how much knowledge each has of the event, and whether there is agreement as to how to proceed. Without fine tuning on the part of at least one participant, there are bound to be breakdowns. At the one extreme, there may actually be two separate events, one for each participant, in which neither recognizes what is going on for the other. An adult "playing" with a child by putting together a complex toy while the child plays with the packaging material would be an example of this. At the other extreme, in which both participants fine tune, both participants would know how to give up or capture turns, which partner will begin the event, how much time each needs for taking a turn, whether there is teasing going on, and if boredom is setting in. The event would proceed smoothly with each participant having expectations about the other, but making adjustments when those expectations need revision. Between these extremes, interactions may have varying degrees of success or breakdown. The adult may accurately assume the child knows how to play hide-and-seek, but overestimate the time the child is willing to "hide" or "seek," leading to disruption of the game format.

In order for interactions to work smoothly, at least one participant must be sensitive to the sense the other has of the event, so that each contribution is consistent with and contributes to the sensemaking. There is also the need to fine tune to the other's knowledge and degree of capability within the event to assure that the sense of the event isn't changed because one partner overestimates or underestimates the other's knowledge or ability. Adults may be perceived as condescending by asking questions that are too easy or intimidating by asking those that are too hard. Children may not recognize signs of confusion in their listener when they supply insufficient background information in their storytelling. An event that begins as "coloring" may become a frustrating exercise in "not crossing the black lines" with the addition of an adult's requirement to "color the house and stay inside the lines." Here there is a mismatch both between the participants' ideas about how the event is done and between the adult's expectation and the child's ability.

Just as sensemaking is an important feature that guides fine tuning, so is functionalism. The fine tuner is sensitive to the goals or agenda of the other and attempts to help his or her partner fulfill this agenda. The individual acts are seen as moves to carry out the agenda and are thus responded to in a manner that facilitates meeting it. If the child is attempting to get something done (e.g., getting all the toy cars to fit in a case), the fine-tuning adult may read the child's comments ("This doesn't go") or questions ("Why doesn't that fit?") as either requests for help and thus offer it, or as a commentary on the child's proficiency in the face of a difficult problem and then respond by confirming both the difficulty and the skill ("I can't believe you got all of those cars in that little case!"). The decision on the part of the adult will depend on both previous experience with and thus knowledge about this child, and sensitivity to the cues that the child is sending regarding self-perceived helplessness or competence in this task.

Sensitivity to agendas sometimes reveals a disparity between the two partners' goals. Perhaps the adult wants to "get a language sample," whereas the child's agenda is to play his entire repertoire of songs on a kazoo into the tape recorder. There is obviously a conflict between these agendas, and the participants cannot simultaneously fulfill their agendas. The partner who is able and willing to fine tune will feel an obligation to resolve this conflict by either dropping or altering his or her agenda or by negotiating some mutual agenda that allows both participants to have their original or new goals at least partially met.

While it seems reasonable to assume that adults, with their greater experience and knowledge about the world, are better equipped to fine tune and thus should bear a greater responsibility to do so in their interactions with children, this is often not the case. When children are described as "not cooperating" or "not paying attention," we are hearing a statement about the expectation that children should fine tune to adult's agendas. Teaching situations often are framed in such a way that the children have to figure out and conform to the adult's structure of the event as well as determine what the adult's agenda is and how to satisfy it. For example, the child's sense of a new event may be "trying to do it right." This involves continual fine tuning to the adult and to the other children as the child tries to answer such questions as: Where do I sit? What objects do I need to pay attention to? How do I know when to talk? What does she want me to say? Am I doing it the same as everyone else? Is she pleased with me? Our assessment approach assumes that adults also bear responsibility for fine tuning to the child's sense of the event and agendas, and evaluates how well different people fine tune to particular children.

ASSESSMENT PROCEDURES

What follows are a set of general procedures for determining children's communicative competence in light of the framework of sensemaking, functionalism, and fine tuning. We will present more detailed assessment procedures in the chapters to follow. Our aim in this chapter is to present our general approach to assessment. The procedures are organized chronologically, beginning with some preparations before meeting with the child, continuing through the language sampling and eliciting structures that are absent or infrequent in the sample, proceeding to analysis of the samples obtained, and concluding with reporting assessment results.

Preassessment

The most efficacious approach to assessing language in light of sense-making, functionalism, and fine tuning, is to be well acquainted with the child being assessed. This is often not feasible. Rather, the clinician may be meeting the child for the first time when assessment begins. Therefore, the clinician needs to devise ways for determining what to do with the child early on to best use the assessment sessions. One approach that has taken on new importance since the advent of pragmatics assessment is to gather information about the child before the first meeting. This information gathering is traditionally done by having the family fill out a preassessment form.

Old versions of the preassessment form varied depending on when the form was developed and for what purposes. For example, those developed during the normative period asked questions about developmental milestones. The forms developed in the etiology period contained questions about the child's medical history. Information gathered from both developmentally and medically oriented forms have been called the child's "case history."

More recently developed preassessment procedures include questions about the child's competence in different contexts (Kjerland and Kovach, 1990; Gallagher, 1983; MacDonald, 1978). We support the use of preassessment information gathering that provides information about the degree of communicative success the child experiences in different contexts. We would include questions about particular everyday contexts of different sorts: ones which are routinized and repetitive such as games and rhymes, ones which are more open such as conversations with familiar interactants, ones that represent typical lessons in classroom settings, and ones in which the focus is not on the child's communication per se but on his or her using communicative devices to get things done such as asking for food in restaurants or at home. It might also be fruitful to find out how a child's typical day is structured to determine which contexts are familiar and what sorts of events occur every day.

In Box 2–1, there are sample questions for gathering information from caretakers. The questions may be part of a preassessment questionnaire and filled out prior to the initial interview or may be asked at the initial interview. The procedure used by Kjerland and Kovach (1990) provides an example of this kind of information gathering.

If the assessment context is in a school rather than in a clinic, teachers can be asked for preassessment information in addition to or instead of family members. That is, teachers can act as informants for indicating how everyday contexts work for the child. The form might be accompanied by a brief cover letter stating the purpose of gathering the information, an indication of what will be done in the assessment session, and an acknowledgment of the important role that the informant plays in the assessment process.

The Family Interview

In clinical contexts, children are often accompanied by their parents and sometimes by other family members for the assessment session. Under these circumstances, the assessment can include information gained from interviews with the family members. The interview not only can provide additional information about the child's communicative competence but also can place the child and the child's problem in the context of a particular family. As the various family members report their observations and concerns, the interviewer begins to see how the child is perceived by the family as, for example, charming, stubborn, bright, lazy, competent, or hopeless. One may hear expressions of

BOX 2–1. *Sample Questions for Gathering Information from Caretakers*

Child's Name:

Date:

Identifying Information

1. What is your full name?
2. Who are the child's primary caretakers?
3. What is your current address?
4. What is your phone number?
5. Are there other children in your household?
6. What are their names and ages?
7. How are they related to your child? (brother, sister, and so on)
8. What adults live in the household?
9. How are they related to your child?
10. What is your child's birthdate?

Family History (select ones which are appropriate for the child)

11. What country is your family from?
12. How long have you lived in the United States?
13. Why did you move to this country?
14. Where did you go to school? For how long?
15. Where did your (husband, wife) go to school? For how long?
16. Where was your child born?
17. Where has your child lived other than this city?
18. What languages are spoken at home?
19. What languages does your child speak and understand?
20. Who does your child talk to at home and in what language?
21. Which is your child's best language?
22. Does your child ever hear English spoken? Where?

Medical History

23. Is your child in good health?
24. Has your child ever had any serious illnesses or injuries?
25. Does your child have any other health problems that your or your doctor are worried about? (allergies, trouble eating, trouble sleeping)
26. Were there any problems with your pregnancy with this child?
27. Were there any problems with this child's birth?
28. Does your child seem to hear well?
29. Has your child's hearing been tested? What were the results?

Developmental History

30. Has your child shown normal growth?
31. How old was your child when he/she learned to crawl and walk?
32. How old was your child when he/she started to say words?
33. Do you think that your child learns more slowly or more quickly than other children?

BOX 2–1. *(continued)*

Educational History

34. Is your child attending school? What is the name and address of the school?
35. What grade is your child in?
36. What languages does the teacher speak to your child?
37. Is your child receiving any other special help? (speech, reading, special instruction in learning English)

Pragmatics Questions

38. Please outline a schedule of activities that your child carries out on a typical day.
39. What activity does your child spend the most time doing? Describe your child's participation in the activity and list who else is usually involved.
40. Do you think your child has any problem with communication? What sort of problem?
41. When does your child communicate best? In what language? To whom? Doing what?
42. When does your child have the most trouble communicating in your language? Why do you think this is so?
43. What are your child's favorite activities?
44. Who are your child's favorite people?
45. How does your child get what he/she wants?
46. What kind of things does your child ask for most frequently?
47. Does your child frequently start activities or conversations?
48. Does your child join in when other people start activities or conversations?
49. Does your child have memorized routines that are repeated regularly? What are they?
50. Does your child seem confused at times? Under what conditions?

anger and fear or optimism and enjoyment. We want to know what the world is like for the child and how well it is managed. Discrepancies between reports from family members might yield valuable insights into the child's differential functioning with different people and under different contextual conditions. Such an interview can contain questions raised from the preassessment responses as well as impressions the family members give of the child's abilities and disabilities.

Initial or subsequent interviews can also include a discussion of videotapes made of family members as they interact in ordinary ways with their children. For example, one might have a member of the family and the child look at familiar books together, or teach and learn something, or just play. The interview about the tape might involve having the family members watch themselves with the child and comment on what they see as significant. A procedure used by Frankel, Leary, and Kilman (1986) and Erickson and Shultz (1982) is to have the interactant identify spots in the interaction that did not seem to go well and to interpret what the problem might have been. This procedure leads to judgments about fine tuning which include the involved adult. It could lead to the family developing better ways to tune to the child's competence and sensemaking. Finally, it could lead to the identification of what the child does which creates interactional problems between the child and his or her family members. Teachers can also be videotaped while interacting with the child and then view their interactions to identify trouble spots or episodes that go very well.

If the family is from a culture or linguistic group different from that of the clinician, it is important to find out about the culture prior to seeing the family. An approach to doing this is to conduct an ethnographic interview with someone who knows the culture and its language. Methods for conducting an ethnographic interview with an informant from the culture are discussed later in this chapter (see also Westby, 1990).

Observing the Child in Naturalistic Contexts

The preassessment information should give some indications as to the kinds of communication competencies and problems that the referred child has. The clinician will know whether those who know the child best have trouble understanding the child's messages and what their perceptions are about the child as a communicator. By reading the preassessment information, the clinician will have some idea about the child's expressive language abilities and whether the child is viewed as understanding language and events. When this information is obtained prior to seeing the child, the first contact can be viewed as a time to confirm or alter these impressions as to the areas of competence and deficit that the child displays. This may precede the interview with the family, so that the interchange can be used to compare the clinician's perceptions and the family's reports. If no previous reliable information about the kind of problems the child is experiencing is available, the first goal is to identify areas to be focused on in the assessment.

We feel it is necessary to observe children and record a sample of their language in several events in order to see their range of proficiency and difficulty and to see the influence of various dimensions of context. As we have pointed out, formal tests present a constrained context and do not show how children respond in events in which they can initiate an activity, ask questions, or choose the topic. Likewise, any other single context has limitations on what can be observed. The clinician cannot possibly observe the child in all contexts, so he or she will want to choose events that vary on several dimensions to provide the most information for the assessment. Our preference is to observe the child with a familiar interactant while engaged in one or more entire events in order to determine how the child interprets the event as well as uses language structure to meet an agenda within the context of the event. We then engage the child in an activity to determine the effect of an unfamiliar partner. Thus we may ask the caretaker to try to teach the child something and then play with an assortment of toys. Our interaction may begin by our entering the play event, and then switch to a structured activity. Events in which talking follows the child's agenda can be compared with prescribed things to say, as in a memorized script or sentences to imitate. Our choice of events is determined by our hypotheses about what will make a difference, based on what we have been told about this child and what structures we suspect are problematic.

Some children talk freely and copiously to any listener in any situation. Most do not, particularly if they have language impairments. It is well to keep in mind that there is no way to *make* children talk; you can only make them want to talk by creating a situation in which there is a reason to talk and an atmosphere that conveys the message that you are interested in what they have to say. If you put yourself in the child's place, this is not a difficult principle to understand. Children, like adults, have the right not to talk unless they feel it is to their advantage to do so. Here some some hints for getting the reluctant talker to want to talk:

1. Keep the focus off your attempt to get the child to talk. With children who are very hesitant to say anything, offer contexts that demand little verbalization for participation, such as drawing pictures or playing a game. This allows the child to become a participant with you in a nonthreatening way. During the event you should comment on what you are doing and allow for, but not directly request, the child's verbal participation.

2. Do not talk too much and do not be afraid to allow silent pauses during the conversations. Do not fill up every empty space with a question because this encourages the child to let you take the lead.

3. Select materials appropriate to the child's interest level. For example, children operating at a preschool level tend to be more interested in toys than in books or games. Older children tend to like unusual objects or things that can be manipulated.

4. Toys with detachable or moving parts and broken toys generally stimulate interest. If possible, you might have the child or caretaker bring in one or two of the child's own favorite toys. Children often have more to say about familiar things than about new ones. When toys become too enrapturing, they tend to inhibit verbal interaction. If that happens, it is best to announce that you will have to put the toy away in a few minutes and do something else or to present an interesting alternative while you quietly remove the distracting toy.

5. Most children are naturally curious. If they know you have something concealed from them, they usually want to find out more about it. Having a big box or bag (or even a pillow case!) from which you withdraw objects may prompt conversation about what else it contains. Likewise, noise sources they cannot see or mechanisms that make toys move stimulate curiosity. It is generally best not to have all of your materials out at once, but you might present alternatives and ask the child which one he or she wants to look at first.

6. If the child will initiate conversation about your materials, let him or her take the lead, and you ask questions or comment briefly on what the child is saying. For a more natural and less "testing" atmosphere, insert your own opinions or comments occasionally.

7. If the child does not initiate, make comments yourself about the materials and ask open-ended leading questions, such as "That looks broken. What do you suppose happened to it?" or "Can you figure out what's going on here?" If these prompts do not elicit verbalization, try more specific questions which require minimum output, such as "Do you. . . ?" "Where. . . ?" "What is. . . ?" and then build up to more open-ended questions, such as "Tell me. . ." or "What about. . . ?"

8. If statements or questions trigger no reaction, demonstrate what you expect of the child. For example, take a toy yourself and play with it, tell about what you are doing, and personalize your account using an imaginary situation. Engage the child in the play as soon as possible and begin to prompt indirectly. For example, make your car crash into the child's car and then ask what happens next.

9. If the child is reluctant to talk about pictures or tell stories, go first and set the

stage. A series of sequence pictures provides more story structure than a single picture and therefore is generally easier for a beginning story. You can have the child tell the same story after you or create a new story using different pictures or characters. Unless you are analyzing for storytelling structures, do not ask the child to tell too familiar a story, since it might be memorized and unlike more natural output.

10. Include another person in the elicitation or collection procedure. This might be another clinician or an aide who can model the responses you expect from the child, or it might be the child's parent, sibling, or friend who can be included in the activities. Having a third party involved tends to take the focus off the child and makes talking more comfortable.

One commonly asked question about language sampling relates to *sample length*. Determination of the length of an adequate sample will depend on the purpose for collecting it. If it is to be used to determine areas of deficit, it should be long and varied enough to reveal potential regularities in syntax, morphology, phonology, vocabulary, discourse, and event management. A minimum time period of one-half hour has been recommended in one or more situations (Bloom and Lahey, 1978; Crystal, Fletcher, and Garman, 1978). As we have indicated, our preference is to collect at least two samples that each cover entire events.

The length of the sample will depend on the structures being assessed. A minimum of fifty to a hundred different utterances spoken by the child is frequently recommended for syntactic analysis (Lee, 1974; Tyack and Gottsleben, 1974), (see Chapter 6). Fifty is generally adequate for phonological assessment as well. Semantic analysis generally requires more than one observation to determine problems with vocabulary choice, word meanings, and conceptual deficits that may appear only in certain contexts. Likewise, pragmatic analysis generally involves multiple observations to sample a diversity of situations. Assessing the communicative competence of a nonverbal child usually requires repeated observations to find regularities in performance.

Our recommendations for assessment procedures may sound somewhat overwhelming for the clinician who works in school settings and has a caseload of forty to sixty children. School clinicians generally must be concerned about obtaining test scores for placement in remedial programs and determining individual educational plan (IEP) goals, and may not see how doing structural analysis fits into the requirements of the systems within which they work. We would like to make some observations about what structural analysis can and cannot do to assist these clinicians. First, structural analysis is a way of thinking about children's language more than a set of techniques to carry out assessment. Thinking structurally obligates the clinician to question the significance of the child's behavior rather than simply to judge it as correct or incorrect. This conceptual shift in orientation does not require additional time or resources. Secondly, the communication of most children in the typical school caseload does not require extensive analysis; our suggested procedures are intended to focus on the patterns of those children that are not readily obvious. Even within this group, there will be few children whose communication difficulties involve all facets of language, and analysis in most cases is confined to a specific area of deficit. Finally, with those children who present us with more questions than answers when we attempt to use standardized assessment procedures, we must be prepared to argue for the necessity of parent conferences, in-class and other situational observations, videotape support, and other means to figure out the nature of the child's communication abilities and disabilities. To write goals and carry out remedial procedures when we have no idea as to the nature of the child's problem is in our view unethical as well as inefficient.

Since structural analysis is not intended to determine if a child's language is normal or delayed, in general it is applied only if a language problem has been identified and thus is not used in making decisions about whether children should be placed or retained in intervention programs. In some cases the results of analysis can be used in this decision making by demonstrating that the children's test responses are consistent with their performance in other contexts. More typically, structural analysis is used to determine and evaluate goals for IEPs. From this perspective, goals are always written with the context specified, which acknowledges the influence of the context on the child's performance. The goals can be stated in quantifiable terms if this is meaningful or required.

Assessing the Child Learning English as a Second Language

Clinicians are likely to find themselves in situations in which they will need to evaluate the language of bilingual children whose first language is not English, and who have limited proficiency in English. The necessity for gathering background information about each child and for learning about the child's family and culture is even greater when evaluating children learning English as a Second Language (ESL children), since clinicians are likely to make incorrect judgments if they use their own cultural norms and values rather than those of the child's culture. An Inuit child may be judged reticent and incorrectly labeled as a verbal noncommunicator (Fey, 1986) if the clinician views the child through the eyes of those raised as white, middle-class Americans rather than from the perspective of those of the Inuit culture (Crago, 1990). Crago found that Inuit mothers seldom ask their children test questions. Further, Inuit mothers and teachers expect children to learn by looking and listening, not by talking. Similarly, a Hispanic child may be incorrectly evaluated as having a language problem based on the absence of third-person singular present forms of verbs, and use of the copula, as a result of the evaluator's failure to realize that those departures from standard English reflect the child's use of Spanish-influenced English, a naturally occurring dialect of English (e.g., Kayser, 1989).

A first step to learning about a cultural group is to talk with members of the group. Anthropologists find out about others' cultures by the tried and true method of ethnographic interview (Westby, 1990; Spradley, 1979). During the interview, the anthropologist asks questions of a cultural member about things such as how people of that culture think and participate in everyday events, about their cultural ceremonies, and about their attitudes toward one another and toward the host culture.

A second step is to evaluate the child. A child should be evaluated in his or her first language by a speaker of that language. Indeed, a child's right to be evaluated in his or her most proficient language has been emphasized by both professional and legislative mandates (ASHA, 1983, 1985; PL 94-142; Title VII of PL 95-561). Some bilingual children may be more proficient in English than in their second language. Before assessing the child's language, some clinicians use language proficiency tests to determine the child's language of greatest competence. Several measures have been designed to determine relative competence in different languages (see Chapter 9 for a listing and description).

For those bilingual children whose best or most dominant language is not English, assessment must be done in their dominant language. Ideally the evaluator would be a clinician who is a member of the child's cultural group, a fluent speaker of the child's first language, and the same person who would be providing follow-up evaluations and therapy. A second possibility would be to have a consulting clinician from the child's culture do the assessment, who would be with the child only during that evaluation. A third option would be for an English-speaking clinician to learn the child's culture and language, developing sufficient fluency to be able to evaluate the child in his or her dominant language.

There will still remain those instances when the clinician will need to evaluate a ESL child in the child's language without knowing the child's language or culture, and when there are no consulting clinicians available to perform the assessment. The clinician may then need to have an informant interview the family members and to elicit and interpret the child's communication. The informant becomes a key person in the evaluation process, providing necessary information about the culture, collecting and translating case history information from family members, and collecting and eliciting language samples from the child. The ideal informant would be very familiar with both languages and both cultures, would have an understanding of the structure of language, and would be able to relate to children with ease.

The following is a suggested procedure for using an informant from the child's culture in the evaluation process (Lund and Duchan, 1990).

Step 1 Interviewing the Informant   The informant is interviewed to allow the clinician to become familiar with aspects of the child's culture which might impact on the assessment of the child's first language or the child's communication in English. Some general issues to be raised in this interview are listed in Box 2–2.

Step 2 Training the Informant for the Interview with the Family   The informant is told the goals and procedures involved in the parent interview and evaluation of the child. Questions such as those in Box 2–2 are shared with the informant, and agreement is reached about which are appropriate to ask. The purpose for each question is carefully explained to the informant.

Step 3 Having the Informant Interview the Family   The informant asks the family members the questions discussed previously with the clinician. The session is taped or video-recorded for later translation.

BOX 2–2. Questions to Ask a Cultural Informant

1. Would questions about any of the following issues be sensitive to members of your culture? Health and illness; pregnancy and birth; family relationships; child-rearing practices; time orientation; schools; health-care providers; employment; level of education
2. How does your culture treat issues related to privacy, courtesy, respect for elders, behaviors related to family roles?
3. What is accepted behavior by your cultural group regarding expression of emotions and feelings, religious expressions, response to handicapping conditions, illness, or death?
4. What are the verbal or nonverbal ways that your culture expresses age, gender, or status? How significant is the age and gender of a professional interacting with members of your culture?
5. What are your culture's views about communication?
   What are the communicative roles children take in different contexts with different people?
   Which people have primary responsibility for child care?
   Which people do children talk to; when do they talk most and least; and what do they talk about?
   How are talkative children and untalkative children responded to?
   What ideas do people have about how children learn to communicate?
   Do adults change their talk when they talk with children?
   If so, how is it changed?
   What are some typical interactive rituals and games engaged in by children with one another and with adults?
   What notions do adults have about the stages children go through when they learn language?
6. What are the features of your language that are different from English?
   What do children have as their first words in your language, and what do they mean?
   What are the phonemes and allowable phoneme combinations in your language, and how does English phonology differ from it?
   How does your language combine morphemes, and how does English morphology differ from it?
   What are the syntactic structures of your language, and how does English syntax differ?
   What are typical types of discourse structures used, and do they compare with those used by teachers in the children's school?
7. Would the professional be better perceived if he or she varied his or her style of communicating; for example, changed tempo of conversation, eye or body contact, distance between speakers?
8. Does your culture use healing systems? Would medical or nonmedical intervention violate beliefs in these systems?
9. What are the culture's traditions about eating (e.g., are meanings of foods, style of food preparation and consumption, frequency of eating, time of eating, and eating utensils culturally determined?). Are there religious influences on food preparation and consumption?
10. What are the most important social networks in your culture (e.g., family, peer, religious affiliation, ethnic/cultural networks)?
11. How does the family participate in the care of and decisions about its members? Are there key family roles? Do all family members participate?
12. How might your culture's attitudes toward the host culture affect how people will respond to professional inquiries or intervention? Do they perceive racism or discrimination from the mainstream culture?

Step 4 Having the Informant Translate the Family Interview and Help Plan the Child's Evaluation Session   The informant translates and explains to the clinician the responses of the family members in light of cultural factors.

Step 5 Eliciting a Language Sample from the Child in the Child's First Language   The informant elicits language samples from the child in the child's first language. A variety of events and interactants are used to elicit language from the child (e.g., child's siblings in a play session, conversation with the informant, storytelling with a parent). All sessions are audio- or videotaped.

Step 6 Assessing of the Child's Communication in the Child's First Language   In this final session, the informant translates and explains the child's language and behavior for the clinician. The clinician provides leading questions about the child's pronunciation, sentence structure, word choices, and general ability to express ideas and achieve communicative aims. Segments of the tape that may reflect confusion or problems by any of the participants are analyzed and discussed in depth.

The analysis of the child's performance in the first language will need to focus both on the language structure and on how the child uses the language. Damico, Oller, and Storey (1983) found that the ways bilingual children used the language (both Spanish and English) was a better predictor of their future academic success than was the linguistic structuring of their sentences. The children who displayed pragmatic problems (e.g., they had a high frequency of revisions in Spanish and abrupt changes in topics) had more difficulty succeeding in monolingual English classrooms than did the children who had trouble with Spanish or English morphology and syntax.

Once the clinician has evaluated the child's first language, he or she can assess the child's English language competence. Since the child's English is likely to be influenced by the first language, any departures from Standard English should be evaluated for whether they may be resulting from legitimate dialect differences coming from the first language, rather than as errors indicative of the child's problems with learning language.

Transcription

After one has elicited a sample of behavior, the next step in performing structural analysis is to transcribe the sample in ways that will achieve the goals of the analyst. This will, of course, vary with different goals. If your purpose is to analyze the phonological system for its structural regularities, the phonological errors should be transcribed in narrow phonetics (see Chapter 4). In this case there is little need to include the adult utterances or notes on the context unless they are needed to determine what the child is saying. In contrast, when investigating aspects of the child's event knowledge, you will want to transcribe the child's and others' verbal productions in standard orthography, and your transcript will have detailed notes on the context (see Chapter 3).

The most commonly used transcript is a *running transcript,* which includes a written version of most of the child's and the interactant's verbal productions in separate columns. Usually it is presented in standard orthography with some commentary on the context in a third column. This is the type of transcript most useful for structurally analyzing the interaction and identifying where breakdowns are occurring. If we are unsure about the nature of the child's problem, we start with a running transcript of at least two events. An example of a portion of such a transcript, along with some conventions we follow in doing these transcripts, are seen in Box 2–3.

BOX 2–3. Running Transcript

Guidelines

1. Child utterances and adult utterances are numbered separately.
2. If the child utterance immediately follows an adult utterance, it begins on the last line of the adult utterance or on the next line if adult utterance takes a single line. Adult and child utterances that are said simultaneously begin on the same line.
3. If the adult utterance immediately follows a child utterance, it begins on the line below that of the child utterance.
4. Pauses between utterances of more than three seconds are shown with blank lines. Longer pauses are indicated with notation of the time elapsed.
5. Significant pauses within utterances are shown with a slash (/).

Examples

Mother	*Child*	*Context*
1. Do your want this now?		M offers milk to C.
	1. Uh-uh	C shakes head "no."
2. What else do you like here?	2. Just a hamburger	
3. OK/but drink some of your milk first.		C gets up from table.

Once the area in which the child is having difficulty has been identified, specific portions of the interaction that contain the problem areas need to be discovered. A *listing transcript* for each structure to be analyzed serves this purpose. If you want to investigate a child's difficulty with the production of spatial prepositions, a listing of the contexts that require the preposition (obligatory contexts) and what the child says and does in those contexts would be necessary. It is useful to group similar productions together, such as correct and incorrect forms. If the listing transcript is derived from a running transcript, the numbers of the original running transcript are retained to allow the analyst to go back and examine the context if indicated. Box 2–4 illustrates such a transcript.

BOX 2–4. Listing Transcript: Obligatory Contexts for Past Tense

Uninflected or Missing Forms	*Context*
11. I do it yesterday.	"When did. . . ?"
13. He not there.	Asked about teacher at school
14. Mommy there, and then come back.	

Overregularized Forms

27. He goed and she goed too.	Pointing at picture

Inflected Forms

4. I did it.	Snaps shirt

Finally, in order to use the nonverbal and intonational aspects of behavior to study pragmatics, we use the *multilevel transcript*. This is a detailed transcription of a brief segment of behavior in which descriptions of simultaneous behavioral changes are made. Condon and Sander (1974) have called these co-occurring changes *whiles*. The transcript involves more detail than can be assimilated in direct observation with note-taking; and because it includes nonverbal and behavioral synchrony information, it requires more information than is available from an audiotape. For these reasons, the multilevel transcripts require that videotaped samples be used as the data base. An example of such a transcript is given in Box 2–5.

BOX 2–5. Multilevel Transcript

Intonation

Levels			
Verbal	măbúbù		ǽ
Nonverbal			
Head	Looks to K's hand		Looks to door
Hand	Touches K's hand		Points to door

The multilevel transcript has been used to analyze for such things as nonverbal performatives (Dore and others, 1976), sensorimotor origins of first words (Carter, 1975), types of requests (Dore, 1977; Read and Cherry, 1978), self-synchrony in behavior (Condon and Ogston, 1967), and functions of echolalia in autistic children (Prizant, 1978; Prizant and Duchan, 1981).

Deep Testing

After the samples collected in naturally occurring events have been analyzed, the clinician may find that there are structures that the child did not use because the event or interaction did not call for them, and other structures that were used too infrequently to find a pattern in production. Under these circumstances you may need to design deep test procedures to elicit several instances of the structure in question to analyze the patterns of usage. The "natural" part of the interaction must sometimes be sacrificed for thoroughness.

Deep testing can be accomplished either by linguistically structuring the session with verbal directions or questions to query the child's knowledge directly or by initiating an adult-directed activity that is likely to elicit the target structure. Linguistic techniques such as patterning, sentence completion, and interviewing for knowledge assess children's metalinguistic abilities; that is, their ability to think and talk about language. Other techniques, such as set ups, pretending, or story retelling encourage children to use structures without involving them in having to explain the rules of their usage. Since children often perform differently in structured elicitations than they do in less structured circumstances, it is important to recognize the constraints of the conditions and not make judgments about their knowledge of language based solely on these contrived situations.

Patterning   Patterned practice has long been used in formal instruction in second-language learning. This technique offers a set of similar utterances in which the learner inserts new, analogous responses derived from the pattern in the presented set. A familiar example comes from children's folklore, where the first child introduces the pattern of alternating turns—"I one it," "I two it," "I three it," and so on until the unsuspecting child is caught saying "I eight (ate) it," when "it" has been described as a singularly unappetizing object.

This elicitation procedure evaluates children's ability to extrapolate patterns from language data as well as demonstrates their knowledge of the structures involve. We describe it as metalinguistic because the attention of the child is on getting the language right, and thus it does not involve the same psycholinguistic processes used in natural conversation. Children may be observed producing structures that they cannot produce in spontaneous conversation, showing the facilitative effect of a routinized task.

A variation on this procedure is to introduce a puppet or doll as a participant in the exercise. This makes it more interesting for young children, and they may be willing to speak to or for the puppet when they are hesitant to talk to strange adults.

We present some examples of pattern activities for deep testing syntactic, morphological, and semantic structures in the respective chapters. For additional suggestions, you might look at drill books for teaching English as a foreign language. Also, Slobin (1967) presents some pattern elicitation techniques that have been used with children.

Sentence Completion   This elicitation procedure works well with forms that occur in the last position of the sentence. The clinician simply says the beginning of the sentence and the child fills in the end—for example, "You eat soup with a _____." Because this cloze procedure depends on the listener's ability to construct what the speaker was going to say and then say it, the speaker must provide enough clues so that the possible correct answers are limited.

A sentence completion task can be designed to elicit linguistic knowledge, as in Berko's (1958) task in which she asked children to extend their knowledge or morphological inflections to nonsense forms: "This is a wug. Now there are two of them. There are two _____." Conceptual knowledge can also be sampled, as when children are asked to base their completion on knowledge about the world or on analogic reasoning. The auditory association subtest of the ITPA offers some examples of both kinds of completions. For example, "Bread is to eat. Milk is to _____." requires only that children have knowledge about milk in order to respond correctly. Interspersed with these simple completion items are others that require knowledge about the analogic relationship between the words in the first sentence, such as "Grass is green. Sugar is _____." Analogies are more difficult for children than are completions in which they must simply provide a word that is semantically and syntactically appropriate for the sentence. The assessor should be clear as to what kind of knowledge is being required.

Multiple-choice items are examples of sentence completion elicitations where children can select an answer from a set of given possibilities. This format is sometimes easier than having to provide the answer spontaneously, but it presents the problem of having to keep all the options in mind while trying to select the correct one. The foils might confuse the issue even when the choices can be presented in written or pictured form.

Interviewing Interviewing is a procedure in which you ask children to tell you directly about their use of language or to indicate which structures are allowable in their rule system. Anthropologists use an interview procedure when they ask a member of another culture to explain some aspect of the culture. When this description is applied to language, it is referred to as a metalinguistic task, meaning that it involves language to talk about language. While adults can be asked directly to be introspective about their own language, children generally lack the ability to be metalinguistic until relatively late in development (Gleitman, Gleitman, and Shipley, 1972; for an exception, see von Raffler Engel, 1965). Roger Brown, for example, tells of asking his famous two-year-old subject, Adam "Which is right—two shoe or two shoes?" to which Adam replied "Pop goes the weasel" (Brown and Bellugi, 1964).

For older children, interviewing has the advantage of providing information that might not be uncovered from structural analysis alone. A second advantage for interviewing over other elicitation techniques is that it treats children as responsible coparticipants in the endeavor of figuring out how they use and understand language. It must be recognized, however, that it is difficult even for adults to explain things they do automatically and to reflect on factors that are usually outside of their awareness. The answers you get may not be an accurate description but will still reflect the child's perception. For example, the child with a phonological problem reports that he has trouble with his tongue, possibly because someone explained his problem to him in that way, when actually his problem has to do with his conceptualization of the phonology of the language and not his tongue movement.

We especially recommend the interview procedure for certain areas of structural analysis, such as speech event analysis. Good interviewing is a highly skilled technique and requires considerable sensitivity and insight on the part of the interviewer. The best interviewers pick up on children's leads and go in the direction their informants are thinking, rather than follow a ready-made format of questions. The late Jean Piaget, a researcher who has perhaps made the most of such interviews, offers a sense of his respect for good interview procedure:

> . . . it is our opinion that in child psychology as in pathological psychology, at least a year of daily practice is necessary before passing beyond the inevitable fumbling stage of the beginner. It is so hard not to talk too much when questioning a child, especially for a pedagogue. It is so hard not to be suggestive. And above all, it is so hard to find the middle course between systematisation due to preconceived ideas and incoherence due to the absence of any directing hypothesis. The good experimenter must know how to observe, that is to say, to let the child talk freely, without ever checking or side-tracking his utterance, and at the same time he must constantly be alert for something definitive, at every moment he must have some working hypothesis, some theory, true or false, which he is seeking to check. (Piaget, 1976, pp. 8–9)

Questions for Information   There are several advantages of asking questions to elicit specific structures or assess the child's understanding of the language and concepts being used. First, question asking is probably familiar to the child (Snow and Ferguson, 1977), and second, it is a direct and therefore quick and efficient means to get particular kinds of information. The disadvantages are that asking many questions might seem like an interrogation, inhibiting spontaneous performance or relaxed interaction. Also, responses to frequently asked questions may be packaged routines rather than productive structures (Duchan, 1980; Thomas, 1979; Gleason and Weintraub, 1976).

As with every elicitation procedure, the context influences its success. Children are more likely to answer questions they feel you really want to know the answer to (e.g., "Where do you live?") as opposed to questions to which you already have the answer (e.g., "What is this?").

Questions for information are most frequently used to elicit particular morphological or syntactic forms, such as asking "when" questions to get tense markers. They also can be used to obtain semantic information, as when asking "What is a spoon used for?" or for eliciting particular word classes.

Retelling or Reenactment   Rather than answering questions about an event or a procedure, children can be asked to recount or act out what went on. This gives the clinician insight as to how they understand the original events, how they handle narrative, and how they take the listener's perspective, among other things. If the interest is in how well the child communicates what actually happened, the clinician needs to know whether the child's rendition matches the event, and thus may want to present or stage new events and have the child recount them.

Reenactments of some events are easier than retellings. For example, showing how the table is set at home would probably be easier than describing how it is done. Other events, such as what happened in a television show, may be easier to retell. It is useful information to note the mode that children use most readily. Language-impaired children may depend much more on reenactment than do children with typical linguistic skills. One of our clinical cases, a Down syndrome child named Mike, was able to enact an elaborate story using one-word utterances to speak for the characters and to narrate the event but could not describe the event verbally. Chapman and Miller (1980) have used this kind of evidence to show a gap in development between cognitive and linguistic understanding in order to determine whether a child would be amenable to learning an alternative communication system.

Pretending   We have used role playing with children to elicit forms such as commands and directions by having the child be the "boss" or the teacher. Having children pretend they are lost and asking directions can elicit question forms. Playing an interpreter for a "blind" friend or a child from another country elicits descriptive terms. The child might also assume the role of a character in a story who speaks in a characteristic way. For example, playing Goldilocks provides good opportunities for using adjectives.

Joining the child in pretending can reveal the child's awareness of roles and events. One can see how the child responds to roles that require expressions of politeness, dominance, uncertainty, and other traits that are conveyed by language. The clinician also can examine the child's knowledge of event structures as the child and clinician pretend to be in a variety of situations.

Games   Games are events which have a prescribed sequence, usually involve competition and taking turns, often involve suspense and resolution, and are usually regarded by children as fun rather than as work. Any number of gamelike elicitiation procedures can be developed. Some familiar games, such as hide-and-seek, can be redesigned to elicit structures such as prepositions by hiding objects and having the child guess where they are rather than searching for them. Board games or card games can be altered or developed to call for the structures in question. Novel games can be designed that sample particular aspects of language performance. We have found games helpful in assessing nonegocentric role taking, conceptual schemes, and classification strategies, as well as vocabulary and language structure.

Set Ups   We are using the term *set ups* to apply to several techniques in which the clinician arranges a naturally occurring event to elicit particular language structures. One version of a set up is where there is an unexpected element to the event, such as offering the child blue milk for a snack. Another version is to have necessary items missing or difficult to obtain, such as having no crayons available when suggesting the child color, or having the top of the paste on too tightly for the child to get it off. These conditions are designed to get the child to act in certain ways—commenting, requesting, or directing the clinician and using particular language forms to do so. Wetherby and Prutting (1984) have called these "communicative temptations." A third type of set up is the use of materials that necessitate the language structure in question in order to get what is needed or to distinguish between similar objects. For example, if a child wants to build with blocks, it is necessary to use the plural form of "block" to get enough items to build with. If the child is dressing dolls, the set up could require the distinction between the "little" clothes for one doll and the "big" clothes for another. Set ups are somewhat more naturalistic than other types of deep tests, because the response is called for by the event rather than by the clinician's request to talk. They also can be very informative in determining which event conditions will be effective in therapy.

Analyzing for Structures

So far we have talked about selecting, recording, and transcribing language samples and about eliciting particular aspects of language that we want to analyze. Now we turn to the analysis of the information gathered. The analysis is done in order to discover regularities. We are calling these regularities *structures,* hence the name for the overall approach is *structural analysis.*

Structures, at first glance, could just as well be called behaviors, since we begin structural analysis by grouping behaviors into types (for example, /s/ sounds). However, structures, unlike observable behaviors, can be abstract constructs and may have a form more general than any particular behavior (for example, "plural"). Nor are structures the same things as behavioral types or classes. Rather, structures are thought of as units which underly behavior. They can be regarded as aspects of knowledge, located in the mind of the child—knowledge which the child can use to understand or produce language. While behaviors that are classified together as types must resemble one another in form, structures can produce behaviors which may not resemble one another. For example, "consonant-vowel structure" can be regarded as the form which underlies a child's speech production and accounts for the way the child produces all words as consonant-vowel syllables irrespective of the particular sounds they contain (pi; so; ra). Structures which do not resemble their associated behavior have been called *deep* or *underlying structures.*

Structural analysis not only reveals the existence of knowledge structures underlying the child's communication but also can be used to determine what expected structures are absent. Absent structures are ones which would be anticipated to occur in normal circumstances, as in the speech of typical children or adults. In the case of absent structures, such as "no plural markers," the term *structure* refers to regularities in the language and not to a knowledge structure in the mind of the child.

Structural Analysis of Events   To assure that the linguistic analysis is related to the child's sense of an event, the analyst needs to look at how the child understands the event in which the language sample was obtained. If the child's conception of interacting with the adult is to do as directed, absence of question forms in the sample is not surprising and indeed is appropriate. If an interaction is seen as an opportunity to talk about the pictures in a favorite book, the concrete vocabulary of the sample is not out of line. While one may try to alter the child's assumptions about interactions such as these, or to introduce contexts in which questions and abstract vocabulary are required, one should not assume the child is missing these structures and proceed to intervene without understanding the sensemaking involved in the sampled events. It is necessary therefore, to begin the analysis with a description of the event from the child's perspective, making note of the nature of the event, how it proceeds, whether there are breakdowns, and which participant takes the interactive initiative. Mismatches in agenda or sense of the event are noted along with behaviors of the child that seem incompatible with what the adult sees as going on. Exchanges are analyzed for the presence or lack of fine tuning they reveal. Procedures for doing event analysis are suggested in Chapter 3.

Some Procedural Steps for Discovering Regularities   The following is a general description of the procedural steps for doing structural analysis. The actual analysis will vary in detail needed and difficulty in finding regularities and will depend on the structures being analyzed. Thus structural analysis for semantic structures will proceed differently from syntax. (See chapters which follow for suggested procedures to use when analyzing different kinds of language structures.)

Some structures are easily identified. They may be clearly expressed by the child, they may be close in form to the behavior which they produce, and they may be definitely required in specifiable and tangible contexts in the adult language. If, for example, a child always produces /t/ for /k/, the task for identifying it as a structure is usually easy and straightforward. To find the desired structure, the clinician examines the running transcript or a tape for the obligatory contexts in which the structures either do occur or should occur (e.g., plural contexts, words which require certain phonemes, questions which require auxiliaries). A listing of the occurrence of the structure in question would reveal the child's use pattern. These readily accessible structures are generally assessed using "error" analysis in which the adult standard is used as a primary guide in deciding what to analyze. The child's performance is examined against a given set of structures in order to find out whether or not the child knows the forms. The standard can be a checklist existing in the mind of the analyst by virtue of being a native speaker of the adult version of the child's language, or it may be an explicitly constructed checklist. If the standard is taken from studies of normal children, in which a child's competence is matched against children of the same chronological or mental age, it is a *norm-referenced* comparison. If the goal of analysis is to determine whether specific forms are present, for example, as a post-therapy measure, it is *criterion referenced*. In both criterion-referenced and norm-referenced approaches, the analyst begins with a list of structures and matches the child's productions against it, indicating whether the child is correct or incorrect.

If the analyst finds that the child seems to produce the target structure in variable ways, more analysis is required to reveal the pattern. The context surrounding the occurrences needs to be investigated to find a reason or a pattern to the variability. Referring back to the running transcript, the analyst makes up a listing transcript of correct and incorrect productions of the structure or of different incorrect patterns and looks for the commonalities within each list. It may be found, for example, that the child uses a grammatical structure in telling a story but omits it in conversation. Or the child may respond better to adults' comments rather than to questions. "Inconsistent" use of *is* can be seen to be very consistent. For example, it may always be omitted as an auxiliary verb but never when used as a copula. Presence or absence of fricatives may be conditioned by the position in the word. While some of the patterns are elusive, a good policy to follow is to assume consistency exists unless you have done the necessary work to prove yourself wrong.

Structures that do not resemble adult forms or those more removed from the surface forms are less accessible to the analyst. Cognitive structures such as the child's concepts about time fit this category, as do the child's restricted phonological rules which result in most words being reduced to consonant-vowel (CV) syllables. In the case of time there is not a simple unambiguous surface manifestation of this concept. In the consonant-vowel example, there is not a clear relationship between the child's structure and the adult word form. In both these instances the error analysis approach does not work because there is no appropriate checklist against which to evaluate the child's performance. Instead, a list might be created of the child's productions of CV syllables, and another that is the child's exceptions to the CV rule. When assessing the child's knowledge of time, the list might include each of the child's references to nonpresent events to find a pattern of expression.

Sometimes the child's productions are so unclear that they need to be analyzed in detail via multilevel transcripts to see if there exists a set of behaviors which are common across productions. For example, Carter (1979) discovered a vocal production of a breathy "h" plus vowel which a child consistently produced in contexts of pleasure along with a smile. Carter concluded that the child was expressing a pleasure-surprise-recognition meaning and assigned the cluster of things the status of a structure.

Analyzing for Communicative Breakdowns In keeping with the sensemaking theme, the analysis of regularities should be done in order to determine whether the deviant structures cause problems in the ongoing interaction. An error which results in confusion or misunderstanding is more serious than one which simply sounds wrong. Thus the analyst might return to the sample and look to see if the structures identified cause interactional breakdowns. Evidence for such breakdowns may be a silence as the partner thinks about what the child has said, a request for revision or clarification from the child, or a misinterpretation of what the child has said. Identifying breakdowns also affords the analyst the opportunity to investigate the repair strategies used by both the adult and the child. This gives useful insight into the degree of fine tuning between the pair.

Analyzing for Relationships Between Discovered Structures Although the structural analysis often focuses on one structure at a time, it does not assume isolation of structures. Rather, the analyst should assume that structures are tied together in a variety of ways to form organized systems. Structures within the same linguistic level may fit together in hierarchical arrangements, as do clause structures in multiple-clause sentences, or in sequential arrangements such as in the rules or processes hypothesized for phonological production.

Structures may also have cross-level affinities. For example, children's problems with deictic terms in semantics, with subordination in syntax, and with discourse devices and polite forms in pragmatics might all be a reflection of their lack of listener perspective taking.

A fruitful way to discover the relationships of structures at different levels is to consider the possible cause of deviations. For example, the deletion of the plural inflectional endings detected in morphological analysis may be due to a problem with weak-syllable deletion or part of a larger problem with fricative omissions instead of an isolated morphological problem. It may also be the case that semantics of particular morphological forms are not yet acquired, such as those involving temporality, so that in the omission of past-tense endings morphological and semantic levels are intertwined.

Finally, as the particular conditions under which the language occurs become more demanding, the language may change systematically. Sometimes called *style shifting,* other times referred to as *task constraints,* these coordinated shifts could be studied by identifying changes that occur together. In rapid or excited speech, for example, there will be a greater likelihood for weak-syllable deletion, stop-consonant underarticulation, syntactic simplification, and deletion of morphological forms. These areas can be regarded as systematically related, and the relationship can be examined in further detail.

Reliability and Validity of Structural Analysis

Two criteria often applied to assessment tools is that they be reliable and valid. Reliability relates to the consistency of the results that are obtained when the measure is used, and validity addresses the issue of how well the results are related to what the assessor hopes to measure. These constructs as they pertain to tests and other tools of assessment are discussed in Chapter 9, but we want to discuss briefly at this point the issues of reliability and validity in relation to structural analysis.

Reliability   A test or measure is said to be reliable if it gives the same results under different circumstances, such as when used by different testers or analysts or when administered at different times of the day. If the language sample is considered to be the "tool" when doing structural analysis, it cannot be expected to be reliable in this sense. The language sample will differ as the child engages with different people and in different events. We cannot even expect that the analysis done on the same sample by two different clinicians will be the same, which would be another way of looking for reliability, because each clinician may focus on different features of the child's language system. When doing structural analysis, we suspend the requirement that the measures be "reliable" and instead concentrate on explaining the differences that occur for different interactants across different events.

Validity   Structural analysts must, however, consider the validity issue. A valid measure is one that gives information on how the behavior or structure being investigated will be used beyond the assessment situation. A common criticism of formal tests is that they are not valid because they cannot predict what behavior will be exhibited outside of the test, either on other tests or in "real world" situations. When doing structural analysis we are interested in how the child functions in real world events and so choose those situations for our analysis. We thus can be quite confident from our analysis that we know how the child will perform when leaving us and going into other similar situations. Again, this is related to the purpose of structural analysis; we do not attempt to say what the child's language structure is like in the abstract, but rather how it functions in different contexts.

DETERMINING GOALS FOR INTERVENTION

The final step in assessment, after analyzing for structural patterns, is to make recommendations for intervention. Information from the analysis will be used to determine the therapy goals. For the child who has multiple problems, the following considerations might be helpful in deciding initial goals for intervention.

Testing the Sturdiness of the Identified Structures

Once the structures have been discovered and attempts have been made to understand relationships among them, the clinician can proceed to a step of the analysis which tests the sturdiness of the structures and their amenability to change. This is a useful endeavor both as verification of the correctness of the analysis and as a prelude to deciding the course of language intervention. Those structures which show lack of stability in that they are inconsistent and change with a bit of environmental juggling—such as changing the context, providing a model for the child to imitate, or asking the child to revise—would be the ones most susceptible to change with language intervention.

Stimulability

Historically speech pathologists have used the term *stimulability* to mean the child's ability to produce a sound correctly following direct stimulation. For example, if the child says /t/ for /s/, the clinician says: "Say this after me: sss, sss, sss." If the child can now produce the /s/, the sound is stimulable.

This ability of the child to reproduce a heard model has been shown to be an indicator of the likelihood that the child is ready to learn the target sound. If the sound is stimulable, it is more likely to change with intervention. We extend the stimulability notion to other structures, such as syntactic structures, phonological processes, and event learning. That is, we suggest that a child who can imitate an example of a structure, may be showing a readiness for learning that structure.

We would also like to use the term *stimulability* to include other techniques which can serve to advance a structure to a more adultlike form. Susceptibility to modeling can also qualify as an indicator of stimulability. For example, if the child is given an example of a structure and spontaneously reproduces it later, the structure can be said to be stimulable with a priori modeling. Or if the child improves on an original production of a form after the adult follows the original with the adult version, the structure can be said to be stimulable with postscript modeling.

Repairs

Breakdowns in interactions also afford an opportunity for the clinician to observe whether the child can change a structure and how the child changes it. For example, Gallagher (1977) studied how normal children at three stages of language development responded when an adult pretended not to understand what they said and used the contingent query "What?" Using children classified according to Brown's stages I through III (see Chapter 6), her results indicated that all the children responded to "What?" by giving a revised version of their original utterance, but they differed in the types of revisions made. Stage I, the youngest children, tended to revise in two ways—by phonetic change (e.g., C: He kit ball A: What? C: He kick ball) or by elaborating on a constituent in the utterance (e.g., C: It ball A: What? C: It big ball). Stage II children had significantly fewer phonetic change in revisions and often changed the grammatical structure of the original sentence by adding new constituents (e.g., C: Big ball A: What? C: It big ball). They also frequently reduced constituents on revision (e.g., C: It big ball A: What? C: It ball). Stage III children displayed the same pattern of adding and reducing constituents and in addition substituted new words in a significant proportion of the revisions (e.g., C: He kick ball A: What? C: He kick it).

Gallagher's questioning technique allows for observation of how a child revises a structure when the situation calls for it, thereby indicating the stability of the structure and its capability for change. Such revisions after breakdowns have been called *repairs*.

Functionality of the Identified Structure

An analysis done in natural contexts can point up which language structures carry more functional weight for the interactants. Question forms, for example, tend to get information that is difficult to get in any other way. Certain vocabulary items are very functional. Other language forms have little obvious utility and seem important only because they are conventional. The distinction between *I* and *me* falls into this conventional category, as does the distinction between *ain't* and *isn't*. While we may choose to target unconventional structures in order to smooth out the child's interactions with others who prefer conventional forms, our first priority should be to address those structures that are functional for the child and to organize our intervention goals by assigning priority to those which are most functional to the child.

To summarize, we have offered four areas of consideration for deciding which of the structures discovered in the structural analysis offer the best candidates for language intervention. (See Box 2–6 for a summary.) The main emphasis is on whether the structure seems to be functional and its sturdiness. The result of the functionality and sturdiness observations can then be incorporated into the recommendation section of the written report, the last step of the assessment procedure.

BOX 2–6. *Selecting Targets for Intervention*

A structure is a good candidate for change through language intervention if it—

1. Is inconsistent—lacks in sturdiness
2. Changes when the child is presented with the adult model—is stimulable
3. Changes when it fails to communicate—improves under repair
4. Carries more communicative import for the child—is functionally significant

---

THE PRAGMATICS OF REPORT WRITING

The pragmatics assessment approach leads to some alteration in the traditional report. The report will focus on the child's ability to make sense of what is going on and how well the child accomplishes what he or she wants to accomplish.

The nature of the events in which the child is engaged while the sampling was done needs to be described in the report. It may also include how well others fine tune to the child's differences. Deficit areas would be treated not as isolated problems but in terms of how the problems relate to the child's ability to perform in everyday life. Thus intelligibility and repair strategies are reported along with phonological, morphological, or syntactic disorders.

Problems should be reported not just in terms of whether the child's communication seems inappropriate to the observing or attending adult, but whether the behaviors judged to be inappropriate or deviant can be deciphered in terms of what the child may be thinking about or trying to achieve. The child's analyzed behaviors might be evaluated not only for their degree of conventionality but also in terms of whether they reflect a different intent or agenda and how well the agendas are achieved.

Writing to Different Audiences

Assessment reports are usually designed to communicate with imagined readers. They tend to be written as if the reader has no knowledge of that child. That is, they contain background information for a naive reader about an unfamiliar child. Some clinicians have commented that these full reports are written for those reading the child's record (Pannbacker, 1975); that is to say, they are written "for the record." The reader is presumed to want to know whether the child has a problem, the origin of the problem, the areas of deficit, the nature of the child's language, and what should be done to remediate the problem. The traditional report attempts to answer all these questions. The report for the record usually begins with identifying information about the child (birthdate, address, phone); contains a section on the reason for the referral and the child's medical, clinical, and developmental history; and then describes the assessment procedures, the results, general impressions, and clinical or educational recommendations.

Assessment reports can also be written to particular people in answer to their specific questions. This is the case when the child is referred by another professional for a particular sort of evaluation—when Doctor X refers to Language Pathologist Y for a language assessment. Sometimes parents have initiated the evaluation and will be the only recipients of the report. The information to be conveyed in the report in these cases is more specific; how was the child observed to communicate and what recommendations are made. Information "for the record" does not need to be included since the referring professional or parent presumably already knows it.

We suggest that assessment reports be confined to the information that can be uniquely provided by the language professional in order to focus on the results of our observation and analysis and the recommendations based on this information. In contrast to traditional reports that attempt to be more comprehensive, a direct and less formal style of reporting can be used. If the report is going to someone who knows the child well, it can be written as a letter that presumes the addressee knows the child and is asking particular questions.

If the report is going to someone who does not have the background information needed for the record, this information can be provided in a different form. For example, the next speech-language pathologist who will be working with the child does not yet know the child and will want to have access to the child's birthdate, medical, developmental, and social history. We recommend a data sheet for this purpose that is designed for the record and therefore is in outline rather than paragraph form. If a report is going to several people or agencies, the data sheet will go only to those that do not have the information. We have included an example of a data sheet which might be adapted for use in Box 2–7. The narrative report can thus be directed to providing the reader with the information that is most central to the language pathologist; that is, how the child is communicating in various contexts and what could facilitate communication.

BOX 2–7. Data Sheet

Child's name: Jose Santiago
Date of report: April 23, 1989
Information provided by mother and classroom teacher

Identifying Information

Birthdate: January 25, 1982
Address: 130 Jewett Parkway, Buffalo, New York 14214
Phone: 836-1363
Guardians' Names: Juanita Santiago (mother)
                Jose Santiago (father)
                Sarita Sanitago (paternal grandmother)
Referral source: Second-grade classroom teacher, Juanita Alvarez, Oliver Wendell Holmes Elementary School
Reason for referral: Does not appear to understand what is going on in class. Has not developed English beyond a few simple phrases over the five months he has been in class

Family Information

Those living with child:
        Mother, father, grandmother (see above)
        Brothers, Juan (age 9) and Samuel (age 3)
Communication problems among family members:
        None except for initial difficulty in this country before knowledge of English was developed
Language spoken in home:
        Primarily Puerto Rican Spanish. Occasional English when visited by English-speaking friends. TV watched on average of two hours per day, English programs

Medical Information

Prenatal birth complications: Caesarean section
Serious illnesses or injuries: Chicken pox with high fever for a week at age three.
Chronic conditions: Periodic bouts of middle ear infection

Consultations with medical specialist: Pediatrician at local health clinic is child's physician.

Health: Good

Hearing test results: Normal acuity Date of test: April 23, 1989

Developmental History

Speech and language development: Learned first words at around two years. Slow to form sentences in Spanish. Difficult to understand if you don't know him well

Other areas of development: Normal

Educational History

First grade in Puerto Rico. Currently in second grade.

Special class? No, but special instruction in English by bilingual teacher

Teacher's name: Juanita Alvarez

School name: Oliver Wendell Holmes Elementary School

School's address: 3200 Standard Street, Buffalo, New York 14260

School's phone: 636-3475

Competence in subject areas: Did well in first grade. Poor performance now. Perhaps because classroom instruction in English

No special tests prior to this referral

Social History

Group activities: Very congenial with Spanish-speaking classmates. Shy with English-speaking peers.

Names and ages of children whom child plays with:
  Manuel Esposito, 7 years, classmate
  David Gonzales, 7 years, classmate and neighbor

Writing Competence Reports

Reports are often written with the aim of outlining "what's wrong with this person." Hence, the report creates a picture of the child that focuses on deficits and conveys a negative attitude on the part of the professional toward that person. A deficit point of view is conveyed in several ways and is frequently pervasive in reports. Finding alternative ways to describe a child's performance or characteristics can instead communicate the professional's recognition and appreciation of the child's strengths and competence. Carefully reviewing our reports for deficit bias may reveal both blatant and subtle examples. Following are some areas to try to avoid when writing reports.

1. *Negative terms* such as *can't, won't,* and *doesn't* obviously emphasize the negative. Less obvious but still negative, are terms such as *rarely, only, except,* and *unless.*
    She *rarely looked at the examiner.*
    He *only* knows the numbers to five.
    She *can't* name any body parts *except* her nose.
    He *wouldn't* talk to the clinician *unless* his mother told him to.

2. *Negative expectations* are often communicated, even when we seem to be making a positive judgment about a child. The following statements seem to presuppose that the child will exhibit negative behaviors and to express surprise that these behaviors are not carried out.

Bob was cooperative, separated easily from his mother, and participated willingly in the tasks.

David was rarely self-abusive. He allowed the evaluator to hold him while completing the puzzle, and he seemed to enjoy being cuddled.

3. *Implied disagreement or disbelief* of the informant's information is often inadvertently conveyed in reports when professionals are reporting second-hand information, especially that from parents. In an attempt to appear "objective," a negative attitude about the informant may be conveyed.

Mrs. S claimed that Jon talks at home.

Cara's father denies that Cara watches television.

The parents defended their choice of preschools by indicating its convenience.

Ms. P maintains that she reads to her children every evening.

4. *Terms that imply pathology* often are used to describe unusual behaviors. These terms give the impression that the behaviors are symptoms rather than meaningful responses, intents, or initiations.

Carlos's play is very *perseverative*.

Echolalia is prominant in Barry's speech.

Celia seems to have an *attention deficit*.

5. *Overall negative judgments* generally do not convey useful information and can be recast more specifically and positively to communicate what was intended.

Robert's play activities indicate he is *not functioning at age level*.

These results indicate a *significant delay* in expressive language abilities.

Because the tendency toward negative reporting is so pervasive and difficult to break, even when the clinician is aware of the problem, reports should be edited after they are written and language and concepts changed if they have a negative connotation. An example of editing to change a deficit to a competence report is given in Box 2–8.

BOX 2–8.   *Changing Negative to Positive in Report Writing*

1. Robert, age 2–11, was referred by pediatrician for suspected speech and language delay. He *had difficulty* separating from his mother.

   Rewrite: He indicated his unwillingness to have his mother left behind by. . .

2. R did not initiate topics of his choice *except* when he wanted to play with puzzles and a Big Bird doll.

   Rewrite: R initiated topics on two occasions, once when he wanted to play with puzzles, and a second time when he wanted to play with a stuffed animal (Bid Bird).

3. He sometimes maintained topics for as long as five minutes; *however*, his average topic maintenance was only one to two minutes.

   Rewrite: On the average he maintained topics for one to two minutes, and on occasion was able to continue topics for as long as five minutes.

4. These results indicate a delay of *at least* one year five months in expressive language abilities.

   Rewrite: His ability to combine words and use word endings was at the level of a one-year-old.

5. R *perseverated* on the words (choo-choo)/(truck) when it was *no longer appropriate*.

Rewrite: Robert had a special interest in vehicles and often preferred them to other tasks being offered.

6. Robert was *distracted* easily by activity outside and was *uninterested* in the pictures.

    Rewrite: He showed a high degree of interest in cars and other vehicles preferring them to pictures.

7. R was able to follow the clinician's point and simple one-step commands ("Put that in," "Don't touch"). He did not, *however*, demonstrate understanding of more complex or compound sentence forms; for example, he did not respond appropriately or did not respond at all to questions such as "Do you see a cup?"

    Rewrite: R was able to follow directions involving one verb. When given longer and more complex directions, he responded to the last words he heard. (Change tells more about what he does do rather than what he does not do.)

8. A formal phonological assessment of R's sound system was not completed during the evaluation due to his *uncooperativeness* during structured clinician-directed tasks.

    Rewrite: Omit

9. His intents were judged to be *limited*. He *did not respond* to yes–no questions and *only* responded to *wh-* questions with single word labels.

    Rewrite: He expressed a variety of intents . . . (how were they limited?) and was able to answer questions about object names with appropriate one-word labels.

10. At times, R's eye contact with his mother and the clinicians was *poor*. Robert was observed to reach for objects and people on his left and right without turning his head to look at what he was doing.

    Rewrite: R often had direct eye contact with his play partner. On occasion he relied on peripheral vision to maintain social contact as well as to locate objects.

11. Robert's pragmatic play abilities indicate that he is *not functioning at age level*.

    Rewrite: Robert's play activities, which involved pretending with more than one person or object, reflect a nineteen- to twenty-two-month-old competence. He has not yet developed the ability to pretend, indicating a slight developmental lag in his play abilities.

12. R's vocal quality and resonance were judged to be good. When requesting, *however*, his pitch tended to become higher and his intonation "whiney," a pattern more characteristic of younger children who are limited in ability to express themselves.

    Rewrite: He was able to use a pitch rise and a "whine" marker to let others know he was requesting something.

13. A formal oral peripheral examination was attempted, *but due to R's lack of cooperation, was not completed*.

    Rewrite: Omit above and tell what was done: Informal evaluation of the oral structures and their functioning revealed symmetrical lip retraction, lip protrusion, and good lip mobility.

14. Phonologically, R demonstrated numerous *errors* including *inconsistent* final consonant deletion, fronting of velars, cluster reduction, and stopping of affricates.

    Rewrite: Robert's speech sound differences were patterned and regular. He preferred stops to fricatives, using final consonants when the words ended in stops and omitting them when words ended in fricatives; producing stops and omitting fricatives from clusters; and substituting stops for affricates. He also substituted front for back consonants.

15. Overall, Robert demonstrated *delayed communicative skills*. There appears to be a *delay* in phonological, expressive, and receptive language, pragmatic and play skills.

    Rewrite: Overall, Robert displays communication style typical of a one-year-old child. He is quite interactive, willing to communicate his desires, and is very interested in what is going on around him, especially if it involves vehicles.

Writing Culturally Sensitive Reports

Reports written about children from different cultures will differ from those about children from the host culture in that they should include relevant information about the culture the child is from, about the child's language learning history (e.g., ages and length of time a bilingual child has been speaking each language), and about family migration history. For children who are assessed in a language other than English, the circumstances surrounding the assessment should be described (e.g., use of interpreter).

Reports written about children from nonstandard American communities (e.g., Native Americans or African-Americans) should take into account ways the child's language reflects a home dialect, and how the child's performance may be reflecting his or her home culture.

Indications of negative bias toward children from different ethnic backgrounds can be found in the presence of terms such as *disadvantaged, culturally deprived, at risk,* and *minority* when used to describe children's family history (Taylor, 1988).

Excerpts from Selected Reports

To give a flavor of what reports might look like and an idea of what is to come as we proceed to later chapters, we conclude this chapter on structural analysis with several examples of reports which have been the outcome of the structural analysis approach. The chapters to follow will analyze structures at various levels of language: the sound system (phonology), words and their parts (morphology), the way words fit together in sentences (syntax), the meanings of words and phrases (semantics), and the organization of language into longer segments of talk (discourse). As one can see from the following excerpts, the method of structural analysis need not be confined to the areas we will be talking about but can be used whenever one needs to find behavioral and structural regularities.

The first two reports, those for Mark and Rick, are written to professionals who referred the child for an evaluation. They do not include background information, since the professional has access to each child's history from previous reports and data sheets of the form presented in Box 2–7. The third report, about Yan Yan Wang, an emerging bilingual child, is written for a future audience who might not have access to background information on the child. For this reason, relevant information about the child's history is provided in the third report.

Analysis of Dysfluency   Mark's speech has an unusual amount of dysfluency which can be classified into at least four different types—unfilled pauses, filled pauses, repeats, and rephrasings. The pauses, both filled and unfilled, seem to fall primarily at the beginnings of sentences and major syntactic units, sometimes before rarer words such as *barrel*. This would suggest that they are formulation pauses where he is trying to decide what to say or how to phrase it. This in itself is not unusual except that they are more frequent for Mark. The filled pauses are noises which are also used by all of us to keep our turn in the conversation (otherwise the other person would start talking). However, most of us use *um's* or *uh's* and Mark's, I think, are fast, unintelligible, and unrecognizable insertions which make the listeners feel they have not understood him. I say "I think" because they may, indeed, be part of the sentence rather than fillers, but judging from the rest of the sentence, I feel they are better categorized as condensed filler phrases. Their frequency, like the unfilled pauses, suggest he is having trouble with formulating an idea or its expression.

Mark's repetitions are usually of a sound or syllable, such as *re re re,* said several times followed by a word which does, indeed, start with the sound being repeated. These seem to occur more with multisyllabic words, especially for those which have similar syllables (*recre*ation) and seem to reflect a problem he has with how to sequence the syllables in the words. To restart then allows him stalling time while he thinks about the way the word goes. In this case, Mark's error patterns suggest that he is not having trouble choosing the word or formulating the idea as with formulation pauses, but rather deciding how to order the syllables.

The rephrasings are yet another kind of nonfluency and are often of a backtracking type where he substitutes a like word (*restaurant* for *building*) or fills in a phrase (*my sister,* changed to *my parents, my brother, and my sister*). Sometimes he doesn't complete the rephrased word, as when he said /kI kI/ and then changed what was possibly going to be *kicked* to *fighting with him.* These seem different from the multisyllabic restarts, since the word is changed and the rephrased units often seem to have already been formulated in terms of word selection in sound sequencing, and in syntactic organization.

Perhaps the most disconcerting rephrasings are those where Mark corrects his pronunciation. These backtracks disrupt the timing of his utterance more and are the hardest for his listeners to follow since they can't recognize what he is saying, as when he pronounced *train* as *chain* when saying *train jumped.*

I believe most of these errors are anticipations of future sounds or sound features. For example, he said *ch* for *tr* in the last example because he was anticipating saying the next word *jump* where the *ch* is said like the *j*. There are many examples of these anticipatory assimilations.

Analysis of Self-Stimulatory Behaviors   Rick displays a variety of self-stimulatory behaviors. There are vocal noises, chin and head hits, and head and body rocks. His vocal noises have an identifiable form which allows one to classify them into two kinds. The first is a *henshui*—a stereotypic form which is two or three syllables in length. The first syllable is usually a very high-pitched consonant and vowel—the consonant is an /h/, the vowel is nasalized. The second syllable is said on a much lower pitch and shorter, and begins with a fricative or affricate followed by a vowel, usually a /u/. The last syllable, if present, is either a vowel or bilabial consonant and vowel. It is also short in duration and low in pitch. Rick's other noises are an *oioioi,* said with a glottal fry, and a buccal fry. The noises all involve extremes in articulatory positioning; that is, front to back vowels, glottal to alveolar movement. The "fry" aspect suggests his focus on kinesthetic as well as, or instead of, auditory features for those sounds.

Rick's hits are most often chin and head hits with the palm or heel of either hand. Sometimes there are quick sequences made with alternating hands on alternate sides of his head. His repetitive sequences were often combinations of several types of behaviors rapidly following one another, such as hits, noises, then rocks. They were sometimes irregular in temporal organization—that is, they were not equally timed, had an unequal number of identical segments per sequence, and were unequal in the amount of time given to each identical sequence. Those sequences which were more regular were where Rick or the adult was talking. In these cases, he hit himself or jerked on the strongly stressed syllable of the utterances. Sometimes every syllable was stressed, as when he said "this is a 'puh' " and hit his leg with his left hand on each word.

In Rick's interaction with his mother, his repetitive behaviors were infrequent, consuming about ten seconds of a two-minute sequence. They occurred between activities or when his mother was looking away from him. Contrastively, his repetitive behaviors were more frequent with his teacher, with the longest sequences following the teacher's nonacceptance of his attempts to perform for her. In both interactions, the adults sometimes continued to talk to Rick during his repetitive sequences. At other times, they waited until the behaviors subsided or told him to put his hands down.

Analysis of a Child Learning English as a Second Language   Yan Yan Wang, a Mandarin-speaking six-year-old, was referred for a language evaluation by his first-grade teacher. His teacher was concerned that Yan Yan does not appear to understand what is going on in the class and that he has not developed his English usage beyond a few simple phrases such as greetings. She felt he should have learned more English, since he has been in this country for five months. He has been getting biweekly special instruction in a kindergarten that emphasizes English-language learning.

Yan Yan comes from a Mandarin Chinese-speaking family. Prior to his arrival, he had not been exposed to English. Yan Yan's parents have been in the United States since 1987, and he joined them after they had been here for two years. Between 1987 and 1989 Yan Yan resided with his grandparents in China. He is an only child and lives alone with his parents. In China he was part of an extended family and lived with several other children and adults. The Wangs speak to each other and to Yan Yan in Mandarin. Yan Yan is exposed to English in school and when he watches TV at home, which he does regularly.

Yan Yan's language proficiency in Mandarin was evaluated with the help of a Mandarin-speaking informant, Mrs. Wen Chen. Mrs. Chen was casually acquainted with Yan Yan and his family through their interactions in local cultural events. Mrs. Chen speaks a dialect of Mandarin slightly different from that of the Wang family, but with the exception of an occasional lexical item, Mrs. Chen and members of the Wang family were mutually intelligible.

Yan Yan was evaluated on March 17, 1990, following an interview with his mother. Mrs. Chen conducted the interview in Mandarin with the mother and interacted with the child; she also provided the translation and needed background information to interpret the mother's information and the child's language behavior.

The evaluation, conducted in the child's native language, involved four events. The child was first engaged in conversation with Mrs. Chen about topics which had previously been determined to be of interest to him. This was followed by a directed play activity where he was required to follow directions.

He then engaged in a storytelling interaction with his mother and a play interaction with a Mandarin-speaking friend who is his age.

The results of the evaluation revealed that Yan Yan performs normally in his native language. He was able to form complex sentences, had adult knowledge of phonology, and was able to tell complex stories at the level of a normal six-year-old Mandarin speaker. He is judged to be a normal language learner.

•   •   •

The child-centered pragmatics framework that we are forwarding as a guide to assessing children's language takes as its method the procedures of structural analysis. The procedures which have been outlined in this chapter follow the step-by-step progression outlined in Box 2–9.

The procedures can be applied to whatever the clinician wants to discover about a particular child's communication. Since there are so many aspects to any single language sample, we have recommended that the clinician focus on those structures which have most to do with sensemaking, functionalism, and fine tuning. We will elaborate more on these three constructs in the next chapter.

BOX 2–9. *Summary of Steps in Structural Analysis*

1. Analyzing the preassessment information
2. Conducting the family interview
3. Observing the child in naturalistic events
4. Transcribing several events
5. Deep testing for structures not adequately sampled
6. Analyzing for structural regularities
7. Determining initial goals for intervention
8. Writing the report

REFERENCES

ASHA. Position of the American Speech-Language-Hearing Association on Social Dialects, 25, 1983, 23–25.

ASHA. Clinical Management of Communicatively Handicapped Minority Language Populations, 27, 1985, 29–32.

BERKO, J. The Child's Learning of English Morphology, *Word,* 14, 1958, 150–77

BLOOM, L., AND M. LAHEY. *Language Development and Language Disorders.* New York: John Wiley, 1978.

BROWN R., AND U. BELLUGI. Three Processes in the Child's Acquisition of Syntax, *Harvard Educational Review,* 34, 1964, 133–51.

CARTER, A. The Transformation of Sensorimotor Morphemes into Words: A Case Study of the Development of "More" and "Mine," *Journal of Child Language,* 2, 1975, 233–50.

CARTER, A. Prespeech Meaning Relations: An Outline of One Infant's Sensorimotor Morpheme Development, in *Language Acquisition: Studies in First Language Development,* eds. P. Fletcher and M. Garman. New York: Cambridge University Press, 1979, pp. 71–92.

CHAPMAN, R., AND J. MILLER. Analyzing Language and Communication in the Child, in *Nonspeech Language Intervention*, ed. R. Schiefelbusch. Baltimore: University Park Press, 1980.

CONDON, W., AND W. OGSTON. A Segmentation of Behavior, *Journal of Psychiatric Research*, 5, 1967, 221–35.

CONDON, W., AND L. SANDER. Neonate Movement Is Synchronized with Adult Speech: Interactional Participation and Language Participation, *Science*, 183, 1974, 99–101.

CRAGO, M. Development of Communicative Competence in Inuit Children: Implications for Speech-Language Pathology, *Journal of Childhood Communication Disorders*, 13, 1990, 73–83.

CROSS, T. Mothers' Speech Adjustments: The Contributions of Selected Child Listener Variables, in *Talking to Children*, eds. C. Snow and C. Ferguson. New York: Cambridge University Press, 1977.

CRYSTAL, D., P. FLETCHER, AND M. GARMAN. *The Grammatical Analysis of Language Disability*. New York: Elsevier North-Holland, 1978.

DAMICO, J., J. OLLER, AND E. STOREY. The Diagnosis of Language Disorders in Bilingual Children: Surface-Oriented and Pragmatic Criteria, *Journal of Speech and Hearing Disorders*, 48, 1983, 385–94.

DORE, J. Children's Illocutionary Acts, in *Discourse Production and Comprehension*, ed. R. Freedle. Hillsdale, N.J.: Lawrence Erlbaum, 1977.

DORE, J., M. B. FRANKLIN, R. T. MILLER, AND A. RAMER. Transitional Phenomena in Early Language Acquisition, *Journal of Child Language*, 3, 1976, 13–28.

DUCHAN, J. Interactions with an Autistic Child, in *Language: Social Psychological Perspectives*, eds. M. Giles, W. Robinson, and P. Smith. New York: Pergamon Press, 1980, pp. 255–60.

DUCHAN, J. Language Assessment: The Pragmatics Revolution, in *Language Sciences*, ed. R. Naremore. San Diego, Calif.: College Hill Press, 1984.

DUCHAN, J. Language Intervention Through Sensemaking and Fine Tuning, in *Language Competence: Assessment and Intervention*, ed. R. Schiefelbusch. San Diego, Calif.: College Hill Press, 1986, 187–212.

ERICKSON, F., AND J. SHULTZ. *The Counselor as Gatekeeper: Social Interaction in Interviews*. New York: Academic Press, 1982.

FEY, M. *Language Intervention with Young Children*. San Diego, Calif.: College Hill Press, 1986.

FRANKEL, R., M., LEARY, AND B. KILMAN. Building Social Skills Through Pragmatic Analysis: Assessment and Treatment Implications for Children with Autism, in *Handbook of Autism and Disorders of Atypical Development*, eds. D. Cohen and A. Donellan. New York: John Wiley, 1986.

GALLAGHER, T. Revision Behaviors in the Speech of Normal Children Developing Language, *Journal of Speech and Hearing Disorders*, 20, 1977, 303–18. Social Skills Through Pragmatic Analysis: Assess-

GALLAGHER, T. Pre-assessment: A Procedure for Accommodating Language Use Variability, in *Pragmatic Assessment and Intervention Issues in Language*, eds. T. Gallagher and C. Prutting. San Diego, Calif.: College Hill Press, 1983, pp. 1–28.

GALLAGHER, T. ed. *Pragmatics of Language: Clinical Practice Issues*. San Diego, Calif.: Singular Publishing Group, 1991.

GALLAGHER, T., AND C. PRUTTING, eds. *Pragmatic Assessment and Intervention Issues in Language*. San Diego, Calif.: College Hill Press, 1983.

GLEASON, J., AND S. WEINTRAUB. The Acquisition of Routines in Child Language, *Language and Society*, 5, 1976, 129–36.

GLEITMAN, L., H. GLEITMAN, AND E. SHIPLEY. The Emergence of the Child as a Grammarian, *Cognition*, 1, 1972, 137–64.

IRWIN, J., ed. *Pragmatics: The Role in Language Development*. La Verne, Calif.: Fox Point Pub. Co., 1982.

KAYSER, H. Speech and Language Assessment of Spanish-English Speaking Children, *Language, Speech, and Hearing Services in Schools*, 20, 1989, 226–44.

KJERLAND, L. AND J. KOVACH. Family-Staff Collaboration for Tailored Infant Assessment, in E. Gibbs and D. Teti, eds. *Interdisciplinary Assessment of Infants: A guide for Early Intervention Professionals*. Baltimore: Paul H. Brooks, 1990, pp. 287–97.

LEE, L. *Developmental Sentence Analysis*. Evanston, Ill.: Northwestern University Press, 1974.

LUND, N., AND J. DUCHAN. The Monolingual Speech-Language Pathologist: An Approach for Assessing Children with Limited English Proficiency. Miniseminar presented at New York State Speech, Language and Hearing Association. Monticello, New York: April 1990.

MACDONALD, J. *Oliver: Parent-Administered Communication Inventory*. Columbus, Ohio: Chas. E. Merrill, 1978.

MILLER, J. *Assessing Language Production in Children*. Baltimore: University Park Press, 1981.

NELSON, K., AND J. GRUENDEL. Generalized Event Representations: Basic Building Blocks of Cognitive Development, in *Advances in Developmental Psychology*, eds. M. Lamb and A. Brown. Hillsdale, N.J.: Lawrence Erlbaum, 1981.

PANNBACKER, M. Diagnostic Report Writing, *Journal of Speech and Hearing Disorders*, 40, 1975, 367–79.

PIAGET, J. *The Child's Conception of the World*. London: Routledge and Kegan Paul, 1929. (Reprinted Totowa, N.J.: Littlefield Adams, 1976.)

PRIZANT, B. An Analysis of the Functions of Immediate Echolalia in Autistic Children. Ph.D. dissertation, State University of New York at Buffalo, 1978.

PRIZANT, B., AND J. DUCHAN. The Functions of Immediate Echolalia in Autistic Children, *Journal of Speech and Hearing Disorders*, 46, 1981, 241–49.

PUBLIC LAW 95-561. The Bilingual Education Act

(Title VI of the Elementary and Secondary Education Act of 1965).

PUBLIC LAW 94-142. The Education of All Handicapped Children Act (November 29, 1975).

READ, B., AND L. CHERRY. Preschool Children's Production of Directive Forms, *Discourse Processes: A Multidisciplinary Journal,* 1, 1978, 233–45.

SLOBIN, D., ed. *A Field Manual for Cross-Cultural Study of the Acquisition of Communicative Competence.* Berkeley, Calif.: University of California, 1967.

SNOW, C., AND C. FERGUSON, eds. *Talking to Children: Language Input and Acquisition.* New York: Cambridge University Press, 1977.

SPRADLEY, J. *The Ethnographic Interview.* New York: Holt, Rinehart & Winston, 1979.

TAYLOR, O. Speech and Language Differences and Disorders of Multicultural Populations, in *Handbook of Speech-Language Pathology and Audiology,* eds. N. Lass, L. McReynolds, J. Northern, and D. Yoder. Philadelphia: B. Decker, 1988, pp. 939–58.

THOMAS, E. It's All Routine: A Redefinition of Routines as a Central Factor in Language Acquisition. Paper presented at the Fourth Annual Boston University Conference on Language Development. Boston: 1979.

TYACK, D., AND R. GOTTSLEBEN. *Language Sampling, Analysis and Training* (rev. ed.). Palo Alto, Calif.: Consulting Psychologists Press, 1974.

VON RAFFLER ENGEL, E. An Example of Ling Consciousness in the Child, *Orientamenti P gici,* 12, 1965, 631–33. Reprinted in *Studies of Language Development,* eds. C. Ferguson a Slobin. New York: Holt, Rinehart & Wii 1973.

WESTBY, C. Ethnographic Interviewing: Asking the Right Questions to the Right People in the Right Ways, *Journal of Childhood Communication Disorders,* 13, 1990, 101–11.

WETHERBY, A., AND C. PRUTTING. Profiles of Communicative and Cognitive Abilities in Autistic Children, *Journal of Speech and Hearing Research,* 27, 1984, 364–77.

3

Pragmatics: Sensemaking, Functionalism, and Fine Tuning

Until recently, researchers and clinicians have studied language as though form and meaning existed independent of the contexts in which language occurs. Research in the last decade has shown the dramatic effect of contexts on the way language is used and interpreted, making it clear that language cannot be realistically assessed if it is isolated from what is going on with the speaker and listener. Pragmatics is the study of the effects of context, and it has been investigated in a variety of ways that offer alternative approaches to analyzing children's use of language. (See Simon, 1985; Duchan, 1984; Gallagher and Prutting, 1983; and Irwin, 1982 for a sampling of many of these approaches.)

The diversity of views on pragmatics is readily apparent in reading the current literature in the field. Some investigators study pragmatics as an additional and separable level of language, along with phonology, morphology, syntax, and semantics (Prutting, 1979; Miller, 1978). Others, the functionalists, regard pragmatics as the force behind the choice of structures in these levels of language and thus of primary importance in understanding language expression and comprehension (Bates and MacWhinney, 1979). They view language structures in terms of their function in carrying out communicative jobs.

We favor the functionalist view of pragmatics and emphasize throughout this book the functions that are served by various linguistic structures. Chapter 2 introduced the idea that language is not separable from the context in which it occurs; one cannot judge the adequacy of a child's syntax or semantics without considering what the child is attempting to do. It may be that once an exchange is viewed from the child's perspective, the structure that "sounds wrong" seems appropriate. Apart from recognizing the centrality of context in all assessment questions, we also believe that some children have "pragmatic" problems that are independent of their linguistic skills. The present chapter is directed toward assessing these children as well as toward providing a conceptual framework for attending to context when doing any language assessment.

We have chosen to organize this chapter around aspects of the context that we feel are the primary determinants of communicative behavior and have identified some of the competencies the child needs in order to function effectively and conventionally in interpersonal situations. We will begin our treatment of pragmatics by concentrating on children's knowledge of events and their ability to make sense out of these events in order to participate effectively in them. We will then discuss our version of functionalism by outlining some aspects of how communicators accomplish their agendas and achieve various intents. Lastly, we discuss the contribution of fine tuning to communication between children and adults. That is, we will be looking at how interactants adjust what they are saying and doing depending on what they think their partner knows. And we will also be emphasizing the role this fine tuning plays in children's language learning.

SENSEMAKING

Sensemaking guides all interactions. Participants in events and observers of those events engage in sensemaking when they create an interpretation of what is going on, bringing their ideas about the world into consideration. Interactants or observers attempt to "make sense" of experiences by relying on their background knowledge, orientation, and theories about how the world operates.

The idea of sensemaking comes from the pragmatic revolution and entails many of the concepts that are discussed under the pragmatic umbrella, such as scripts, turntaking, intent, and topic maintenance. Rather than seeing these themes as separate aspects of pragmatics, we view them as all being unified in their sensemaking role.

The Event

The most critical determinant of the communicative exchange between children and their partners is the event in which they are participating, or more precisely, their sense of what the event is. If you were to ask children "What's going on here?" in different events, they would answer on different occasions "We're playing," "We're telling jokes," "We're in speech class." The sense of the event, then, is the participant's conceptualization of the kind of interaction he or she is having. This defines that person's event and sets the scene for particular kinds of exchanges.

Although the setting may be closely tied with the participant's sense of an event, such as being in speech class and "doing speech," the setting is not the event. A therapy room full of toys and furniture is not an event. It is only after something significant happens that one can say an event has taken place—a party, a game, or a conversation. Events happen; they require some kind of change or action sequence.

Likewise, although events are tied to actions, actions are not events. Playing ball can be broken down into a sequence of actions, such as throwing and catching, but it is only when these actions are thought of within a structure that one can identify the event. For example, the event of "the pitcher warming up" and the event of "playing catch" will involve throwing and catching the ball, but participants and observers would generally agree that different events are occurring. Actions may be seen as constituting events when they all fall under a single plan or script or when they are part of a single ritual.

The event may or may not be the same for all participants. The interpreters' perspective on a sequence of actions may vary and thereby create a different sense of the event. The adult may view a given exchange as "teaching," whereas it may be a play session or talking about a television show for a child. Or the adult may be conceptualizing a conversation event, whereas the child perceives the same exchange as a quiz in which there are right and wrong answers.

Events come in many varieties. There are talking events in which the focus is on a verbal exchange, and action events in which the focus is doing some activity. Talking events include exchanges that we think of as conversations, storytelling, verbal descriptions, and verbal routines. Action events may be goal directed, such as putting ingredients together to make something, or "autotelic," that is, consisting of an activity that is an end in itself, such as sliding down a slide (Hubbell, 1981). Some action events will be seen as dramatic play or games. An action event may involve talking, but it differs from talking events in the focus. In action events, talking relates to the activity and serves the purpose of starting or accomplishing the event. Examples would be giving directions preceding or during an activity or speaking for characters in dramatic play.

The participants' sense of the event is very influential in determining the manner in which they act and interact. We know how to participate in an event only when we have identified what that event is and call on our previous experience with like events. If, for example, we perceive a gathering of people to be a study group, we act differently than if we perceive it to be a party. Our behavior and verbal contributions are different when a verbal exchange is viewed as an interview and when it is seen as an argument. This is because we have conventions for these events that are different, and we act accordingly. Most people are uncomfortable when the event is ambiguous, and they hesitate to participate until the nature of the exchange is clear. We generally attempt to determine in advance what an event will be. When asked to someone's home, for example, we often want to know how many other people will be there, whether we will be served a meal, and how we should dress. Without prior knowledge, we risk embarrassment if we misjudge the nature of the event. Similarly, participating in a novel event may cause discomfort or hesitation. It is typical to look to others and to the situation for cues for how to "do" the event when we have no experience with it.

Events make sense because they have coherent organizational structures or "interpretive frames." There are many ways events can be organized, and different events have different sorts of organization. Four such organizational structures have been laid out in Duchan (1991) as a guide for tracing children's acquisition of event knowledge and for assessing particular children's event knowledge. The first is the *role structure*, which involves children's interpretation of the roles carried out by the event participants, and the ways actions and goals are in keeping with those roles. Role structure emphasizes the participants. Both *temporal structure* and *logical structure* involve how the actions in the events relate to one another. Some actions, such as those necessary in setting a table, are ordered sequentially, yet the order is arbitrary. Spoons may be put down before forks, but the opposite order would work just as well. Other actions, such as those which are causally related, are ordered logically. Lids must be removed before contents can be poured. A fourth structure for events, *the deictic structure,* is one in which events and participants are structured from a point of view. Gifts can be either seen as given or received, depending upon the perspective taken.

Not only is our language production influenced by our sense of the event but so is our comprehension of others' language. Children first interpret language in light of the ongoing event and comprehend best when language is embedded in a familiar event. For example, the child is more likely to understand "Where is your belly button?" in a routine involving naming body parts than if the utterance were to occur outside of the routine context. Shatz (1975) studied this phenomenon and found that children interpreted the same utterance in different ways, depending on their sense of the event. "Can you talk on the telephone?" was interpreted as a request to act by talking on the phone when it was given with other such requests ("Come get the telephone"; "Push the buttons"; etc.). However, when it was presented with utterances that solicited information (e.g. "Who talks on the telephone in your house?"), it was treated as a request for information.

Scripts of Action Events   There are many everyday events that are engaged in that have predictable elements such as meal times, getting ready for work or school, and going to the supermarket. These events are done in essentially the same way each time because participants have a mental representation of them that includes the necessary features and the sequence of actions. Schank and Abelson (1977) first proposed the existence of mental representations of events that organize experiences, calling them scripts. Scripts consist of a general outline of temporal and causal sequences of activity, with each portion allowing for variation in how it is carried out. A restaurant script, according to Schank and Abelson (1977) has in it being seated, ordering, being served, eating, getting and paying the check, and leaving. Variation is introduced in each component, such as where to sit, how many people can eat together, whether to order from a counter or a menu, or what to eat. The script would not provide guidelines for what to do in unforeseen circumstances such as sitting in a broken chair.

Frames of Discourse Events   While action events are most easily characterized by their scripts, talking events have different characteristics that distinguish them from one another. We refer to the characteristics that define each type of discourse event as the *event frame.* The frame specifies the characteristics that distinguish that form of discourse from others, such as the distinction between an argument and an interview. The frame thus may include the manner in which the discourse begins, the number of participants, the nature of turn taking, or any other feature that serves to make that discourse event what it is. An event may be organized both in action and in talk, such as a trip to the zoo. The action script would contain information about where to go, what to do, and what to say during the zoo event. The discourse frame might involve a conversation about the zoo, a quiz about what was remembered, or an argument about what is supposed to happen. Each type of discourse has a characteristic frame. These discourse events will be further discussed in Chapter 8. For now, we will look at various kinds of action events that one may observe in assessment or may wish to ask the family about.

Routines   Some events are very predictable because they begin, progress, and end in essentially the same way each time they occur. These events are thought of as *routines*. The "trick-or-treat" exchange on Halloween and peek-a-boo are both examples of routines. Routines are prefabricated units involving established verbal and nonverbal exchanges through which children conceive of and participate in repeated events. Just because we see children respond appropriately to a verbal initiation, we must not assume that they understand it as a linguistic entity. Rather, they may be working from a routine package conceptualization—a tight frame which, when triggered, moves automatically and unanalytically through a particular sequence.

The effect of routines on children's language comprehension has only recently begun to be appreciated and is still undefined. What is apparent is that there are many routine exchanges in the language of adults to children (Duchan, 1980, 1991; Thomas, 1979) and that these routines may be one important way that children move from their prelanguage stage of situational comprehension to their beginning language comprehension. Thomas's (1979) description of the routines used by fathers to children suggests that the children understand the parent's routine "syntactic amalgams" and that these forms may, in the early stages of child language development, function as vocables do in their language production; that is, the utterances in routines do not yet mean anything but rather are part and parcel of the complex cluster of happenings within which they occur. For example, the attention-getting routines such as "Look it" are probably construed by the child as a signal that an event is about to begin rather than as a command meaning "Look over here."

Scripted Events   Scripted events are those that have been done previously, and thus contain for the participants an expectation of how they will progress. Unlike routines, these events have variations in their execution. One time a child plays with the doll house, for example, the mother doll may be the focus of the activity, whereas the next time it may be the boy doll. Each time, however, the central theme may be that the family disperses and then returns to the house to eat.

Scripts may be idiosyncratic for a participant. For example, "going to a restaurant" for a particular child may involve going to McDonalds and ordering a Big Mac and fries. A script may be highly specific (going to McDonalds with Grandpa) or very general (going to any eating establishment). Scripts are like guidelines which can be violated. The very feeling that "this is not supposed to be what happens" that is engendered by such violations is evidence that scripts exist.

Events which do not occur so frequently, such as going to the zoo or buying a car, are not so highly scripted. These events proceed with some knowledge and expectation based on previous experience of the participant, but the particular actions and sequence of actions can't be predicted at the outset. Still other events are totally unfamiliar and are carried out without much preconceived structure and so involve more problem solving. One's first visit to a sushi bar or the first lesson in how to use a computer leaves the participant with little prior experience to rely on and thus structure the present event. These novel events are unscripted unless they seem similar to one that is familiar, or until enough experience is accrued with the new event that a script is developed.

Events and Turn Taking   In the enactment of an event, the partners often take turns. Sometimes those turns are prescribed by the script or by the frame. For example, in playing a board game, there are explicit rules about turns. A lesson frame may likewise have clear turn-taking patterns, such as teacher question, child answer, and subsequent teacher evaluation. Some types of discourse events such as lectures or sermons, specify that one participant gets most or all of the turns, and other participants get turns only when granted them by the primary speaker. Sometimes turn taking must be negotiated, with specific bids needed to get a turn (Sacks, Schegloff, and Jefferson, 1974). A conversation, for example, will involve two or more participants who are equally free to initiate turns, but each must signal when he or she is willing to give up or take the floor.

Developing Sense of Events   Infants, like adults, are continually engaged in events. Their events tend to be more restricted than adult events and generally show relatively little variation in the way they are carried out. Everyday events such as eating, bathing, and getting dressed all have predictable patterns that are followed. It is likely that child's first sense of participating in an event is in these familiar, repetitive situations. We begin to see evidence of the child's awareness of an event when there is anticipation, either of the beginning of an event or of the next step in a familiar event. For example, the child reacts with excitement to the sight of the stroller or lifts a foot in anticipation of having a sock put on. Later, we see more complex indications of event knowledge, as when a child assembles the materials needed for coloring or instructs someone how to play school. We will first examine the literature on the development of early routines.

EARLY PLAY ROUTINES   Jerome Bruner has extensively studied early events. He notes that much of the initial acquisition of communicative skill occurs in the context of the mother and infant jointly carrying out tasks together, such as getting something to eat or getting a game to be repeated, and he sees early language closely linked to joint actions (Bruner, 1977). Bruner has paid particular attention to the kind of routine events that are usually characterized as play, such as peek-a-boo, hide the object, and exchange games that involve passing objects back and forth. He believes that the ambience of play provides the ideal context for numerous joint activities between mother and child in a tension-free atmosphere (Bruner, 1975). In this context, mother and child develop a variety of procedures for operating jointly and in support of each other.

Bruner and his colleagues (Ratner and Bruner, 1978; Bruner, 1977; Bruner and Sherwood, 1976; Bruner, 1975) have shown that these early play activities have predictable characteristics. We believe these characteristics facilitate the child's perception of them as events. First, they have restricted formats with a limited number of objects, people, and actions that are familiar to the child. Second, they involve highly repetitive structure with clearly marked beginnings, middles, and endings, which allow both for anticipation of the order of events and for variation of the individual elements. Within this structure vocalizations are used to mark transitions within the event such as just before or just after an action. Finally, the role structure is almost invariably reversible; so, for example, either party can play the role of "hider" in peek-a-boo. This latter characteristic would seem to contribute to the sense of participating in an event (playing peek-a-boo) rather than simply doing an action (watching for mom's face).

Children need to learn how to participate in these routine events, and the role they play in them changes over time. Bruner (1977) describes the evolution of "give and take" games from three months to fifteen months, and Ratner and Bruner (1978) trace the development of appearance and disappearance games from five months to approximately fourteen months. Both of these accounts demonstrate how mothers *scaffold* events for their children; that is, mothers begin by taking responsibility for the entire event and thus demonstrate to the child how it is done. As the child becomes more capable of participation, the mother's dominance gradually decreases until the child is an equal partner in the event.

At three months, the exchanges are notoriously one sided. The mother devotes much of her attention to getting and maintaining the child's attention with devices such as shaking brightly colored objects and holding them in front of the baby's eyes or rubbing them against the cheek. Along with this manipulation, she frequently verbally highlights the object with questions such as "Do you want this?" or "You want your rattle, don't you?" When attention is gained, the mother places the object in the baby's hand, and the episode ends when the baby drops the rattle. The next round then begins with the mother's renewed attempt to get the baby's attention by offering the same object or introducing a new one. In the next stage, at about six months, the attention-getting phase is markedly reduced and can be characterized more as an offering. A brief action or "Look" is now sufficient to get the child's attention, and the child responds with a reach. A variety of objects is typically used to maintain interest, and at times two objects are offered simultaneously. At this point, the mother no longer takes all of the responsibility for the event but expects the child to signal with a vocalization or gesture when the object is out of reach. The child's role as receiver becomes more pronounced in the next two months, in demanding objects and being quite possessive of them once obtained. A significant change takes place in the routine when at around ten months the child begins to initiate the exchange game and also to act as the giver. Initially, the "give" may consist of showing and offering, retaining the object and considerable hesitancy in the process. Before long, however, the action becomes smooth. The child at this stage also regularly inserts vocalizations at those transitions in the event previously marked by the mother's comments. Increasingly, the event structure is routinized and the child assumes more responsibility. Also, there is evidence that the task of exchanging becomes paramount for the child rather than the possession of the objects being exchanged.

A parallel sequence of development is identified for appearance and disappearance games, including peek-a-boo (Ratner and Bruner, 1978; Bruner and Sherwood, 1976). This would seem to indicate that children's sense of an event, at least those that can be identified as routine play events, builds slowly and is accomplished with the help of a responsive adult who scaffolds the event, thus providing a tutorial about what is involved and how to participate.

DEVELOPMENT OF SCRIPTS   As we have indicated, there have been various descriptions of the knowledge that guides participants through familiar events. Schank and Abelson (1977) refer to scripts; Nelson and Gruendel (1981) to generalized event representations, which include scripts; and Rumelhart (1975) to schemata. Nelson (1978) elaborates on the predictive value of scripts when commenting on how the child forms concepts:

> As long as most of what the infant has to deal with is novel and unpredictable, the task of living will take enormous cognitive effort. Much of the time will need to be spent in extracting information from the ongoing scene. To the extent that the infant has already established event structures into which she can set the ongoing sequence, and to the extent that objects and people fit into those structures, she can be free of the necessity of constant monitoring of events to figure out what it is all about. The previously established structures provide expectations for the present experience. (Nelson, 1978)

There has been considerable study in recent years of children's understanding of use of scripts from an early age (e.g., Furman and Walden, 1990; Price and Goodman, 1990; Nelson, 1986). Some have commented that young infants who become upset when their daily sequence is violated are showing their knowledge of scripts (Nelson, 1985; Schank and Abelson, 1977). Most research on the acquisition of scriptal knowledge is based on the children's verbal descriptions of familiar routines (Fivush and Slackman, 1986, but see Price and Goodman, 1990, who use reenactmant of events as a performance measure). Children of about three years of age can formulate multi-utterance event descriptions (Nelson and Gruendel, 1981). Older children describe events in more detail and with more temporal and hierarchical complexity (Fivush and Slackman, 1986).

There appear to be stages in which children learn scripts. Nelson and Gruendel (1981) see script learning for children of all ages as deriving from an initial episodic memory of a particular event. Further experience with the same event will activate this memory and will fuse with the previous experience if the relevant parts are similar. If the second experience differs from the first, modifications and additions to this fused memory may take place. With repeated experience, a well-known script develops that is the generalized event representation, rather than the representation of any single instance of the event. Only after a script is developed can the child recognize something as novel in the event and recall a specific occurrence of the event. For example, "The time I got sick at Grandma's" can be recalled as a specific event only against the background of a script for "going to Grandma's, " which doesn't include getting sick since it does not usually happen.

Farrar and Goodman (1991) have hypothesized two stages in processing familiar events, both for children and adults. The first stage involves *schema confirmation*. It occurs at the time an event is experienced and as it becomes identified with a known schema. Also during this stage the person matches the experienced event with what is already known about events of that type. In doing so, the processor focuses attention on what is expected. For new events, the processor will try to formulate a new schema based on past experience, generalizing from existing schema.

The second stage of schema processing is termed *schema deployment*. In this stage, information from the event that is consistent with what is already known is readily processed, while inconsistent information requires more time and attention to process. Farrar and Goodman (1991) found that four-year-olds are more involved in schema confirmation than seven-year-olds. The younger children also had more difficulty than older children in remembering aspects of idiosyncratic episodes which did not fit with their general schema knowledge, which is attributed to their difficulty with schema deployment.

FUNCTIONALISM

Not only do participants work to make sense of an event, they take an active role in using the event to accomplish a premeditated purpose. The entire event can function to achieve a single purpose. We refer to this as the participants' *agenda*. Furthermore, each act in an event can be performed to serve a purpose. The purposes behind individual acts have been called *intents* or *intentions*.

Agenda

To identify the goals of the participants in an event is to discover their agendas. In some cases, agendas are obvious; for example, washing dishes or practicing for a play. Sometimes the agenda may be "hidden," such as getting a language sample or making someone angry. An agenda typically spans a whole event; if the agenda changes, most likely the event also changes, but this is not always the case. A game that begins with the agenda of having fun may become a battleground for control over rules.

The listener's interpretation of what the speaker is saying will vary depending on their assumptions about what the speaker wants; that is, the speaker's perceived agenda. Clinicians will be familiar with the experience in which they ask a child to repeat an utterance and the request is taken as a correction because the child sees the clinician as seeking "good speech" rather than simply requesting clarification.

The importance of agenda becomes clear when the participants in an interaction have different agendas. For example, language pathologists who use a game to teach a child a structure may be disappointed when the child gets very involved with strategies for winning and misses the "point," which was to learn the structure. In this case, at least the clinician's agenda of teaching and the child's agenda of winning are compatible. In other cases, incompatible agendas lead to breakdown of the interaction. This would be the case, for example, if a child wants to play with blocks and the therapist wants the child to paste pictures. Since agenda mismatches are frequent, agenda analysis of both participants is called for (Lubinski, Duchan, and Weitzner-Lin, 1980).

Intentions

When adults or children perform meaningful nonverbal or verbal acts, they are not just expressing the meanings but are trying to accomplish something. When a speaker says "That's too noisy," he or she is saying something about the noise conditions as well as asking the listener to do something about it. Whether or not the listener does what the speaker intends is also significant, and determines the success or failure of the utterance from the point of view of the speaker.

These three factors—the actor's intent, the conventional meaning of the act, and the effect of the act—have been identified as the components of a communicative act (Searle, 1969). The intent is called *illocutionary force*, the meaning is referred to as the *propositional meaning*, and the effect is called the *perlocutionary force*. Our shorthand terms will describe the intent as *intent*, the propositional meaning as the *semantics*, and the effect as the *function*.

Some utterances explicitly state their intent in their semantics. For example, they may use verbs that indicate the intent. Such verbs are called *performative verbs* and include *ask, tell, promise*, and *declare*. They actually perform an act rather than describe it (e.g., "I promise to do it"). Most acts do not contain performative verbs, so we have to look at the context to derive the speaker's intent. Sometimes the intent is obvious, as those expressed by direct requests or transparent nonverbal gestures (e.g., "give me a drink"; "drink"; grunt accompanied by a point to the glass of milk and a look to an adult). Less obvious acts are those expressed indirectly (e.g., "I'm thirsty") or nonconventionally (repetition of an offer to indicate you want what is offered), or nonexplicitly (crying to indicate discomfort).

People performing communicative acts may or may not achieve a successful result. When children or adults do not achieve what they intend they are left with the problem of what to do next. The lack of success may be due to a miscommunication, in which case the intender may want to revise the act and try again. These repeated attempts to achieve an intent have been called *repairs* and are seen as an integral part of communication in which speakers and listeners, or actors and receivers, work together to achieve communication and to accomplish the goals surrounding the communicative act.

A healthy research literature has developed on the types of intents commonly expressed by children and adults and the route by which normal children learn to construct intents. We turn first to the classification systems commonly used to categorize intents in normal children and in adults.

Classification of Intents

A favorite endeavor of researchers who subscribe to the *use theory* of language is to classify intents. Philosophers, linguists, and psychologists alike have subdivided the utterances performed by adult language users into subtypes. For example, the philosopher Searle (1975) identified the following five illocutionary types:

1. Representatives: utterances which describe the world as it is (e.g., event descriptions such as "The boy is running.")

2. Directives: utterances which attempt to get the listener to do something (e.g., "Go home.")

3. Commissives: utterances which commit the speaker to do something (e.g., "I promise.")

4. Expressives: utterances which are expressions of feelings (e.g., "Wow!")

5. Declarations: utterances which change social truths (e.g., "I pronounce you man and wife.")

Halliday (1975), a linguist, also has taken a functional approach to his study of adult language and has arrived at the following seven functions (what we are calling intents) which serve adults in their language expression: *instrumental* ("I want"), *regulatory* ("do as I tell you"), *interactional* ("me and you"), *personal* ("here I come"), *heuristic* ("tell me why"), *imaginative* ("let's pretend"), and *informative* ("I've got something to tell you"). Some of Halliday's functions have subdivisions. For example, interactional intent is divided into actions in which the child is initiating and those in which the child responds. The personal category includes expression of interest and of withdrawal or lack of interest. Heuristic intent involves both requests for information and imitations which are presumed to be used to find out information.

Taking a more narrow focus than Searle or Halliday, Ervin-Tripp (1976) has studied the linguistic form used for expressing one type of intentional act, the directive. Her results are a six-category subclassification: *need statements* ("I need an X"), *imperatives* ("Give me an X"), *embedded imperatives* ("Could you give me an X?"), *permissive directives* ("May I have an X?"), *question directives* ("Have you got an X?"), and *hints* ("The X's are all gone").

Ervin-Tripp and Gordon (1986) view requests, or what they call *instrumental acts*, as involving the following requisites for success:

1. Attention: the speaker must have or gain the attention of the addressee who is to carry out the desired act.

2. Clarity: the speaker must identify by gesture or word what is desired whenever the goal or action wanted is not apparent in the context.

3. Persuasion: if the desirability or necessity of the action is not obvious to the addressee, the speaker must explain, persuade, or threaten to move the addressee to action.

4. Social relations: because instrumental speech acts are at the same time social moves, the speaker must choose appropriate social markers.

5. Repairs: when the first move fails, the speaker must identify the reason and make a correction for a second try.

Child-language researchers studying the normal language learner's illocutionary acts have taken two approaches, one which uses the adult categories as a basis for classifying children's intents (Mitchell-Kernan and Kernan, 1977; Halliday, 1975), and one which is derived from children's use without regard to adults (Bates, 1976; Dore, 1974). Those studying the children's system alone, without regard to what adults are doing, often make a two-part subdivision between those acts which have social goals and those which are object identified (Sugarman, 1984; Bates, 1976). Bates (1976) calls the social-goal acts *protodeclaratives*, in which the child's act is interpreted as a declaration whose purpose is to convey information to the listener. The object type Bates calls *protoimperative*. Here the child is attempting to obtain something other than social approval, such as having someone perform an action or get him or her an object. In both cases Bates sees the act as a means to a goal, in both the act serves a communicative function, and in both there can be attention to objects and people. Where the types differ is in their focus. For the protodeclarative, the child uses the object as a means to obtain a social goal; and for the protoimperative, the child uses the person as a means to obtain a nonsocial goal, an object.

Dore's often cited classification scheme (Dore, 1974) was derived from the acts expressed by two children at the one-word stage of language development. It typifies the sorts of classification schemes which are used to identify intents expressed by beginning language users and contains the following nine categories: labeling, repeating, answering, requesting action, requesting answer, calling, greeting, protesting, and practicing.

Halliday (1975), in a longitudinal study of his son, found his adult classification scheme was useful for classifying his child's utterances between the ages of nine months to two and one-half years. An attempt to match Dore's and Halliday's categories offers an instructive exercise in understanding the problems as well as the advantages of classifying children's utterances into intent types.

Dore (1974)	*Halliday (1975)*
1. Label (doll's body parts)	1. Personal (that's interesting)
2. Repeat (overhears and repeats "doctor")	2. Heuristic (imitating)
3. Answer (M: What's this? C: bow wow)	3. Informative (I've got something to tell you)
4. Request action (uhuhuh = help)	4. Regulatory (do as I tell you)
5. Request answer (C: book? M: right)	5. Heuristic (tell me why?)
6. Calling (mama)	6. Interactional (initiation)
7. Greeting ("Hi" as person comes in)	7. Interactional (response)
8. Protest ("No" + resisting)	8. Personal (withdrawal)
9. Practice ("daddy" when daddy not present, mother doesn't respond)	9. _____
10. _____	10. Instrumental (I want)
11. _____	11. Imaginative (let's pretend)

Some of the matches between the two lists seem direct, such as Dore's request for action when compared with Halliday's regulatory function, and Dore's greeting compared with Halliday's interactional response. Other matches require a bit of category stretching. For example, Dore has the child label and repeat without presuming a feeling on the child's part that the objects of labeling and repetition are interesting or being learned. Dore's answer category requires a preceding question whereas Halliday's informative category does not. Halliday's interaction category is broader or perhaps quite different in its definition from Dore's "calling." Halliday's interaction initiation includes the situation in which the child vocalizes as he begins looking at a book with his mother, certainly not a calling situation if calling is taken to mean calling someone's name. Halliday's withdrawal example has the child indicating he is sleepy, an example with a weaker force than the emphatic protest described in Dore's taxonomy. Finally, there are three categories which do not have a correlate in the other list (Dore's practice category, Halliday's instrumental and imaginative categories).

Some of the differences between Dore and Halliday seem to stem from the perspective taken by the authors. Dore sees vocal play as practice; Halliday either ignores it or classifies it as something the child regards as interesting. Other differences between the two classification systems may be related to the sampling, in which the child being studied does not express a particular function because there was no inclination or opportunity to do so. A third source of difference may be that the children were indeed different. If we are to derive a classification system to be used as an assessment tool, we might want to use a composite system incorporating aspects of a group of studies. We will return to this point later, after we outline the developmental literature on normal children's acquisition of intentionality.

Development of Intentionality and Intent Types

PREVERBAL STAGE The origins of communicative intents lie in the child's preverbal development and have been identified as early as four and five months. Sugarman (1984) studied the development of seven babies, three between four and nine months, and four between eight and fourteen months. She found a consistent and gradual evolution in their development toward their eventual expression of communicative intent. The babies' actions at four months were oriented to either people or objects. The people orientation behaviors involved looking and smiling as initiations as well as responses to an adult's looking and vocalizations. The object orientations involved actions on objects such as beating or mouthing them.

Between five and eight months the babies began to add to both their people- and object-orienting actions an additional act such as simultaneously looking, smiling, and hugging. This was described by Sugarman (1984) as the stage of complex single orientations. At twelve months or so, they were able to coordinate actions between people and objects, doing such things as looking at a jar and holding it toward the adult in a showing gesture.

It is in this combined people + object action stage that researchers ascribe intentionality to the child. Bates (1976), in her study of preverbal children, placed the onset of intentionality at around ten months, when they were able to request by looking at an adult and identifying a requested object or by showing an adult an object. These behaviors, which Bates identified as protoimperatives and protodeclaratives, provide the cognitive and social origins to later verbal expressions of intentionality.

At a year or so children begin adding phonetically consistent vocalizations to their gestural expressions of intentionality. For example, Halliday's (1975) son Nigel expressed four intents between the ages of nine and sixteen months: instrumental, regulatory, interactional, and personal. His expression involved the use of a single or repeating syllable, a characteristic intonation pattern, and a gesture or focus on a person or object. Nigel said /da/, which Halliday interpreted to mean "look at picture." These nonconventional sounds accompanying acts have been called *vocables* (Werner and Kaplan, 1963). Nigel's vocables seemed to have no external or internal referent. That is, the vocables had no propositional content but were taken to be direct expressions of the child's intent.

Carter studied the vocables of a normal two-year-old child named David, analyzing in detail the patterns in his gestures and vocalizations (Carter, 1975a; 1975b; 1978). David produced eight action-vocable schemes at two years. Each scheme contained a characteristic vocable and gesture. Carter ascribed functions to some of the schemes on the basis of David's productions and traced the evolution of the schemes over a series of play sessions occurring as he progressed from two to two and one-half years. David's request for objects involved an open-handed reach plus /m/ sound, and attention to objects a reach plus a syllable beginning with *l, d,* or *y.* He also produced a pleasure expression and had separate vocable-gesture units for attention to self, for giving or taking objects, for changing an unpleasant situation, for requesting that something be moved, and for getting help to remove an object.

ONE-WORD STAGE   The difference between intents in the preverbal and first word stages, according to Griffiths (1979), is that vocables in the preverbal stage mark only the intent, but the word replacing the vocable has a referential meaning separate from the intentional force. Carter's child David, for example, signaled requests at the preverbal stage with an /m/ and reach, but at the first word stage he requested objects by naming them (Carter 1975a; 1975b; 1978). Griffiths sees these first words as the beginning of referencing (see Chapter 8 for more on referencing).

From her astute and detailed review of the literature on intentionality, Griffiths (1979) concluded that children just beginning to learn first words confine their communicative attempts to making requests and gaining and directing attention through the use of referring expressions (single words). Only later in the one-word stage do they use their single words to comment on objects or to gain information. During this later one-word period their comments may occur after the children have made reference to objects. A typical exchange at this late one-word period is the vertical construction described by Scollon (1974) (Child: "book"; Adult: "uh huh"; Child: "funny"). The first utterance has an attention-to-object force; the second conveys information through predication.

McShane (1980), in his longitudinal study of six children from the ages of twelve to twenty-four months, developed a sixteen-category taxonomy for classifying the intents of children's vocables and first words. The categories are grouped under five general headings: regulation, statement, exchange, personal, and conversation.

The regulation intents include:

1. Attention: attempts to get the observer to attend to an object or event
2. Request: requests for action or permission
3. Vocative: calls to another to get him or her to a location

The statement intents are

4. Naming
5. Description: says something about the object or event
6. Information: comments about an event beyond the here and now

The exchange intents include

7. Giving: says something as gives
8. Receiving: says something as receives

The personal intents are

9. Doing: descriptions of an act being performed or just performed
10. Determination: intent to carry out an act
11. Refusal: refusals of objects or requests
12. Protest: expressions of displeasure

The conversational intents are

13. Imitation: immediate repetitions of preceding utterance
14. Answer
15. Follow-on: a conversational response that is neither an imitation nor an answer
16. Question: requests for information

PRESCHOOL STAGE: TWO- TO FIVE-YEAR-OLDS   Dore (1979) identified three primary intents for conversational acts spoken by preschool children (two- to five-year-olds): conveying content, regulating conversation, and expressing attitude. Dore subdivided the content-conveying intent into *conversational initiation*, which is performed by requestive, assertive, and performative acts; and *conversational response*, which is performed by a responsive act. Each of these general content-conveying categories is divided into specific intents. *Assertives*, for example, are classified as assertions about perceived information, about internal phenomena, and about social phenomena. For each of these intents there are particular conversational acts specified that perform that function. Assertions about internal phenomena are expressed as internal reports ("I like it"), evaluations ("That's good"), and attributions ("He wants to"). At this level there are twenty-six particular illocutionary acts derived through a five-level hierarchy from the content-conveying intent of conversational acts. The other two general intents, regulating conversation and conveying attitude, are not as elaborate and together include only nine categories of particular acts at the terminal level. Conversational regulators act as discourse markers and ways to get in and out of conversations (e.g., attention-getting acts such as "Look"). Acts which convey attitude are nonpropositional comments (e.g., "Wow") or repetitions of prior utterances.

Gordon and Ervin-Tripp (1984) have studied the emergence of direct and indirect requests. In their formulation, the direct requests are conventional, are usually in the form of an imperative sentence, and specify the action desired. Indirect requests require inferencing in that they do not have the identifying form of a conventional request, and operate as hints in that they do not directly state their objective.

In their detailed study of a four-year-old boy, Gordon and Ervin-Tripp (1984) found a predominance of direct forms, as might be expected, along with a surprising number of indirect forms. The number was surprising, given that four-year-olds are usually unable to devise inferences from nonexplicit information (see Chapter 8 for more on the development of inferencing).

Adding to the evidence that young children can form indirect requests, Newcombe and Zaslow (1981) found that children as young as two and one-half were able to express requests in indirect ways. In their study, nine children of two and one-half years expressed 67 percent of their requests directly and 36 percent indirectly by identifying a problem which required an adult solution.

Gordon and Ervin-Tripp (1984) address the question of why young children seem so advanced in their indirect request. When their four-year-old subject said "The macaroni's boiling," Gordon and Ervin-Tripp classified it as an indirect request to get his mother to do something about it. They then hypothesized that the child is not being indirect but rather is directly describing his cause of concern. The inference is made by the adult that the comment is a request for her to do something and is not necessarily intended by the child.

The four-year-old studied by Gordon and Ervin-Tripp used different language forms for expressing what the authors take to be his three types of requests: (1) *self-oriented wants* expressed in situations in which the child wanted an object or to carry out an action ("I want"; "can I"); (2) *corrections,* which were expressed in situations in which the child wanted to change what was going on ("you should"; "you're supposed to"); and (3) *difficult to obtain requests* expressed when he expected problems in getting what he wanted ("why don't you").

FINE TUNING

Adult-to-Child Talk

In the early 1970s researchers began looking at the adult side of conversations with children. The goal was to evaluate the role adult language plays in children's language learning. The early studies were directed at refuting the theory that children were born with a set of transformational rules in their innate *Language Acquisition Device* (Chomsky, 1965). The theory, which has come to be called the *nativist theory,* argues that children evolve through stages of language learning in much the same way that they grow taller—through genetic preprogramming. The nativist theory was built on the assumption that the knowledge children needed in order to use language was not readily available in the language the children heard. Nativists argued that because adult talk is very complex, is often ungrammatical, and contains deep structure regularities not manifest in surface talk, beginning language learners cannot learn language simply by listening to the language that goes on around them.

To counter the nativist view, researchers began studying the structure of language addressed to children. Their attempt was to find out whether it was, indeed, too complex, too agrammatical, and too opaque for young children to learn. What ensued was a spate of research studies which showed that language spoken to children in English-speaking environments was different from that which the nativists were hearing in their conversations with adults (Newport, 1977; Snow and Ferguson, 1977; Broen, 1972; Snow, 1972; Drach, 1969).

The language spoken to young children has come to be called by some *motherese,* although it is spoken not only by mothers but also by some fathers (Rondal, 1980; Gleason, 1975), by other adults (Snow, 1982), and by older children (Sachs and Devin, 1976). The following are features commonly found in motherese spoken to young children of middle-class families in North America (see Kaye [1980] for an elaboration).

Phonology	clear enunciation, reduplication ("make peepee")
Prosody	high pitch, exaggerated intonation contours, slow rate, pauses between sentences
Syntax	short, well-formed sentences, telegraphic speech ("baby go byebye" for "the baby is going byebye"), frequent questions
Vocabulary and single word semantics	restricted diversity, high use of concrete nouns and frequent words, words for things present in the child's current context
Discourse	frequent self-repetition and repetition of what child says, restricted topics

Blount (1982) found that the features differ in when they are used. Results of his study of Spanish- and English-speaking families in Austin, Texas, revealed that certain features, such as the intonational ones, are used in contexts where the mothers are trying to attract their child's attention; other features, such as self- and child repetition, occur in contexts where the adults are trying to maintain interaction with the child.

Cross-cultural research on talk to children has revealed that the features of motherese listed above are culturally specific (Schieffelin and Eisenberg, 1984). For example, Brice Heath (1983) studied a lower-class black community in the southern United States where adults do not talk to the children directly until the children have developed basic sentence structure. She found the children began talking by imitating the ends of utterances and then they began varying these utterances as they came to understand constituent structures. During this constituent structure stage, the adults corrected the child's talk, scolding them for inaccuracies.

Pye (1986) also found departures from the motherese style used by North American middle-class mothers when he studied Guatemalan mothers speaking Quiche to their children. He found that the mothers did not alter their intonation patterns when speaking to the children, nor did they engage in language-learning routines or speak in simple sentences. The Quiche-speaking mothers did have special forms directed to children which they did not use with adults. For example, they often told their children what to say in response to questions posed them by an unfamiliar adult, and their phonological variations involved omitting unstressed syllables at the beginning of words and adding diminuitives at the ends of words. Pye concludes from his findings that motherese is a culturally determined style of talk and not one which derives from the adults tuning to their particular child's language competency.

Current research on motherese has moved in at least two new directions from its original emphasis on finding evidence for the existence of a motherese register. The current work presumes the existence of motherese as a form of language commonly spoken to children and goes from there to examine whether there is variation in the motherese spoken to different children within the same culture. In the case of variability, the aim of the research has been to try to determine whether the adult gears the motherese to fit different children's capabilities and interests. This is what we will be calling the "fine tuning" focus. It is countered by a theory which argues that motherese derives from social conventions and has little to do with the adult's responsiveness to the particular child with whom he or she is talking.

Another focus for motherese research has been to examine the effect of motherese on the child's language learning. Factors such as the frequency of the words spoken to the child have been analyzed for their effect on the child's learning patterns. We will call this second type of research the study of "motherese effects."

The Fine Tuning Focus

Fine tuning is the term we have been using to describe how adults alter what they say to children in response to what the child is presumed to be thinking or doing. One assumption in the literature on fine tuning has been that the closer the match between the language input and the child's thinking, the better the conditions are for the child to understand and learn about language (Duchan, 1986; Shatz, 1982).

Evidence for adult fine tuning to infants' understandings occurs in middle-class English-speaking families when the children are about nine months old. Several researchers (Murray, Johnson, and Peters, 1990; Stern and others, 1983; Sherrod and others, 1977) have found a decrease in the length of mother's utterances to their nine-month-old children. Prior to children's arrival at nine months, mothers' mean length of utterance (MLU) averages 3.6 to 4.0 and at the time of nine months, the average MLUs drop to 2.8 (Murray, Johnson, and Peters, 1990). The shift in MLU coincides with the children's first understandings of individual words (Benedict, 1979), the onset of intentionality as evidenced by use of gestures (Bates and others, 1977), and the beginnings of object play (Snow, 1977). It is as if the mother is responding, and fine tuning, to the child's new interests in the world (Murray, Johnson, and Peters, 1990).

Book reading activities offer an interesting context for examining the ability of an adult to fine tune to a particular child's understanding. Many adults in middle-class English-speaking homes conduct book reading activities with children by enacting a labeling game where the goal is to name the identified picture. Ninio and Bruner (1978) found a regular predictable interaction sequence between mothers and beginning language learners. The activity begins with the mother directing the child's attention to a picture which she has selected to be named (e.g., "Look"). Then the child either looks at the picture or points to it. Once the child is focused on the picture, the mother asks for a name ("What's that?"), whereupon the child names it or the mother does. The event progresses to the point where the child can offer the name and eventually to where the child assumes the role of soliciting a name from the adult.

These vocabulary lessons build on one another, with the mother keeping track of which words the child knows and "raising the ante" when the naming task becomes too easy. Chapman (1981) characterizes the mother's role in picture-labeling activities as "historian, gamesleader, and informant."

One might argue that the activity is culturally determined and that the adult is following the cultural specification for what to do rather than carrying out a finely tuned sequence in response to the child. On closer examination, however, it becomes apparent that the adult does have to make decisions based on her model of what the particular child knows. For example, the adult must select the object to be named, decide when to offer the name as opposed to requiring the child to supply it, and when to raise the ante. When finely tuned, such an activity is a concrete example of adults gearing their interaction to the competence level of the child.

Fine tuning one's syntax to fit the child's language learning needs has been the most studied and most controversial area in the motherese literature (Furrow and Nelson, 1986; Gleitman, Newport, and Gleitman, 1984). There are those who say adults do adjust their syntax to the children's language level and others who say they don't. Newport, Gleitman, and Gleitman (1977) found in their investigation that mothers of two-year-olds are not particularly finely tuned to changes in the child's linguistic capacities. These researchers were looking for whether adults seemed to provide particular syntactic structures in their language to their children which aided the child in learning those structures. They conclude that while adults use shorter sentences they do not necessarily use less complicated ones. For example, the adults frequently asked the children questions which contain difficult-to-learn syntactic structures such as auxiliaries.

Using a more general index of syntax—sentence length—other researchers have found a match between the mean length of the utterances (MLU) spoken to the children and the child's utterance length (Chapman, 1981). This correlation between adult and child MLU was especially strong for children between eighteen months and twenty-four months. Mothers of children at that age tended to talk to children using utterances two to three morphemes longer than their offspring (Furrow, Nelson, and Benedict, 1979; Cross, 1977; Seitz and Stewart, 1975). Judging from these results, adults seem to be doing some fine tuning at the level of syntax, where they shorten their sentences to be slightly longer than the sentences spoken by the child to whom they are talking.

Examination of the match between motherese and the children's utterances has shown more fine tuning going on in the area of semantics than in syntactic structure (Snow, 1986; Cross, 1977). Snow (1977) and Van der Geest (1977), in their study of the relationship between semantic relations expressed by caregivers and children, found that the majority of mother's utterances express only those semantic relations that the children have in their linguistic repertoire. For example, a mother might significantly increase her talk about object location once she hears or sees the child indicating an interest in the location of objects.

The most recent work in fine tuning has been in the area of discourse. Researchers have begun to examine what speakers of motherese say following children's utterances. Cross (1977) and Snow (1977) have found that adults often comment on what the child is saying or doing. They have called this feature of motherese *semantic contingency*. When Cross (1977) examined the language of mothers of linguistically advanced children, she found an abundance of semantic contingencies such as *expansions,* in which the mother repeats and elaborates on the semantics of the child's utterances,

CHILD: Daddy bowl.
MOTHER: That's daddy's bowl.

and *extensions* in which the mother adds additional information to the child's meaning, expressing semantically related contents,

CHILD: Daddy bowl.
MOTHER: It got broken.

Contingent queries, or questions about what the child has just said, often find their way into adult–child discourse (Garvey, 1977). This form of discourse structure has been viewed as a way to provide feedback to the child as to the success or correctness of his communication. Queries may be of the general form (e.g., "What?" "Huh?") or more specific in nature to direct the child to the questionable element in his or her utterance (e.g., "You did what?" "You saw a man on a what?")

The Effect of Motherese on Children's Language Learning

The previous section outlined some features of motherese and examined whether these features are tuned to the child's language and cognitive level. It did not address the question of whether motherese, even finely tuned motherese, helps move children along their way to learning the adult language. Researchers who study motherese hold varying opinions as to its effect on language learning. Those who believe motherese aids in language learning are proponents of what has been dubbed the "motherese hypothesis." In its strongest version the motherese hypothesis claims that language to children plays an essential role in their language acquisition (Furrow, Nelson, and Benedict, 1979). A weaker version of the motherese hypothesis contends that listening to motherese helps, but that the child also determines what is to be learned (Barnes and others, 1983; Shatz, 1982). Finally there is an antimotherese hypothesis which gives little importance to language input as a source for children's language learning (Pye, 1986; Gleitman, Newport, and Gleitman, 1984; White and White, 1984).

Impressive research evidence is accumulating in favor of the strong version of the motherese hypothesis. (However, see Shatz [1982] and Gleitman, Newport, and Gleitman [1984] for arguments against this strong version.) Underlying most of the research supporting the strong version is the assumption that the influence of motherese is direct in that children pick up particular language forms from the language they hear. Direct learning is supported by the literature which shows that the child learns best those language forms which occur frequently and which are most salient.

A less direct kind of learning from motherese is one which results from the feedback adults provide the child. In this second kind of learning, adults respond to what a child says by recasting it in a different form, or they provide positive acknowledgment of the child's communicative attempts and thus help the child better express what he or she was trying to say.

Motherese may also influence children's language learning indirectly by providing the child with a rich source of information to draw from contexts which encourage the child to communicate. Evidence for influences of motherese that can be attributed to direct learning, feedback, and indirect learning are reviewed below.

Direct Learning from Motherese One view of why children learn certain parts of language before others is that the forms they learn occur more frequently than other forms in the language they hear. The frequency view was especially prevalent when language learning was viewed under the behaviorist framework in which children were thought to learn language by imitating a stimulus. The proponents of behavioral theory feel that frequently occurring stimuli which children imitate are learned best because the imitated responses have more of an opportunity to be positively reinforced. From the more recent mentalistic view of language acquisition, the frequency of reinforced imitated responses no longer was seen as an advantage to learning, and frequency was no longer regarded as an important factor in learning.

Research on adult input of language to children has raised the issue of the role of frequency once again, as there is some evidence in recent work on motherese that the frequency of occurrence of the language form can influence children's order of acquisition. For example, when mothers ask their children a lot of yes–no questions, their children learn auxiliaries earlier (Furrow, Nelson, and Benedict, 1979; Newport, Gleitman, and Gleitman, 1977). The same was true for information questions (Hoff-Ginsberg, 1990; Yoder and Kaiser, 1989). Similarly, Brown, Cazden, and Bellugi (1973) found a relationship between the frequency of *wh-* questions in motherese and the childrens' later development of the ability to answer these questions. They were asked *where, why, how,* and *when* in that order of frequency, and the children learned to answer in the same order. Finally, Farrar (1990) found that the more frequent morphemes in the input language to the child were learned first.

Under the behavioral view, the focus was that children must imitate a form in order to learn it. Under the mentalist view, as demonstrated in the above studies, frequently heard forms are seen as having a positive influence in that they may offer the children more of an opportunity for understanding or processing the form, thereby increasing the chances that the frequent form will be learned before equivalent nonfrequent forms.

Frequency of occurrence in mothers' talk has also been studied in relation to the acquisition of semantic relations. Retherford, Schwartz, and Chapman (1981) studied six mothers with their children and analyzed changes in the semantic relations expressed by mothers and children before and after a six-month interval. The researchers found that the mothers expressed the semantic relations which have been found to occur in the speech of all young children (Brown, 1973) and did not change the relative frequency of these relations during the six-month period. However, the children changed in two ways: They increased the number of semantic relations expressed, with their additions being independent of the mother's frequency of expression; and they decreased their expression of the relations which were infrequently used by their mothers. In seven cases the semantic relations which were among the infrequently expressed categories in the mother's speech at the beginning of the study became less frequent in the children's speech after the six-month interval.

Both mentalists and behaviorists recognize that merely increasing the frequency and subsequent reinforcement of the language form to be learned will not assure learning. Rather, those forms must be noticed by the child. Behaviorists call this notice *stimulus discriminability* and mentalists call it *perceptual* or *cognitive salience*.

Evidence for the positive effect of increased salience on children's language learning has begun to accumulate. An area of interest has been how mothers make particular language features salient so that their children will attend to them. Fernald (1981) found that four-month-old babies tend to pay more attention to highly intoned language and nonspeech sounds than to the more modulated forms. Another attention-getting device which is common in motherese is what Ninio and Bruner (1978) have called the *attention vocative*. For example, the mother in their study tended to say "look" as she pointed to a picture in a book. This attention-getting device occurred in contexts in which the child was not looking at the picture that the mother wanted named. One assumes that the child would not have named or learned the name of the object in the picture had he not been looking at the same picture as the mother. Thus the attention vocative, accompanied by the indicating gesture, offers a necessary condition for the activity to be successful and for the child to learn the labels for the pictures.

Shatz (1982), in a study of eight children ranging from nineteen months to thirty-four months, studied whether gestures of their mothers, such as points, increased the child's success in responding to the mother's directives. She found that her eight subjects performed slightly better when asked to name or perform an action on an object if the request were accompanied by a gesture. However, the difference between their performance with and without gesture did not reach statistical significance.

Once attending, the child must segment the language into interpretable units. Efforts on the part of the speakers of motherese to aid the child in this segmenting process are evidenced by their careful articulation and slowed down speech and their pauses between syntactic constituents. The special significance of pauses has been revealed by Kemler Nelson and others (1989) who artificially inserted one-second pauses in the utterances spoken by adults to their infants (ranging from seven to ten months old) and to other adults. The pauses were inserted within clauses in one condition and between clauses in the second. The children attended longer to messages addressed to them (rather than to adults) and to messages in which the pauses occurred between rather than within clausal boundaries. This would suggest that they are aware of clausal units.

Being able to detect clausal boundaries is particularly important for children whose language input is not of the shortened "motherese style" type, but rather is primarily long utterances. Brice Heath (1983), for example, has described a culture in which the children were not "taught to talk" through simplification. They were thus required to pick up the language presented to them in large units. Brice Heath found the children used a "gestalt strategy" (named by Peters, 1983) as exemplified by Lem, a nineteen-month-old who tended to repeat segments from the conversation taking place around him. Below are examples from Lem's talk, extracted from the ongoing conversations. Included are the utterances just preceding his:

NELLIE: What dat thing?
LEM: What dat thing?

BENJY: You can turn right dere.
LEM: Can turn right dere.

NELLIE: Miz Hea', leave Lillie Mae.
LEM: (unintelligible) De go roun' here, duh, right dere (pause) a truck.

HEATH: That's a furniture store.
LEM: Dat ting.

HEATH: That's a church. That's a big church.
LEM: Dat a church.

BENJY: What dinda truck dat is?
HEATH: That's a Pepsi-cola truck.
LEM: Kind dat truck.

Adult Feedback One of the more consistent findings about how adult talk impacts on child language learning is the positive effect of semantic contingency. Children's language seems to develop faster when their language input consists of adults frequently commenting on what the children are thinking (Barnes and others, 1983; Cross, 1978). For example, Barnes and others (1983) studied the language development of two-year-olds as a function of motherese and found that the children who progressed most over a nine-month interval were those whose mothers frequently expanded on the child's meanings. Not surprisingly, the major area in which semantic contingency affected language development was in the child's progressing from one- to two-word semantic relations.

Scherer and Olswang (1984) found that two-year-old boys at the one-word stage imitated their mother's expansions more than the rest of their mother's speech. Further, when the researchers had the mothers participate in a controlled experiment in which they expanded certain semantic relations in a picture description task, they found that the children first imitated and then spontaneously produced the two-word semantic relations which had been expanded. Interestingly, the children also spontaneously produced two-word relations which had not been expanded in the controlled experiment, suggesting that the learning going on had to do with forming two-word utterances rather than particular meaning relations.

Masur (1982), in a study of the effect of child gesturing on mother's subsequent behavior, followed the development of four children through their infancy. The study began when the children were three months old and ended at one and one-half years after they had learned their first words. Masur identified three gestural types having to do with objects: pointing at an object, extending an object toward the mother as in a give, and open-handed reaching toward an object. She looked to see what the mothers did in response. All of the mothers tended to label the objects in response to the pointing gesture more than to the giving and reaching gestures. The mothers' labeling of objects increased for giving and reaching after the children had learned their first words. Once the children learned words (at a year or so), the children tended to name objects more often when they pointed than when they gave or reached for them. Masur takes this pattern as evidence that children learn from the adults' contingent responding that points go with naming.

Semantic contingency has been studied as a general phenomenon, with each adult utterance classified as being either contingent or noncontingent with the child's last utterance. Recent research has revealed subtypes of contingency, with different contingent types having differential effects on children's language learning. For example, Farrar (1990) distinguished three types of contingent responses:

> *Recasts,* where the adult reformulates the child's preceding utterance by adding a grammatical morpheme (C: "Phone ring"; M: "The phone is ringing"), substituting one morpheme for another (C: "I can move," M: "You will move"), or moving a morpheme to another place in the sentence (C: "It is raining," M: "Is it raining?").
>
> *Expansions,* where the adult uses some of the same words as the child but does not recast them (C: "The ball"; M: "The ball is rolling").
>
> *Topic continuation,* where the adult maintains the child's topic but does not use the same morphemes (C: "Truck in garage"; M: "Are you parking it?").

Farrar found that children's learning of different morphological inflections related to different types of contingent responses; their acquisition of plurals and progressives were associated with maternal recasts, and their learning of regular past tense and copulas were associated with maternal expansions and topic continuations.

Conti-Ramsden (1990) also subclassified semantically contingent responses of adults into different types. Her system was similar to that of Farrar (1990) except that she distinguished simple recasts, which alter only one component of the child's previous utterance (C: "Big?" M: "Too big"), and complex recasts which involve changes in two or more of the main components of the child's preceding utterance (C: "It fell"; M: "The barrel fell off the wagon"). Conti-Ramsden (1990) studied the adult language addressed to both language-impaired and normally developing children and found an interesting negative correlation between impaired children's intelligibility and their mother's number of recasts. The mothers issued more recasts to children when they were less intelligible. The author concludes that the mothers were finely tuned to their children, responding to their need to receive an easy-to-process input. Conti-Ramsden says it this way:

> [Simple recasts] provide the child with a simple, informative, and easy-to-process reply that helps the child to find out new ways of forming utterances. Complex recasts . . . are more informative and, thus, not so easy to process . . ." (p. 267).

Conti-Ramsden (1990) concludes that the mothers of children with language problems are "providing them in some sense a more appropriate environment for their children's language development" by supplying them with recasts (p. 268).

Adult responses to children's errors provide another source of feedback. There has been a set of studies looking at the effects of correction on language learning. Studies by Gruendel (1977) and Mervis (1984) have been directed to examining how mothers respond to children's errors of overextended word meanings (e.g., the child says *car* for *truck*). Gruendel (1977) found the following three feedback strategies among the responses of her mothers:

Correction   That's a truck.
Negative acceptance   That's not a car.
Negative acceptance plus correction   That's not a truck, it's a car.

Mervis (1984) found parents not only providing a new label but also pointing out the feature which distinguishes the new label from the child's incorrect classification:

Correction plus explanation   That's a truck. See, it has a place to put things in.

Chapman, Leonard, and Mervis (1986) designed an experimental study to determine which of these varieties of feedback lead the children to the best learning. They found that all five of their one-year-olds benefited most from the correction plus explanation condition, second best from the negative acceptance plus correction condition, and least well from simple acceptance with information about the incorrectness of the response.

Parents accept and correct their children's talk when they understand it; what do they do when they fail to understand what their children have said? The adults have been found to respond to such breakdowns by guessing what the child meant to say (e.g., Child: "It hut"; Adult: "A hat?"); by requesting the child to repeat the whole thing ("huh?"); or by requesting the part that was not understood ("You're going *where?*"). These forms of feedback from adults have been studied under the category of "contingent queries" (Garvey, 1977) or as "requests for clarification" (Brinton and others, 1986; Corsaro, 1976).

Although there is a developing literature on children's ability to answer contingent queries and their revision strategies for making their language more acceptable (e.g., Anselmi, Tomasello, and Acunzo, 1986; Gallagher, 1977, 1981), there is none, as far as we know, which examines the long-term language-learning effect of such exchanges.

Indirect Learning from Motherese   The conversational style used by many speakers of motherese is one which regards children as conversational partners, encouraging them to offer their own contributions to a conversational exchange. An alternative to the conversational style is a directive one, designed to teach or control the child. McDonald and Pein (1982) and Olsen-Fulero (1982) found that those using directive styles use a high incidence of test questions (ones to which the mother knew the answer), imperatives, attention-getting devices, and comments and corrections on the child's performance. For the conversational mothers, the researchers found a high incidence of open-ended "real" questions (ones to which the mothers did not know the answer), and briefer conversational turns.

One of the consistent findings in the literature on effects of motherese on children's language learning is the negative effects of imperatives (White and White, 1984; Kaye and Charney, 1981; Furrow, Nelson, and Benedict, 1979; Newport, Gleitman, and Gleitman, 1977; Nelson, 1973). This finding has led a number of researchers to advocate parent-training programs in which parents who are directive are taught to become more conversational in their interactions with their children (e.g., Cross, 1984; Tiegerman and Siperstein, 1984).

Before we proceed to such a conclusion, we need to examine some of the possible reasons for motherese users to be directive. In a recent insightful and revealing study, Murray and Trevarthan (1986) observed eight mothers interacting with their two-month-old infants under two conditions, both involving face-to-face contact through a two-way video system. In the first condition the mother and child saw and heard each other immediately, as they would in a live interaction. In the second condition the mother saw and responded to a replay of the child creating a mismatch between what the adult was seeing the child do and when the child did it. While the mother's verbal content was child centered in the immediate context, it became more direct in the lag context, when their utterances were not responded to by the child. The changes were as follows:

In the more "live" condition there was a greater incidence of

1. Genuine questions: those in which the mother is judged not to know the answer and that relate to the infant's activity (e.g., "What can you see up there?")
2. Expansions: references to the infant's activity or to the infant as focus of interest that are not elaborated (e.g., "Whoops, there's that hand again.")
3. Extensions: further developed expansions to give added meaning (e.g., "What a big yawn for a little boy.")
4. Contentless utterances: affective, musical speech and vocalizations, verses and songs
5. Answers to one's own questions

In the time-lagged condition there was a greater incidence of

1. Directives: strong commands or suggestions (e.g., "Sit up.")
2. Prompt questions: those in which the mother is judged to know the answer, or explicitly requests a particular action (e.g., "Are you looking up?")
3. Calls for attention: calling to the baby or uttering exclamations (e.g., "Oy, little man.")
4. Utterances about or for herself (e.g., "Here I am.")
5. Corrections (e.g., "Oh, no, that's not a smile.")
6. Other-centered comments: references to events, persons, or objects in the immediate or nonimmediate situation
7. Negative statements (e.g., "You're not interested in your mummy, eh?")

These findings of Murray and Trevarthan (1986) reveal that the same mothers can perform in two styles, a conversational and directive style, and that their performance is related to the responsiveness of the child.

Besides child responsiveness, the goal or agenda or the adult can lead to the selection between a directive and conversational style (Duchan, 1983). In contexts in which adults see themselves as trying to get the child to perform for another person or to teach the child something new, the adult resorts to a directive mode. We know from Bruner's research (Ninio and Bruner, 1978; Ratner and Bruner, 1978), for example, that mothers, even the most conversational ones, have certain contexts which are conducted as tutorials through a procedure which Bruner has called scaffolding. Such exchanges are controlled by the adult and contain more features of the controlling mode than of the conversational mode.

A third factor contributing to use of directive or conversational style is the adult's cultural or professional identity. Directive style is characteristic of some cultural groups (see Lieven, 1984, and Schieffelin and Eisenberg, 1984, for reviews). Professional enculturation also leads to style determination, as can be seen from the research on the directiveness of speech-language pathologists (Ripich and Panagos, 1985; Prutting and others, 1978) and classroom teachers.

There is also evidence that the degree of directiveness will vary depending on the judged competence of the child. The use of imperatives diminishes with normal children as they get older and more competent but tends not to diminish as rapidly for communicatively disordered populations (White and White, 1984).

Finally, and perhaps most crucially, the degree of directiveness in Western middle-class cultures is a reflection of the power relationship of the participants. Watzlawick, Beavin, and Jackson (1967) have proposed that every communication not only involves the content of the message but also conveys information about the relationship between the communicators. The *relationship message* carries implications about the participants' balance of power and the degree of intimacy.

Power can be thought of as the relative influence of each participant on the outcome of any activity (Aponte, 1976). Power accrues to an individual through the cooperation of others. Adults typically have more power than children because they are more self-sufficient and capable of managing their world through greater size, knowledge, and resources, and also because they are in a position to manage the child's world through meting out pleasures and punishments. Children may gain power through negotiation or resort to gaining it by withholding some behavior that is expected or desired by an adult.

Power relationships are revealed in discourse as well as through the language of *test questions, terms of address,* and *directives.* The patterns involved in turn interruption and turn overlap are ones which can be interpreted as reflections of power, competition, and status relationships. Eder (1982), for example, found that teachers allow more interruptions of reading group sessions for children in low groups than they do for children in the better groups. Other researchers have found that, in general, the partner that assumes greater power interrupts more frequently (Fisher, 1984; West, 1979). (See Lund, 1986, for a review of the literature on power relationships.)

Comparing the Relative Impact of Direct and Indirect Learning on Children's Acquisition of Syntax Hoff-Ginsberg (1986, 1990) conducted two studies in which she attempted to sort out the relative contributions of direct and indirect learning on children's acquisition of auxiliaries and verb phrases. She found in her 1986 study that certain types of utterances from twenty-two mothers were predictive of later learning in their two-and-one-half year-old offspring. Utterance types were judged beneficial if they led to increased learning months later. Hoff-Ginsberg found, for example, that children whose mothers used more real questions at Time 1 had more auxiliaries in their language four months later.

Hoff-Ginsberg's concern in her 1990 study was to determine whether the children in the earlier studies responded better because of indirect influences, which she casts as a *conversational providing function,* or because of direct learning, which she calls a *data providing function.* She defined her notion of "responded better" as responding more often and with more complex syntax (more auxiliaries or verb phrases) than the comparison types. Adults' *real questions,* such as "What do you want to eat?" tended to lead to use of a greater number of utterances with auxiliaries than did other utterances such as *acknowledgments* ("Yes, that's right") or *declarative sentences.*

Hoff-Ginsberg found both positive and negative evidence for the indirect influences of motherese. In the positive vein she found that children responded more often to certain utterance types such as real questions, than to others such as declarative utterances. She argued from this that children who hear more of these beneficial utterances get more practice in using language structures. This effect, she contended, can indirectly lead to improved language learning. The negative evidence for indirect influences was that the average length and complexity of the children's responses to adult utterances was not correlated with the degree to which the adult's utterance type was beneficial.

Hoff-Ginsberg (1990) also found support for the effects of direct learning. Her subjects, for example, used utterances with auxiliaries more often following utterance types which contained auxiliaries (e.g., real questions), than they did following types without auxiliaries (e.g., declaratives).

In order to determine the impact of motherese on children's language learning, researchers such as Hoff-Ginsberg used correlations between adult talk at an early time period (Time 1) and the children's performance at a later time period (Time 2). Yoder and Kaiser (1989) added another correlational analysis; they also examined the children's language at Time 1 and compared it with their mother's performance at Time 1 and their own performance at Time 2. Yoder and Kaiser found that not only were the number of real questions used by adults in Time 1 correlated with the increase in the child's MLU at Time 2, but also that the number of real questions used by adults at Time 1 correlated with the child's ability to respond to requests for confirmation at that same time. The researchers conclude that the child's advancement at Time 2 not only depends upon the adult's language at Time 1, but that it also depends upon the child's abilities at Time 1. These authors thus argue against the direct influence theory and in favor of the indirect influence of motherese on children's language development.

ASSESSMENT OF PRAGMATIC COMPETENCIES

Assessing Sensemaking

Sensemaking involves examining how participants make sense out of events. Thus an event analysis needs to be done with the purpose of determining what the child thinks about events as they are taking place.

Event Analysis

IDENTIFY THE BEGINNINGS AND ENDINGS OF EVENTS   Once a variety of events have been recorded, they should be transcribed with indicators included that would help identify event boundaries and transition points within events. Markers should be placed on the transcript to indicate event beginnings and endings; for example, a line across the page indicates those events with clear onsets or offsets. Indicators of event beginnings can be used such as:

> Let's pretend that . . .
> Once upon a time . . .
> Do you want to help me . . .

Such beginnings can both mark the onset and define the nature of the event such as a dramatic play event, a storytelling event, or a goal-directed action event.

Most events begin without such clear announcements. They may begin abruptly with no apparent tie to the previous event, or the beginnings may be subtle and involve transition from another event. For example, a child may be playing "cars" by building a road and running the cars along the road, and then begin to make a car fly through the air and recount a story seen on TV. In this case, the child seems to shift from an action event to a storytelling event that uses the same toy as a prop. In the following transcript excerpt the transition is more abrupt. Michael, at three years, one month, and the adult have been playing with toy cars for some time. Twice the adult (A) begins a new event (indicated by a horizontal line) with only a minimal transition from the previous event:

A: What happened?
M: They crashed.
A: They crashed?
M: Yeh.

A: I got you (grabbing M. and tickling him).
M: I'm the driver.
A: You can't tickle the driver, right?
M: No.

A: Look at those jeans you have on.
M: They're blue.
(Discussion of clothing continues and cars are abandoned.)

Often event endings involve a tacit transition to the next event. Some endings, however, are explicitly marked, such as in any of the following:

Child puts down toy and leaves the room.
"I don't want to do this anymore."
"It's time to put the game away."

Sometimes there is a transition period between events during which the participants negotiate what the next event will be. This may be evidenced as partners make "bids" for the next event. We see such a transition in this portion of a transcript of an interaction between Josh, at three years, one month, and an unfamiliar adult:

A: Do you want to do something else, Josh, or do you want to keep reading your book?
J: Wanna do something else.
A: You wanna do something else? What do you want to do? I see something.
J: What?
A: What's that Jigbits Men? Can we see those? Would you like to show those to us? Do you want to play with your favorite toy?
What's your favorite toy?
J: Uh . . . nothing.
A: Do you want to play with these or something else?
J: I wanna play with these.

Sometimes events involve preevents, such as verbal discussions about how the play will transpire, or giving directions for an activity. In the following excerpt, Brian, at four years, three months, sets the conditions for the event of "telling the secret":

B: Will you tell if I tell you?
A: I won't tell. Then it wouldn't be a secret, would it?
B: No, but I want it to be a secret for you and me. Not for girls.
A: Oh, O.K., this is man to man.
B: Don't tell.
A: I won't.
B: Now this is one secret and that's for you. (Whispers secret.)

Events don't always progress smoothly from beginning to end. They may be interrupted or temporarily ended and then resumed. When the two participants have different events going on simultaneously, they may briefly interrupt their own event to participate in their partner's. In the following exchange, Stephen, at two years, six months, is playing with cars, while the adult is attempting to get "conversation" about the cars, which Stephen acknowledges begrudgingly:

S: Car, this car.
A: What color is that car?
S: Let go. I don't know.
A: You know. What color is the car?
S: I can't get out. This car? Red.

A: No.

s: Yellow car?

A: What color is that? You know.

s: Get the cars for you.

DETERMINE THE CHILD'S IDEA OF THE EVENT FRAME Children's difficulty in understanding the speech event might be manifest in their inattentive behaviors, inappropriate responses, lack of initiative, or lack of cooperation. They may be willing or able only to respond to tightly framed familiar events, and inept or uncooperative in more negotiated events. Thus, an analysis of their sense of speech events and frames could lead to insight into their erratic or poor performance in particular events.

Children's as well as adults' ideas about speech events are impossible to divorce from their ideas about the event frame. Thus, their sense of the event frame will likely be elicited along with their ideas about the event. The most direct way to elicit their event and frame sense is through an interview procedure in which they are asked to name the event or in which they are asked about an event already named by the clinician or by them. This interview procedure is a common one in ethnographic analyses and has been used successfully with verbally competent and reflective children (Spradley and McCurdy, 1972).

The interview would involve asking the children about a particular kind of event, such as playing house—asking what the event is called, when it might occur, and what it entails in terms of action sequences, participants, necessary props, rules, and so on. The interview, then, becomes one basis for the transcription. An analysis of such an interview would perhaps involve discrepancies between the child's conceptualization and that of other participants or that of the adults in the culture, or perhaps a comparison between what the children say about the event and their actual behavior when they participate in the event. They may have one rendition in the interview and another when they are in the event itself.

A second way to find out about children's conceptualization of events is to ask them to reenact them, perhaps inserting commentary along the way. For example, ask them to pretend they are in speech class. Comparisons of several reenactments would allow you to make some judgment about what is incidental and what is prescribed as necessary to the event. This is the distinction between frames and circumstantial aspects of the event structure. A variant of this reenactment plus commentary technique is to allow children to observe a videotaped segment of the event and to comment on it.

Finally, the most natural way to learn about children's sense of events is simply to observe them participating in the event and to analyze their performance in relation to the culturally prescribed frame and in relation to previous and subsequent performances of the same event. From this you can extract the action or discourse sequences common to all enactments of the event and thereby determine its frame.

A running transcript with descriptions of most important actions would be the most obvious means for transcribing the event. If temporal relations are important to the analysis, then aspects of the event may need to be transcribed in a multilevel way. The transcript is most logically begun at the beginning of the speech event. If there are shifts in the sample to a new activity, this could be indicated by designating it as a separate speech event and by specifying the defining features which led to its separate classification.

Platt and Coggins (1990) have devised a coding scheme for analyzing children's performance in routinized events. The codes yield a three-level differentiation in children's performance from noninvolvement (inattentive behaviors) at level 1, to minimal involvement (neutral interaction behaviors) at level 2, to full involvement (conventional behaviors) at level 3. These authors traced twenty-nine children as they progressed from nine to fifteen months of age and found that the children developed from level 2 to level 3 in their performance in games such as peek-a-boo and patty cake. The children's performance levels improved when the mother provided more prompting.

ANALYZE AN EVENT'S INTERPRETIVE FRAME The following questions, based on four possible interpretive frames as presented in Duchan (1991, and see above) can serve as a guide to analyzing an event's organizational structure.

> *Role frame:* Who are the participants in the event? Are they the same each time the event gets carried out or do they vary with different instantiations? What are the role relations of the participants? Can the child assume different roles in the event (e.g., speaks or acts for both teacher and student)?
>
> *Temporal or logical structure:* How do the actions in the event relate to one another? Is the ordering obligatory or optional? Do early events cause or enable later ones?
>
> *Deictic structure:* From what point of view is the event enacted or described? Does the child seem to take the other person's point of view (e.g., hides from the other person during hide-and-seek games)? Does the child use deictic terms (personal pronouns, motion verbs such as *come*, past tense) which are consistent with a particular perspective?

IDENTIFY THE TIGHTNESS OF FRAMING Some events have a routine or well-rehearsed quality that is apparent even if it is the first time we observe it. An exchange such as the following has this quality:

MOTHER: Ooh, what's this?
CHILD: Kitty.
MOTHER: What's the kitty say?
CHILD: Meow.
MOTHER: And what's this?
CHILD: Doggy.
MOTHER: What's the doggy say?
CHILD: Bow wow.

Action events are scripted when they are performed in the same manner each time they occur. For example, each time the child plays with dolls, the same sequence may be followed indicating a scriptal base for the play.

Some children have difficulty acting or interacting in novel or loosely framed events. They may become silent or seem "inappropriate" because they are uncertain as to what is expected of them or how to proceed. Their language proficiency can thus not be judged independent of their event knowledge.

DETERMINE EVENT COMPATIBILITY BETWEEN PARTNERS   As was indicated previously, an activity may not be the same event for all participants. The child may be involved in an action event while the adult is attempting to make it into a conversational event by bringing in new topics. Or the adult may be telling a story while the child considers it a conversation and regularly takes turns to ask questions or make comments. In these cases we must consider the child's performance in light of his or her own sense of the event rather than judging the adequacy of performing the adult's event.

IDENTIFY SUCCESSFUL AND UNSUCCESSFUL CONTEXTS OR TURNS   When attempting to evaluate the relative success of an event from the child's point of view, the clinician can first examine the event for whether it contains distress indicators. These indicators of the child may not match those of the adult interactant or observer. For example, the adult may judge an event unsuccessful because the child did not talk very much or did not use a particular language form enough, or because the child gave too many "wrong responses." The same interaction from the child's perspective may have been successful because the child was "having fun."

Common behaviors which indicate that the child may be experiencing communicative distress or communicative "breakdowns," are (1) noncompliance, where the child attempts to change the event by doing something else, (2) passive stance by nonparticipation or minimal participation, (3) inattentiveness, and (4) emotional reactions such as those which are interpreted as indicators of unhappiness, anger, or fright. These signs of distress, noninvolvement, or discontent, when they occur throughout an event suggest that the child does not experience the event as a communicative success. Successful events, on the other hand, progress with a minimum of distress or disruption and are often accompanied by pleasure indicators such as enthusiasm or laughter.

To determine whether an event is successful from the child's point of view, the clinician may want to mark instances of distress, noncompliance, or noninvolvement in the transcript with minuses. For example, the abundance of negative indicators in the following transcript shows that K is feeling harassed by J and interpreting his brother's initiatives to help as attempts on the part of his brother to take his cup away from him. Similarly, the brother, J, would probably judge the interchange as a communicative failure because K never turns over the desired cup to him, despite J's use of both power and conciliation in his pursuasive efforts.

K—Kyle 2;6
J—K's brother, 5;0

	K	*J*
(K drops a covered cup, the lid comes off. K tries to put it on and asks attending adult for help)	—	
(K looking at adult)		
1. K—Put this on for me.		
2. J—I'll put on for you if you give me it.		
3. J—It's *my* cup, ha ha.		

	K	J

(K leaning forward over cup)
4. K—*I* cup.   —
5. J—No, it's my cup.   —

(J approaches K, reaching toward cup)
6. J—I'll show you how to put it on.
7. J—You want me to?

(K shouting)
8. K—No.   — —
9. J—Here, I'll put it on.

(K shouting)
10. K—No.   — —

(J with high tone, pleading, conciliatory)
11. J—Please.

(K quietly)
12. K—No.   — —

(K drinks from cup leaning backward)
(J backing away, talk directed to no one in particular)
13. J—It's gonna dump on him.

To summarize, the recommended steps in analyzing children's ideas about events have been intended to lead to an idea of how a child makes sense of what is going on. The steps which have been recommended for determining the child's sensemaking for particular events are listed in Box 3–1.

BOX 3–1. Steps for Determining How a Child Makes Sense of an Event

1. Identify the beginnings and endings of events.
2. Determine the child's idea of the event frame.
3. Analyze an event's interpretive frame.
4. Identify the tightness of framing.
5. Determine event compatibility between partners.
6. Identify successful and unsuccessful contexts or turns.

Sample Report: Event Analysis   The following summary is the result of an event analysis for language-impaired, five-year-old George. The preponderance of George's comments relate to the ongoing action structure of events, indicating that perhaps for some children the major sensemaking focus of their language is the action sequence of familiar events.

GEORGE   George's talk revolves around his ideas about routine events. He often requests routines by asking for the first action in the routine. For example, he asks "I go to the rug?" for the event which begins when all children are seated on the rug, and "I want to see the green line?" for the event which begins with them lining up behind the green line. These action requests are made during activities that occur just prior to the one being requested.

Once a routine has begun, George's talk has to do with the prescribed utterances involved in the routine. For example, he asks the teacher's questions before she does during the calendar routine (e.g., "What was yesterday?"). He can substitute elements appropriately such as the name of the day or the weather, indicating that he is not just rotely reciting routine structure, but is understanding what is being asked for.

When routines do not go according to plan, George comments on the departures or assures himself that it's okay. For example, he marks what should have been done by saying "later." He said "I do 'g' later" when the teacher missed his turn.

George's dependency on routines for his communications is apparent from his behavior in nonroutinized events. During snack preparation in his classroom, George is not involved in the event but rather comments on what seem to be irrelevant aspects of what is going on. For example, he comments on where children are sitting rather than on what the teacher is demonstrating. Often, after the nonpredictable event has continued for a while, George begins to misbehave and eventually he asks to be removed from the activity by asking to be put on the time-out chair ("Karen will put me on the chair?").

In summary, George's language can be characterized as "stage manager talk." His goal is to stage the sequence of scenes and to recite his lines, with little interest in the events for their own sake and with little facility for contributing to what goes on in a spontaneous, unprescribed way.

Assessing Functionalism

Agenda Analysis An analysis of an agenda would best be done for those speech events in which agenda questions are at issue, such as events involving persuasion, arguments, or conversations in which one of the partners is inattentive. Thus, an elicitation procedure would be one of structuring situations, as did Brennis and Lein (1977), who asked children to argue with one another; or naturalistic interactions in which agenda or lack of agenda becomes a determining force (Lubinski, Duchan, and Weitzner-Lin, 1980). For those children who can evaluate an event, an interview in which the assessor asks the participants what they or others were trying to do could lead to insight about their notions and enactments of agendas.

The transcription, at least at first, would be a running transcript which could then be evaluated, utterance by utterance, for whether the illocutionary force of each utterance is in concert with and therefore is a manifestation of a hypothesized agenda. For example, if the child wants to leave, one could imagine several utterances which would stem from that agenda and then perhaps a period which departs from that agenda where the child becomes diverted or gives up, only to return to it later. This "agenda tracking" could perhaps account for topic shifts; it could also reveal how well children can make their needs known and how well interactants can respond to their expression of agenda.

In the following segment the adult seems to be behaving as if her agenda is to ensure that Jordan, a five-year-old, does not wake up his younger sibling, whereas Jordan's agenda is to get the blocks out of the box

Adult	Jordan	Context
		J carrying box with blocks.
23 Over on the rug if you're gonna play with that.		
	20 OK.	J moves to rug.
	21 I know.	
	22 I do like this.	
	23 I empty them.	J picks up box of blocks.
	24 I gotta lift the box up and I turn it over.	
24 Well, I take them out this way so it doesn't make as much noise.		Adult takes blocks out gingerly, one at a time.
25 Cause we don't wanna wake up Rosie.		

Intentionality Analysis The most commonly used clinical approach for assessing intentionality is to adopt a taxonomy of intents and to classify a child's acts or utterances into the categories of the taxonomy (Wetherby and others, 1988; Leonard and others, 1982; Wollner and Geller, 1982; Coggins and Carpenter, 1981; Bloom and Lahey, 1978; Skarakis and Prutting, 1977). After the intentional acts are tallied against the taxonomy, they are evaluated in terms of the following questions:

1. Does the child express a variety of intent types, and which are missing?
2. Do some types occur more frequently than others?
3. Are the child's intents equivalent in form, content, or type to other children at his or her age or cognitive level?

One source of concern for those who use existing category systems is deciding which one should be used. Clinicians might choose category systems based on whether the categories can be reliably used. By the same token, researchers have tried to develop systems using the categories from the many available that are most reliably identified by different observers. In this approach, a system is made up of categories which meet criteria of observer reliability (Creaghead, 1982; Coggins and Carpenter, 1981).

A second basis for choosing which category system to use would be to match it with the age or developmental level of the child being evaluated. If the child is at the one-word stage in language development, Dore's nine-item category system (1975) would be more appropriate to use than the system Dore developed for older preschoolers (Dore, 1979).

For the preverbal, one-word, and beginning multiword stages a recent instrument developed by Wetherby and her colleagues might be selected (Wetherby, Yonclas, and Bryan, 1989; Wetherby and others, 1988). These authors developed a system for distinguishing growth in intentionality among children between one and two years of age. It includes three types of communicative acts, those involving *behavioral regulation* (requests for objects and actions and protests), *social interaction* (requests for permission and for social routines, showing off, greeting and calling), and *joint attention* (commenting, requesting information and clarification). The stages covered by the instrument progress from prelinguistic, through single-word, to multiword utterances.

Finally, one might want to choose an intention checklist by picking the system which focuses on the questions being asked about a particular child's competencies. Some of the systems focus on a wide variety of intents (McShane, 1980); others focus more narrowly on subtypes of intents such as directives (Ervin-Tripp, 1977; Mitchell-Kernan and Kernan, 1977). Some systems focus on the object or goal of the intent, such as the categories by Coggins and Carpenter (1981) that specify goals such as getting action, attention, or information. Others emphasize the nature of the expression or accompanying gesture for each intent. For example, Halliday (1975) analyzed his careful transcription of intonation and gesture to distinguish among intentional categories. Some systems confine themselves to communicative acts (McShane, 1980) whereas others include noncommunicative acts such as Dore's categories (1975).

There are several problems with using preexisting taxonomies for assessing a child's expression of intents. One difficulty is that these systems do not work well for the child who expresses intents in nonconventional ways. The a priori lists lack the flexibility needed to evaluate intents behind immediate echolalia, or self-stimulatory behaviors, or those expressed in unintelligible language or with idiosyncratic vocables. Nor do these systems allow for analysis of intents expressed which do not appear on the checklists. Also, the systems presuppose that all contexts offer the opportunities for expression of a wide variety of intents, failing to recognize the close connections between a child's expression of intents and the social and event contexts in which those intents occur. Finally, the lists are geared only to middle-class American children and are subject to cultural bias when used with children from other cultures. A Kaluli child from Samoa would, for example, be penalized under these systems for not responding to shame questions, which, in their culture do not require a response (Schieffelin and Eisenberg, 1984).

Procedures for discovering children's intents without the use of a checklist have been developed (Wetherby and Prutting, 1984; Prizant and Duchan, 1981; Carter, 1979). They follow the pattern-discovery approach which we have been advocating throughout this book. In this approach the clinician examines the child's behaviors and language in light of the surrounding event in an attempt to discover regularities. The regularities we are looking for here are those which we will take to be expressions of intents. The following procedures are recommended as a general guide for assessing intentionality.

For assessing early communicative attempts the goal is to determine whether the child's behaviors are intentional and, if they are, what it is the child is intending. The procedures involve two steps: identifying and classifying intents.

IDENTIFYING NATURALLY OCCURRING INTENTS We recommend that intents be identified by using the approach of the researchers who discovered intent categories by close examination of individual acts and their composite movements, noises, and the like (Prizant and Duchan, 1981; Carter, 1975a, 1975b, 1978, 1979). Multilevel transcriptions of such acts should be made to include the various aspects of the act and its context. For example, the following aspects of the context and activity can offer insights into the underlying intent: nonverbal accompaniments such as reaches and the direction of gaze, rises and falls in intonation and volume, and the nature of preceding and subsequent acts.

The multilevel analysis involves looking for repeated clusters of behaviors exhibited by the child across different levels in the transcription. For example, Prizant and Duchan (1981) found through multilevel analysis that autistic children's echoes were expressions of different intents. An echo that meant "yes" in response to an offer contained the following features: an offer of the object to the child just preceding the echo; the child's look to the person or object being offered so that the echo seems directed to the conversational partner; a similarity of intonation between the echo and the statement being echoed; and an acceptance of the offered object as the child echoes, or just after.

Carter (1979), using the same multilevel structural approach, found that her two-year-old's expression of intents also involved a cluster of predictable elements. For example, the intent to get rid of objects included an object-ridding action such as a push, tap, nudge, or pound; a crisp explosive vocalization with initial /b/ and falling intonation; the goal of getting the receiver's help in removing an object.

In order to identify acts as intentional, one needs to examine the transcripts for evidence that the act being transcribed is goal directed. A two-phase movement, one involving a means (e.g., climbing on a chair) and another an end (e.g., getting an object), would provide evidence for intentionality. It is easiest to detect intents where the means act and end are related, although this is not always the case. Children may be using a means which is not obviously connected to an end (e.g., throwing a tantrum to achieve a change in activity).

Other sources of evidence for assigning acts intentionality are (1) when an act persists until a goal is achieved; (2) when an act terminates when the goal is reached; or (3) when other means are used because the original act does not work. Reactions to achievement and failure to reach a goal, such as expressions of excitement and disappointment, also give clues that an act is intentional. Under these criteria, the following action sequences would not qualify as intentional:

1. Unrelated activities, such as banging the headboard then throwing a toy
2. Cyclical action sequences such as in several games of patty-cake
3. A repetitive series such as banging a spoon
4. Actions that are not separable from their end, such as putting food in the mouth and eating

CLASSIFYING INTENTS Once individual intentional acts are identified, they should be classified into general types, the goal being to capture when, what, and how the child expresses intents. Some questions which might be answered by the analysis are

Does the child have different forms of expression for the different intents? (e.g., different vocables for different wants?)

Are the child's nonconventional acts expressions of intent? (e.g., self-stimulatory behaviors, immediate or delayed echoes, head banging?)

Are there certain contexts which promote more intentional behaviors than others? (e.g., obtaining favorite objects, asking for food, protesting an unfavorite situation?)

Does the child use communicative acts to initiate interactions? (e.g., requests, attention getters, greetings, initiating an object exchange?)

Does the child issue acts with the focus on responding to others initiations? (e.g., answers, repetitions, protests, turn taking?)

Does the child communicate things to others which he or she considers worthy of note? (e.g., labels, comments, acknowledgments, descriptions, providing information?)

Does the child perform noncommunicative acts with the intent to regulate his or her own action or thought? (e.g., practicing, noninteractive labeling, imagining?)

How does the child communicate affect? (e.g., vocal play, whining, pleasure noises, self-stimulatory behavior?)

Adult	*Jordan (4-year-old)*	*Context*
23 Over on the rug if you're gonna play with that	20 Okay	J moves to rug.
	21 I know.	
	22 I do like this.	
	23 I empty them.	J picks up box and
	24 I gotta lift the box up and I turn it over.	motions to dump blocks out.
	25 The blocks come out pouring out out.	
24 Well, I take them out this way so it doesn't make as much noise.		M takes blocks one at a time.
25 Cuz we don't wanna wake up Rosie.	26 No.	
	27 You said Brosie.	
26 I said Rosie.		
	28 No you said Brosie first.	
27 Brosie?		
28 Cuz I said we're going to wake up/Rosie and I said Rosie right after up, so it sounded like Brosie, right?		M removes tape from box.
	29 Yeah.	

Adult	Jordan (4-year-old)	Context
	30 That was strange how come we got that.	
29 Got what?		
	31 Got that thing from here.	J points to tape and box.
		M puts tape in playpen.
30 A piece of tape.		
	32 You shouldn't put it in the playpen!	
31 I guess I didn't think about it.		
32 Do you want to get it out?	_____	
	33 No, I can't go in there.	J points to playpen.
33 Why?		
	34 Cuz my mom and dad don' allow me.	
34 Cuz you're not a baby, right?		
_____		
	35 But I go in there sometimes when Aunt Sarah's here and she catches me.	
35 And she gets angry, I bet.	36 No, she just gits me.	
	37 I say Aunt Sarah, can you git me? and then she'll say I'll git you.	
	38 Then she still smile.	
	39 Hey, this could be a garage for 'um.	J looks at blocks.
36 Can they fit?		
	40 Noo.	

SAMPLE ANALYSIS FOR INTENTIONALITY   To show an example of a classification scheme of a child's intents, we present first a portion of a transcript and then the worksheets used to analyze it (see Box 3–2). The transcript has been segmented to show abrupt shifts and transitions from event talk to discourse. The intentional categories were derived by grouping together Jordan's utterances that seem to serve the same function and then assigning the group a label to capture the common thrust.

BOX 3–2. *Functionality Assessment*

Name: Jordan L.
Event: Play with blocks and conversation

Acknowledgements				*Comments*		
E	20	Okay.		E	22	I do like this.
E	21	I know.		E	23	I empty them.
E	26	No.		E	24	I gotta lift the box up and I turn it over.
D	29	Yeah.		E	25	The blocks come out pouring out out.
				E	39	Hey, this could be a garage for 'um.

Initiations		
D	27	You said Brosie
E	30	That was strange how come we got that.

Protests				*Clarification/Expansion*		
D	28	No you said Brosie first.		E	31	Got that thing from here.
E	32	You shouldn't put it in the play-pen.		ED	34	Cuz my mom and dad don' allow me.
ED	33	No, I can't go in there.		D	35	But I go in there sometimes when Aunt Sarah's here and she catches me.
D	36	No, she just gits me.		D	37	I say Aunt Sarah, can you git me, and then she'll say I'll git you.
E	40	Noo.		D	38	Then she still smile.

E = Event talk; D = Discourse; ED = Fading from event talk to discourse.

This sample was collected while Jordan was playing with blocks with his speech-language clinician who was visiting his home. The play is interrupted first by a brief discourse segment when Jordan misunderstands the adult and seeks clarification, and then by his attention to a piece of tape. A brief segment of event talk about the tape gradually fades to discourse about play with his aunt. He then returns abruptly to the block play. Jordan displays a variety of intents in this sample and uses several forms to express each. Jordan initiates both discourse exchanges and event talk. In event talk, he most typically comments on his own activity while acknowledging the adult's comments. His intents are more varied in discourse segments, where he shows more expansions and clarifications. He effectively registers protests against the adult's actions, conclusions, and statements in several forms in both types of exchanges.

ELICITING INTENTS   Various procedures designed to get young children to express particular intents have been recently developed. Wetherby and Prutting (1984) and Wetherby, Cain, Yonclas, and Walker (1988) have developed a procedure in which children are tempted into responding. These contexts involving "communicative temptation" are exemplified by the following: Eat a desired food item in front of the child without offering any to the child.

Like Wetherby and her colleagues, Coggins, Olswang, and Guthrie (1987) developed procedures for eliciting intents from children. Coggins and his colleagues elicited children's requesting and commenting and compared these responses with those gained under naturally occurring conditions. The study was a longitudinal one where they followed thirty-five normally developing children as they developed from nine months to two years of age. The researchers found that the nine-month-olds did not express requests or comments under either elicitation or spontaneous conditions. Between one and two years the children issued more requests with elicitation than spontaneously. But for comments, the elicitation conditions were not productive until the children were twenty-one months old, despite the fact that children were producing comments spontaneously. At twenty-one months, children commented under both elicited and spontaneous conditions. The authors conclude that eliciting requests is far easier than eliciting comments from children older than nine months, and explain their results by observing that requests and comments serve different communicative needs. Requests require action from adults, whereas comments solicit their attention and express the child's desire to share information. These differences make requests more amenable to control through elicitation (e.g., withholding needed objects) than comments.

Assessing Fine Tuning

Fine tuning analyses have been designed to answer such questions as the following:

> How semantically contingent is the adult to what the child is doing or saying?
> How directive is the adult when interacting with the child?
> Does the child tune to his or her listener?

The problem with these questions as they are posed is that they presume a black-and-white approach to fine tuning and disregard the particular circumstances under which an interaction between two people take place. For example, the positive value typically placed on semantic contingency assumes that children's sensemaking is always focused on what they are saying or doing, when, in fact, it is easy to imagine a child whose focus is on something else, such as what will be happening next. Similarly, the devaluation of directiveness presumes that directives and directiveness are by their very nature inappropriate, ignoring the literature which indicates that directive activities (e.g., naming pictures) are commonplace and productive in language learning and ignoring as well the research findings that directiveness is effective for certain purposes such as getting a nonattentive child to attend. Because of such difficulties in analyzing for fine tuning, we recommend that clinicians consider the nature of the exchange transpiring rather than simply using the literal content of a transcript. For example, when an adult asks a child "How old are you?" it may be a directive test question in one situation, whereas under other circumstances it represents playful teasing.

Given these cautions, the following procedures can serve as guidelines for evaluating the interactive style of adults, the degree of semantic contingency of adults, and the ability of children to fine tune to their communicative partner.

Contingency Analysis   An adult may or may not be responding to what the child has just said or done. The related responses are considered semantically contingent. An analysis that separates contingent from noncontingent responses may offer the clinician a gross index of whether the adult is accepting the child's communicative attempts as well as offering the child a means for expanding on what he or she knows. The following indices may be used to determine the degree to which an adult is contingent for a particular interaction. A high frequency and percentage for the first three items indicate high contingency; a high frequency or percentage for the last three indicate low contingency. Compute the percent or number of adult utterances that are the following:

1. Expansions, semantically related comments (extensions or answers) or questions (contingent queries) related to child's preceding utterance
2. Comments related to child's activity
3. Acknowledgments of child's activity or utterance (uh huh; I see; no)
4. Comments unrelated to child's focus
5. No response to child's communicative attempt
6. Interruption of child's talk

Interaction Mode Analysis   The two extremes of interaction style or mode are directiveness and nurturance. When investigating the degree of directiveness, the clinician needs to consider the event structure, the adult goals, and the cultural patterns within which the adult and the child are operating before judgments are made as to whether the directiveness is appropriate or effective. If the goal of the assessment is to determine whether the caretaker can interact nondirectively with the communicatively handicapped child, the clinician might arrange conditions which usually lead to nondirective interactions. For example, the adult might be asked to interact with the child as the child manipulates toys so that the clinician can observe how the child plays. In contrast, if the adult is asked to get the child to do a specific task, it is likely that the adult's style will be more directive. If the goal is to determine the effect of adult directiveness on the child's performance, we would compare across different events such as these.

Since the event to be analyzed is created and managed by the interactants, it is impossible to devise a set of norms whereby one can judge whether a particular adult is too directive, or judge how many directive features in a given event is excessive. It is possible, however, to characterize an event as being primarily directive or nurturant by identifying features of these modes in the transcript and determining which is most frequent. Some of the features which may indicate interactive mode are shown in Box 3–3. Events can be compared by determining the relative frequency of adult and child utterances, the frequency with which various features occur in each event, and the percentage of utterances that display each feature. The features that relate to adult performance would be calculated as a percentage of the total number of adult utterances, while the child features would be calculated as a percentage of the total number of child utterances.

BOX 3-3. Indicators of Interactive Mode

Indicators of Directive Mode

1. Adult test questions
2. Adult imperatives
3. Adult bids for child's attention
4. More adult utterances than child utterances

Indicators of Nuturant Mode

1. Adult acceptance or acknowledgment of child's initiations
2. Adult questions for information
3. Adult comments or expansions
4. Child initiations

Child's Fine Tuning Analysis   Besides measuring the adult's ability to fine tune to the child, clinicians can focus on the child's ability to fine tune to the adult or to a peer. This involves looking for evidence that the child is sensitive to the interactive partner's message, knowledge, and perspective, or conversely, that such sensitivity is lacking. Following are some indicators that the child is fine tuning:

1. Responses to adult utterances are topic contingent
2. Explanations and background information are supplied when needed.
3. Appropriate repairs are made when partner does not understand.

A high frequency or percentage of the following features would indicate that the child is not fine tuning:

1. Responses to partner's utterances are not topic contingent.
2. Child turn ignores or interrupts partner.
3. Adult requests for clarification of unclear meaning.

Comparisons across Events   It is generally found that the same pair of interactants have different styles of interacting in different types of events, so one needs to conduct analysis such as those just discussed for several events. This comparison is useful to identify the kind of events that promote the most fine tuning on the part of both the child and the adult and also to determine which features of fine tuning appear to impact most effectively on communicative success.

Sample Analysis for Fine Tuning   We now present a transcript to illustrate some facets of analysis for fine tuning (Box 3–4). The sample was collected while Patty, a retarded adult, was playing a card game with her speech-language pathologist. We are using the transcript to do three kinds of analysis.

I. Clinician's semantic contingency with Patty's focus of attention.
   1. In the first column following each clinician utterance, we have indicated whether that utterance is contingent with Patty's focus (C for contingent), departs from Patty's focus (NC for noncontingent), or is the beginning of a new exchange where the focus of Patty's attention is undetermined (—). The judgment of contingency is based on what we presume Patty is thinking about rather than necessarily what activity is transpiring. We also indicate in this column instances when Patty seems to expect a response from the clinician and does not receive one (NR for no response). In cases where Patty's utterance does not appear to call for a response from the clinician, we do not use the NR designator even though Patty may have said something and the clinician did not respond. We do not want our analysis to presume that all talk should be responded to.
   2. Next we totaled the adult utterances, and subtracted from that total all those which we have indicated as not appropriate for this analysis (—) since they are initiations of new exchanges or if it is unclear whether or not they are contingent (Box 3–5).
   3. The remaining clinician utterances that are contingent and noncontingent were counted and a percentage was calculated using the subtotal in Step 2 as a denominator.
   4. The number of non-responses in situations that call for a response were totaled.
II. Interactive mode: One gets a general impression of this interaction as being quite evenly controlled because the number of utterances produced by the two participants is roughly equal and Patty frequently takes the initiative in beginning new topics. Thus we decided that the relevant analysis is to investigate the amount and type of directiveness used by the clinician, and to determine if the directiveness had a particular function. We followed these steps in analysis:
   1. The clinician's utterances were examined for directive features and coded for those present.
      D1 = Test questions
      D2 = Imperatives
      D3 = Attention getter
   2. Percent of the clinician's utterances that are directive was computed.
   3. The context in which the directive utterances occurred was examined to determine what the directiveness might be related to.
III. Client's fine tuning
   1. Patty's utterances were examined for instances when she did not appear to respond to the clinician's confusion. Utterances were identified that needed clarification or confirmation, as evidenced by the clinician's contingent queries. These were coded in the column following Patty's utterance as Conf. (for confused). Following each confused utterance, there is an indication of whether the confusion is repaired (Rep.) or not repaired (No Rep.) by Patty in her subsequent utterance.

BOX 3–4. Transcript for Analysis of Fine Tuning

Patty		*Clinician*		
1. Me waiting for you.		1. You ready?	C	
2. OK.		2. You want to go first?	C	
3. OK.		3. I'm going to win today.	C	
4. That's what you think.		4. Patty.	NC	D3
5. Huh?		5. Patty, take a card.	NC	D2, 3
6. This one.		6. Do you need it?	C	
7. Yea.		(P. picks up card)		
8. Oh boy.		(P. looks at card)		
		(C. takes card)		
		7. Take the next one.	NC	D2
9. Now?		8. Go ahead.	C	D2
10, 11. Oh boy.		9. Can you lay some down?	C	
12. Where is dat?	Conf.	10. What?	C	
13. Where is dat?	No Rep.	11. I guess it's my turn.	NC	
14. Go.		12. I'm not doing so well.	C	
15. Me do it better.				
16. Me know where it is.		13. Patty, hold your cards right.	NC	D2, 3
(section omitted)				
23. Do it good?		19. You sure are.	C	
24. How much me got?		20. Two pairs already.	C	
		21. Can you count them?	NC	D1
25. Yeah want see how much you got.			NC	D2, 3
		22. Patty, count your cards.		
26. Dis sure better for me.	NC	23. You like this game better?	C	
27. One more.	Conf.	24. You want to play another hand after this one?	C	
28. One more.	No Rep.	25. We'll see.	C	
29. Oh boy.		26. You like that one, huh?	C	
30. Me.		27. Oops, my card fell.	—	
31. Nothin fall down you drop it.				
32. You got it?				
(section omitted)				
		32. Have you played this before?	—	D1
36. Me do it before mommy go out.		33. You've played it with me too, haven't you?	C	

(*continued*)

BOX 3–4. *(continued)*

37. Yea.				
38. Now?		34. Yes.	C	
39. Oh boy.				
40. Tomorrow's Friday.		35. No. tomorrow's Thursday.	C	
41. What day is?		36. Today is Wednesday.	C	
(section omitted)				
59. Yellow one.		51. You like yellow?	C	
60. Yup.				
61. Yellow one.				
62. Me like come over			C	
here.		52. I'm glad.		
		53. Take a card, Patty.	NC	D2
63. Oh boy.				
64. Know what?		54. What?	C	
65. My brother coming			C	
out two more days.	Conf.	55. Who's coming out?		
66. My brother.	Rep.			
67. My Bobby coming out.		56. He is!	C	
68. Yup coming out two			C	
more days.		57. That'll be nice.		
69. Call up last night.				
70. He go be home two			NC	D2
more days.		58. Let's keep going.		
71. Two more days.		59. Good job.	NC	
		(P. takes card.)		
72. You know me lucky?		60. You are?	C	
73. Yup, see.		61. Hold your cards right,	NC	D2
		Patty.		
74. Peter Rabbit!		62. I don't know where to put	NC	
		these.		
75. All mixed up got no				
room where you are.				
76. Me got enough room this				
way.				
77. Dis chair real			C	
comfortable.		63. I'm glad you like that		
		chair.		
		64. What's this?	NC	D1
78. Me like dat.	NC	65. Good. Take a card.	NC	
79. You?	Conf.	66. Do I like that chair?	C	
		67. Yeah I like that one.	C	
81. Me like dis chair.		68. Good. What's this?	NC	D1
82. Clown.		69. Right.	C	
83. Oh boy.		70. A good one?	C	
84. Look dere's a little one	NC			
too.				
85. Oh my god that's real			C	
good.		71. Sure is.		
		72. Is that the big one or	NC	D1
		the little one?		
86. You know the big one.				

BOX 3–4.   *(continued)*

#	Utterance	Code
87.	That's real small.	
	(section omitted)	
92.	You eat that at home?	
93.	Me eat carrot home all time now.	
94.	Me got one in my lunch.	
95.	Carrot and celery taste real good.	
96.	Carrot.	
97.	Do it good.	
98.	How many me got?	
	(section omitted)	
106.	Watch your ring don't come off.	
107.	(unintelligible)	
108.	Oh boy.	
109.	Better this way.	
110.	Look!	
111.	Me don't wanna kick you.	
	(section omitted)	
123.	How bout do dis one too.	
124.	See?	
125.	Oh boy.	
126.	Me. (unintelligible)	
127.	Put that round me see that better.	
128.	Yeah.	
	(section omitted)	
137.	Me tell you bout my brother coming up?	
138.	Yeah, me lucky.	
139.	Me lucky.	
140.	Do dis one too.	
141.	Me like see that.	Conf. No Rep.
142.	Better for me.	
143.	See how much you got in here.	Conf. No Rep.
144.	Yeah.	
145.	Put all that stuff in here.	
146.	See what you got in here.	
	(section omitted)	

#	Utterance	Code	
73.	That's right.	C	
77.	Yes, do you?	C	
		C	
78.	Do you?		
		C	
79.	Mmm, sounds good.		
		NC	
81.	Super.	C	
82.	More than I do.	C	
91.	What do I have on?	—	D1
		C	
92.	It won't.		
93.	It's too tight.	C	
94.	Hmm.	C	
95.	Hold them like this.	NC	D2
96.	What did you get? (P. kicks chair.)	C	
		C	
97.	No you won't.		
106.	I think we're done.	—	
		C	
107.	Alright we can do that one next.		
108.	I see!	C	
		C	
109.	Like this?		
		C	
110.	Yeah.		
		NR	
		NR	
111.	Alright.	C	
112.	You'd like to see this one?	C	
		NR	
113.	See how much I have in here?	C	
		C	
114.	I have this.		

(continued)

BOX 3–4. *(continued)*

	144. Look out it rolls.	—	D3
152. Stupid marble.	145. Oops, stay there.	C	
153. Stay there.			
154. Stupid marble.	146. Sure is.	C	
155. Me put all this away for you?		C	
	147. No, I'd like to leave it out please because I need it later. (C. takes out list.)		
	148. Point to your hair. (P. points to head.)	NC	D2
156. (sigh) Hair.			
157. Me know that suppose have off tomorrow.		C	
	149. You are?		
	150. Point to your elbow.	NC	D2
158. You funny you.	151. I'm funny? How come?	C	
159. You foolin (unintelligible)		C	
	151. I'm not fooling you.		
	152. They're questions.	C	
160. Me turn it?	NC	153. First we're going to finish this.	C

2. Patty's utterances are generally semantically contingent with the clinician in this sample, so contingency is not coded. Utterances that indicate noncontingency or instances of no response were coded (NC or NR). Utterances that signal topic shifts were not coded as noncontingent unless there is evidence that the clinician's utterance calls for a different response.

3. Patty's noncontingent responses were examined to determine if they were related to event structure or agenda differences with the clinician.

The interaction between Patty and her speech-language pathologist generally has the flavor of an interaction where control is being shared by the participants. Each has approximately the same number of turns, and each initiates topic changes and ask questions of the other. In most exchanges, both of them are aware of and respond to the focus of their partner's attention. There are occasions, however, when each participant does not follow the other's bid with a contingent response. In the case of the speech-language pathologist, these noncontingent utterances are primarily aimed at moving the activity along when Patty spends too much time looking at one card or engaging in conversation. These clinician utterances consist most frequently of directive turns and take the form of calling Patty's name to get her attention and issuing imperatives. The speech-language pathologist also directs the activity by asking questions to prompt Patty to take the next step in the activity or to test her knowledge of some aspect of the materials being used. Patty also seems to use noncontingent responses to further her own agenda. This most frequently occurs for her when she has been asked to do something that seems irrelevant or silly. She then abruptly shifts the topic rather than respond to the request of the speech-language pathologist. This shift appears to be due to agenda differences rather

---

BOX 3–5. *Fine Tuning Analysis*

Name: Patty C.

Event: Playing card game

I. Adult semantic contingency

Total adult utterances	83
(−) Adult initiations	−4
Utterances analyzed	79
Number of contingent utterances	59
Percent of utterances analyzed	73%
Number of noncontingent utterances	20
Percent of utterances analyzed	27%
Number of no response	4

II. Interactive mode

Total adult utterances	83
Total client utterances	98
Directive features	
Test questions	6
Imperatives	11
Attention getters	5
Total	22
Percent of total adult	
utterances	26%

III. Client fine tuning

Confusion index	
Confusing client utterances	6
Percent of total client utterances	6%
Client repairs	1
Percent of confusing utterances	1.6%
Noncontingency index	
Noncontingent responses	5
No response	0
Total noncontingent responses	5
Percent of total client utterances	5%

---

than an inability to fine tune to the intent of her partner. Patty does seems to have some difficulty recognizing when her listener is confused about her meaning. In several instances the speech-language pathologist used a contingent query to indicate she needed clarification or confirmation of what she thought Patty had said. In only one case did Patty attempt to repair the breakdown.

REFERENCES

ANSELMI, D., M. TOMASELLO, AND M. ACUNZO. Young Children's Responses to Neutral and Specific Contingent Queries, *Journal of Child Language,* 13, 1986, 135–44.

APONTE, H. The Family-School Interview, *Family Process,* 15, 1976, 303–10.

BARNES, S., M. GUTFREUND, D. SATTERLY, AND G. WELLS. Characteristics of Adult Speech Which Predict Children's Language Development, *Journal of Child Language,* 10, 1983, 65–84.

BATES, E. *Language and Context: The Acquisition of Pragmatics.* New York: Academic Press, 1976.

BATES, E., L. BENIGNI, I. BRETHERTON, L. CAMAIONI, AND V. VOLTERRA. From Gesture to First Word: On Cognitive and Social Prerequisites, in *Interaction, Conversation, and the Development of Language*, eds. M. Lewis and L. Rosenblum. New York: John Wiley, 1977.

BATES, E., AND B. MACWHINNEY. A Functionalist Approach to the Acquisition of Grammar, in *Developmental Pragmatics*, eds. E. Ochs and B. Schieffelin. New York: Academic Press, 1979.

BENEDICT, H. Early Lexical Development: Comprehension and Production, *Journal of Child Language*, 6, 1979, 183–200.

BLANK, M., M. GESSNER, AND A. ESPOSITO. Language Without Communication: A Case Study, *Journal of Child Language*, 6, 1979, 329–52.

BLOOM, L., AND M. LAHEY. *Language Development and Language Disorders*. New York: John Wiley, 1978.

BLOUNT, B. Culture and the Language of Socialization, in *Cultural Perspectives on Child Development*, eds. D. Wagner and H. Stevenson. New York: W. H. Freeman, 1982, pp. 72–74.

BRENNIS, D., AND L. LEIN. "You Fruithead": A Sociolinguistic Approach to Children's Dispute Settlement, in *Child Discourse*, eds. S. Ervin-Tripp and C. Mitchell-Kernan. New York: Academic Press, 1977.

BRICE HEATH, S. *Ways with Words: Language, Life, and Work in Communities and Classrooms*. New York: Cambridge University Press, 1983.

BRINTON, B., M. FUJIKI, D. LOEB, AND E. WINKLER. Development of Conversational Repair Strategies in Response to Requests for Clarification, *Journal of Speech and Hearing Research*, 29, 1986, 75–81.

BROEN, P. The Verbal Environment of the Language Learning Child, *Monograph of the American Speech and Hearing Association*, No. 17, December 1972.

BROWN, R. *A First Language: The Early Stages*. Cambridge, Mass.: Harvard University Press, 1973.

BROWN, R., C. CAZDEN, AND U. BELLUGI. The Child's Grammar from I to III, in *Studies of Child Language Development*, eds. C. Ferguson and D. Slobin. New York: Holt, Rinehart & Winston, 1973, pp. 295–333.

BRUNER, J. The Ontogenesis of Speech Acts, *Journal of Child Language*, 2, 1975, 1–19.

BRUNER, J. Early Social Interaction and Language Acquisition, in *Studies in Mother–Child Interaction*, ed. H. Schaffer. New York: Academic Press, 1977, pp. 271–89.

BRUNER, J., AND V. SHERWOOD. Early Rule Structure: The Case of Peekaboo, in *Play: Its Role in Evolution and Development*, eds. J. Bruner, A. Jolly, and K. Sylva. New York: Penguin, 1976.

CARTER, A. The Transformation of Sensorimotor Morphemes into Words: A Case Study of the Development of "Here" and "There," *Stanford Papers and Reports on Child Language Development*, 10, 1975a, 31–47.

CARTER, A. The Transformation of Sensorimotor Morphemes into Words: A Case Study of the Development of "More" and "Mine," *Journal of Child Language*, 2, 1975b, 233–50.

CARTER, A. From Sensorimotor Vocalizations to Words: A Case Study of the Evolution of Attention-Directing Communication in the Second Year, in *Action Gesture and Symbol: The Emergence of Language*, ed. A. Lock. New York: Academic Press, 1978.

CARTER, A. The Disappearance Schema: Case Study of a Second Year Communicative Behavior, in *Developmental Pragmatics*, eds. E. Ochs and B. Schieffelin. New York: Academic Press, 1979.

CHAPMAN, K., L. LEONARD, AND C. MERVIS. The Effect of Feedback on Young Children's Inappropriate Word Usage, *Journal of Child Language*, 13, 1986, 101–17.

CHAPMAN, R. Mother–Child Interaction in the Second Year of Life: Its Role in Language Development, in *Early Language: Acquisition and Intervention*, eds. R. Schiefelbusch and D. Bricker. Baltimore: University Park Press, 1981.

CHOMSKY, N. *Aspects of the Theory of Syntax*. Cambridge, Mass.: M.I.T. Press, 1965.

COGGINS, T., AND R. CARPENTER. The Communication Intention Inventory: A System for Observing and Coding Children's Early Intentional Communication, *Applied Psycholinguistics*, 2, 1981, 235–51.

COGGINS, T., L. OLSWANG, AND J. GUTHRIE. Assessing Communicative Intents in Young Children: Low Structured Observation or Elicitation Tasks? *Journal of Speech and Hearing Disorders*, 52, 1987, 44–49.

CONTI-RAMSDEN, G. Maternal Recasts and Other Contingent Replies to Language Impaired Children, *Journal of Speech and Hearing Disorders*, 55, 1990, 262–74.

CORSARO, W. The Clarification Request as a Feature of Adult Interactive Styles with Young Children, *Language in Society*, 6, 1976, 183–207.

CREAGHEAD, N. Children with Disorders of Pragmatics, in *Pragmatics: The Role in Language Development*, ed. J. Irwin, La Verne, Calif.: Fox Point Publishing, 1982, pp. 29–47.

CROSS, T. Mothers' Speech Adjustments: The Contributions of Selected Child Listener Variables, in *Talking to Children*, eds. C. Snow and C. Ferguson. New York: Cambridge University Press, 1977.

CROSS, T. Mothers' Speech and Its Association with Rate of Language Acquisition in Young Children, in *The Development of Communication*, eds. N. Waterson and C. Snow. New York: John Wiley, 1978.

CROSS, T. Habilitating the Language-Impaired Child: Ideas from Studies of Parent–Child Interaction, *Topics in Language Disorders*, 4, 1984, 1–14.

DORE, J. A Description of Early Language Development, *Journal of Psycholinguistic Research*, 4, 1974, 423–30.

DORE, J. Holophrases, Speech Acts, and Language Universals, *Journal of Child Language*, 2, 1975, 21–40.

DORE, J. Conversation and Preschool Language Development, in *Language Acquisition*, eds. P. Fletcher and M. Garman. New York: Cambridge University Press, 1979, pp. 337–61.

DRACH, K. The Language of the Parent: A Pilot Study. Working paper 14, Language-Behavior Research Laboratory, University of California, Berkeley, Calif., 1969.

DUCHAN, J. Interactions with an Autistic Child, in *Language: Social Psychological Perspectives*, eds. H. Giles, W. Robinson, and P. Smith. New York: Pergamon Press, 1980, pp. 255–60.

DUCHAN, J. Autistic Children Are Noninteractive: or So We Say, *Seminars in Speech and Language*, 4, 1983, 53–61.

DUCHAN, J. Language Assessment: The Pragmatics Revolution, in *Language Sciences*, ed. R. Naremore. San Diego, Calif.: College Hill Press, 1984.

DUCHAN, J. Language Intervention Through Sensemaking and Fine Tuning, in *Language Competence: Assessment and Intervention*, ed. R. Schiefelbusch. San Diego, Calif.: College Hill Press, 1986, pp. 187–212.

DUCHAN, J. Everyday Events: Their Role in Language Assessment and Intervention, in *Pragmatics of Language: Clinical Practice Issues*, ed. T. Gallagher. San Diego, Calif.: Singular Press, 1991.

EDER, D. Differences in Communicative Styles Across Ability Groups, in *Communicating in the Classroom*, ed. L. Wilkinson. New York: Academic Press, 1982.

ERVIN-TRIPP, S. Is Sybil There? The Structure of Some American English Directives, *Language in Society*, 5, 1976, 25–66.

ERVIN-TRIPP, S. Wait for Me Roller Skate, in *Child Discourse*, eds. S. Ervin-Tripp and C. Mitchell-Kernan. New York: Academic Press, 1977.

ERVIN-TRIPP, S., AND D. GORDON. The Development of Requests, in *Language Competence: Assessment and Intervention*, ed. R. Schiefelbusch. San Diego, Calif.: College Hill Press, 1986.

FARRAR, M. Discourse and the Acquisition of Grammatical Morphemes, *Journal of Child Language*, 17, 1990, 607–24.

FARRAR, M., AND G. GOODMAN. Developmental Differences in the Relation Between Scripts and Episodic Memory: Do They Exist? in *What Young Children Remember and Why*, eds. R. Fivush and J. Hudson. New York: Cambridge University Press, 1991.

FERNALD, A. Four-Month-Olds Prefer to Listen to "Motherese." Paper presented at the meeting of the Society for Research in Child Development, 1981, cited in *The Development of Language*, ed. J. Gleason. Columbus, Ohio: Merrill, 1985.

FISHER, S. Institutional Authority and the Structure of Discourse, *Discourse Processes*, 7, 1984, 201–24.

FIVUSH, R., AND E. SLACKMAN. The Acquisition and Development of Scripts, in *Event Knowledge: Structure and Function in Development*, ed. K. Nelson. Hillsdale, N.J.: Lawrence Erlbaum, 1986, pp. 71–96.

FURMAN, L., AND T. WALDEN. Effect of Script Knowledge on Preschool Children's Communicative Interactions, *Developmental Psychology*, 26, 1990, 227–33.

FURROW, D., AND K. NELSON. A Further Look at the Motherese Hypothesis: A Reply to Gleitman, Newport, and Gleitman, *Journal of Child Language*, 13, 1986, 163–76.

FURROW, D., K. NELSON, AND H. BENEDICT. Mothers' Speech to Children and Syntactic Development: Some Simple Relationships, *Journal of Child Language*, 6, 1979, 423–42.

GALLAGHER, T. Revision Behaviors in the Speech of Normal Children Developing Language, *Journal of Speech and Hearing Research*, 20, 1977, 303–18.

GALLAGHER, T. Contingent Query Sequences with Adult–Child Discourse, *Journal of Child Language*, 8, 1981, 51–62.

GALLAGHER, T., AND C. PRUTTING, eds. *Pragmatic Assessment and Intervention Issues in Language*. San Diego, Calif.: College Hill Press, 1983.

GARVEY, C. The Contingent Query: A Dependent Act in Conversation, in *Interaction Conversation, and the Development of Language*, eds. M. Lewis and L. Rosenblum. New York: John Wiley, 1977.

GLEASON, J. Fathers and Other Strangers: Men's Speech to Young Children, in *Georgetown University Roundtable on Language and Linguistics*, ed. D. Dato. Washington, D. C.: Georgetown University Press, 1975.

GLEITMAN, L., E. NEWPORT, AND H. GLEITMAN. The Current Status of the Motherese Hypothesis, *Journal of Child Language*, 11, 1984, 43–79.

GORDON, D., AND S. ERVIN-TRIPP. The Structure of Children's Requests, in *The Acquisition of Communicative Competence*, eds. R. Schiefelbusch and J. Pikar. Baltimore: University Park Press, 1984.

GRIFFITHS, P. Speech Acts and Early Sentences, in *Language Acquisition: Studies in First Language Development*, eds. P. Fletcher and M. Garman. New York: Cambridge University Press, 1979, pp. 105–120.

GRUNDEL, J. Referential Extension in Early Language Development, *Child Development*, 48, 1977, 1567–76.

HALLIDAY, M. *Learning How to Mean: Explorations in the Development of Language*. London: Edward Arnold, 1975.

HOFF-GINSBERG, E. Function and Structure in Maternal Speech: Their Relation to the Child's Development of Syntax, *Developmental Psychology*, 22, 1986, 155–63.

HOFF-GINSBERG, E. Maternal Speech and the Child's Development of Syntax: A Further Look, *Journal of Child Language*, 17, 1990, 85–99.

HUBBELL, R. *Children's Language Disorders: An Integrated Approach.* Englewood Cliffs, N.J.: Prentice-Hall, 1981.

IRWIN, J., ed. *Pragmatics: The Role in Language Development.* La Verne, Calif.: Fox Point Publishing, 1982.

KAYE, K. Why We Don't Talk "Baby Talk" to Babies, *Journal of Child Language,* 7, 1980, 489–507.

KAYE, K., AND R. CHARNEY. Conversational Asymmetry between Mothers and Children, *Journal of Child Language,* 8, 1981, 35–50.

KEMLER NELSON, D., K. HIRSH-PASEK, P. JUSCZYK, AND K. WRIGHT CASSIDY. How the Prosodic Cues in Motherese Might Assist Language Learning, *Journal of Child Language,* 16, 1989, 55–68.

LEONARD, L., S. CAMARATA, L. ROWAN, AND K. CHAPMAN. The Communicative Functions of Lexical Usage by Language-Impaired Children, *Applied Psycholinguistics,* 3, 1982, 109–26.

LIEVEN, E. Interaction Style and Children's Language Learning, *Topics in Language Disorders,* 4, 1984, 15–23.

LUBINSKI, R., J. DUCHAN, AND B. WEITZNER-LIN. Analysis of Breakdowns and Repairs in Aphasic Adult Communication. Proceedings of the Clinical Aphasiology Conference, Bar Harbor, Maine, 1980.

LUND, N. Family Events and Relationships: Implications for Language Assessment and Intervention, *Seminars in Speech and Language,* 7, 1986, 415–31.

MCDONALD, L., AND D. PIEN. Mother Conversational Behavior as a Function of Interactional Intent, *Journal of Child Language,* 9, 1982, 337–58.

MCSHANE, J. *Learning to Talk.* New York: Cambridge University Press, 1980.

MASUR, E. Mothers' Responses to Infants' Object-Related Gestures: Influences on Lexical Development, *Journal of Child Language,* 9, 1982, 23–30.

MERVIS, C. Early Lexical Development: The Contributions of Mother and Child, in *Origins of Cognitive Skills,* ed. C. Sophian. Hillsdale, N.J.: Lawrence Erlbaum, 1984.

MILLER, J. Assessing Children's Language Behavior: A Developmental Process Approach, in *Bases of Language Intervention,* ed. R. Schiefelbusch. Baltimore: University Park Press, 1978, pp. 269–318.

MITCHELL-KERNAN, C., AND K. KERNAN. Pragmatics of Directive Choice Among Children, in *Child Discourse,* eds. S. Ervin-Tripp and C. Mitchell-Kernan. New York: Academic Press, 1977.

MURRAY, A., J. JOHNSON, AND J. PETERS. Fine-tuning of Utterance Length to Preverbal Infants: Effects on Later Language Learning, *Journal of Child Language,* 17, 1990, 511–25.

MURRAY, L., AND C. TREVARTHAN. The Infant's Role in Mother–Infant Communications, *Journal of Child Language,* 13, 1986, 15–29.

NELSON, K. Structure and Strategy in Learning to Talk, *Monographs for the Society of Research in Child Development,* 38 (serial no. 149), 1973.

NELSON, K. How Young Children Represent Knowledge of Their World in and out of Language, in *Children's Thinking: What Develops?* ed. R. Siegler. Hillsdale, N.J.: Lawrence Erlbaum, 1978.

NELSON, K. *Making Sense: The Acquisition of Shared Meaning.* New York: Academic Press, 1985.

NELSON, K., ed. *Event Knowledge.* Hillsdale, N.J.: Lawrence Erlbaum, 1986.

NELSON, K., AND J. GRUENDEL. Generalized Event Representations: Basic Building Blocks of Cognitive Development, in *Advances in Developmental Psychology,* eds A. Brown and M. Lamb. Hillsdale, N.J.: Lawrence Erlbaum, 1981, pp. 131–58.

NEWCOMBE, N., AND M. ZASLOW. Do 2½-Year-Olds Hint? A Study of Directive Forms in the Speech of 2½-Year-Old Children to Adults, *Discourse Processes,* 4, 1981, 239–52.

NEWPORT, E. Motherese: The Speech of Mothers to Young Children, in *Cognitive Theory* (Vol. 2), eds. N. J. Castellan, D. Pisoni, and G. Potts. Hillsdale, N.J.: Lawrence Erlbaum, 1977.

NEWPORT, E., H. GLEITMAN, AND L. GLEITMAN. Mother, I'd Rather Do It Myself: Some Effects and Noneffects of Maternal Speech Style, in *Talking to Children: Language Input and Acquisition,* eds. C. Snow and C. Ferguson. New York: Cambridge University Press, 1977.

NINIO, A., AND J. BRUNER. The Achievement and Antecedents of Labeling, *Journal of Child Language,* 5, 1978, 1–15.

OLSEN-FULERO, L. Style and Stability in Mother Conversational Behavior: A Study of Individual Differences, *Journal of Child Language,* 9, 1982, 543–64.

PETERS, A. *The Units of Language Acquisition.* New York: Cambridge University Press, 1983.

PLATT, J., AND T. COGGINS. Comprehension of Social-Action Games in Prelinguistic Children: Levels of Participation and Effect of Adult Structure, *Journal of Speech and Hearing Disorders,* 55, 1990, 315–26.

PRICE, D., AND G. GOODMAN. Visiting the Wizard: Children's Memory for a Recurring Event, *Child Development,* 61, 1990, 664–80.

PRIZANT, B., AND J. DUCHAN. The Functions of Immediate Echolalia in Autistic Children, *Journal of Speech and Hearing Disorders,* 46, 1981, 241–49.

PRUTTING, C. Process/pra/ses/n: The Action of Moving Forward Progressively from One Point to Another on the Way to Completion, *Journal of Speech and Hearing Disorders,* 44, 1979, 3–30.

PRUTTING, C., N. BAGSHAW, H. GOLDSTEIN, S. JUSKOWITZ, AND I. UMEN. Clinician–Child Discourse: Some Preliminary Questions, *Journal of Speech and Hearing Disorders,* 43, 1978, 123–39.

PYE, C. Quiche Mayan Speech to Children, *Journal of Child Language,* 13, 1986, 85–100.

RATNER, N., AND J. BRUNER. Games, Social Exchange and the Acquisition of Language, *Journal of Child Language,* 5, 1978, 391–401.

RETHERFORD, K., B. SCHWARTZ, AND R. CHAPMAN. Semantic Roles and Residual Grammatical Categories in Mother and Child Speech: Who Tunes into Whom? *Journal of Child Language,* 3, 1981, 583–608.

RIPICH, F., AND J. PANAGOS. Accessing Children's Knowledge of Sociolinguistic Rules for Speech and Language Lessons, *Journal of Speech and Hearing Disorders,* 50, 1985, 335–46.

RONDAL, J. Father's and Mother's Speech in Early Language Development, *Journal of Child Language,* 7, 1980, 353–71.

RUMELHART, D. Notes on a Schema for Stories. In D. Bobrow and A. Collins (eds.), *Representation and Understanding: Studies in Cognitive Science.* New York: Academic Press, 1975.

SACHS, J., AND J. DEVIN. Young Children's Use of Age Appropriate Speech Styles in Social Interactions and Role Playing. *Journal of Child Language,* 3, 1976, 81–98.

SACKS, H., E. SCHEGLOFF, AND G. JEFFERSON. A Simplest Systematics for the Organization of Turn-Taking for Conversation, *Language,* 50, 1974, 696–735.

SCHANK, R., AND R. ABLESON. *Scripts, Plans, Goals and Understanding: An Inquiry into Human Knowledge Structures.* Hillsdale, N.J.: Lawrence Erlbaum Associates, 1977.

SCHERER, N., AND L. OLSWANG. Role of Mothers' Expansions in Stimulating Children's Language Production, *Journal of Speech and Hearing Research,* 27, 1984, 387–96.

SCHIEFFELIN, B., AND A. EISENBERG. Cultural Variations in Children's Conversations, in *The Acquisition of Communicative Competence,* eds. R. Schiefelbusch and J. Pikar. Baltimore: University Park Press, 1984, pp. 379–420.

SCOLLON, R. *One Child's Language from One to Two: The Origins of Construction.* University of Hawaii: Working Papers in Linguistics, 6, no. 5, 1974.

SEARLE, J. *Speech Acts.* New York: Cambridge University Press, 1969.

SEARLE, J. Speech Acts and Recent Linguistics, in *Developmental Psycholinguistics and Communication Disorders,* eds. D. Aaronson and R. Rieber, New York: New York Academy of Sciences, 1975.

SEITZ, S., AND C. STEWART. Expanding on Expansions and Related Aspects of Mother–Child Communication, *Developmental Psychology,* 11, 1975, 763–69.

SHATZ, M. How Young Children Respond to Language: Procedures for Answering, *Papers and Reports in Child Language Development,* 10, 1975, 97–110.

SHATZ, M. On Mechanisms of Language Acquisition: Can Features of the Communicative Environment Account for Development? in *Language Acquisition: The State of the Art,* eds. E. Wanner and L. Gleitman. New York: Cambridge University Press, 1982.

SHERROD, K., S. FRIEDMAN, S. CRAWLEY, D. DRAKE AND J. DEVIEUX. Maternal Language of Prelinguistic Infants: Syntactic Aspects, *Child Development,* 48, 1977, 1662–65.

SIMON, C., ed. *Communication Skills and Classroom Success.* San Diego, Calif.: College Hill Press, 1985.

SKARAKIS, E., AND C. PRUTTING. Early Communication: Semantic Functions and Communicative Intentions in the Communication of Preschool Children with Impaired Hearing, *American Annals of the Deaf,* 122, 1977, 382–91.

SNOW, C. Mothers' Speech to Children Learning Language, *Child Development,* 43, 1972, 549–65.

SNOW, C. Mothers' Speech Research: From Input to Interaction, in *Talking to Children: Language Input and Acquisition,* eds. C. Snow and C. Ferguson. New York: Cambridge University Press, 1977.

SNOW, C. The Development of Conversations Between Mothers and Babies, *Journal of Child Language,* 4, 1977, 1–22.

SNOW, C. Conversation with Children, in *Language Acquisition,* eds. P. Fletcher and M. Garman. New York: Cambridge University Press, 1979, pp. 363–76.

SNOW, C. Conversations with Children, in *Language Acquisition: Studies in First Language Development* (2nd ed.), eds. P. Fletcher and M. Garman. New York: Cambridge University Press, 1986.

SNOW, C., AND C. FERGUSON, eds. *Talking to Children: Language Input and Acquisition.* New York: Cambridge University Press, 1977.

SPRADLEY, J., AND D. McCURDY. *The Cultural Experience: Ethnography in Complex Society.* Chicago: Science Research Associates, 1972.

STERN, D., S. SPICKER, J. BARNETT, AND D. MacKAIN. The Prosody of Maternal Speech: Infant Age and the Context Related Changes, *Journal of Child Language,* 10, 1983, 1–15.

SUGARMAN, S. The Development of Preverbal Communication, in *The Acquisition of Communicative Competence,* eds. R. Schiefelbusch and J. Pikar. Baltimore: University Park Press, 1984.

THOMAS, E. It's All Routine: A Redefinition of Routines as a Central Factor in Language Acquisition. Paper Presented at the Fourth Annual Boston University Conference on Language Development, Boston, Mass., 1979.

TIEGERMAN, E., AND M. SIPERSTEIN. Individual Patterns of Interaction in the Mother–Child Dyad: Implications for Parent Intervention, *Topics in Language Disorders,* 4, 1984, 50–61.

VAN DER GEEST, T. Some Interactional Aspects of Language Acquisition, in *Talking to Children,* eds.

C. Snow and C. Ferguson. New York: Cambridge University Press, 1977.

WATZLAWICK, P., J. BEAVIN, AND D. JACKSON. *The Pragmatics of Human Communication.* New York: W. W. Norton, 1967.

WERNER, H., AND B. KAPLAN. *Symbol Formation.* New York: John Wiley, 1963.

WEST, C. Against Our Will: Male Interruption of Females in Cross-Sex Conversation, *Annals of the New York Academy of Sciences,* 327, 1979, 81–95.

WETHERBY, A., D. CAIN, D. YONCLAS, AND V. WALKER. Analysis of Intentional Communication of Normal Children from the Prelinguistic to the Multiword Stage, *Journal of Speech and Hearing Research,* 31, 1988, 240–52.

WETHERBY, A., AND C. PRUTTING. Profiles of Communicative and Cognitive Abilities in Autistic Children, *Journal of Speech and Hearing Research,* 27, 1984, 364–77.

WETHERBY, A., D. YONCLAS, AND A. BRYAN. Communicative Profiles of Preschool Children with Handicaps: Implications for Early Identification, *Journal of Speech and Hearing Disorders,* 54, 1989, 148–58.

WHITE, S., AND R. WHITE. The Deaf Imperative: Characteristics of Maternal Input to Hearing-Impaired Children, *Topics in Language Disorders,* 4, 1984, 38–49.

WOLLNER, S., AND E. GELLER. Methods of Assessing Pragmatic Abilities, in *Pragmatics: The Role in Language Development,* ed. J. Irwin. La Verne, Calif.: Fox Point Publishing, 1982.

YODER, P., AND A. KAISER. Alternative Explanations for the Relationship Between Maternal Verbal Interaction Style and Child Language Development, *Journal of Child Language* 16, 1989, 141–60.

4

PHONOLOGY

In pragmatics the emphasis is on the ways in which language changes in different contexts. In phonology, or the study of the sound system of language, the emphasis has traditionally been to study it as if it does not vary. In phonology contextual variability has been considered an aberration. There is strong evidence from various sources, however, against this fixed view of phonology. One set of studies is of style or code shifting. It documents the fact that the sounds you use can depend on the person you are talking to and the formality of the situation. A second influence of context on phonology is that of linguistic context. For example, a well-known phenomenon to speech-language pathologists is that children's speech sounds vary depending on the phonological and syntactic difficulty of the surrounding language. This influence of adjacent sounds on one another is studied under the titles of *coarticulation* and *assimilation*. Finally, there is evidence from the developmental literature that children's early language forms are highly context bound. They are closely intertwined with the accompanying action in both timing and form and also are tightly related to the accompanying intonation pattern.

Some of the following discussion about phonology is context focused, such as our sections on context-sensitive analysis and context-sensitive rules. Other parts ignore the role of context and leave it to you to keep in mind that children's performance will vary depending on the person they are talking to, the event, and the phonological and syntactic environment of the particular sound in question.

PHONOLOGY AND WHAT IT INCLUDES

Phonology, as an area of linguistics, has to do with the way the sounds of a language are organized. It can include the documentation of what the sounds are (the sound inventory), their component features, how the sounds are strung together, and the various underlying rules or processes which operate to influence how the sounds change when they are produced under certain circumstances and in certain contexts. Sometimes intonation is included as an aspect of phonology, probably because it too can be heard and measured acoustically, using such instruments as sound spectrographs. However, components of intonation are at least as closely tied to meaning and sentence structure as they are to the sound system of the language. Therefore, we regard the treatment of intonation as an aspect of only the phonological system as a mistake; the same mistake, incidentally, which is made when one views the study of speech sounds as only the study of what is heard.

Let us elaborate this idea by filling in some background information. Our account will lead to the opinion that the sounds of a language, and of any child's speech, come from a nonobservable or underlying set of structures, instead of to the mistaken view that one can determine what the sound system of a language is by studying the sound waves which it produces.

Phonemes

We, as speakers, readers, writers, and listeners of the language have an elaborate and abstract sense of what the sounds are that make up the language. However, we develop this sense as much from our meaning system as from the way the words sound. That is, we learn in English that /p/ and /b/ are different because we use the difference to distinguish words with different meanings. It is also the case that speakers of English produce /p/ sounds differently, but when they do it does not result in a word of different meaning. Said another way, /p/ and /b/ are contrastive, and the various /p/ sounds are not. It is usual, therefore, to refer to /p/ and /b/ as *phonemes* and the different /p/ sounds as *allophonic variants* of the same phoneme.

Because we know that /p/ and /b/ make a meaning difference, we as adult native listeners ignore the subvarieties of each and treat what we hear as an abstract category or phoneme. A phoneme, then, is like a concept, and not an observable phenomenon. As speakers of English, we would agree, for the most part, on what the phonemes of English are. Linguists who have listed our phonemic inventory of English conclude that there are over forty in number.

Distinctive Features

The abstract phonemes which speakers and listeners of English have as categories differ from one another along particular dimensions. Some are prolonged, some are quick; some are hissing in quality, some are not. These differences are ones of *manner*. Phonemes also differ in where they are said in the mouth, a difference of *place*; and whether or not they are said with laryngeal vibration, a difference in *voicing*. These three features—manner, place, and voicing—can characterize the basic distinctions which make a difference in English; that is, each phoneme differs from every other phoneme along one or more of these three dimensions.

Table 4–1 outlines the distinctive features of English consonants along these place, manner, and voicing dimensions. The various place features have to do with the articulators and the place involved in creating the narrowest point of constrictions as the sound is said. Thus, for bilabial sounds, the

TABLE 4–1   Manner, Place, and Voicing of English Phonemes

Place in Mouth from Front to Back	Manner of Production					
	Stop	Fricative	Affricate	Glide	Liquid	Nasal
Bilabial	p*	hw				
	b			w		m
Labiodental		f				
		v				
Tip dental		θ				
		ð				
Alveolar	t	s				
	d	z			l	n
Blade-prepalatal		ʃ	tʃ			
		ʒ	dʒ			
Front-palatal				j		
Central-palatal					r	
Back-velar	k					
	g					ŋ
Glottal		h				

* The top line within a category is voiceless; bottom line is voiced.

narrowest point is between the lips; for labiodental, between the lips and teeth, and so on. The manners have been subclassified in Table 4–1 into six types: stops, fricatives, affricates, glides, liquids, and nasals. Other classification systems may distinguish manners. Finally, there are sounds which contrast only in that one is voiced and the other is voiceless. The table follows the format used by Fisher and Logemann in their Test of Articulatory Competence (1971).

We have picked this feature system as our frame because it is easier to work with in doing structural analysis and has, in our experience, captured the essence of most of our children's phonological problems. That is to say, it is psychologically real to children. Other feature systems can be borrowed from when needed. One is the system of Chomsky and Halle (1968), which consists of a classification based on data from acoustic phonetics rather than using the articulatory focus of a place, manner, and voicing classification. That is, Chomsky and Halle derived their features from differences portrayed in an examination of physically measured aspects of the sound waves. Those subscribing to any feature system agree that the distinctions between phonemes are not clear-cut, and the features, like the phonemes themselves, operate as abstract categories which are used by speakers, listeners, and structural analysts to distinguish the sounds from one another.

Phonological Rules

So far, we have been concentrating primarily on sound and feature inventories and pretending that once these inventories are discovered they are stable, and all is said and done about phonology. However, as we will see throughout this book, nothing is so easy. Rather, phonemes and features are different when they are produced in combinations. They combine in prescribed ways with one another. The entities which describe and govern these combining processes have been called *rules*.

There are a number of phonological rules which have been found to occur in languages of the world as well as in the language of developing children. For example, an assimilation rule which occurs in English is that the plural morpheme becomes voiced, voiceless, or syllabic depending on features of the last sound of the word to which it attaches. Thus, the plural is said as [z] in *dogs* and the /g/ is voiced; it is said as [s] in *cats* because the /t/ is unvoiced; and it is said as [iz] in *dresses* because the /s/ is a fricative.

The assimilation rule we have mentioned is based on what phonemes or distinctive features surround the changed element. Other rules depend not on phoneme or feature influences but on the syllable structure, or consonant-vowel relationships in the word. For example, if a voiceless stop such as /p/, /t/, or /k/ occurs at the beginning of a syllable, it becomes aspirated [pʰat]. This rule, as well as the assimilation rule, is context sensitive; but with this rule the relevant context is the syllable and not the feature or phoneme.

PHONOLOGICAL DEVELOPMENT

Perceptual and Phonological Discrimination

Apparently children are born with the ability to distinguish complex sounds through which languages of the world are organized. That is, when infants as young as one month are presented with a repetitive stimulus, they first adjust to the repetition and ignore it. When that stimulus is changed only slightly, for example, in place-feature, changing a /ba/ to a /da/, or in voicing, changing a /pa/ to /ba/, the babies show awareness as evidenced by a change in their heartbeat or in their sucking rate (Morse, 1972). What is also true, however, is that they do not understand these changes as meaningful phonological contrasts, since they do not yet have the ability to understand or produce words. These distinctions, then, are not linguistic but are perceptual ones that are later applied to language learning.

The linguistic distinctions children make between minimal-difference pairs of monosyllables have been studied by Schvachkin (1973) and Garnica (1973). When Schvachkin studied ten- to twenty-one-month-old children, he taught them meanings for what at first were nonsense syllables. His subjects were comparable in the order in which they learned distinctive features. Garnica (1973), on the other hand, found considerable variability among her seventeen- to twenty-two-month-old English-speaking subjects.

Barton (1976, cited in Menyuk and Menn, 1979) found that children's familiarity with a word aided them in their performance on discrimination tasks, suggesting that Schvachkin and Garnica's results are conservative, since the words they used were new to the children. Barton's results for children distinguishing meaningful and familiar words were that children between twenty-seven and thirty-five months were able to distinguish between two words with single-feature contrasts for all the features of English.

Menyuk and Menn (1979) summarize this sparse literature on children's acquisition of phonetic and linguistic distinctions between similar sounding syllables and words as follows:

> The human infant at age 1 month is capable of discriminating between some acoustic parameters that mark speech sound differences; by age 9 to 13 months, the infant appears to be able to comprehend the meaning of phonological sequences in certain contexts; that is, gestalt comprehension of phonological sequence plus context, rather than phonological differentiation of sequences; the child is able to learn to associate objects and nonsense syllables that contrast many of the initial consonant features during the period of 10 to 22 months; the child can distinguish between minimal pair words that contain most English singleton phonological contrasts by 35 months. (Menyuk and Menn, 1979, p. 52)

Menyuk and Menn (1979) warn against our believing that children at this age are making their distinctions on the basis of single-feature discriminations. Instead, based on naturalistic rather than laboratory studies, children appear to be attending to the phonological sequence as a whole and are using situational cues in assigning meaning to the words they hear. Thus, although infants can hear the differences between syllables which contrast on features of voicing or place, they do not use this fine a distinction until later in their language development, when they become more analytical and can separate sounds from one another and from the linguistic and situational contexts in which they occur. The rich interpretation fallacy which Menyuk and Menn warn us against would have its parallel in visual perception in which one would assume from watching children distinguish the written letters *b* and *p* that they could read words containing this distinction.

Prelinguistic Stages in Sound Development

Children's early production of sounds proceed through a series of stages, from mere vegetative noises to the production of sounds which resemble those used in language or languages the children are exposed to. Stark (1986) and Oller (1980), in their reviews of their own and others' research on prespeech sound development, have divided this progression into six differentiable stages as follows:

Stage 1, from Birth to Two Months: Reflexive Crying and Vegetative Noises These are burps, coughs, sneezes, and swallowing.

Stage 2, from Two Months to Three Months: Cooing During this stage the child produces back sounds which resemble velar consonants (e.g., /k/, /g/, and /x/). They are combined with back vowels, which are nasal in quality. Cooing begins with single-syllable productions and extends to a period where syllables are produced in series of from three to ten segments. The cooing sequences tend to be produced in contexts of comfort, and as conversational responses to the smiling and talking of a familiar adult.

Stages 3, from Four to Seven Months: Vocal Play   During this stage the child produces longer syllable sequences. The sounds within the syllable are more anterior, and the vowels are of longer duration than those produced in cooing. Also appearing at this time are affective sound sequences such as growling and squealing. A vocal play sequence may contain varying levels of pitch and can be used in a range of communicative play situations.

Stage 4, from Six Months to Twelve Months: Reduplicated Babbling   Babbling first begins with the child's repeated production of a single consonant across a syllable sequence (e.g., *nanana*). The consonants in the sequences resemble those of the adult language in some ways. For example, they frequently include alveolar stops and nasals, and /w/ and /j/ glides. However, they do not reflect differences between languages such as the different timing distinctions between voiced and voiceless consonants, or final syllable prolongation. In conjunction with reduplicated syllables is the emergence of single-syllable sequences such as /ba/ which Oller (1980) dubs "single-consonant babbling."

Unlike cooing and vocal play, reduplicated syllables tend to occur in nonsocial contexts and have been described as "self-stimulatory" in function (Stark, 1986). Hilke (1988), in a study of eight-month-old children, found a relationship between the frequency of vocalizations and shifts in the children's attention. There was an increase in vocalizations with changes in the child's experience of the ongoing event.

Stage 5, from Nine Months to Eighteen Months: Variegated Babbling   This stage, also referred to as *jargon*, is characterized by the child's use of different sounds across the syllable sequence. Oller (1980) distinguishes two types of variegation—one confined to the sound structure, with little variability in intonation, and the second with varied sound and intonation, resulting in sequences resembling sentences in the adult language. Both types of variegated sequences contain a larger variety of sounds than those used in reduplicated babbling, including newly emerging fricatives and high, front and back vowels.

The context for variegated babbling involving both sounds and intonation variation, is usually social and often in situations calling for monologues such as one-sided phone conversations or book reading. The child seems to be simulating lengthy adult talk, using meaningless forms to do so. This jargon-like stage is prolonged for some children, those Dore (1973) has called the "intonation babies" and brief or absent in the development of others—Dore's "word babies."

Stage 6, Ten Months: Vocables   These are short segments, ranging from one sound to two-syllable segments, which are both phonetically consistent and context specific. They are often accompanied by identifiable gestures (Carter, 1979) and tend to occur as part of ritualized games (peek-a-boo), emotional states ("uh-oh"), or frequently occurring communicative acts ("hi" + greeting; grunt + reach; "da" + point). The vocables do not qualify as words because they are not used apart from the contexts and appear to be one component of the action sequence rather than a symbol which can stand in its stead (Blake and Fink, 1987; Carter, 1979; Dore and others, 1976; Ferguson, 1978; and Halliday, 1975).

Relationship between Prelinguistic Stages and First Words

What is the relationship between the sounds used in prelinguistic development and those used for first words? Some researchers have argued that there is little relationship. Indeed, some have suggested a developmental discontinuity between the prelinguistic and linguistic periods of speech-sound development. The debate usually revolves around the relationship between babbling and first words. Those advocating discontinuity divide into (1) the temporal discontinuity types, or those who argue that children stop babbling for a while before they begin speech (Jakobson, 1968); and (2) the phonological discontinuity types, or those who argue that the particular sounds produced in babbling are not like those used in first words. Advocates of temporal discontinuity have been proven wrong. Babbling and first words have often been found to occur simultaneously. For example, intonation babies, who use a jargon-like babbling, have been found to produce first words as part of their jargon (Sachs, 1989).

Advocates of phonological discontinuity have been shown to be both incorrect and correct—correct in that there are many sounds produced in babbling which are not used in first word production indicating support for sound discontinuity, and incorrect in that sounds used for first words tend to be ones frequently produced during the babbling stage (Lieberman, 1970; Oller and others, 1975).

Continuity is further supported by the similar sound structuring and selection found in both developmental periods. Oller, Weiman, Doyle, and Ross (1975) and Oller (1980) summarize features common to both babbling and first words:

1. More singleton consonants than consonant clusters
2. More initial than final consonants
3. More initial stops than fricatives and affricates
4. A greater proportion of fricatives and affricates than stops in final position than in initial position
5. More unaspirated than aspirated initial stops
6. More voiceless than voiced final consonants
7. More prevocalic glides than liquids
8. More apical than velar consonants

Cross-Linguistic Similarities in Prelinguistic Development

Evidence that children tend to babble the sounds they later use in their first words might lead to the assumption that children from different linguistic communities will babble using the sounds and sound patterns of their home language. However, the regularities found in babbling have not been found to be language specific. American children exposed to English reduce consonant clusters in their babbling and first words, even though their target language calls for those clusters.

Several researchers have tried to determine whether children from different language communities show different babbling patterns. For example, Oller and Eilers (1982) compared the sounds used in babbling by 8 one-year-old children exposed to Cuban Spanish with 8 one-year-olds from English-speaking homes. The children's utterances were transcribed in Spanish and English by speakers of each language trained in phonetic transcription. The two groups of children did not differ in the sounds they produced and followed the patterns described in Oller and others (1975; see the eight features listed above).

Like Oller and Eilers (1982), de Boysson-Bardies, Sagart, and Bacri (1981), and de Boysson-Bardies, Sagart, and Durand (1984) found that the babbling of children from different languages was indistinguishable when compared on their sound structure. However, the French-speaking judges were able to identify babbling from infants from their own language community if the examples included long coherent intonation patterns. The adult judges were able to distinguish the babbling of eight- and ten-month-olds who came from French communities from those who came from Arabic and Cantonese communities on the basis of their intonational differences.

Phonological Stages Accompanying First Words

At about ten months, most normal children start producing their first words. These tend to be words whose referents are familiar objects or events. The words have a simple consonant + vowel syllable structure (e.g., *da*) which may or may not be reduplicated (e.g., *dada*). The consonants are typically front stops or nasals, although children vary in their choice of favorite sounds and syllable structures. Some children confine their choice of words to fit their phonology, only saying words whose adult forms conform to their structural competences. These children avoid words which they cannot produce. Other children are more imperialistic in their productions and make adult words conform to their limited phonological capabilities. Menyuk and Menn (1979) call these children the "modifiers."

Another phenomenon reported for this period is that the first words can fluctuate considerably in how they are said, suggesting that for some children the phonemes and features are still in broadly circumscribed categories (Ferguson and Farwell, 1975). One view of this phenomenon is that these children have large overlapping phoneme categories with considerable allophonic variability within each. Within their systems this fluctuation could be seen as phonetic variability (Ferguson and Farwell, 1975). The problem with this view is described by Menyuk and Menn (1979), who have noticed that, for their subjects, some words vary much more than others and that the variability may be more related to the lexical item than to the sounds which make it up. Menyuk and Menn (1979, p. 73) put it this way: "In such a state of affairs, a feature bundle (phonemic) specification is inadequate; lexical (word particular) specification is necessary. Near the onset of speech, we may find many forms which similarly do not decompose into entities which are comparable across words." These two renditions of what is going on have been called the *across the board* versus the *lexical diffusion* hypotheses (Menyuk and Menn, 1979). In the first, a feature or phoneme will be rendered the same way across lexical items; in the second, the pronunciation will vary depending on the lexical item. What all this says about first words, perhaps, is that for some children they are highly rule constrained phonologically; for other children, there is a tendency toward a high degree of phonetic variability, which is not rule governed but depends upon the particular word being produced.

In sum, this early word stage is different for different children. Children vary in their sound and syllable structure preferences; they vary in the degree to which they impose these preferences on adult forms; and they vary in whether they organize their phonological systems by rules which work across words, or by memorizing individual lexical items. What seems to be common to all children is that this is a stage in which the phonological ability is highly restricted, and it is followed by another which is qualitatively different and in which there is rapid phonological progression (Menyuk and Menn, 1979; Ferguson, 1978; Ingram, 1976).

Acquiring the Phonemic Inventory

Several studies have attempted to determine the age at which normally developing children learning standard English acquire the various phonemes of English (e.g., Templin, 1957; Poole, 1934). It is difficult to compare across studies because different standards were used to determine when a sound was considered to be acquired. Templin (1957), for example, used the criterion of correct production in all three positions of a word by 75 percent of children of a particular age. Olmstead (1971) identified two ages for each phoneme—the first when it is produced in either one out of two, or two out of three possible word positions by more than half of an age group, and the second when more than half of an age group produces it correctly in all possible word positions. Templin's data came from giving children articulation tests, which assumed that all sounds were equivalent in importance, whereas Olmstead used spontaneous speech samples that reflect the relative frequencies with which different phonemes occur in spoken language. Both of these measures indicate a statistical average but do not necessarily represent what is normal and expected for a particular child learning standard English.

Sander (1972) reviewed several studies of phoneme acquisition and proposed that it is more appropriate to identify an age range rather than a single age within which normally developing children acquire a sound. He determined the age at which 50 percent of the children use the sound correctly in all word positions and also the age when 90 percent of an age group produces the sound. He identified this range as the range of typical acquisition. Since half of all children begin to produce the sound before the age identified as the lower limit of the typical range, it is inappropriate to describe those children as advanced, but rather, we should see them as developing normally. The upper limit would provide clinicians with a way of determining if their child's productions are significantly slower than is typical. If, for example, a seven-year-old learning standard English is not producing the /l/ phoneme, we can see from reference to Sander's data (see Box 4–1) that this child is within the slowest 10 percent to develop this sound.

Recent approaches to phonological acquisition have studied the variability in children's learning of individual phonemes for different dialects and different languages. The variability is the rule rather than the exception, so reliance on the earlier norms is no longer considered an appropriate way to determine whether or not a child is delayed in his development of phonology. Within this

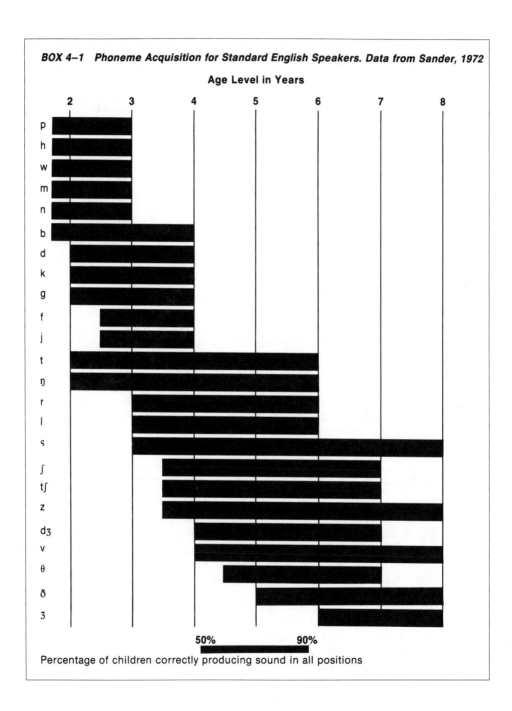

BOX 4–1 *Phoneme Acquisition for Standard English Speakers. Data from Sander, 1972*

Age Level in Years

50%   90%

Percentage of children correctly producing sound in all positions

picture of considerable variability are the following regularities for standard English speakers (adapted from Dyson, 1988; Edwards and Shriberg, 1983; and Ingram, 1976, 1981):

1. The earliest acquired sounds (around one to two years of age) tend to be from the following manner groups: nasals (/m, n, ŋ/), glides (/w, j/), or stops (/p, b, t, d, k, g/).
2. Among the later acquired manners (four to six years of age) are liquids (/l, r/), fricatives (/θ, ð, ʃ, v, s, z/), and affricates (/tʃ, ʤ/).
3. Front sounds (e.g., labials) tend to be learned before back sounds.
4. Stops tend to appear first in the initial position in a word.
5. Fricatives tend to be acquired in final position in a word and often are learned only after the stop cognate (e.g., /s/ is learned after /t/, /f/ after /p/).
6. Velars tend to emerge first in final position of a word.
7. Voiceless consonants tend to be acquired before voiced, although for some children this will depend on the position of the sound in the word.
8. The /a/ vowel tends to be the first vowel learned followed by /i/ or /u/.
9. Sounds tend to be learned more easily in word initial than word final position (Dyson, 1988).

Studies of phoneme acquisition of children learning languages other than English have revealed certain commonalities with standard English learners, as well as significant differences. Of particular interest are the differences involving the sounds common to the languages being compared. For example, Anderson and Smith (1987) found that two-year-olds learning Puerto Rican Spanish had already acquired palatals, showing much earlier learning than that evidenced by monolingual children learning English. Similarly, Pye, Ingram, and List (1987), in their study of the initial consonants acquired by Mayan children learning Quiche, found the children already learned /l/ and /tʃ/ quite early and use them often during their one-word language stage, unlike their English-speaking counterparts who learned the same sounds much later.

Acquiring Phonological Rules and Eliminating Error-Producing Processes

As we described earlier, phonologists have devised techniques for discovering sound changes and phonological environments in which these changes occur. The changes or phonological processes may be (1) *substitution*, in which segments are modified, often depending on their position in a word; (2) *assimilation*, in which adjacent phonemes or features become more alike; or (3) *syllable structure changes*, in which the number of syllables or the consonant-vowel patterns of syllables is systematically changed. Stampe (1969), in an influential article, forwarded the hypothesis that children are born with an adultlike knowledge of phonological processes which are common to all languages. The processes make up "an innate system . . . revised in certain ways by linguistic experience" (p. 441). The child then revises the innate processes by suppressing some, partially limiting others, and ordering others.

Stampe's theory differs from other theories of phonological development in that he sees the child's phonological knowledge as consisting of phonological processes, rather than seeing phonological development as acquiring context-sensitive rules, or acquiring an inventory of individual phonemes (Templin, 1957), features (McReynolds and Engmann, 1975), or feature opposition (Jakobson, 1968).

While Stampe's (1969) formulation was made at a highly abstract level and began with phonological universals from languages of the world, Ingram (1976) used his idea of phonological processes in a more descriptive way to characterize error patterns in phonological acquisition. The processes which Ingram lists as characteristic of normal standard English-speaking children are

Substitution Processes

Stopping—substituting stops for fricatives
Fronting—substituting alveolars for velar and palatal consonants
Gliding—substituting glides for liquids
Vocalization—substituting vowels for syllabic consonants (*m, n, l, r*)
Vowel neutralization—changing vowels to oral and central position

Assimilation Processes

Voicing—consonants tend to be voiced before a vowel and unvoiced at the end of a syllable
Consonant harmony—two consonants tend to become more alike when they are near one another
Progressive vowel assimilation—unstressed vowels become like a nearby stressed vowel

Syllable Structure Processes

Cluster reduction—consonant clusters are reduced to a single consonant
Deletion of final consonants—consonant-vowel-consonant (CVC) syllables become CV syllables
Deletion of unstressed syllables—unstressed syllables are deleted
Reduplication—a syllable is repeated in a multisyllabic word (*wawa for water*)

The processes above are commonly occurring ones for both normal and abnormal language learners and for children learning different languages. While Stampe's (1969) original description of phonological processes was based on normal adult productions, the identification of processes in children's speech is usually taken as evidence that the child does not yet have full adult competence. Their progression is usually thought of as one in which processes become eliminated.

Recently researchers have begun to trace developmental trends in children's elimination of error-producing phonological processes. Hodson and Paden (1991) have found that by age four normally developing English-speaking children have eliminated most developmental processes which lead to errors. Except for liquid deviations (problems with /l/ and /r/), their four-year-old subjects achieved adult phonological competence. Hodson and Paden (1991) have reported similar findings for four-year-old Spanish-speaking children.

Preisser, Hodson, and Paden (1988) studied the phonological processes used by three groups of two-year-olds (eighteen to twenty-one months; twenty-two to twenty-five months; twenty-six to twenty-nine months) by asking them to name twenty-four objects. Three fourths of all the children's responses involved cluster reductions (73 percent) and liquid deviations such as omissions or distortions (77 percent). The youngest group exhibited final consonant deletions (45 percent occurrence) and syllable deletions (43 percent occurrence), but by twenty-six months these processes were no longer prevalent (3 percent for both processes). Other, less frequently occurring processes were omission of prevocalic consonants (8 percent occurrence), omission and stopping of stridents (40 percent), fronting velars (28 percent), and omitting nasals and glides (27 percent).

Lowe, Knutson, and Monson (1985), in study of 1,048 children ranging from two and one-half to four and one-half, found that a small percentage used fronting of velar and palatal consonants (e.g., t/k; ts/ch) (6 percent), with the youngest children exhibiting a higher incidence (23 percent) than the oldest (3.5 percent).

In a more detailed study of three- to five-year-old children, Haelsig and Madison (1986) found that their 10 three-year-old subjects exhibited cluster reduction, weak syllable deletion, glottal replacement, labial assimilation, and gliding of liquids. They conclude that "these processes should be expected in children's speech at or under the age of three" (p. 113). The four- and five-year-olds exhibited weak-syllable deletion and cluster reduction. There was a considerable change in performance between the three- and four-year-olds, with over 50 percent diminution in the four-year-olds' use of each of the following: deletion of final consonants, stopping, fronting, and gliding of liquids.

Acquiring Awareness of Phonology

It is not until children begin to learn to read that they come to consciously know that words are units and that they are made up of sounds (Hakes, 1982). This ability to think about the components of language requires a special kind of knowledge, what has been called *metalinguistic knowledge*. Metalinguistic knowledge is learned for particular areas of language after the direct knowledge of that area is acquired. For example, children learn to use sounds first and only later do they begin to think about how words are made up of sounds. Children start using sounds in words around age one and one-half, but they do not know about sounds as such until they begin to read. For example, Fox and Routh (1975) asked three- to seven-year-old normal language learners learning standard English to divide bisyllabic words into syllables and to divide syllables into sounds. The syllable task was successfully accomplished by the three-year-olds, but breaking one syllable words into component sounds was not accomplished by children until they were six years old.

Kamhi, Lee, and Nelson (1985) borrowed the Fox and Routh procedure and asked normal language learners and language-disordered children to break one syllable words into sounds. Their procedure involved the following instructions:

> Now I'm going to say something to you; it will be a word. I want you to say just a little bit of it. If I say "sailboat" you could say "boat." Say just a little bit of sailboat. If I say "boat" you could say "boa." Say just a little bit of "boat." (p. 209)

Kamhi, Lee, and Nelson (1985) found that their four- and five-year-old normal subjects averaged six out of eight correct items on the syllable division task and three out of eight on the sound division task. The six-year-old normal subjects were correct in answering the syllable task and averaged six out of eight on the sound task. The language-impaired six-year-old children averaged three out of eight on the syllable task and were unable to perform the sound task.

Other metalinguistic tasks may involve rhyming and comparable types of sound analysis. For example, Calfee, Chapman, and Venezky (1972) found that five-year-old children, when given word pairs in which one contained an initial sound and the other did not (*feel–eel*; *shout–out*), had difficulty recalling the second word when given the first. Bruce (1964), using a more difficult task, found that normal children as old as seven years were unable to determine what word would be left upon removal of a sound from a stimulus word (e.g., "What would happen if I took the /n/ out of *snail?*")

PHONOLOGICAL ASSESSMENT

Assessment of phonology has traditionally been called *articulation testing*, and the most common testing procedure is to administer an articulation test requiring the child to say each sound in the beginning, middle, and end of words. The objective of such a procedure is to identify mismatches between the child's sound production and the correct or *target* phoneme.

Problems with this approach have long been recognized by clinicians. For example, (1) it is a common phenomenon to see children who have many more misarticulations in connected speech than are revealed in test samples; (2) describing a production of a sound as a distortion does not capture the fact that it is still a substitution, but one in which a nonstandard allophonic variant is used in place of a standard allophone of the target sound; (3) the traditional approach tends to operate with broad or phonemic transcription and does not recognize errors which fall within the phoneme class, such as a production of the aspirated /t/ in *butter* ([bʌtʰɚ/bʌtɚ]); (4) there is no focus on patterns of consistency across substitution errors with this approach (the child who devoices all final consonants would appear to have many errors if all substitutions were simply listed, and the critical interaction of voicing and position in the word might be missed); (5) there are frequent error-to-target matching problems especially when the number of segments in the child's production are not the same as the number in the target production, and it is unclear which elements are omitted and which are substituted or distorted (e.g., /tʌpaɪ/ for *butterfly*); and (6) children who are "inconsistent" defy description in substitution analysis with a single sampling approach—no test captures accurately the variety of productions they have for a given target phoneme in their nontest speaking situations.

There have been several alternatives to this traditional approach described in the literature. Recognition that single productions of sounds are not representative of the sound in all contexts has been highlighted by McDonald (1968), as well as by studies of coarticulation (Liberman, 1970; MacNeilage and de Clerk, 1969; Daniloff and Moll, 1968).

Feature approaches, such as those suggested by McReynolds and Engmann (1975) or Fisher and Logemann (1971), have been designed to meet some of the criticisms of the traditional approach. The feature approaches are based on the recognition that sounds can be analyzed in bundles of features and that any given feature can occur in a number of sounds. Application of this approach to defective articulation has taken the form of identifying the features that are not used or are used incorrectly. The focus is thus on the pattern of consistency. The feature approach is an improvement over traditional analysis because it requires moving away from single-sample testing and because it may reveal a consistent error pattern related to features. However, as generally used, it has many of the same disadvantages of the traditional approach in that it does not allow within-phoneme error detection, it does not treat distortions, it does not solve the error-to-target matching problem, and it fails to reveal consistencies which are not related to features.

A broader based approach is currently popular—one which we have been describing. As we have said, it derives from the linguistic literature on phonology (Hooper, 1976; Hyman, 1975; Schane, 1973; Chomsky and Halle, 1968) and has been applied to the study of language acquisition (Ferguson, 1978; Ingram, 1976) as well as to language assessment (Stoel-Gammon and Dunn, 1985; Edwards and Shriberg, 1983; Ingram, 1976, 1981; Hodson, 1980; Shriberg and Kwiatkowski, 1980; Lund and Duchan, 1978; and Weiner, 1978). It has been called the *phonological process approach*. We prefer calling it the *multifaceted approach*, since we would like it to do more than discover phonological processes. It incorporates analyses from traditional and feature approaches and adds to them analysis of deviations which are not mere substitutions of the child's production of the adult form. In cases in which the phonological context is the relevant determinate of the deviation, *context-sensitive analysis* captures the consistency. *Syllable-structure analysis* is appropriate when the child's errors are alterations of consonant-vowel relationships within a syllable, or are additions or reductions in the number of syllables in a word. Finally, for those patterns which remain and which are idiosyncratic to the child, *idiosyncratic analysis* can be devised.

Substitution Analysis

Feature Analysis   Substitutions can be analyzed in terms of features that reveal regularities in the child's phonology. The feature analysis should be flexible enough to discover features which not only describe the variation across phoneme boundaries, usually called *substitutions*, but also describe the allophonic variations in the child's production, usually called *distortions*. Narrow transcription of the child's production is necessary to record the allophonic variations and reveal the significant feature substitutions—that is, those features which make the child's articulation deviant.

A feature system developed by Fisher and Logemann (1971) uses narrow transcription, thus providing for analysis of the allophonic variations within a phoneme as well as substitutions of one standard phoneme for another. Using the features of place of production, manner of production, and voicing, the child's misarticulation is precisely described. For example, if a child produces a voiced bilabial fricative [b̌] in place of a bilabial stop [b], this is described as the substitution of manner (fricative for stop) rather than as a distorted /b/.

Referring back to Table 4–1, we can see that errors which are substitutions of sounds in one column for those in another are described as *manner* errors—that is, sounds of one manner are substituted for sounds of another manner. Often these errors are consistent across several sounds. For example, when there is a pattern in which stops are substituted for fricatives of like voice and place, the pattern is *stopping* (refer back to Ingram's list given earlier). Similarly, fricatives for stops can be described as a problem of *frication*, nasals for like stops is *nasalization*, and affricates for like fricatives, *affrication*. The common substitution pattern of w/r and j/l is *gliding*. It is often accompanied by substitution of a rounded vowel or *w* for postvocalic *r* and *l*. This is referred to as *vocalization*.

Substitution errors of sounds in one row for another are *place* errors. In this case, as we have said, sounds made in one place in the mouth are substituted for sounds made somewhere else in the mouth. Sometimes these place errors are patterned across several substitutions, as t/k, d/g, in which case front or alveolar sounds are substituted for velars. This is an example of *fronting*. *Backing* is, as one would guess, the tendency to substitute back sounds for those more forward. Often children have preferences for a particular articulatory position, such as the alveolar ridge, in which case they substitute alveolar sounds for those made in other places, as t/k, t/p, d/g, d/b. This has been called *tetonism* but could more descriptively be called *alveolarizing*. One can easily imagine, then, what the patterns would be for children who display *labializing* or *velarizing*.

Examining Table 4–1 again, a within-cell substitution pattern can also occur in which voiced sounds are substituted for their voiceless cognates, or vice versa. In the first case, the problem is one of *voicing*, in the second a *devoicing* error.

Position Plus Feature Analysis Children often have feature substitutions that are specific to a particular position of a sound in a word. The child who, for example, omits final stop consonants while producing them in initial position may appear inconsistent. Consistencies can be found through an analysis which lists substitutions according to their position in the word.

Traditionally, sound positions are classified as initial, medial, and final. These categories can lead to inaccurate classification. For example, words such as *faster* and *sister* contain two consecutive consonants in the position which would be identified as medial in traditional analysis. This identification fails to distinguish a medial cluster or blend from two adjacent consonants, one terminating the initial syllable and the other initiating the final syllable. Description of the position of consonants in relation to vowels in the syllable unit leads to more precise classification. If the child produces two sequential consonants as a cluster, the cluster can be classified as a postvocalic unit (re*st* + room) or prevocalic unit (re + *st*ore). If the child separates the consonants by a juncture (si*s* + *t*er), the first consonant would be classified as postvocalic, the second as prevocalic. Thus a child may say *sister* correctly but omit the fricative in the clusters in *restroom* or *restore*. We suggest that the position of consonants and clusters be described relative to vowels, that is, pre-, inter-, or postvocalic.

Traditional substitution analysis has been adapted here to describe more accurately children's misarticulations. Using narrow transcription allows one to view "distortions" as allophonic substitutions. Once a comparison is made between different error and target sounds, the manner, place, or voicing feature can be discovered which characterize the within-phoneme as well as across-phoneme substitutions. Manner errors could be those of stopping, fricating, or nasalizing. Place errors could be fronting, backing, alveolarizing, labializing, or velarizing. Voicing errors could be voicing or devoicing. A position and feature analysis reveals consistency in patterning in which children have different feature substitutions depending on where the consonant is located in the syllable unit.

Context-Sensitive Patterns

While adaptation of substitution analysis helps to circumvent some problems, there remain some inherent difficulties with the substitution procedures which cannot be remedied without using a different kind of analysis. One such problem is that misarticulations are often produced because of the influence of sounds and syllables on one another. For example, later sounds can affect earlier ones in a word or a syllable, and vice versa. These *context-sensitive* effects cannot be discovered by an error segment to target segment match. For example, although a child's production of *pup/cup* looks like a /p/ for /k/ substitution, it is possible that the final /p/ in *cup* is affecting the production of the initial /k/, especially if the initial /k/ is produced correctly in other contexts. Context-sensitive analysis abandons the error-to-target matching procedure and instead looks for patterns in errors which might be due to the sequential relationship of sounds and syllables to one another within or across word boundaries.

Assimilation Assimilation or harmony describes the phenomenon wherein sounds in a word change under the influence of other sounds. When a child said *pup* for *cup*, as mentioned before, it was suspected that the initial /k/ in *cup* was influenced by the final /p/. On reexamining the data, it was found that in words in which /p/ occurred, the /p/ influenced other stops and fricatives. For example, the child produced /pɪpɚ/ for *zipper*, /pʌmpɪ/ for *jumping*, /pəpæmʌz/ for *pajamas*, as well as /pʌp/ for *cup*. Thus, the concept of assimilation of adjacent sounds to /p/ explains the child's misarticulations, which might have appeared to be inconsistent substitutions when using substitution analysis.

Assimilation in which an earlier sound influences a later one may occur—for example, /dɑdi/ for *doggy*, and /dɑɪdɪ/ for *diaper*. We will call this *perseverative assimilation*. Assimilation can also occur in which a later sound influences an earlier one—for example, /gɔg/ for *dog*. We are calling this *anticipatory assimilation*. Ingram (1976) has described a child's production wherein the liquid becomes a stop through anticipation, as seen in the production of /dado/ for *ladder*, /tɛto/ for *letter*, /taɪt/ for *light*, and /tɪp/ for *lamp*. In some cases, the influenced sound is not completely assimilated, but only some of its features are—for example, /gʌk/ for *duck*, in which the place feature of a final voiceless stop influences the initial voiced stop, but the initial stop maintains its original voicing feature. Smith (1973) describes his son, who through assimilation produces velar stops in place of fricatives when the target word has a velar stop. Thus /s/ and /θ/ appear as /g/ initially in *thank you*, *sing*, and *sock*; medially in *glasses*; and finally in *kiss* and *cloth*. This child displays both velar perseveration and anticipation. We would call his overall problem *bidirectional assimilation*. This means that the influence of a sound can operate in both directions. It can influence sounds which occur before as well as after it in a word.

Coalescence Children's misarticulations which have fewer syllables than the target word may also be the result of syllables coalescing. Menn (1971), for example, found such productions in her two-year-old child, exemplified by /mɛn/ for *melon*, where the single syllable retains /m/ from the initial syllable in the target word and /n/ from the final; /æʃ/ for *radish*, where /æ/ is derived from the initial syllable and /ʃ/ from the final; and /gæʒ/ for *garage*, where /g/ is retained from the initial /ʒ/ from the final. A more familiar example is *sketi*/ *spaghetti*, where the /s/ from the first syllable is coalesced with the second syllable. Coalescence can also take place at the level of individual phonemes such as when a child says /f/ for /sp/ combining features of frication and bilabial to make one sound from two.

Transposition When children change the order of sounds from the target word, we say they are transposing. A common example of transposition is /ækst/ for *asked*. Other examples would be /ful/ for *flu* or /bɛts/ for *best*. Phonological transposition may occur across syllables as well as within syllables. For example, /pɑsgɛti/ for *spaghetti* maintains all the phonemes and syllables in the word but reorders the elements. Some phonologists use the term *metathesis* to refer to transposition.

Context-sensitive analysis leads to the discovery of how phonetic context influences error patterns. It will reveal patterns of feature or of whole phoneme *perseveration* and *anticipation*, syllable *coalescence*, wherein two syllables or sounds are coalesced into one, and *transposition*, wherein elements are reordered.

Syllable Structure Patterns

Words have characteristic syllable structure in that the consonants and vowels must be ordered in prescribed ways and there must be a predetermined number of syllables in a word. Some types of phonological errors reflect a problem with the syllable structure of words rather than with individual phonemes.

Weak-Syllable Deletion Certain multisyllabic words are often misarticulated by children and adults alike, resulting in familiar forms such as bʌflo/ *Buffalo*, or membɚ/*remember*. Children with phonological problems might have an abundance of such errors. Since the sounds omitted will vary with the word (/ri/ in *remember*; /ə/ in *Buffalo*), it is inappropriate to characterize the errors by listing them as sound omissions; instead, what is common to all the errors is that the weakest syllable in the word is being dropped, thereby warranting the description of *weak-syllable deletion*. For example, Moskowitz (1970) noted that

Erica, a two-year-old, omits unstressed syllables when they are followed by stressed syllables, as seen in her production of /tɑtɑ/ for *potato*, /dʒæmʌs/ for *pajamas*, /meitos/ for *tomatoes*, and /nɑnɑ/ for *banana*. Ingram (1976) found weak-syllable deletion for a three-and-one-half-year-old with a language problem. This was seen in the child's production of /tʌpo/ for *telephone* /tʌtʌt/ for *elephant*, and /tʌpɑi/ for *butterfly*.

Reduplication   Another example of a problem which acts on syllable structure is that of reduplication, often exhibited by normally developing children. The most common form of reduplication occurs when the child repeats the initial consonant and vowel for a two-syllable word, as in *mama* and *dada*, or as in Waterson's (1971) examples of her one-and-one-half-year-old son's production of /pʊpʊ/ for *pudding*, and /tɪtɪ/ for *kitty*. It would be inaccurate to think of his production of /tɪtɪ/ as a t/k substitution. Rather, he selects a syllable from the target word and duplicates it.

Cluster Reduction   Children's developing phonological systems often do not accommodate two adjacent consonants in a syllable. They then deal with target words with consonant cluster structure by reducing the cluster to a singleton consonant, as, for example, with the production of /tap/ for *stop*. The child's cluster reduction rule may apply to all clusters, or only to certain consonant combinations, such as clusters beginning with *s* (*sn-*, *st-*, *sp-*, etc.) or to stop + liquid combinations (*pr-*, *kl-*, *tr-*, etc.). Postvocalic cluster may be produced correctly while those in the prevocalic position are reduced. Some clusters may be reduced by retaining the first consonant (e.g., *fag/flag*) while others retain the second element (e.g., *tar/star*). (See coalescence for an example of features of two consonants being combined into a simple consonant.) In a description of cluster reduction patterns, it is always necessary to specify both the type of clusters that are affected and the nature of the reduction.

Final Consonant Deletion   While consonant omission sometimes occurs in other word positions as well, the most common pattern is omission of final consonants. Final consonant deletion has been described as the *open syllable* by Renfrew (1966). As with other rules, the child may apply the deletion rule generally and produce no final consonants or, more typically, will delete some classes of consonants when they occur in the word final position while producing others. Final nasal consonants often appear even when no other final consonants are produced.

Restricted Syllable Structure   Sometimes children's words can be described as having a particular consonant-vowel patterning, and this patterning in turn can account for children's sound and syllable omissions. For example, children who say /ta/ for *stop* and /ta/ for *bottle* may be displaying a pattern of producing a consonant + vowel syllable for all their productions. Children who operate in this way may be said to have a consonant-vowel (CV) structuring. We would predict that these children would reduce consonant clusters and consistently omit final consonants. Panagos (1974) gives the example of a child's production of /pi dɪ mi ɪ nɑ/ for *please give me it now*, the initial /pl/ is reduced to /p/ as well as omission of /z/, /v/, and /t/. It can be postulated that this child's phonological system is based on *CV structure*, which would account for both his consonant cluster reduction in *please* and omission of final consonants. We do not know from this sample of his speech what he would do with a two-syllable word. He might reduce the entire word to one CV structure (such as /sɪ/ for *sister*) or preserve the two syllables and make the utterance into a CVCV form as /sɪtə/ for *sister*. We can indicate the first as CV structuring and the second as CVCV structuring.

Syllable Addition   Finally, changing the syllable structure of words can involve *adding syllables*, as when children add /i/ to a word, producing a diminutive form. While many conceive of these forms as adult-to-baby talk, they can be productive for the child, as was noted in our observation of a one-and-one-half-year-old child who said /buki/ for *book*, a form unlikely to have been produced by the adult. The same child, for a one-week period, added /jɑ/ to the base form of words designating animate objects, as in /mɑmɪjɑ/ for *mommy* and /dædijɑ/ for *daddy*. This again suggests that baby talk to children is not necessarily how this child learned the syllable addition but that the addition is a productive phonological rule in that she applied it to particular forms to generate combinations she had never heard.

Sometimes children insert vowels between consonant sequences, a process that has been called *epenthesis*. The result of this vowel insertion is to add an extra syllable to the word as when *blue* is pronounced /bʌlu/ or *crayon* is pronounced /kʌreijʌn/. This insertion of an epenthetic vowel is familiar to speech-language pathologists who have worked with children on consonant clusters, since the children sometimes go through a period at first of saying a neutral vowel between the two consonants.

Syllable structure deviations are those which involve changes or restrictions in the consonant-vowel relationships in a word. They can take several forms: *weak-syllable deletion, reduplication, cluster reduction, final consonant deletion, restricted syllable structure*, and *syllable addition*.

Idiosyncratic Structures

In many of our examples, the target forms are more varied than the child's productions. The similarity with which the morphemes are produced by children suggest that children are taking the adult form and making it fit their own phonological structures. The structural consistencies can be manifested in ways other than those previously mentioned under context-sensitive analysis.

Waterson (1971) described five specific structures which her one-and-one-half-year-old child used in his word production. These structures had a characteristic number of syllables and consonant-vowel sequences that usually did not correspond to the adult configuration. For example, the child's *nasal structure* included /ŋẽːŋẽ/ for *finger*, /ŋeːŋe/ for *window*, /ŋɑŋɑ/ for *another*, and /ŋɑŋo/ for *Randall*. Menn (1989) has called such structures *canonical forms*.

One seven-year-old child with multiple articulation problems presents a striking example of this phenomenon. He has a *two-syllable structure*; that is, a CVCV pattern, with the medial consonant always being the glottal stop (ʔ). This pattern underlies his production of two-syllable words as disparate as *zipper, feather, scissors,* and *fishing.* Their productions in this child's structure become /wʌʔi̅/, /hʌʔi̅/, /dʌʔi̅/ and /wʌʔi̅/, respectively. The productions are not determined by the features of the phonemes in the target words so much as their bisyllabic configuration; so it is clearly erroneous to assume his productions are phoneme-for-phoneme substitutions.

Phonological Strategies

So far, we have been presenting ways to discover patterns in children's sound production and to cast them as separable phonological rules. Once you have a set of rules formulated, you may find that they seem similar; the effect of cluster reduction, final consonant omission, weak-syllable deletion, and epenthesis all seem to work together to produce a CV structure. These rules can be seen as being in *conspiracy* with one another (Kisseberth, 1973) and can be thought of as rules fulfilling a child's phonological strategy to simplify to a CV form.

The notion of *strategy* is perhaps too rich in the sense that it implies consciousness on the part of the child. We find it a useful way to think about how rules work together for the child and do not intend to imply that the child is thinking in any conscious way about what he or she is doing.

It pays, then, to ask yourself what strategies or general processes may be operating for children you are evaluating. Strategies which have been found by those studying monolingual normal children are (1) avoidance of words with unattainable phonological structures (Ferguson and Farwell, 1975) and (2) favorite sound strategies, wherein sounds are used either instead of others or words are learned because they have those favorite sounds in them (Ferguson, 1978). These two strategies are selection strategies for a perfectionistic learner whose constructions match adult forms. A third strategy is to change the adult form to fit a limited phonology, a modifying strategy. A fourth is to select single sounds as the target around which to organize phonology. A fifth strategy is more holistic, in which children concentrate on learning forms such as familiar intonation contours or sound combinations (Peters, 1983).

The bilingual language learner is met with the need for additional strategies, since, unlike the monolingual child, the child learning two languages must learn two phonological systems. Watson (1991) comments:

> Differentiation, avoidance of interference, learning to categorize acoustic input in two contrasting ways are all tasks which must be carried out by the bilingual and which the monolingual escapes. Obviously, all of these assume a degree of mental processing, involving strategies which will remain undeveloped in those exposed to only one language. The nature of these strategies may vary from individual to individual and according to the type of bilingualism. (p. 44)

Children who learn each of their languages separately have been found to approach the second language with strategies different from ones typically used by children learning one language or children learning two languages at the same time. The second language learner who already has a well-developed first language can fit the new language system to the old. For example, Fantini's son Mario learned Spanish first, completing his consonantal knowledge at two and one-half years (Fantini, 1985). His subsequent learning of English showed

Spanish influences, such as the substitution of a velar fricative /x/ for the English /h/. Later his Spanish became influenced by his English phonological knowledge as when he violated rules of Spanish by aspirating consonants in Spanish words using English phonological rules. The child's approach to the two phonologies was to integrate them, building his knowledge of one from the other.

THE IMPACT OF THE PHONOLOGICAL PROBLEM ON COMMUNICATION

Children with phonological problems may or may not be difficult to understand. Their intelligibility will depend on a variety of factors: the number of misarticulations (Shriberg and Kwiatkowski, 1982), the number of homonyms (Ingram, 1981), the type of misarticulations (Hodson and Paden, 1983), familiarity of the listener with the child, and whether the listener has an idea of what the child is talking about.

Measures of intelligibility often are done with listeners knowing little about what the child is trying to say. Shriberg and Kwiatkowski's (1982) recommended procedure involves asking strangers to listen to a minute of an audiotape of the child engaging in conversational speech. The listener is asked to judge the severity of the child's problem. The authors found that a measure of percent of correct consonants can predict the degree of severity judged by the listeners with no knowledge of the context or of the child. For example, children with 85 to 100 percent correct consonants were judged as mild; those with 65 percent correct were judged mild to moderately severe; those with 50 to 60 percent correct consonants were moderately severe; and those below 50 percent were ranked as severe by the naive listeners. Bleile and Wallach (1992) identified the phonological patterns of African-American preschoolers that were judged to be deviant by speakers of their dialect.

Ingram (1981) has included in his procedures for doing phonological analysis a measure of homonymy, in which the clinician tracks the number of different lexical items associated with the same phonological form. For example, a child may say /ba/ and mean *ball* on one occasion, *box* on a second occasion, and *bike* on a third. A child who has excessive homonymy is likely to have considerable difficulty in making herself understood.

Ingram's analysis of homonymy involves a charting procedure where the clinician lists phonetic forms in one column and the adult word (gloss) in the adjacent column. Ingram's index of homonymy includes two measures. One is a ratio of the number of phonetic forms (e.g., /ba/) which occur as a homonym to the number of phonetic forms which are associated with only one gloss. This he calls the *proportion of homonymous forms*.

Ingram's second index is to calculate the number of glosses (e.g., *ball, bat, bike* = 3) which occur as a homonym against those glosses with only one associated pronunciation. The separation between forms and glosses allows for the distinction between children who have a few favorite forms which serve as homonyms for many different words, and those whose homonymous language consists of a wide variety of different pronunciations.

In a comparison study of the phonological processes used by sixty unintelligible three- to seven-year-olds and by sixty intelligible four-year-olds, Hodson and Paden (1981) found that there were certain phonological processes that set them apart. They administered an object naming test (Hodson, 1980). The unintelligible children used cluster reduction, stridency (/s,z,ʃ,ʒ/) deletion, stopping, final consonant deletion, fronting of velars, backing, syllable reduction, prevocalic voicing, and glottal replacement. The intelligible children exhibited processes which were less different from the sounds in the target language such as devoicing of final consonants, lisping, vocalization of final /l/ and /r/, /f/ for /θ or ð/ substitutions, gliding, and metathesis.

The above measures involved determining intelligibility in context-free situations. That is, listeners judging the child's intelligibility tended to be unfamiliar with the child, and unaware of what the child was talking about. The exception was the Hodson and Paden study (1981) in which the children labeled objects, creating a situation in which words were not produced in the context of connected discourse. Since we know from the pragmatics literature that context boundedness influences the ability to understand what a person is saying, intelligibility indices are needed which compare a child's intelligibility in context-bound and context-free situations. The context-bound situations would be ones with familiar listeners, ones in which the listener has access to what the child is talking about, and ones in which the context effect is maximal, thereby enhancing intelligibility. Contrastively, a more difficult task for a listener would be one in which the child and the topic is unfamiliar, resulting in an impression of less intelligibility.

Communicative competence also involves the child's ability to revise the language when a listener fails to understand. Thus it is important to determine whether the child can revise what and how he says something when the listener indicates that the message is not understood. Gallagher (1977) and Gallagher and Darnton (1978) found that both normal and language-disordered children revised what they said in response to a "what?" request. For the normal children, revisions involved phonetic changes, adding some content to the original, shortening the original, or paraphrasing. For the language-disordered children, the phonetic change revisions involved adding or deleting consonants.

A study by Weiner and Ostrowski (1979) offers an elaboration of the "what?" questioning procedure used by Gallagher and Darnton (1978). Normal children were asked to name pictures involving words they had previously mispronounced. When the children said the word incorrectly, the experimenter asked, "did you say. . . ?" and filled in the blank with either the correctly produced word (e.g., *cat*), the child's error (e.g., *dat*), or a different word and an incorrect interpretation (e.g., *pat*). The children were required to respond "yes" or "no, I said. . . ." The results indicated that children correctly revised their original production significantly more often if the examiner said the wrong word (*pat*) than for the other two conditions. The authors report, in fact, that children emphatically corrected the experimenter ("NO!"), indicating a strong need to fix things if they thought they were being misunderstood.

The revision index is an indicator of the percentage of times a child repairs in the direction of the target form. In light of Weiner and Ostrowski's (1979) results, it would be worthwhile not only to look at the percent of progressive phonological repair but also to examine the nature and context of the breakdown to see if the more intelligible form occurs under particular discourse conditions.

These measures of revision are more pragmatically situated versions of what speech-language pathologists used to call "stimulability testing." The older version of stimulability testing involved presenting the child with the sound in isolation and requiring an imitation. The revision measures offered here also indicate the child's potential ability to produce a misarticulated sound, but in this case the means for asking the child to try harder to do something different are naturally situated.

STEPS TO PHONOLOGICAL ASSESSMENT

When working with this multifaceted approach to phonology, one can discover regularities in deviations which have traditionally been characterized as inconsistencies. When a child appears to be phonologically inconsistent, further analysis of the results of standard articulation tests as well as language-sample analysis can reveal consistencies. Following is a suggested set of steps for carrying out such an analysis. However, not all of the patterned regularities that occur in children's speech production can be discovered through using these steps. They are meant to be suggestive of an analytic approach to phonological analysis rather than an exhaustive list of procedures. Using this approach, clinicians will no doubt discover new kinds of patterns in the speech production of children and become aware that most children are not phonologically inconsistent.

1. Recognize productions that are typical of everyday speech patterns and ones which do not reflect phonological deviations. These are productions that even the most proficient speakers may use in situations when they are hurried or when they are using a casual speaking style. These productions would not be considered deviations and would not be included in your analysis. These include productions such as

> *gettum* for *get them*
> *runnin* for *running*
> *howdja* for *how did you*

When assessing the phonological knowledge of children who speak dialects of English other than Standard English dialect, care must be taken not to penalize or see as deviant the sound changes which occur as a result of normal learning; that is, changes that are part of the child's dialect group. Wolfram (1985) has identified a group of sounds which tend to be different in nonstandard English dialects. An adaptation and short version of Wolfram's list follows:

> *Final cluster reduction*: When clusters occur in the final position of a word (e.g., *find, test*), dialect speakers often omit the final stop.
> *Addition of syllabic plural following final clusters*: Words ending in an /s/ + stop cluster may take the *-es* plural, producing forms such as *tesses* for *tests*.
> *Changes in th sounds*: The voiced and voiceless *th* is often changed in nonstandard dialects. For example, t/th and d/th in word initial positions are common as are f/th or v/th in medial or final position.
> *Reduction of postvocalic /r/ and /l/*: Speakers of Southern and New England dialects typically omit final /r/ and /l/ sounds resulting in productions such as /sɪstə/ for *sister* and /ba/ for *ball*.

BOX 4–2. Modifiers for Allophones

⌢	—lateral	[ŝ]	x	—fricative	[b̠]
⌐	—dental	[t̪]	·	—stop	[z̧]
ω	—rounded	[r̫]	h	—aspirated	[pʰ]
ɯ	—unrounded	[w̫]	=	—unaspirated	[p⁼]
⌣	—lax	[f̫]	:	—lengthened	[a:]
			~	—nasal	[ā]

Deletion of unstressed initial syllables: The tendency for weak syllables to be deleted occurs in standard English dialect in informal speech styles (e.g., *'cause/because*) and is more pervasive in other dialects (e.g., *'member/remember*).

Substitution of /n/ for /ŋ/: A commonly occurring change in most nonstandard dialects of English is the alteration on *ŋ* in weak syllables, such as in the progressive marking on verbs such as *buyin* for *buying*.

Vowel changes: Particularly susceptible to regional variability are the back vowel /ɔ/, the front vowel /ae/, and vowels preceding the /r/ sound.

2. When administering an articulation test, it is suggested that you transcribe in narrow transcription the child's production of the whole word rather than recording only the particular sound being tested. Further, if the child is prompted on some items, this should be indicated so that differences between imitated and spontaneously produced utterances can be revealed. Some symbols to facilitate narrow transcription are given in Box 4–2. Other symbols can be found in Fisher and Logemann (1971) or Trager (1972) or can be created by the clinician as the need arises to describe a distinctive production. If the word is produced correctly, it need not be transcribed phonetically but simply marked as correct.

3. For those children who are intelligible, a narrow phonetic transcription of a sample of the errors in a child's spontaneous language should be made so that production of the sounds in connected speech can be displayed. The addition of the adult translation of the child's utterances and notes on the situation can facilitate analysis.

4. Listing transcripts, as shown in Box 4–5, should be made for each sound found to be in error, including correct productions as well as error productions. The error list should be compared to those productions that are correct to see the effects of context and identify instances of assimilation or coalescence. Deviations that are identified as due to these or other phonological processes where there is lack of one-to-one correspondence between the child's production and the adult form of the word, are not treated as substitutions.

5. Examine the errors in the listing transcripts for syllable structure patterns or idiosyncratic forms. Create new lists by grouping similar productions together to discover the existence and strength of the patterns. For a deviation to be judged as due to syllable structure restriction (e.g., CV or CVCV), you should find many examples that fit the pattern. One or two words do not warrant identification of this structure. The following list offers a possible organization for this analysis:

Context-Sensitive Errors

Assimilation
Coalescence
Transposition

Syllable Structure Errors

Weak-syllable deletion
Reduplication
Cluster reduction
Final consonant deletion
Restricted syllable structure
Syllable addition

Idiosyncratic Structures

6. Going back to the listing transcripts of error sounds, the substitutions can be identified as those productions that cannot be accounted for by phonological processes. *Substitution analysis* can be done on these errors by entering the misarticulations in a chart such as Box 4–3. Here the specific occurrences of manner errors, place errors, and voicing errors are listed together. Some will involve more than one feature, in which case it is entered in several places.

7. An inventory of the sounds that the child has produced in the samples can be taken by marking them in the appropriate columns of a phonemic inventory chart such as Table 4–2. If a sound is produced correctly in the context where it appears in the adult target, place a check in the column. If the only instance of the sound is in a word where it is used as a substitution for another sound, write the word in the space provided. For example, if the only initial /s/ in the sample is when the child says *sue* for *shoe*, write "sue/shoe" in the space for initial /s/. If the child attempts a sound but does not produce

---

BOX 4–3. Substitution Analysis

	Prevocalic	Intervocalic	Postvocalic
Manner			
Stopping			
Fricating			
Nasalizing			
Other			
Place			
Fronting			
Backing			
Other			
Voice			
Devoicing			
Voicing			

TABLE 4–2   Phonemic Inventory Chart

		Prevocalic	Intervocalic	Postvocalic
Stops	p			
	b			
	t			
	d			
	k			
	g			
Fricatives	hw			
	f			
	v			
	θ			
	ð			
	s			
	z			
	ʃ			
	ʒ			
	h			
Affricates	tʃ			
	dʒ			
Glides	w			
	j			
Liq.	r			
	l			
Nasals	m			
	n			
	ŋ			

BOX 4-4.   Cluster Inventory

Sample: (Test/Conversational)

Prevocalic Clusters	*Postvocalic Clusters*
Stop + liquid	Liquid + stop
Fricative + liquid	Stop + fricative
s + stop	Fricative + stop
s + liquid	Nasal + stop
s + nasal	Nasal + stop + fricative
s + stop + liquid	

---

it correctly, put an *X* in the column to indicate that it was sampled and do a listing transcript.

A separate inventory should be done of the child's consonant clusters, and also of vowels if there is evidence of vowel deviations. The cluster inventory should group similar clusters together and distinguish between prevocalic and postvocalic clusters. A cluster inventory chart is shown in Box 4-4.

8. *Deep testing* should now be carried out to confirm suspected patterns, and also to elicit sounds that were not included in your samples. The inventory charts will have blank spaces where there are sounds that were not sampled; pictures, questions, or sentence imitation can be used to elict those sounds that are in question. Phonemes with variable production should be elicited in various contexts to determine what contextual features condition the variability. An example of patterns to investigate is shown in Box 4-5.

9. Once the phonological patterns have been discovered, their effect on intelligibility should be examined to help determine which sounds should be

---

BOX 4-5.   Sample Listing Transcript

Structure: /t/

Child's productions

Correct	Errors
to	/kekɪ/ for *taking*
two	/kʌgbok/ for *tugboat*
Tom	/kɪpɪ/ for *Tippy*
tell	

(no intervocalic or postvocalic /t/ sampled)

Possible patterns

Correct in one-syllable words and replaced by /k/ in two-syllable words
Assimilation of velar place of /k/ and /g/ (*Tippy* an exception because of idiomatic production)
/t/ becomes /k/ whenever there is another stop consonant in word

---

targeted for intervention. *Intelligibility analysis* should be carried out first under context-bound situations, in which the intelligibility is measured using a familiar listener in a familiar context as an informant. The listener should be asked to listen to an audio- or videotape and to write down or repeat what the child is saying. The percent of intelligible words over total words (or syllables, if words are not determinable) can serve as the index. This percent should be compared in a context-free situation in which the listener is unfamiliar with the child and with what the child is talking about. Sounds or words which are unintelligible to both familiar and unfamiliar listeners might be a place to start. Or you might want to begin with the sounds which are the greater contributors to the unintelligible segments.

10. A final analysis, a *phonological repair analysis*, can also offer some aid in determining sounds on which to work. Following the idea of the more traditional stimulability testing, the sounds which the child repairs spontaneously may be the ones most readily remediable (Carter and Buck, 1958). A repair analysis would involve tracking the phonological changes which the child makes when asked to repeat what he or she has said.

In conclusion, a variety of phonological analyses might be used to answer different questions about the regularities in a child's phonological system. Ten steps have been presented for doing a complete analysis, with the different steps revealing different sorts of regularities about the data. It is not recommended that all steps be followed for every child with a phonological problem but rather that the appropriate analyses be chosen to answer the questions presented in the data.

REFERENCES

ANDERSON, R., AND B. SMITH. Phonological Development of Two-Year-Old Monolingual Puerto Rican Spanish–speaking Children, *Journal of Child Language*, 14, 1987, 57–78.

BARTON, D. The Role of Perception in the Acquisition of Speech. Ph.D. Dissertation, University of London, 1976.

BLAKE, J., AND R. FINK. Sound-Meaning Correspondences in Babbling, *Journal of Child Language*, 14, 1987, 229–53.

BLEILE, K., AND H. WALLACH. A Sociolinguistic Investigation of African American Preschoolers, *American Journal of Speech Language Pathology*, 1, 1992, 54–62.

BRUCE, D. Analysis of Word Sounds by Young Children, *British Journal of Educational Psychology*, 34, 1964, 158–69.

CALFEE, R., R. CHAPMAN, AND R. VENEZKY. How a Child Needs to Think to Learn to Read, in *Cognitition in Learning and Memory*, ed. L. Gregg. New York: John Wiley, 1972.

CARTER, A. Prespeech Meaning Relations: An Outline of One Infant's Sensorimotor Morpheme Development, in *Language Acquisition*, eds. P Fletcher and M. Garman. New York: Cambridge University Press, 1979, pp. 71–92.

CARTER, E., AND M. BUCK. Prognostic Testing for Functional Articulation Disordered Children in the First Grade, *Journal of Speech and Hearing Disorders*, 23, 1958, 124–33.

CHOMSKY, N., AND M. HALLE. *The Sound Pattern of English*, New York: Harper & Row, 1968.

DANILOFF, R., AND L. MOLL. Coarticulation of Lip Rounding, *Journal of Speech and Hearing Research*, 11, 1968, 707–21.

DE BOYSSON-BARDIES, B., L. SAGART, AND N. BACRI. Phonetic Analysis of Late Babbling: A Case Study of a French Child, *Journal of Child Language*, 8, 1981, 511–24.

DE BOYSSON-BARDIES, B., L. SAGART, AND C. DURAND. Discernible Differences in the Babbling of Infants According to Target Language, *Journal of Child Language*, 11, 1984, 1–15.

DORE, J. The Development of Speech Acts. Unpublished doctoral dissertation, City University of New York, 1973.

DORE, J., M. FRANKLIN, R. MILLER, AND A. RAMER. Transitional Phenomena in Early Language Acquisition, *Journal of Child Language*, 3, 1976, 13–28.

DYSON, A. Phonetic Inventories of Two- and Three-

Year-Old Children, *Journal of Speech and Hearing Disorders*, 53, 1988, 89–93.

EDWARDS, M., AND L. SHRIBERG. *Phonology: Applications in Communicative Disorders*. San Diego, Calif.: College Hill Press, 1983.

FANTINI, A. *Language Acquisition of a Bilingual Child: A Sociolinguistic Perspective*. Brattleboro, N.Y.: The Experiment Press, 1976.

FERGUSON, C. Learning to Pronounce: The Earliest Stages of Phonological Development in the Child, in *Communicative and Cognitive Abilities: Early Behavioral Assessment*, eds. F. Minifie and L. Lloyd. Baltimore: University Park Press, 1978, pp. 273–97.

FERGUSON, C., AND C. FARWELL. Words and Sounds in Early Language Acquisition, *Language*, 51, 1975, 419–39.

FISHER, H., AND J. LOGEMANN. The Fisher–Logemann Test of Articulation Competence. Boston: Houghton Mifflin, 1971.

FOX, B., AND D. ROUTH. Analyzing Spoken Language into Words, Syllables, and Phonemes: A Developmental Study, *Journal of Psycholinguistic Research*, 4, 1975, 331–42.

GALLAGHER, T. Revision Behaviors in the Speech of Normal Children Developing Language, *Journal of Speech and Hearing Research*, 20, 1977, 303–18.

GALLAGHER, T., AND B. DARNTON. Conversational Aspects of the Speech of Language-Disordered Children: Revision Behaviors, *Journal of Speech and Hearing Research*, 21, 1978, 118–35.

GARNICA, O. The Development of Phonemic Speech Perception, in *Cognition and the Acquisition of Language*, ed. T. E. Moore. New York: Academic Press, 1973, pp. 215–22.

HAELSIG, P., AND C. MADISON. A Study of Phonological Processes Exhibited by Three-, Four-, and Five-Year-Old Children, *Language, Speech, and Hearing Services in Schools*, 17, 1986, 107–14.

HAKES, D. The Development of Metalinguistic Abilities: What Develops? in *Language Acquisition: Language, Cognition and Culture*, ed. S. Kuczaj. Hillsdale, N.J.: Lawrence Erlbaum, 1982, pp. 163–210.

HALLIDAY, M. *Learning How to Mean: Explorations in the Development of Language*. London: Edward Arnold, 1975.

HILKE, D. Infant Vocalizations and Changes in Experience, *Journal of Child Language*, 15, 1988, 1–15.

HODSON, B. *The Assessment of Phonological Processes*. Danville, Ill.: Interstate Printers and Publishers, 1980.

HODSON, B., AND E. PADEN. Phonological Processes Which Characterize Unintelligible and Intelligible Speech in Early Childhood, *Journal of Speech and Hearing Disorders*, 46, 1981, 369–73.

HODSON, B., AND E. PADEN. *Targeting Intelligible Speech*. San Diego, Calif.: College Hill Press, 1983.

HODSON, B., AND E. PADEN. *Targeting Intelligible Speech* (2nd ed.). Austin, Tex.: Pro-Ed, 1991.

HOOPER, J. *An Introduction to Natural Generative Phonology*. New York: Academic Press, 1976.

HYMAN, L. *Phonology: Theory and Analysis*. New York: Hold, Rinehart & Winston, 1975.

INGRAM, D. *Phonological Disability in Children*. London: Elsevier North-Holland, 1976.

INGRAM, D. *Procedures for the Phonological Analysis of Children's Language*. Baltimore: University Park Press, 1981.

JAKOBSON, R. *Child Language, Aphasia and Phonological Universals*. The Hague: Mouton, 1968.

KAMHI, A., R. LEE, AND L. NELSON. Word, Syllable, and Sound Awareness in Language-Disordered Children, *Journal of Speech and Hearing Disorders*, 50, 1985, 207–212.

KISSEBERTH, C. The Interaction of Phonological Rules and the Polarity of Language. Mimeographed. Indiana University Linguistics Club, 1973.

LIBERMAN, A. The Grammar of Speech and Language, *Cognitive Psychology*, 1, 1970, 301–23.

LOWE, R., P. KNUTSON, AND M. MONSON. Incidence of Fronting in Preschool Children, *Language Speech and Hearing Services in Schools*, 16, 1985, 119–23.

LUND, N., AND J. DUCHAN. Phonological Analysis: A Multifaceted Approach, *British Journal of Disorders of Communication*, 13, 1978, 119–26.

McDONALD, E. *A Deep Test of Articulation*. Pittsburgh: Stannix House, Inc., 1968.

MACNEILAGE, D., AND J. DE CLERK. On the Motor Control of Coarticulation in CVC Monosyllables, *Journal of the Acoustical Society of America*, 45, 1969, 1217–33.

McREYNOLDS, L., AND D. ENGMANN. *Distinctive Feature Analysis of Misarticulation*. Baltimore: University Park Press, 1975.

MENN, L. Phonotactic Rules in Beginning Speech, *Lingua*, 26, 1971, 225–51.

MENN, L. Phonological Development: Learning Sounds and Sound Patterns, in *The Development of Language*, ed. J. Gleason. Columbus, Ohio: Chas. E. Merrill, 1989, pp. 59–100.

MENYUK, P., AND L. MENN. Early Strategies for the Perception and Production of Words and Sounds, in *Language Acquisition: Studies in First Language Development*, eds. P. Fletcher and M. Garman. New York: Cambridge University Press, 1979.

MORSE, P. A. The Discrimination of Speech and Non-Speech Stimuli in Early Infancy, *Journal of Experimental Child Psychology*, 14, 1972, 477–92.

MOSKOWITZ, A. The Two-Year-Old Stage in the Acquisition of English Phonology, *Language*, 46, 1970, 426–41.

OLLER, D. The Emergence of Sounds of Speech in Infancy, in *Child Phonology*, Vol 1, eds. G. Yeni-Komshian, J. Kavanaugh, and C. Ferguson. New York: Academic Press, 1980, pp. 93–112.

OLLER, D., AND R. EILERS. Similarity of Babbling in Spanish- and English-learning Babies, *Journal of Child Language,* 9, 1982, 565–77.

OLLER, D., L. WIEMAN, W. DOYLE, AND C. ROSS. Infant Babbling and Speech, *Journal of Child Language,* 3, 1975, 1–11.

OLMSTEAD, D. *Out of the Mouths of Babes.* The Hague: Mouton, 1971.

PANAGOS, J. Persistence of the Open Syllable Reinterpreted as a Symptom of a Language Disorder, *Journal of Speech and Hearing Disorders,* 39, 1974, 23–31.

PETERS, A. *The Units of Language Acquisition.* New York: Cambridge University Press, 1983.

POOLE, E. Genetic Development of Articulation of Consonant Sounds in Speech, *Elementary School Review,* 11, 1934, 159–61.

PREISSER, D., B. HODSON, AND E. PADEN. Developmental Phonology: 18–29 Months, *Journal of Speech and Hearing Disorders,* 53, 1988, 125–30.

PYE, C., D. INGRAM, AND H. LIST. A Comparison of Initial Consonant Acquisition in English and Quiche, in *Children's Language,* Vol. 6, eds. K. Nelson and A. Van Kleek. Hillsdale, N.J.: Lawrence Erlbaum, 1987, pp. 175–90.

RENFREW, C. Persistence of the Open Syllable in Defective Articulation, *Journal of Speech and Hearing Disorders,* 31, 1966, 370–73.

SACHS, J. Communication Development in Infancy. In J. Gleason (ed.), *The Development of Language.* Columbus, Ohio: Merrill Publishing Co., 1989, pp. 35–57.

SANDER, E. When Are Speech Sounds Learned? *Journal of Speech and Hearing Disorders,* 37, 1972, 55–63.

SCHANE, S. *Generative Phonology.* Englewood Cliffs, N.J.: Prentice-Hall, 1973.

SCHVACHKIN, N. The Development of Phonemic Speech Perception in Early Childhood, in *Studies of Child Language Development,* eds. C. Ferguson and D. I. Slobin. New York: Holt, Rinehart & Winston, 1973, pp. 91–127.

SHRIBERG, L., AND J. KWIATKOWSKI. *Natural Process Analysis of Continuous Speech Samples.* New York: John Wiley, 1980.

SHRIBERG, L., AND J. KWIATKOWSKI. Phonological Disorders III: A Procedure for Assessing Severity of Involvement, *Journal of Speech and Hearing Disorders,* 47, 1982, 242–56.

SMITH, N. *The Acquisition of Phonology: A Case Study,* New York: Cambridge University Press, 1973.

STAMPE, D. On The Acquisition of Phonetic Representation. Papers from the Fifth Regional Meeting of the Chicago Linguistic Society, 1969, Chicago.

STARK, R. Prespeech Segmental Feature Development, in *Language Acquisition: Studies in First Language Development* (2nd ed.), eds. P. Fletcher and M. Garman. New York: Cambridge University Press, 1986.

STOEL-GAMMON, C. AND C. DUNN. *Normal and Disordered Phonology in Children.* Austin, TX.: Pro-Ed, 1985.

TEMPLIN, M. *Certain Language Skills in Children.* Minneapolis, Minn.: University of Minnesota Press, 1957.

TRAGER, G. *Language and Languages.* San Francisco: Chandler Publishing, 1972.

WATERSON, N. Child Phonology: A Prosodic Review, *Journal of Linguistics,* 7, 1971, 179–211.

WATSON, I. Phonological Processing in Two Languages, in *Language Processing in Bilingual Children,* ed. E. Bialystok. New York: Cambridge University Press, 1991, Chap. 2, pp. 25–48.

WEINER, F. *Phonological Process Analysis.* Baltimore: University Park Press, 1978.

WEINER, F., AND A. OSTROWSKI. Effects of Listener Uncertainty on Articulatory Inconsistency, *Journal of Speech and Hearing Disorders,* 44, 1979, 487–93.

WOLFRAM, W. The Phonologic System: Problems of Second Language Acquisition, in *Speech Disorders in Adults,* ed. J. Costello. Austin, Tx.: Pro-Ed, 1985, pp. 59–76.

5

Morphology
and Word Classes

Morphemes are regularly occurring units of a language that have meaning. Every word contains at least one morpheme and may have several. If a word has only one morpheme, that morpheme is described as *free* since it can stand independently. Other morphemes which do not have this independence characteristic are called *bound* morphemes. Bound morphemes serve several functions. The *derivational* morphemes add semantic information to the free morphemes to create new or altered word meanings, as in *re*construct and *un*happy. These derivational morphemes can be applied to more than one word class while retaining their own meaning, as the negating *un-* in *untie* (verb), *unhappy* (adjective), and *unwisely* (adverb). Derivational morphemes can change the word class of the free morpheme to which it attaches, as when the adjective *lovely* becomes the noun *loveliness*, the adjective *happy* becomes the adverb *happily*, or the verb *farm* becomes the noun *farmer*.

Inflectional morphemes, like derivational morphemes, tend to be bound forms. They differ from derivational morphemes in that they change neither the meaning nor the word class of the free morphemes to which they are attached, but rather add grammatical information to indicate features such as the time of action (past or present) and number of entities (singular or plural). Inflectional morphemes are a closed set of forms that are attached only to specific word classes, unlike the derivational morphemes which can be used in more varied ways. It is therefore customary to discuss the inflectional morphemes in connection with a given word class, which we will do.

Some bound morphemes change their form, depending on the word they attach to. The derivational morpheme that expresses negation, for example, is expressed as *un-* (*unhappy*), *in-* (*incoherent*), and *im-* (*impossible*). These different forms are referred to as allomorphs of the same morpheme. Inflectional morphemes also may have allomorphs, which are generally conditioned by the phonology of the free word to which they are attached. The regular past tense morpheme, for example, may be pronounced as /t/ in *walked*; /d/ in *leaned*, and

/Id/ in *wanted*. Since these allomorphs are determined by phonology, they are sometimes referred to as *morphophones*.

Free morphemes can be divided into word classes, depending on how they function syntactically and to what bound morphemes they are connected. The first class has been called *form* words or major word classes. These include nouns, verbs, adjectives, and adverbs. *Structure* or minor word classes, which include prepositions, conjunctions, and pronouns, have only free forms and do not combine with derivational or inflectional morphemes. (Some classification systems distinguish between content words and function words, which roughly correspond to our distinction between form and structure words.)

Following a review of the word classes, our discussion in this chapter will focus on the inflectional morphemes associated with the different form-word classes. Analysis of the derivational morphemes and free morphemes falls within the realm of semantics and will be discussed in that chapter.

FORM WORD CLASSES

Nouns

The first definition of nouns learned in school is that nouns are names of "persons, places, or things." This definition is too narrow in that it incorrectly excludes some of the more abstract nouns that express ideas (*liberty*), processes (*conceptualization*), or nonentities (*energy*). Nouns are generally easy to recognize by their ability to be modified by an article (the *book*; a *democracy*) and their ability to be made plural (*books*; *democracies*) or possessive (the *book's* cover; *democracy's* promise). Most nouns can be modified in all three ways, but some nouns are more restricted than that.

Proper nouns are names of particular people, places, brand names, or created works such as dramas or ships. They differ from *common nouns*, which refer to nonspecific entities. They can be inflected to show possession, but because they signify a unique entity, only a limited set of created works can take an article, and they can take plurals only under unusual circumstances. (starred items indicate ungrammatical forms.)

> Chicago's mayor
> Mary Smith's aunt
> Macbeth's director
> Let's see the *Queen Mary*.
> * Let's see the Chicago.
> * Let's see the Mary Smith.
> *but*
> Of all the Mary Smiths, she is the oldest.

Mass nouns are applied to quantities that are perceived as indivisible into smaller countable portions, such as *milk* or *spaghetti*. They differ from *count* nouns, which name entities that can be counted. They can be modified by the definite article (*the*) but not the indefinite articles (*a, an*). They cannot be made plural, since the concept of quantity is already conveyed by the free morpheme. They can become possessive, but generally appear in an altered form:

> The milk's smell—the smell of the milk
> Your hair's shine—the shine of your hair

There are minor dialectal differences as to which nouns belong in this category. Most commonly, for example, *hair* is treated a mass noun, but in some dialects it is correct to say "I washed my hairs" as a parallel expression to "I washed my hands."

Nouns without singular forms are those that occur only in plural form; some of these refer to multiple entities that are not being distinguished and thus are actually mass nouns (*police, furniture, cattle*). Others refer to single entities but with plural forms (*scissors, eyeglasses, pants*).

Noun Inflections

NUMBER There is no inflectional morpheme to indicate the *singular* form of a noun; therefore, an uninflected noun is generally taken to be singular in meaning. *Plural* forms are inflected in several ways. *Regular plural nouns* are those that indicate multiple instances by adding -*s* to the singular form in standard English. This morpheme has three allomorphs; /s/ following most voiceless consonants (*cats*), /z/ following most voiced consonants (*dogs*), and /Iz/ following the voiced and voiceless fricative consonants /s, z, ∫, ʒ/ and affricates /tʒ, dʒ/, as in *buses* and *churches*. *Irregular plural nouns* are formed in other ways. Some may change the free morpheme (*man/men*; *mouse/mice*), whereas others add, change, or delete endings (*ox/oxen*; *datum/data*). Still others employ both a change and an addition (*child/children*; *leaf/leaves*). A small class of nouns have no change between singular and plural forms in standard English (*sheep, soap, deer, fish*).

CASE Case is the indication of the grammatical relationship between nouns and other word classes in a sentence. Most case relationships in English are conveyed through word order rather than through inflections. It is the placement of the nouns rather than their form that alerts one to noteworthy action in "Man bites dog." The only case that is indicated with an inflectional morpheme in standard English is the *possessive* or *genitive* case, and this is done in the same way with all nouns, by ending the noun with the morphophone of -*s*. The possessive relationship is generally clear from word order, as with other case relations, so the possessive morpheme is somewhat redundant. The possessive case is not obligatory in all dialects in which the noun plus noun structure alone conveys the relationship. In some instances, however, the possessive marker serves to eliminate ambiguity as to the relationship between two nouns; for example,

> The boy's doll   versus   The boy doll
> My grandfather's clock   versus   My grandfather clock

Pronouns

Pronouns also refer to entities such as people and things and in this sense function like nouns. They differ from nouns, however, in several ways. First, they are not explicit labels; they depend exclusively on the context in which they occur for interpretation. They are described as having *phoric* reference; that is, their meaning is found by looking at the linguistic or nonlinguistic context for their meaning. Pronouns also involve shifting reference; the referent (i.e., the person or thing referred to) for *me* or *it* shifts continually, depending on who is speaking and what they are talking about, unlike a name which stays attached to a person or object. Pronouns also differ from nouns in that they cannot be modified to specify something about the entity to which they refer, to identify it, or to comment on its characteristics. Finally, most pronouns have no inflectional morphemes for number and case. Instead, different pronouns are used to indicate these distinctions. Pronouns are classifiable as personal, indefinite, demonstrative, relative, and interrogative.

Personal pronouns are used when the reference is to one or more specific persons or objects. Whereas nouns are inflected only for number and possession, pronouns have additional case, person, and gender inflections. Thus they require much more grammatical knowledge to be used correctly. The inflectional possibilities for personal pronouns are shown in Table 5–1.

Indefinite pronouns refer to unknown, unspecified, or general referents (e.g., *somebody, anything, no one*). Some indefinite forms do not seem to have any referent. These are the *existential* forms, such as

It's a nice day.
There's nothing I can do.

Demonstrative pronouns indicate a specific referent or referents but do not name them. Demonstrative pronouns are used to direct the attention to a specific unnamed referent or set of referents. They include such words as *this, that, these, those, both, either,* and *all*. These forms also can be used along with a noun, in which case they are modifiers and not pronouns. Pronouns take the place of a noun rather than appear with it.

That is mine.   PRONOUN
That cup is mine.   MODIFIER

TABLE 5–1 Personal Pronouns

	Singular				Plural			
	Subj.	*Obj.*	*Poss.*	*Reflex.*	*Subj.*	*Obj.*	*Poss.*	*Reflex.*
First person	I	me	mine	myself	we	us	ours	ourselves
Second person	you	you	yours	yourself	you	you	yours	yourselves
Third person	he	him	his	himself	they	them	theirs	themselves
	she	her	hers	herself				

Either will do.   PRONOUN
Either color will do.   MODIFIER

Relative pronouns are clause-linking pronouns that refer back to an earlier mention of the referent in the first clause. The common relative pronouns are *who, which, what,* and *that.*

The man, *who* has red hair, is my brother.
That's the boy *whose* father drove.
That's the book *which* I finished.

Interrogative pronouns are *who, what,* and *which,* or *which one.* They differ from their use as relative pronouns in that the referent is not given, and thus there is a question as to its identity. They may be used in direct or in embedded questions.

Direct Questions	*Embedded Questions*
Who is that?	I know *who* that is.
What do you mean?	I see *what* you mean.
Which one is best?	I wonder *which one* is best.

Verbs

Verbs are by far the most varied and complex of the word classes. They, therefore, are an excellent indicator of the child's progress in mastering the grammatical rules of the language. Verbs can be classified in a variety of ways. We will first distinguish among four types of verbs in order to facilitate discussion of the verb inflections.

Lexical Verbs   Lexical verbs add content to the utterance; they indicate the action or the state of the subject being discussed. Lexical verbs are often divided into *transitive* and *intransitive* verbs, depending upon words that follow them.

She *ate.*   INTRANSITIVE
I *run* every day.   INTRANSITIVE
He *likes* the bike. TRANSITIVE
I *had* the mumps.   TRANSITIVE

Copulas   Copulas also are called *linking verbs* because they have no meaning in themselves but serve only to link or join the subject with a description or *complement.* It is the complement rather than the verb that adds new information about the subject. The most common forms of the copula are derived from the *be* verb, with the form depending on the subject.

I *am/was*
You, we, they *are/were*
He *is/was*

Comparing utterances with and without copulas, one can see that apart from the tense (present versus past), they add no information and in fact can be eliminated when one chooses to incorporate the information relayed by the complement into a noun phrase.

He is here.	He here	
He was here.	He here	
The girl is tall.	The girl tall	The tall girl
The window is broken.	The window broken	The broken window

When subjects and complements are reversed, there is no change in the meaning although it may not always seem "grammatical."

The boy is here.	Here is the boy.
The girl is tall.	Tall is the girl.

Other copulas are verbs of the senses (*feel, smell, taste*), of appearance (*appear, look, seem*), and change or duration (*turn, become, stay, remain*). Although these verbs seem, unlike the *be* verb, to add new information, it can be seen by substituting the *be* that they add only subtle meaning.

The steak *tastes* delicious.	The steak *is* delicious.
The leaves *turned* brown.	The leaves *are* brown.
He *looks* sick.	He *is* sick.

Some of these verbs can also function as lexical verbs, in which case they would not meet this *be* substitution test and would not be serving as copulas in those instances.

I *turned* the handle.	*I was the handle.
He *tastes* the soup.	*He is the soup.

Auxiliary Verbs   The lexical verb or copula that is the main verb in an utterance may have an auxiliary or helping verb accompanying it to indicate the tense or mood of the utterance. There are several types of auxiliaries that affect the main verb in distinctive ways.

"BE" AUXILIARIES   The same forms of *be* that can act as main verb copulas can also serve as auxiliary verbs.

I *am* eating.
She *was* becoming an adult.
The dog *is* chasing his tail.

They differ in that a lexical verb is present to add information about the subject to the utterance.

"HAVE" AUXILIARIES   *Have* and its various forms (*has, had*) can also occur as either an auxiliary verb or a main verb. As a lexical verb, it is the only verb in the clause and has a distinct meaning.

I *had* the mumps.
She *has* the money.   LEXICAL
They *have* all the luck.

As an auxiliary verb, forms of *have* always are accompanied by a main verb.

I *have seen* it myself.
She *has taken* the money.   AUXILIARY
They *have had* their shots.

MODAL AUXILIARIES   Some auxiliary verbs have been identified as modal verbs, in that they indicate something about the attitude or mood of the speaker. These include the moods of wish or intention (*will, shall*), certainty or possibility (*can, could, may, might*), and necessity and obligation (*must, should*). A set of early-appearing and frequently used spoken expressions called *catenatives* are also considered modal verbs. These include *wanna, hafta, gonna, gotta*.

I *wanna* go.   I *shall* go.
I'm *gonna* go.   I *will* go.
I *gotta* go.   I *should* go.
I *hafta* go.   I *must* go.

"DO" AUXILIARIES   *Do*, like the *have* and *be* forms, can either be a main verb in a sentence ("I *do* the dishes") or occur along with another verb ("I *do* run fast"; "*Do* you like it?"). When it occurs in a statement along with another verb, the *do* form acts to emphasize the speaker's affirmation of the statement ("I *do* run fast" versus "I *don't* run fast"). This is called the *emphatic do*. In other cases, it acts as an auxiliary verb but does not convey any grammatical information or mood, as do true auxiliaries. Rather, it "stands in" to form questions ("*Do* you like it?") when there is no auxiliary in the underlying statement. We call this the *dummy do* to distinguish it from true auxiliaries and will discuss it further in relation to questions. *Do* forms in both statements and questions can take negative forms (*don't*) and can be inflected for tense (*did*) and person (*does*).

Nonfinite Verbs   Nonfinite verb forms have been variously identified as verbals, secondary verbs, or verbids. They differ from the examples of lexical verbs and copulas just discussed in that they function as nouns or adjectives despite their verblike appearance.

INFINITIVES   Most infinitives can be recognized by the occurrence of *to* before a verb. While historically this was the preposition *to*, and no grammatical distinction was made between to + noun (*to the fence*) and to + verb (*to run*), we now identify the first form as a prepositional phrase and the second as an infinitive. Following some verbs, the *to* is no longer used as part of the infinitive, resulting in a "plain" infinitive as the verb in the second clause.

I heard him *sing*.
Make him *sit* down.   PLAIN INFINITIVES
Help me *lift* it.
She let it *go*.

I asked him *to sing*.
Tell him *to sit* down.   "TO" INFINITIVES
Help me *to lift* it.
She wanted it *to go*.

The main verb and plain infinitive may be adjacent, as in "let go" or "I'll help cook," in which the intervening noun or pronoun is deleted. The infinitive may be incomplete in dialogue, in instances in which only the *to* appears. In these cases previous utterances provide the infinitive verb.

Can you go?
I want *to* (go), but I can't.   INCOMPLETE INFINITIVE

Infinitive phrases are formed when the infinitive has an object noun that follows it. When we refer to infinitives, we include these infinitive phrases as well.

I went *to visit my aunt*.
He asked *to take the test*.

Infinitives serve a variety of functions in utterances. We will outline some here and elaborate these further in our discussion of syntax.

Infinitives as Modal Verbs   Some verbs preceding infinitives can express mood and intention in a manner parallel to the modal verbs and the catenatives. Just as *gonna* is considered a modal, so is its expanded form *going to* when it precedes an infinitive, as in "going to go." It can be seen that it is actually the verb preceding the infinitive, along with the *to*, that becomes the auxiliary verb, while the infinitive becomes the main verb in these cases. It is only with a small set of preceding verbs that this can occur.

I *need to* see him.
It's *got to* move.
You're *supposed to* be there.
You *ought to* go.
I *used to* shop there.

Infinitives as Sentence Objects

I asked *to go home*.
He started *to cry*.
I want *to laugh*.

Infinitives as Complements

It is easy *to fix*.
She is *to choose*.
I'm sorry *to say* it's true.

Infinitives as Adverbials

I went *to buy bread*.
I need money *to buy it*.
I stopped *to help*.

Infinitives in Subordinate Clauses

1. Clauses with *for*
   a. That's for me *to know*.
   b. For me *to go*, I need a ride.
2. Verb of object clause
   a. You want me *to do* it?
   b. Let me *ask* him.
3. Embedded questions
   a. Ask him where *to go* next.
   b. Tell me how *to start* it.

Infinitives as Sentence Subjects

To fix it is easy.
To do well is my only choice.

GERUNDS Gerunds are formed by adding *-ing* to the base form of a verb, with the resulting form used as a noun. Gerunds serve some of the same functions as infinitives. Like other nouns, some gerunds can be modified or inflected. Gerunds can form *gerund phrases* when they have an object.

Gerunds as Sentence Subjects

The swimming here is dangerous.
Chasing cars is my dog's favorite pasttime.

Gerunds as Complements

My favorite sport is *skating*.
His hobby is *oil painting*.

Gerunds as Sentence Objects

I like *getting* up early.
He avoided too much *walking*.

Gerunds as Objects of Prepositions

I did it by *stepping* on the branch.
I can ride without *holding* on.

PARTICIPLES Participles are verb forms that take on the characteristics of adjectives. *Present participles* are formed like gerunds, that is, by adding *-ing* to the base verb. *Past participles* are formed in several ways. Most commonly, past participles are identical to the past tense. Others are formed with either the present or past tense verb plus the *-n* ending. Still others have a root that differs in the vowel from both the present and past tenses and may or may not have an *-n* ending. These options are illustrated in Table 5–2.

In traditional grammars, participles have been treated as adjectives, with the following sets of utterances considered to have parallel functions:

The man is tall.	ADJECTIVE
The man is sleeping.	PRESENT PARTICIPLE
The man is wanted.	PAST PARTICIPLE

TABLE 5–2   Past Participles

	Root			Suffix			
	Present	Past	Vowel Changed	-ed	-n	Unmarked	Perfective
Walk	walk			-ed			have walked
eat	eat				-n		have eaten
run	run					√	have run
choose		chose			-n		have chosen
feed		fed				√	have fed
ride			rid-		-n		have ridden
ring			rung			√	have rung

All of these structures can be transposed into noun phrases, with the information in the complement depicted as a modifier. This demonstrates how the complements act as descriptors.

> The tall man
> The sleeping man
> The wanted man

In most modern grammars, the distinction is made between participles that are part of the verb phrase and those that have primarily adjective force, with the former having an auxiliary verb rather than a copula.

> The girl is sleeping.   AUXILIARY + LEXICAL VERB
> The girl is interesting.   COPULA + ADJECTIVE

Despite the surface similarities, some manipulations can show that the lexical verb and adjective are different structures. Since the participle as verb form indicates actions in progress, it can be restated as

> The girl is [engaged in] sleeping.

while the same cannot be demonstrated with the adjective form.

> The girl is [engaged in] interesting.

On the other hand, the adjective form can be modified in ways that is not possible with the verb form.

> The girl is very interesting.
> *The girl is very sleeping.

We can now identify the major roles played by participles according to their function as verbs or as adjectives.

PARTICIPLES AS MAIN VERBS   Participles as main verbs are accompanied by an auxiliary verb. The present participle almost always occurs with a *be* form.

The only exceptions are when a verb like *keep* or *continue* is used to emphasize the continuous nature of the action. The present participle is generally known as the *progressive* form of the verb when it is used as a main verb.

I *am running* away.
You *keep going* too fast.
They *were leading* the way.

The past participle occurs either with a *have* or *be* auxiliary, or more colloquially with a form of *get*.

I *have eaten*.
It *was broken* by the wind.
He *got bitten*.

PARTICIPLES AS SENTENCE COMPLEMENTS   Participles function as adjectives when they are complements, as can be seen by substituting conventional descriptive adjectives in the same position.

The toy is *fascinating*.   PRESENT PARTICIPLE
The toy is *broken*.   PAST PARTICIPLE
The toy is *old*.   ADJECTIVE

Participles also are adjective complements following copulas other than the *be*.

It seems *broken*.

Participles as Object Complements

I got the machine *running*.
I found the window *broken*.
There is a bear *sleeping* on the pillow.

Participles as Adverbs

He's out *getting* wet.
Waiting until dark, she got cold.

Verb Inflections   Verbs can be inflected for tense, aspect, voice, number, and person. Some of these inflections are applied only to the main verb, while others involve the auxiliary verb. Some only apply to certain classes of verbs.

TENSE   The current time in which a speaker is talking has been called the *speech time* (Reichenbach, 1947; Smith, 1980), whereas the time of the event being discussed is described as the *event time*. Tense indicates the relationship between speech time and event time. If speech time and event time are seen as the same, the present tense is used. If event time is thought of as prior to speech time, past tense is used. If the event is anticipated in the future, the present tense verb is modified with an auxiliary verb to indicate this expectation. This latter form is discussed under modal verbs.

The *present tense* of most lexical verbs is conveyed by the uninflected verb form.

I *want* some lunch.
You *hold* the flag.

The exception to this rule is when the subject of the present tense verb is in the third person (that is, not the speaker or the person addressed) and is singular. Under this condition, the verb is inflected by adding an *-s* to the verb.

Susan *wants* some lunch.
He *holds* the flag.

The present tense copulas depend on the person and number of the subject.

First person   I am (singular)   We are (plural)
Second person   You are (singular)   You are (plural)
Third person   She is (singular)   They are (plural)

Regular past tense verbs are formed by adding *-ed* to the uninflected verb, with no variability for person or number. Three allomorphs, /Id, d, t/, appear in spoken productions.

I *rested*.
They *called*.
She *washed*.

Much more frequent in English are *irregular past tense* verbs. These are formed in other ways, including changes in the vowel from the present:

steal   stole
drink   drank
blow   blew

Vowel change plus addition of final consonant:

say   said
do   did
sell   sold

Vowel change plus change or loss of final consonant before addition of /t/:

catch   caught
lose   lost
think   thought

Final consonant change to *t* or *d*.

make   made
have   had
build   built
send   sent

There are some invariable verbs that have the same form in present and past tense:

hit	shut
hurt	cost
cut	put
let	quit

There are two verbs, including the copula, that have distinctively different forms in present and past tense:

go	went
be	was/were

ASPECT   Whereas tense serves to establish an event in the past or present, aspect addresses the internal temporal characteristics of the event, such as its duration and progress toward completion. As speakers and listeners of English, we are generally not as aware of conveying aspect by our choice of vocabulary and inflections as we are of tense, but it is always part of our message. There are three major categories of aspect that have been named in different ways: terminate or perfective, progressive or imperfective, and perfect. They are based on the observer's perspective relative to the event. Along with inflectional morphemes, aspect is conveyed by the inherent meaning of many words. We will discuss the lexical indicators of aspect in Chapter 7.

Perfective aspect places the observer outside of the event, viewing it as a whole, as a fact, or as a habitual, characteristic, or general truth. Verbs with perfective aspect are inflected only for tense since there is no inflection for the perfective aspect; it is sometimes described as *simple* aspect.

I *work* at Wendy's.
She *slept* eight hours.
Water *runs* downhill.

Imperfective aspect places the observer within the event, from which vantage point features such as the duration, repetition, and progress toward completion can be reported. Imperfective aspect can be conveyed by using the progressive verb form, in which case the auxiliary is inflected for tense.

She *was sleeping* again.
He *will be going* to school in September.
I'm *working* until noon.

PERFECTIVE AND IMPERFECTIVE EVENTS   Some events can be thought of as perfective events because by their very nature they involve completion, such as making a cake or climbing the stairs. Unless they are complete, that is, viewed as a whole, one cannot be described as having done these things. The duration of some activities is so brief they they can only be thought of as a whole, and thus also are perfective events.

She *shot* the arrow.
He *fell* down.
It *broke*.

Imperfective events, on the other hand, can be stopped at any moment and still retain the notion of what the event is. This would include actions such as swimming or walking. With these activities, the statement "I was Xing" would imply "I Xed" (e.g., "I was swimming"; "I swam"). The same is not true for perfective events, since "I was painting the house" does not necessarily imply "I painted the house."

Since it is grammatical to say "I was painting the house," it obviously is possible to refer to perfective events with imperfect aspect. Likewise, imperfective events can be discussed with perfective aspect, as in "I swim every day." Some activities can be either imperfective if they are ongoing or perfective if they have a specified endpoint. The choice for the speaker depends largely on discourse features, which we discuss in Chapter 8.

Perfective Aspect

I swam in the ocean.   IMPERFECTIVE EVENT
I swam to the dock.   PERFECTIVE EVENT

Imperfective Aspect

I was swimming in the ocean.   IMPERFECTIVE EVENT
I was swimming to the dock.   PERFECTIVE EVENT

Perfect aspect is used to talk about the results or persistence of events that occurred in the past or are anticipated in the future but have current relevance. Perfect verbs are formed with *have* auxiliaries inflected for tense and the past participle verb form. They can be contrasted with actions or events that have their results in the past. This is illustrated in the following pairs of sentences:

1. a. I *have finished* my dinner; (can I leave the table?)
   b. I finished my dinner (and left the table).
2. a. I *have lived* here for four years (and still do).
   b. I lived here for four years (and then moved).

The first of each pair specifies an action with persistence into the present, and the second of each pair specifies an activity that is over and done with in the past. In 1a we have an action that is completed in the recent past but is relevant to the present. In 2a, the action extends into the distant past and is still continuing at the time of mention.

VOICE   There are two voices, active and passive, which indicate the relationship between the subject and the verb of a sentence.

Active voice is most frequently used, particularly in spoken language. The active voice is used whenever the subject does or is something named by the verb or verb and complement. Uninflected verbs always have active voice; those inflected for tense or aspect are active unless they have passive inflection.

Passive voice is used to indicate that the action of the verb is carried out by someone or something other than the subject, with the subject being acted upon by that force. The passive voice is conveyed by the past participle with a *be* auxiliary verb, or more colloquially, with *get*.

We paint the house every year.	ACTIVE
Our house gets/is painted every year.	PASSIVE
John ate the last cookie.	ACTIVE
The last cookie was eaten by John.	PASSIVE
Someone broke the toy.	ACTIVE
The toy got broken.	PASSIVE

NUMBER AND PERSON   Typically, lexical verbs are not inflected to indicate the number and person of the subject. The exception is when the subject is singular and third person, and the verb is present tense and perfective in aspect. In this case the verb is inflected by adding -*s* to the base form.

He run*s* (third person)	but	I run (first person)
She swim*s* (present)	but	She swam (past)

Most lexical verbs are regular for this *third person singular* inflection. The only common exceptions are *have*, which becomes *has*; *do*, which becomes *does*; and *say*, which becomes *says*.

Adjectives

Adjectives are words that describe or point out the entity designated by a noun or a pronoun. A variety of forms fit this description and, like adjectives, also function as noun modifiers. Among them are articles (*a, the*), genitive articles (*my, your*), demonstratives (*this, that*), ordinals (*first, next*) and quantifiers (*several, many*). The descriptive adjectives (e.g., *old, red, cold*) are the only forms that can be inflected. Following a discussion of these inflections, we will briefly discuss the other invariable modifiers.

Derived adjectives are formed from other word classes by the addition of suffixes. These include -*ish* (*childish*), -*ly* (*friendly*), -*less* (*homeless*), -*able* (*workable*), and others. The semantic meaning of these derivational morphemes becomes clear when we see the ease with which they are used to create new forms.

I'm computerless.
Let's walk fastish.

Adjective Inflections   In many languages, adjectives are inflected to agree with nouns, but this is not the case in English. In English the only inflectional forms on adjectives are those denoting comparison.

COMPARISON   The simple or uninflected adjective is the *positive* form. The *comparative* indicates that the quality described by the adjective is of a higher degree in comparison to another entity or previous state.

This branch is *bigger* than that one.
It got *bigger* and *bigger*.

The *superlative* indicates that the quality is in the highest degree. This may be in an absolute sense ("He is the tallest man in town") or relative to others being compared ("He is the tallest of the three boys"). The superlative is sometimes used to indicate a high degree without a comparison being made.

> I saw the *best* movie.
> We're the *closest* of friends.

Some adjectives convey the same sense of comparison by combination with *more* or *most* instead of the inflected forms. These adjectives can then also take a negative form with *less* or *least*.

> He is *kinder* than his father.
> He is *more kind* than his father.
> He is *less kind* than his father.

Although some adjectives can take either of these configurations, in general, adjectives of one syllable or those ending in certain vowels take the inflected endings, and the rest take the *more* or *most* form. There are a few *irregular* comparisons that use neither form.

good	better	best
bad	worse	worst
far	farther	farthest
little	less	least

Other Noun Modifiers

DETERMINERS Determiners indicate how generally or specifically the noun is to be understood. Included are *articles*: the indefinite article *the*, the definite article *a*, and the genitive articles (*my, your, their,* etc.); *demonstratives* (*this, that, those, these*); and *qualifiers* (*any, each, either, enough, much, neither, no, some*). Note that some of these forms can also act as pronouns (e.g., *his, those, one*). The distinction is that pronouns replace nouns (e.g., It is *his*; I want *one*), whereas determiners occur with nouns and modify them (e.g., It is *his* book; I want only *one* button). The definite and genitive articles along with the demonstratives indicate specific entities, whereas the indefinite article and some of the qualifiers express more general interpretation. Other qualifiers set limits on the class to which they refer without indicating a specific entity.

> I want *the* book you have.
> I want *that* orange.   A SPECIFIC ONE
> That's *my* sandwich.

> I need *a* book.
> I'll take *any* orange.   ANY WILL DO
> I need *some* food.

> I'll take *either* one.
> Look at *each* one.   LIMITED CHOICE

Adjectivals   In addition to the descriptive adjectives (e.g., *big, cold*), adjectivals include *ordinals*, or terms of relative position (e.g., *first, next*) and *quantifiers* (e.g., *one, six, several, many*), which indicate generally or precisely how much quantity or how many occurrences there are of the entity named by the noun.

Adverbs

Adverbs supply information about the time, place, manner, degree, or cause of action, entities, or conditions being discussed. Some adverbs have no other function. They are always adverbs. Others can have other functions, as we will show below, and are adverbs only if they modify a verb, an adjective, or other adverb. Some adverbs are derived from other word classes by addition of prefixes or suffixes. The most common of these *derived* forms are the adjective + *-ly* forms (*timidly, carefully*). Adverbs are also derived from combinations of *some-, any-, every-,* and *no-* with *how, why, where, place,* and *time.*

Adverbs take many forms and can be classified in a variety of ways. We choose to classify them according to meaning.

Adverbs of *place, direction, or arrangement* indicate where things or actions are located (e.g., *here, there, where, somewhere, no place*).

> *Here* it is.
> I put it *somewhere.*

Some forms that can also be prepositions (e.g., *in, out, around, at*) are adverbs when they have no object noun and thus specify a general direction or location.

Adverbs	Prepositions
Put it *down.*	Put it *down* the hole.
It's *around* somewhere.	It's *around* the tree.
I'm going *out.*	I'm going *out* the door.

Some nouns become adverbs when used to designate the place or direction and thus indicate *where,* rather than their usual function of indicating *what.*

He is *home.*	Where?	ADVERB
His *home* is for sale.	What?	NOUN

Adverbs of *time* indicate when an action occurs. They include *now, then, soon, immediately, when, after,* and others.

> I knew *immediately* that something was wrong.
> We're going *now.*
> I'll go there *someday.*

Again, some nouns (*yesterday, tomorrow, Sunday*) become adverbs when they place the event in relative time rather than express an identity with a copula.

As complements, they may switch places with the subject, but as adverbs, they can move much more freely in the sentence or can be eliminated and leave the sentence grammatically complete.

My birthday was *yesterday.*   What?   NOUN
Yesterday was my birthday.

I had a party *yesterday.*   When?   ADVERB
Yesterday I had a party.
I, *yesterday,* had a party.

Adverbs of *manner* express how the action is done (e.g., *well, fast, neatly*).

She ran *quickly* to the door.
That was *fast.*

Adverbs can also indicate *degree, amount,* and *number* (e.g., *very, nearly, almost, twice*).

He *almost* died.
She won *twice.*

Adverbs of *cause* and *result* generally take the form of the interrogative *why* to express "for what reason," and *so* or less commonly *therefore* or *thus* to express "as a result."

Why did you do that?
No one was home *so* I left.
I'm broke. *Therefore,* I can't go.

Adverb Inflections   Most adverbs have only one form; that is, they are always uninflected and do not have variable morphological forms. They are described as invariable. There are only a few variable adverbs, and they vary only to indicate comparison in a manner parallel to the adjectives. That is, *comparative* is indicated with *-er, superlative* by *-est* attached to the base adverb. These are primarily monosyllabic words (*fast, near, late*), with one exception (*early*). Most adverbs, including the derived forms, make comparisons through use of *more, most, less,* and *least,* which are also adverbs.

Move *more* quickly
He's here *less* often
It should be done *more* carefully

There are also a few irregular adverbs that change the base form.

well   better   best
badly   worse   worst

STRUCTURE WORD CLASSES

The structure or minor word classes (sometimes called function words) include the prepositions, conjunctions, and interjections. They are all invariable; that is, they have no inflectional morphemes and so have only one form. Prepositions and conjunctions have much in common and are sometimes grouped together as connectives. At times the distinction between them is subtle. A few examples illustrate why conjunctions could be viewed as sentence prepositions. We will be discussing the relevant differences as part of syntax.

It sounds *like* rain.	PREPOSITION
It sounds *like* the rain is starting.	CONJUNCTION
Do it *before* school.	PREPOSITION
Do it *before* school is out.	CONJUNCTION

Prepositions

Prepositions connect nouns or pronouns with other parts of the utterance and indicate the nature of the relationship between the connected units. Prepositions most often express spatial and temporal relations along with several other less common relationships. Prepositions always precede an actual or implied object noun or pronoun.

Jerry is *at* the door.	SPATIAL
Before school, I watch TV.	TEMPORAL
Do it *with* care.	MANNER
Hit it *with* a hammer.	INSTRUMENTAL
He's *with* his friend.	ACCOMPANIMENT

When these words are used without actual or implied objects, they are not prepositions. As we have indicated, they may act as adverbials when they specify a general direction or location.

I'm going *out*.
Put it *down*.

Some preposition-like words occur along with specific verbs and without an object noun, such as *turn on*, *think over*, and *set up*. These *particles* are properly considered part of the verb and not prepositions. Particles, unlike prepositions, change the meaning of the verb and can be separated from it by a noun or pronoun but cannot be followed by a pronoun. Conversely, prepositions can be separated from the verb by adverbs, whereas particles cannot be.

Compare the sentences that follow and determine why those marked with asterisks are ungrammatical:

Particle	*Preposition*
He ran *up* the flag.	He ran *up* the hill.
He ran the flag *up*.	*He ran the hill *up*.
He ran it *up*.	*He ran it *up*.
*He ran *up* it.	He ran *up* it.
*He ran quickly *up* the flag.	He ran quickly *up* the hill.

Conjunctions

Conjunctions are another class of connectors that indicate the relationship between joined parts of an utterance. The two general classes of conjunctions usually identified are coordinate and subordinate conjunctions. The distinction between them is not always clear. We have tried to concentrate on the features that will be relevant to analysis of children's language.

Coordinate conjunctions join two separate units in a manner that gives them equal emphasis. The three conjunctions generally agreed to be coordinate are *and, but,* and *or.* There is less agreement among linguists as to which other words fit into this class. We choose to define coordinate conjunctions as those that can join single words of the same word class as well as separate clauses. These include *not, than, as well as, rather than, like,* along with correlative pairs such as *either–or* and *both–and* when they are used to join together units that have the same explicit or implied structure.

> She washes dishes *and* he dries them.
> Kathy (will go) *or* Tom will go.
> I wanted a roll, *not* (I wanted) bread.
> She'll eat it *rather than* (she'll) waste it.
> Maria is tall *like* Tanya (is tall).

Subordinate conjunctions, like coordinate conjunctions, join clauses together to make them into single sentences. Whereas coordinate conjunctions join single words or clauses that have equal emphasis or importance, subordinate conjunctions join only clauses, and always in such a way as to make one of them the main clause and the other subordinate to the main clause. Some subordinate conjunctions have no other function. These include *because, if, whether,* and *although.* Others in this group function at other times as adverbs or prepositions or both (e.g., *since, before, so, when, until*). It is necessary to determine their function in a sentence before they can be classified as conjunctions. Examples of subordinate conjunctions are

> She left *because* it was dark.
> *Since* you are here, have some lunch.
> Don't go *until* you see this.
> I did it *like* you told me.

Interjections

Interjections are words or phrases that stand apart from the rest of the utterance as exclamations, starters, or fillers. They are common in informal spoken language.

> *Oh,* I forgot to tell you.
> *Ouch.*
> It's, *you know,* not quite done.
> You know, *like,* I can't.

DEVELOPMENT OF MORPHOLOGY

The development of inflectional morphology was one of the first areas of child language to receive extensive attention following the landmark study by Roger Brown of three normally developing children—Adam, Eve, and Sarah. Brown (1973) reported that the three children, despite differences in their rate of language acquisition, developed inflectional morphemes in essentially the same order and at the same points in their development. He identified fourteen morphemes that occurred with sufficient frequency in young children's speech to track their development, and identified the contexts in which these morphemes are obligatory; that is, where they are required rather than optional. A morpheme was considered to be acquired by a child when it was used in 90 percent of the obligatory contexts. Brown's findings were replicated by de Villiers and de Villiers (1973), who used a larger group of twenty-one children at different stages of development. Table 5–3 shows the average order in which the morphemes met the criterion of acquisition.

The average order of acquisition presented in Table 5–3 does not necessarily represent the order of acquisition for any given child. In fact, none of Brown's original three children followed this order exactly (Brown, 1973, p. 271).

As development of languages other than English are studied, it is clear that the order of acquisition of the grammatical markers of these various concepts is not universal. Kvaal and others (1988) investigated that morphological development of young Mexican-American Spanish speakers and found articles, copulas, masculine and feminine demonstratives, and present indicative to be the earliest acquired forms.

Lists that present order of acquisition do not reveal the extensive time and variability in the amount of time over which a morpheme is acquired. For example, for Sarah, one of Brown's subjects, sixteen months elapsed from the time the present progressive morpheme was used 50 percent of the time correctly until it reached criterion for acquisition at 90 percent. Brown states

TABLE 5–3   Brown's Acquisition Order for Fourteen Morphemes

  1. Present progressive
2–3. *in, on*
  4. Plural (regular)
  5. Past irregular
  6. Possessive
  7. Uncontractible copula
  8. Articles
  9. Past regular
 10. Third person regular
 11. Third person irregular
 12. Uncontractible auxiliary
 13. Contractible copula
 14. Contractible auxiliary

It is true of all the grammatical morphemes in all three children that performance does not abruptly pass from total absence to reliable presence. There is always a considerable period, varying in length with the particular morpheme, in which production-where-required is probabilistic. (Brown, 1973, p. 257)

Thus determining the order in which these morphemes appear in children's speech and are finally mastered is less important than tracing their changes over time.

Early Verb Inflections

When children begin to use verbs in their early word combinations, the verbs are uninflected; that is, they are not marked with grammatical information such as tense and aspect. Brown (1973) describes this early "generic" verb as interpreted in four ways by parents: as an imperative (get milk = you get milk), as past tense (milk spill = milk spilled), as an expression of intention or prediction (baby sleep = baby is going to sleep), or as an expression of present temporary duration (fish swim = fish is swimming). When inflections begin to appear in the child's productions, it is the indicators of these same interpretations that appear first. The progressive (*-ing*) inflection develops to indicate actions that are in progress at the time of mention, while the past tense form signals activities just completed. Anticipated actions are first indicated with early modals or catenatives (*gonna, wanna, hafta*). When these inflections appear, the uninflected verb serves to convey imperatives and is often accompanied by a *please*, thus further marking its function as a directive. The progressive inflection is usually the first to appear in children's production, and its occurrence generally heralds the emergence of these other early verb forms. It appears then, that the forms serve several functions. They signal the child's ability to comment on events in the past or completed events, they indicate present and future events, and they direct their listeners to do something.

Present Progressive

Children learning English as their first language often use the progressive verb form, initially without the auxiliary verb, as their first grammatical morpheme. Not all verbs take the progressive form, but children rarely apply it incorrectly. This makes it rather remarkable in contrast to all other inflections, especially when we examine the rather complex pattern of progressive usage in English.

The distinction can be made between "process" verbs, which involve change moving toward an end, and "state" verbs, which express an unchanging condition. The observation that process verbs can take the progressive inflection whereas state verbs cannot has led to the hypothesis that children learn a semantic distinction between these two types of verbs, and thus apply the progressive rule appropriately to new verbs (Kuczaj, 1978). The distinction between verbs that can and cannot take the progressive form, however, is not quite along the lines of the progressive and stative distinction. Process verbs clearly can take the progressive inflection.

The snow is *melting*.
I'm *baking* a pie.
He's *thinking* about it.
I'm *learning* to ski.

State verbs are not as clear in their relationship to the progressive inflection. Many cannot take the progressive.

I *know* how to read. (NOT *am knowing*)
The glove *fits* me. (NOT *is fitting*)
I *see* the next one. (NOT *am seeing*)

However, some state verbs can be progressive, even though no change to an end is involved.

He's *standing* still.
They're *hanging* over the door.
She is still *sleeping*.

Other state verbs that have temporary duration are not inflected progressively.

I *like* this movie. (NOT *am liking*)
I *want* a cookie. (NOT *am wanting*)
I *need* an nap. (NOT *am needing*)

Brown (1973) resolves these seeming contradictions by pointing out that verbs that can be inflected in the progressive tense all involve voluntary activity, whereas those state verbs which cannot, express involuntary actions. Thus, *want*, *need*, *like*, *believe*, *have*, *see*, *know*, and others are viewed as involuntary action, as contrasted with *learn*, *look*, *hang*, *sleep*, and others, which are voluntary. It is interesting to note that the same distinction holds for verbs that can be put into imperative forms to request actions of others.

Learn this.
Hang it up.

It is likely that there are other factors that conspire to make the progressive form an early one to appear. The progressive form is completely regular in English; that is, it always takes the *-ing* form. This may contribute to its ease of acquisition relative to irregular forms with multiple manifestations. The perceptual saliency of the *-ing* as a separate syllable may also be an advantage in noticing and in learning the inflection. Finally, it has frequently been observed that children pay attention to action, and action is precisely what is marked by this inflection. *Eat*, *ate*, or *gonna eat* only indicate potential action, whereas *eating* describes the attention-catching event as the child watches the kitty eating her dinner. The progressive form of the verb is thus the only form that describes the actual motion expressed by the verb whereas the other forms express only the abstract sense of the action. It is likely that these factors work together to make the progressive inflection the first to appear in most children's production.

Past Tense

Whereas the present progressive verb expresses an event in time that is being shared by the speaker and the listener, the other early verb inflections serve to inform the listener that the speaker's reference is not in the present. Past tense indicates "earlierness" in that the referred-to event has already transpired at the time of talking about it. Brown (1973) reports that appropriate use of the past tense began for his three subjects "with a small set of verbs which name events of such brief duration that the event is almost certain to have ended before one can speak. These are: *fell, dropped, slipped, crashed, broke*." These verbs can all be described as *punctual* verbs, in that they represent actions that occur so quickly that they scarcely can be viewed while in progress. Thus, the first reference to past is the immediate past, most likely when a jarring and highly salient event is referred to immediately upon its completion. The degree of earlierness is thus initially very slight, and likely expands gradually over time to reference events increasingly more removed from the present.

These punctual verbs include both regular (*dropped, slipped, crashed*) and irregular (*fell, broke*) past tense forms. It is unlikely at this stage that the child has a rule for past tense and recognizes some verbs as exceptions to that rule. Instead, it is likely that children consistently hear the punctual verbs expressed by adults in their past tense form, and learn them simply as an expression of the event that has occurred, rather than as a contrast to the present tense form of the verb. It may be more appropriate, therefore, to consider these early punctual verbs as expressing the perfective aspect rather than past tense.

Most high-frequency verbs in English are irregular and take a perceptually distinct form in the past tense. It is likely that children's first meanings for these readily distinguishable forms (e.g., *go* and *went*) are unrelated and do not refer to the same action. Eventually children discover the regularities of the language and the relationship between past and present action; this leads to the well-documented phenomenon of *overregularization*, in which the irregular verbs are transformed to fit the regular rule. For example, *went* is replaced temporarily with *goed* and *did* by *doed*. With increased experience children somehow sort out which verbs must follow the rule and which can depart from it.

Anticipated Events

Whereas past tense evolves to orient the listener to the completion of an activity, early reference to not-yet-happened events seems to serve two functions for the child. These utterances may serve a directive function in that they signal someone to make an event occur, or they may be an expression of what the child intends imminently to do. Directives specify the desired participation of the listener. They have verbs of voluntary action and strike us as imperatives.

Hold this.
Stand it up.

The early expressions of imminent action are characterized by catenatives.

Gonna go.
Hafta pee-pee.
Wanna eat.

It can be argued that at least some of these latter forms are also directives involving expression of the child's state and implying a request for listener participation. Brown's examination of the context of these utterances with catenatives, however, rejects this interpretation. He found no semantic distinction between the various catenatives, but rather found that the children showed partiality for a particular form and used it to name actions which they were just about to perform.

It seems plausible that children first distinguish between anticipated events over which others have control and those which the child controls. The grammatical distinctions then reflect this awareness and signal different intentions, with the uninflected verb indicating a request for help and the catenative being a comment on the child's own upcoming action.

Other Investigations of Morphological Development

In addition to Brown's studies of Adam, Eve, and Sarah, there have been numerous experimental and naturalistic studies of children's morphological development. We will comment on some of these that have been influential or are potentially applicable to assessment procedures.

Berko's Study   The first experimental study of morphological development was done by Jean Berko (1958), who is now Berko Gleason. She demonstrated that children's use of morphological inflections is based on grammatical rules rather than memorization of what adults say by giving the children nonsense words to inflect. For example, while showing a picture of a nonidentifiable creature, she said, "Here is a wug. Now there is another one. There are two _____." In this manner she elicited from preschoolers and first graders progressive, past tense, possessive, and third person inflections in addition to the plural. The results of Berko's investigation revealed that at least by four years of age standard English speaking children can apply morphological rules to new words, yet their morphological knowledge is still developing at age seven, as shown by errors among her oldest subjects. She also found that different allophones of the same morpheme have different levels of difficulty. Allophones that require separate syllables (*tasses*; *motted*) were consistently more difficult than those that followed a simple phonological form (*wugs*; *ricked*). If the more difficult allophones are disregarded, the order of difficulty parallels quite closely the order of development identified by Brown (1973). The children in the experimental study, however, seemed to be developing the same morphemes at a much later age than did Brown's subjects. This appears to be the effect of the nonsense words, since her children responded much more accurately to the few real words in the sample than they did to the synthetic counterparts.

Berko's methodology has spawned many other experimental investigations with different groups of subjects (e.g., Kernan and Blount, 1966, Natalicio and Natalicio, 1971, with Spanish speakers; Bellamy and Bellamy, 1970, with older children; Goodglass, 1968, with aphasic patients; Dever, 1972; Newfield and Schlanger, 1968, with mentally retarded children; Cooper, 1967, with hearing-impaired and deaf children). A discussion of the limitations of the design and alternative interpretations of the data is presented by Natalicio and Natalicio (1969).

Investigations of Specific Forms Investigation of the process of development of a single grammatical morpheme or related groups of morphemes has been more common in recent years than have further studies of overall order of development. We now turn to these studies and group together those investigating the same grammatical meanings.

VERB ASPECT AND TENSE There is ongoing debate among psycholinguists as to whether children's early inflectional morphemes mark tense or aspect. The difficulty arises because these two grammatical systems are intertwined in most languages. As we have indicated in discussing the punctual verbs, these could be seen as expressing either earlierness or completion. Some researchers (Antinucci and Miller, 1976; Bloom, Lifter, and Hafitz, 1980; Bronckart and Sinclair, 1973) view early past tense inflections as marking aspectual features rather than earlierness. Other researchers argue that the children are in fact indicating past tense (Weist and others, 1984; Sachs, 1980; Di Paolo and Smith, 1978). This theory that children's first use of past tense markers is really to indicate just finished events has been called the "defective tense hypothesis" (Weist and others, 1984).

The perfectivity interpretation of past tense markers was first forwarded by Antinucci and Miller (1976) when they found that their Italian-speaking two-year-olds used past tense only when the events they referred to came to completion in the current present. Weist and others (1984) found that their two-year-old Polish subjects used different grammatical markers for indicating perfectivity and pastness. If these results generalize from Polish-speaking children to English-speaking children, it would appear that use of past tense is not a defective but rather a real marker of pastness.

There is only a small body of research that uses data collected in natural settings to investigate development of aspect. Fletcher (1979) in his analysis of diary studies of young children and of a child named Daniel found beginning use of past tense to occur at around two years. Fletcher raised the question of whether the tense marker might be an expression of perfectivity; that is, maybe children are marking the event as having just been completed. Herring (1981) looked at the development of past tense and the perfective-imperfective distinction, using data from one child between twenty-seven months and four years. He found that the children initially relied on lexical choices to convey temporal notions. The child in Herring's study initially used verbs that encoded the appropriate aspectual meaning, and a variety of directives to signal completion and result such as *throw away* and *fix together*. These findings would seem to argue against the prevalent view in the literature that verbal inflections are the first and predominant markers of temporal notion (Bloom and Lahey, 1978). (The development of lexical indicators of aspect will be further considered in Chapter 7.)

Several experimental studies have examined children's use of verb inflections to mark perfective and imperfective aspect (Harner, 1981; Bloom, Lifter, and Hafitz, 1980; Smith, 1980; Kuczaj, 1977; Antinucci and Miller, 1976). Their findings do not resolve the dispute concerning the interpretation of early inflections as tense or aspect. There is general agreement that by age three children have developed the concept of temporal ordering and can indicate pastness with past tense inflection. Some investigations have examined whether children distinguish aspectual differences in past events. An experimental design used by Bronckart and Sinclair (1973) with French-speaking children was adapted by Smith (1980) for use with English speakers between four years, seven months and six years, six months. The children were presented with four perfective activities with definite endpoints (e.g., climb stairs) and four imperfective actions with no such endpoint (e.g., dance), and asked to recount what they had seen immediately upon completion. Unlike the French speakers, the English children used past tense almost exclusively, and all of them used both progressive and simple past to relate both kinds of activities. There was, however, some variability with age. The youngest children tended to use progressive aspect (-ing) mostly to express imperfective actions and applied simple past primarily for perfective actions. The oldest group showed more variability; they expressed both kinds of activities with both indicators of aspect. Since no context was given to the children, there was no correct or incorrect way to express the actions. The greater variability of the older children may correspond to their greater linguistic skill and thus their ability to choose more freely the manner of expression. It could also relate to their increasing sensitivity to their listener's needs, since in real-life situations, the appropriate aspect is related to what a listener already knows and what new information is being presented.

Unlike perfectivity, imperfectivity, and tense, children's learning of perfect constructions to indicate current relevance are acquired after they are well along in their language acquisition. For example, Johnson (1985) asked normal four- and five-year-olds to imitate and reenact a short dialogue between dolls, in which one of the dolls used a sentence with the perfect construction (e.g., "I *have been riding* in Mr. Howard's truck all day" or "I *have ridden* this bike for a couple of years"). About half of Johnson's children omitted the perfect marker. Those who included it favored the present with the *-ing* progressive ("I *have been riding*"), using it more frequently than the present perfect without the progressive.

"BE" FORMS   The allomorphs of the verb *be* (*am, are, is, was, were*) are used in two distinctly different ways; as main verbs (i.e., copulas) and as auxiliaries with the progressive. Brown (1973) showed this distinction to be relevant when studying children's acquisition of these forms. He also found that another distinction was necessary in order to explain children's apparent inconsistencies in their use of both the copula and auxiliary verbs. This distinction is based on the linguistic context in which the *be* form is used. In some contexts, it is possible to contract the *be*, whereas in others this is not possible. For example,

"What is that?" can be produced as "What's that?" but no parallel contraction is possible for "What is it?" Brown found that children first used both copulas and auxiliaries in contexts in which contractions are not allowed in standard adult speech. In contrast to Brown's findings, de Villiers and de Villiers (1973) found the contractible forms to be acquired before the uncontractible versions. Their findings would also indicate that the contractibility distinction is significant, but the nature of the difference is unclear.

Acquisition order of the *be* forms is thus seen as related both to the grammatical role of the verb and to the linguistic context. The uncontractible copula occurred relatively early for all three of Brown's children, with utterances such as:

> I *be* good.
> Here I *am*.

In Brown's data, the uncontractible auxiliary lagged considerably behind the uncontractible copula and was closely followed by the contractible forms of first the copula and then the auxiliary. The data of both Brown and the de Villiers show the *be* forms as relatively late morphemes to be mastered.

THIRD PERSON SINGULAR VERB   It appears that, contrary to the usual pattern of development, children begin to use the third person singular form of the verb earlier than they demonstrate their comprehension of the form. Keeney and Smith (1971) found that when four-year-old children had to rely on the verb inflection to determine if the subject was singular or plural, they responded at chance level, indicating they were ignoring the verb inflection. They were, however, using the inflection correctly. Keeney and Wolfe (1972) then assessed comprehension of verb forms for three- to five-year-olds with two procedures. In the first, children were given the verb of a sentence and asked whether the subject should be "one bird" or "two birds." They used both lexical verbs and *be* auxiliaries (*is, are*) to assess the children's judgment of singular and plural. In the second procedure, children also heard only verb phrases (*is singing; sing*) and were to point to pictures of one or two birds. The children's spontaneous speech was examined for verb inflections to compare production and comprehension. Their findings on the picture task confirmed the results of the previous study; the children did not make judgments based on the verb inflection. In the verbal task, however, their choice of the appropriate subject was significantly better than chance. It appears then that the children made the judgment based on what "sounds right" rather than on understanding the significance of the inflection. These authors indicate that the children had difficulty attending to the task and question the usefulness of this kind of task with young children. Certainly it is unusual for children to be requested to make judgments without any supporting context. In their production data, these investigators found that the children produced significantly fewer auxiliary *be* forms than lexical verbs to indicate number, but that the auxiliary forms that were used were consistently correct, whereas the lexical markers were sometimes incorrect. This would lead to the prediction of mastery of the auxiliary forms (*is, are*) before the third person singular form of the lexical verb (e.g., *sings*), which is inconsistent with Brown and other investigators. It is unclear why this discrepancy occurred.

MODAL VERBS   In his study of two-year-old Daniel, Fletcher (1979) found his use of modals confined to those (1) which indicate his own willingness, inability, or request for permission, and (2) which indicate prohibition of an action by someone else. Most were in questions or responses to questions and had no other verb ("I will"; "I can't"; "won't you?") At two, Daniel was not yet using modals to express the possibility and probability of propositions and events or the abilities and wishes of other people. Kuczaj and Maratsos (1975) also found modals to request permission (e.g., *can*) to occur as early as two years, six months, whereas modals of possibility (e.g., *might*) did not appear until three years, three months. They also found that the youngest children most frequently use modals to indicate a logically inferred outcome ("They must be in the box"), rather than in moral or ethical consideration ("You must do it"). Their four-year-old subjects produced proportionately more of the latter type. The distinction in meaning between the future indicators *will* and *gonna* was investigated using spontaneous samples of 2 three-year-old children by Gee and Savasir (1983). Their findings indicate that *will* carries with it an implication of commitment to or responsibility for an ongoing or immediately subsequent undertaking, whereas *gonna* tends to be used for more distant ends.

In an investigation of comprehension of modals, Hirst and Weil (1982) looked to see if children interpret modals as different from copulas ("It is here" versus "It may be here") and distinguish between the forcefulness of *must, may,* and *should* in conditions in which either logical conclusions or moral choices were involved. Their task involved items such as "The peanut must be under this cup or it may be under this cup. Where is it?" To look for comprehension under the condition of moral judgment, the children were told that a doll, Andy, was given instructions by two teachers, such as one that tells him he *must* go into the red room and another that tells him he *should* go into the green room. The child is asked where Andy would go if he is a good boy. Under these conditions, the three-year-olds understood the contrast between *is* and *may* in the logical condition, but they seemed to grasp no other contrast. By three years, six months to four years, the distinctions between *is* and *should* and between *must* and *may* in this condition were made. At four years to four years, six months, the contrast between *is* and *must* emerged, followed by *must* and *should* six months later, and *should* and *may* at five years, six months to six years. The various contrasts were made approximately a year later in the moral judgment condition.

NOUN PLURALS   Children appear to grasp the distinction between one and more than one instance of something before they are marking that distinction with inflections. Miller and Ervin (1964) identify four stages in the development of plurals. In the first stage, children make no contrast between singular and plural nouns but may use modifiers such as *two* or *more* to mark the plural. In the second stage, the *-s* is attached to plural nouns in only a few contexts, and in stage three the use becomes more generalized. At this point, there is evidence of overregularization, with forms such as *mans* and *feets* being expressed. In the fourth stage, the distinction between regular plurals (i.e., those that are formed with *-s* and its allophones) and irregular plurals is made. Graves and Koziol (1971) further distinguish stages of development within this fourth stage, noting that certain phonological patterns are mastered first. They found that first graders in their study had largely mastered the simple plural allomorph (-*s* or -*z*) but many of the third graders had still not acquired the /-ez/ form. Some irregular forms also showed patterns of development, with final /f/ words (*leaf*) becoming correct for most children between first and second grade, whereas words ending in the /-sk/ (*desk*) were not correctly pluralized by many children until the third grade. Ansfield and Tucker (1967) found the same order of difficulty in production of these allophones, but comprehension data showed a different pattern. When they asked children to indicate the best name for a picture and gave two nonsense syllables to choose from, they found that children most consistently interpreted the word-final /-z/ to indicate plurality, making fewer plural judgments from either /-s/ or /-ez/. The authors speculate that this is due to the greater frequency with which the /-s/ and the /-vowel + z/ do not indicate plural as in *horse* and *breeze*, making the final consonant + /z/ a more reliable plural marker.

Brown (1973) found that by the time his three children were correctly using the plural noun inflection, they were also using singular and plural pronouns correctly. At the same time, the children continued to show lack of comprehending the plural inflection under experimental conditions. For example, they did not perform any differently when asked for "the pencil" or "the pencils." Brown speculates that this may be due to the effect of the experimental conditions in contrast to the natural situation where the plural is typically marked twice as in "Give me those pencils."

POSSESSIVES As with plurals, children express possessive relationships with pronouns and also with word order before they mark them with inflections. In early word combinations, this is accomplished with noun + noun constructions, such as "Daddy chair." Brown (1973) observed that in all of the children's early constructions of this type, the relationship between the possessor and the possessed was of a particular kind. That is, in virtually all cases, the possession was optional or temporary.

ARTICLES Two questions are addressed by investigations of children's acquisition of articles—when do they learn them and what do they express with their early articles. The most common finding is that children first master the indefinite article in situations in which the referent has already be identified. (e.g., "That's a hot dog"). Somewhat later, they begin to use articles to introduce unidentified referents and first use the definite article to do so (e.g., "The kitty went meow"). Still later, they use the indefinite article to introduce a previously unmentioned referent to their listener (e.g., "A kitty went meow"). The situation in which children are asked to use naming and referring expressions determines which ones they use and how close their performance matches that of adults. Maratsos (1976) told children stories and then asked them questions to elicit articles. He found that his youngest three-year-old subjects could correctly produce answers with the indefinite article ("What did he see?" "A cow"). They frequently failed to use the definite article, however, when the referent had been previously established ("And what did he ride on?" "The cow"). Maratsos found that his most proficient four-year-olds could correctly manage all forms. Warden (1976), on the other hand, concluded that children younger than five years old do not take their listener's knowledge into account and thus frequently do not use the definite article when mentioning a referent the second time, as is required for adults. His results indicated that it is not until nine years that many children have full mastery of articles in referring expressions. In his task, children were to tell a story from three adjacent pictures, so that there would be first and second mention of several referents. Emslie and Stevenson (1981) used a similar task, but with explicit directions that the story was to be directed to the parent who could not see the pictures and with colorful pictures that clearly indicated that the same referents were in each picture. Under these conditions, correct usage of all forms corresponded more closely to Maratsos' (1976) findings. These authors speculate that children use more egocentric definite reference when the cognitive demands of the task are greater and that children from the age of three can correctly use the articles for identifying and referring if the task is consistent with their cognitive ability.

COMPARATIVES AND SUPERLATIVES The few studies that have looked specifically at the development of the use or understanding of both comparative and superlative inflections do not distinguish between adjective and adverb inflection with these forms. In a comprehension task in which the task was to show objects (Layton and Stick, 1979), children did about equally as well for superlative forms ("Show me the biggest horse") as for comparatives ("Show me the truck that is smaller than this car"). The youngest subjects, who were two years, six months, were correct over 60 percent of the time, whereas the children who were four years, six months were correct in their choice over 90 percent of the time. The children's production of the spoken form in this study was sampled through sentence completion ("This truck is big, but this car is ＿＿"). The youngest subjects frequently did not use either inflectional form but conveyed dimensional relationships with lexical choice, most commonly with *big*. Between three and four years of age, there was a tendency for children to add both *-er* and *-est* to the base to indicate either comparative or superlative, with the appropriate distinction between them not generally made until children were between four and four years, six months. An earlier study by Wales and Campbell (1970) found that superlatives were understood somewhat earlier than comparatives.

An interesting study by Gitterman and Johnston (1983) distinguishes between different meanings that young children have for the comparative adjective forms. They found that the five-year-olds used comparative forms to indicate change in the state of an item ("It got bigger") but not to compare across items ("This one is bigger than that one"). These same children were unable to correctly order a set of objects on the basis of size. It thus appears that the *-er* adjective form is first used before children are able to systematically compare different objects on a single dimension. Seven-year-olds, in contrast, who were proficient at the ordering task, used the *-er* adjective form for comparisons between objects. Gitterman and Johnston also found that some kinds of comparisons were much easier for their subjects to make than others. Contrasts based on visual comparisons (tall, short) were made more frequently than those relying on tactile comparisons (light, soft). The contrasts that were least frequently made correctly depended on a combination of visual and tactile judgments (smooth, rough).

The procedures used in this study to elicit the comparative forms could also be used by clinicians in deep testing. To test the child's use of the form to indicate a dynamic change, the adult manipulated the material to actively create a change. For example, the child held a piece of material while the adult used a squirt gun to make it *wetter*, asking the child "What is happening? How is it getting now?" and "What happened?" To elicit comparison between two objects, the adult presented the first exemplar, naming the dimension such as "This is big"; two additional exemplars were then presented, with the comment "These are not big, but how are they different from each other?" Children were expected to indicate their relative comparison on the dimension mentioned (e.g., "That one is littler").

DIALECTICAL VARIATIONS

There have been extensive sociolinguistic studies of some regional and ethnic American English dialects that can help the clinician identify if a deviation from standard patterns may be attributable to a learned dialectical pattern for a given individual (Labov and others, 1968; Wolfram and Fasold, 1974; Baugh, 1983; Wolfram and Christian, 1976; Christian, Wolfram, and Dube, 1984). Likewise, features of languages other than English have been published to assist the clinician in identifying the possible source of deviations from English structure if the individual is learning English as a second language (Spanish, Asian, Native American). We will not attempt to duplicate that information here but will identify some grammatical features that are frequently handled differently in dialects or languages other than standard English. Most of this summary is taken from Wolfram (1986).

Verb Phrases

Irregular verb usage may show a variety of patterns that differ from standard forms. Some common patterns are (1) past tense as participle ("I had went down there"); (2) participle as past ("She done her homework"); (3) uninflected verb as past ("She come to my house yesterday"); (4) regularization ("Everybody knowed he was late"); and (5) different irregular form ("I hearn a noise"). Wolfram (1986) points out that categories 1, 2, and 3 are common in both Northern and Southern vernaculars while category 5 is more likely to be found in Southern vernacular and regularization; category 4 is frequent in individuals learning English as a second language.

Completive "Done" Use of *done* to indicate a completed action or event is distinguished from the simple past in that it emphasizes the completeness ("I *done* forgot") or intensity of the message ("I *done* told you not to do that"). This is found most frequently in Southern vernaculars.

Habitual "Be" When an event or activity is distributed intermittently over time or space, this aspect is conveyed with *be* in vernacular black English ("Sometimes she *be* sleeping late").

Verb Subclass Shifts Patterns identified in vernacular dialects include the following: (1) shifts from transitive to intransitive ("If we *beat*, you have to pay") or intransitive to transitive ("He *learned* me how to swim"); (2) formation of verb complement structure ("The wall needs *painted*"); and (3) different semantic domain covered by verb ("He *took* sick").

Absence of "Be" Forms In those contexts where *is* and *are* can be contracted in standard English, they often are not used in some vernaculars and by second language learners ("He big"; "They taking the bus"). In contrast, these same forms are typically present in uncontractible contexts ("I know who he *is*"; "That's where they *are*"), as are past forms ("He *was* here"; "We *were* worried") and *am* ("I'*m* ready").

Subject-Verb Agreement Agreement between subject and verb is most apparent when the subject is third person, since this is when a grammatical distinction is made between singular and plural in standard English. Several vernacular dialects have different patterns and variations and are common for people learning English as a second language. Some variations include (1) consistency between singular and plural forms of *be* ("The girl/girls *is* ready"; "The cat/cats *was* sleeping"); (2) use of singular with existential *there* ("There *is* several ways to do this"; "There *was* two of us"); (3) uninflected *don't* auxiliary ("He *don't* want any part of it"); and (4) uninflected verb with third person singular subjects ("She *walk* on the side of the road").

Uninflected Past Tense Absence of a regular past tense marker often is due to consonant cluster reduction, a phonological process previously discussed ("I already *walk* too far"). Past tense may be unmarked and time conveyed adverbially ("Yesterday I *play* it for the first time"). This is most common for second language learners. American Indian English generally uses the un-marked verb to indicate a habitual activity in the past ("In those days, we *work* very hard").

Ain't The auxiliary *ain't* corresponds to a variety of forms in standard English, including *be* + *not* ("He *ain't* home"), *have* = *not* ("She *ain't* been gone long"), and *do* + *not* ("I *ain't* finish my part").

Noun Phrases

Plurals Absence of a regular plural marker is the accepted pattern in some English dialects when the noun is one of weight (*five pound*), measure (*six mile*), or time (*four year*). General absence of the plural suffix is more common for those whose English is influenced by previously learned languages ("All the *dog* were barking"). Regularization of irregular plurals may also occur (*deers*; *snowmans*).

Possessives The adjacency of two nominals ("the woman car") without a possessive marker can signal the possessive relationship in black English vernacular. There may also be regularization of the possessive pronoun (*mines*).

Pronouns A common pattern in several vernacular varieties of English is the use of object pronouns in compound subjects ("*Me and him* are going together"). The objective form may extend to demonstratives as well ("*them guys*"). Regularization of reflexive forms, by analogy with possessive pronouns, is also a common feature (*hisself*; *theirselves*). There are several regional variations of the second person plural *you* to distinguish it from the singular form (*y'all*; *youse*; *you'uns*).

Existential It or They   In contexts where standard English would use *there* as an existential subject rather than as a locative adverb, some dialects would use *it* or *they* ("*It*'s a bug on your arm"; "*They*'s a bug on your arm").

ASSESSING INFLECTIONAL MORPHOLOGY

Of all the systems involved in language, the system of inflectional morphology is the easiest for the clinician to assess. Although we have generally argued against using a checklist approach to assessment, this seems to be the most efficient way to proceed with morphological analysis. The reason for our shift on this point is that there is a finite set of grammatical morphemes that modulates the meaning of the major word classes. Children we have seen either use these inflections—correctly or incorrectly—or do not use them; they do not create new inflections or appear to create new categories of information to express with inflections. This is not to say that their use of grammatical morphemes is necessarily consistent, either within their samples or with adult usage. We have not found the need, however, to go beyond the description of conventional morphology to capture children's productions. There is always the possibility, of course, that the next child we see will be the exception and will present a new challenge for structural analysis.

Morphological analysis of inflectional morphology is most appropriately carried out with children who have relatively intact language systems, since inflections are essentially refinements in conveying content. If a child has no syntactic structure, that is, if he or she is using primarily one- and two-word utterances, we would not be concerned with morphology. Likewise, if a child shows pragmatic problems, such as echoing or undeveloped dialogue structure, morphology would take on lesser importance because it impacts less on conveying the intended message. Finally, if a child has severe phonological problems, morphological competence again would be of secondary importance, since most inflections would probably not be produced intelligibly even if they were part of the child's linguistic structure.

The morphological inflections used in a sample greatly depend on the event or the topic, so it is best to have samples collected in at least two different events. A brief description of the events should be included in your summary of morphology so that the findings can be interpreted in light of what was going on. For example, if the child is engaged in play with action figures, the absence of past tense in the sample is less significant than if she had been discussing an event that occurred in the past. The structures that are not found in either sample can be elicited with events that have obligatory contexts for the targeted inflection. We present some suggestions for elicitation procedures following our discussion of analysis of the samples.

Screening for Morphological Inflections

Sometimes it is necessary or desirable to quickly analyze the language of several children, as when determining comparability of groups or matching subjects in a research study. While standardized tests have been used for this purpose, they fail to provide more than a very rough description of a child's language ability. We prefer to use a procedure that relies on language sample analysis. One such procedure, the Index of Productive Syntax or IPSyn, has been proposed by Scarborough (1990). He lists fifty-six grammatical forms in four subscales: noun phrase, verb phrase, question/negative, and sentence structure, thus combining morphological and syntactic features. Language samples are "scored" by assigning points for each of the features used, with a maximum of two exemplars counted for each feature. Reliability has been found to be good with samples as small as fifty utterances, excluding unintelligible utterances, imitations, self-repetitions, and routines, but use of a hundred utterances is recommended. Scarborough (1990) provides a chart for converting samples of different lengths to a common index for comparison. If this procedure is used to judge the normalcy of a child's language development, local norms should be developed. Other forms may be included for children of different ages or from different linguistic groups.

Structural Analysis

While a screening procedure may be useful for a quick overview of a child's morphological development, it does not provide a detailed analysis of error productions or distinguish mastery from emergence of a form. When there are few or inconsistent exemplars of a structure, more detailed analysis is called for.

A listing transcript of the child's utterances is recommended for use as a worksheet for this analysis. You may want to begin with separate listing transcripts for each sample. If they seem quite similar, the results can be combined in your final summary. If the child's morphological regularities are different in the two samples, however, the summary should include a comparison. Utterances are not included if they are part of memorized material or are direct imitations of someone else. You also can exclude utterances that obviously have no inflectional forms, such as "yes" or "no way." If the same utterance is said more than once by the child, it is included only the first time. Utterances in the listing transcript retain their number from the running transcript so they can be easily located if needed for further analysis. The running transcript should be referred to in order to determine if morphological structures are correct. If, for example, the child says "cat" while pointing to a picture of two cats, the plural morpheme is missing; this judgment can only be made based on the context.

Each utterance in the worksheet should be examined for inflectional morphemes and personal pronouns that are correct, incorrect, or missing. Indefinite pronouns can be included if it appears that the child makes errors on these forms. Table 5–4 illustrates a format for a morphology worksheet. The child's correct and incorrect morphological forms can be summarized as in Table 5–5. Any form that shows error production should be further analyzed

TABLE 5–4   Morphology Worksheet

For each utterance, indicate grammatical morphemes that are missing with a slash (/). Underline those that are present.

Utterance	Inflections Present	Pronouns Present	Words Missing	Error Forms
1. /Boy/ runn<u>in</u>	Progressive participle		Art; Aux.	
3. I <u>wanna</u> go in/ car	Modal	I	Art. def.	
4. It brok<u>ed</u>				Irreg. past
8. I need<u>s</u> mittens	Reg. plural	I		3rd pers. overreg.
10. That/ mine			Copula	

to determine the nature of the regularities that affect that form. If the form is sometimes correct and other times incorrect or missing, all instances of the form should be listed to compare the different contexts in which they occur. It may be determined, for example, that present tense copulas are omitted whereas past tense forms are present and correct. If a form is inconsistently correct, the consistency of the error should be determined. For example, the child may sometimes regularize the irregular past tense verb and at other times use an uninflected verb for this form. A sample listing transcript of errors is shown in Table 5–6.

TABLE 5–5   Summary of Morphological Inflections and Pronouns

	Number Correct	Number Error	Percent Correct
Noun forms Regular plural			
Irregular plural			
Possessive			

Articles
  Definite
  Indefinite
  Genitive			

Verb forms Regular past			
Irregular past			
3rd person singular			

continued

TABLE 5–5 Summary of Morphological Inflections and Pronouns (*continued*)

	Number Correct	*Number Error*	*Percent Correct*

Progressive
  Participle
  "Be" auxiliary			

Perfect
  Participle
  "Have" auxiliary			

Passive
  Participle
  "Be/get" auxiliary			

Modal/catenative			
"Do" auxiliary			

Copula
  Present
  Past			

Nonfinite forms
  Infinitives
  Gerunds
  Participles			

Adjective/adverb forms Comparative			
Superlative			
Pronouns Subject			
Object			
Possessive			
Reflexive			

TABLE 5–6 Error Analysis Form

Target structure: Irregular past tense

Correct Productions	*Error Productions*
11. I went. 46. I went too.	4. It broked. 44. I sawed it. 51. He dided it.

Summary: Generally uses redundant past tense (irreg + reg). <u>Went</u> seems to be idiomatic.

TABLE 5-7 Morphology Worksheet

Name: Patty C.
Event: Playing card game

Utterance	Inflections Present	Pronouns Present	Words Missing	Error Forms
1. Me /waiting for you. (I am waiting for you.)	Progressive participle	you (obj.)	Aux.	me/I
4. That's what you think.	Copula's	you (sub.)		
6. This one.				
12. Where is dat?	Copula is			
15. Me / do it better. (I can do it better.)	Comparative adv.		Modal	me/I
16. Me know where it is.	Copula is			me/I
23. //Do/ it good? (Am I doing it good?)			Aux. 1st pers. subj. Do aux.	Prog. part.
24. How much / me got? (How much do I have?)				me/I
25. Yeah / want / see how much you got. (I want to see how much you have.)		you (obj.)	1st pers. subj.	Modal inf.
26. Dis sure / better for me. (This sure is better for me.)	Comparative adj.	me	Copula is	
31. Nothing fall/ down you drop/ it. (Nothing fell down, you dropped it.)		you (sub.)		Irreg. past Reg. past
32. You got it?		you (sub.)		
36. Me do/ it before mommy go/ out.				me/I Irreg. past (2)
40. Tomorrow's Friday.	Copula 's			
41. What day is /? (What day is it?)	Copula is		Subj.	
52. /Me do/ it good? (Am I doing it well?)			Aux.	me/I Prog. part.

continued

TABLE 5-7 Morphology Worksheet (*continued*)

Name: Patty C.
Event: Playing card game

Utterance	Inflections Present	Pronouns Present	Words Missing	Error Forms
62. Me like (/) come(/) over here. (I like to come over here.) (I like coming over here.)				me/I Inf./Ger.
65. My brother / coming out /two more day/. (My brother is coming out in two more days.)	Art. gen. Prog. part.		Aux. Prep.	Reg. plural
67. My Bobby / coming out. (My Bobby is coming out.)	Art. gen. Prog. part.		Aux.	
68. // Coming out / two more days.) (He is coming out in two more days.)	Prog. part. Reg. plural		3rd pers. subj. Aux.; Prep.	
69. [kʌp] call/ up last night. (? called up last night.)				Reg. past.
70. He /go be home / two more days. (He is going to be home in two more days.)	Copula *be* Reg. plural	he	Aux. Prep.	Modal inf. Prog. part.
72. You know me / lucky? (You know I'm lucky.)		you (sub.)	Copula *am*	me/I
75. //All mixed up / got no room where you are. (You are all mixed up so you have no room where you are.)	Copula *are*	you (sub.)	2nd pers. subj. Copula *are*	
76. Me got enough room this way				me/I
77. Dis chair / real comfortable. (This chair is real comfortable.)			Copula *is*	

178

No.	Utterance				
78.	Me like dat.				me/I
79.	/ You? (Do you?)			*Do aux.*	
81.	Me like dis chair.				me/I
84.	Look dere's a little one too.	Copula's Art. indef.			
85.	That's real good.	Copula's			
86.	You know the big one. (You know (which is)? the big one.)	Art. def.	you (sub.)		
87.	That's real small.	Copula's			
92.	/ You eat that at home? (Do you eat that at home?)		you (sub.)	*Do aux.*	
93.	Me eat carrot/ / home all / time now. (I eat carrots at home all the time now.)			Prep. Article	me/I Reg. plural
94.	Me got one in my lunch.	Art. gen.			me/I
95.	Carrot and celery taste real good.				
98.	How many / me got? (How many do I have?)	Art. gen. *Do aux.*			me/I
106.	Watch your ring don't come off.			*Do aux.*	3rd pers.
109.	Better this way.	Comparative			
111.	Me don't wanna kick you.	*Do aux.*	you (obj.)		me/I
123.	How bout / do dis one too? (How about we? do this one too?)			Subj.	
127.	Put dat round / me / see dat better. (Turn that around so I can see it better.)	Comparative adv.			Modal me/I
137.	/ Me tell you bout my brother coming up? (Did I tell you about my brother coming up?)	Art. gen. Prog. part.	you (obj.)	*Do aux.*	me/I
140.	Do dis one too.			*Do aux.*	

continued

TABLE 5–7 Morphology Worksheet (*continued*)

Name: Patty C.
Event: Playing card game

Utterance	Inflections Present	Pronouns Present	Words Missing	Error Forms
141. /Me like / see that. (I would? like to see that.)			Inf.	
143. See how much you got in here.		you (sub.)		
145. Put all that stuff in here.				
146. See what you got in here.		you (sub.)		
155. /Me put all this away for you? (Should/Can I put all this away for you?)			Modal	me/I
157. Me know that // suppose// have off tomorrow. (I know that I'm supposed to have tomorrow off.)			Subj. Copula	me/I Modal inf.
160. / Me turn it? (Can/Should I turn it off?)			Modal	me/I

TABLE 5–8 Summary of Morphological Inflections and Pronouns

	Number Correct	Number Error	Percent Correct
Noun forms			
Regular plural	2	2	50
Irregular plural			
Possessive			
Articles			
Definite	1	1	
Indefinite	1		
Genitive	4		100
Verb forms			
Regular past		2	
Irregular past		3	0
3rd person singular		1	
Progressive			
Participle	5	3	63
"Be" auxiliary		7	0
Perfect			
Participle			
"Have" auxiliary			
Passive			
Participle			
"Be/get" auxiliary			
Modal/catenative		8	0
"Do" auxiliary	2	5	33
Copula			
Present	10	3	80
Past			
Nonfinite forms			
Infinitives		4	100
Gerunds		(1)	
Participles			
Adjective/adverb forms			
Comparative	4		100
Superlative			
Pronouns			
Subject	10	25	29
Object	5		100
Possessive			
Reflexive			

TABLE 5–9 Error Analysis Form

Target structure: Regular plural

Correct Productions	*Error Productions*
68. Coming out two more days.	65. . . . coming out two more day.
70. He go be home two more days.	93. Me eat carrot home all time now.

Summary: Form seems to be developing, but too few instances to tell if it has generalized beyond "two more days."

Target Structure: Progressive participle

Correct Productions
   1. Me waiting for you.
  65. My brother coming out. . . .
  67. My Bobby coming out.
  68. (He is) coming out. . . .
 137. Me tell you bout my brother coming up?

Error Productions
  23. (Am I) do it good?
  52. (Am) me do it good?
  70. He (is) go be home. . . .

Gerund/Infinitive
  62. Me like come(ing) over here. or
      Me like (to) come over here.

Summary: Progressive forms are consistently produced without the auxiliary; the participle seems to be used on specific verbs and omitted on others. Deep testing on other verbs is needed to determine if there is a rule to this variable use. The lack of verb inflection on *come* in no. 62 seems to reflect her pattern of not inflecting nonfinite verbs.

Target Structure: Infinitive/auxiliary

Correct Productions

106. Watch your ring don't come off.
111. Me don't wanna kick you.

Error Productions

Aux Be
   1. Me (am) waiting for you.
  23. (Am) (I) do it good.
  52. (Am) me do it good.
  65. My brother (is) coming out. . . .
  67. My Bobby (is) coming out.
  68. / (is) coming out two more days.
  70. He (is) go be home. . . .

Aux Do
  24. How much (do) me got?
  79. (Do) you?
  92. (Do) you eat that at home?
  98. How many (do) me got?
 137. (Did) me tell you bout my brother coming up?

Aux Can
  15. Me (can) do it better.
 127. . . . me (can) see that better.
 155. (Can) me put all this away for you?
 160. (Can) me turn it?

Infinitive
  25. Want (to) see how much. . . .
  62. Me like (to) come over here.
  70. He go (to) be home. . . .
 157. . . . / suppose (to) have off tomorrow.

Target Structure: Infinitive/auxiliary
(*continued*)

Summary: Patty rarely uses more than one verb in a clause. *Do* auxiliary is used in negative form, but all other auxiliaries are consistently omitted. She uses two verbs in several constructions that call for either catenatives or infinitives to be complete.

Target Structure: Copula

Correct Productions	*Error Productions*
4. That's what you think.	26. (This) sure (is) better for me.
12. Where is (that)?	72. You know me (am) lucky.
16. Me know where it is.	75. (You are) all mixed up. . . .
40. Tomorrow's Friday.	
41. What day is (it)?	
70. He go be home. . . .	
75. . . . got no room where you are.	
84. (There's) a little one.	
85. That's real good.	
87. That's real small.	

Summary: Generally uses contractable and uncontractable forms of *is* correctly; may delete *is* after *this* because of final *s*; deep testing needed to sample other forms.

Target Structure: Subject pronouns

Correct Productions	*Error Productions*
9 × you is used correctly	18 × object me is used in place of subject I
1 × he is used correctly	1st person subject missing 2 ×
	2nd person subject missing 1 ×
	3rd person subject missing 1 ×
	Undetermined subject missing:
	123. How bout (we/I/you) do this one too?
	157. Me know that (I/we) suppose have off
	tomorrow.

Summary: Use of object for subject pronoun seems to be confined to the first person; production of *she* should be elicited. Do further analysis to determine if missing subjects have discourse regularities.

Sample Analysis: Morphology

A sample morphological analysis is presented to demonstrate how the various forms can be used. The running transcript of the interaction in which Patty was playing a card game with her speech-language pathologist is presented in Chapter 3. Here we present only Patty's utterances that would be included for morphological analysis (Table 5–7). A gloss is given when Patty's meaning is not clear from her utterance. In places where alternative interpretations are possible, the gloss contains a question mark (?). Following the identification of deviations on the general morphological worksheet, the frequency of correct and error productions is calculated (Table 5–8). If three or more instances of the structure are present, the percentage of correct usage is given. The identified deviations are next organized with the error analysis form (Table 5–9). Some of the errors in this sample are syntactic rather than morphological. They will be analyzed in the next chapter.

MORPHOLOGICAL STRUCTURES

Events That Elicit Morphological Inflections

1. Have the child narrate the activities of the clinician to someone else. Activities can include sustained or repeated actions to elicit imperfect aspect (*blowing, stirring*), and punctual actions to elicit past tense (*fell, dropped*). This procedure can be altered to have the child relate the actions after they are completed to elicit more variety in past tense verbs.

2. Have the child retell stories that are chosen for the variety of morphological forms. "Three Little Kittens," for example, is likely to elicit plurals, and "The Three Bears" has many possibilities for possessive forms. Stories could also be created specifically for elicitation tasks.

3. Create events in which the structure is needed to proceed as expected. For example, give the child only one checker or card when the game calls for a full set in order to elicit the plural. A play situation can require that the child ask for items that are distinguished by the person they belong to in order to elicit possessives ("the Daddy's hat"; "Baby's shoe"). Offering the child materials that are not adequate for the task can elicit comparatives ("I need a bigger one").

4. Create the unexpected. Ask the child to do something on the pretense that you are not aware she is doing it or that it has been done. This can be effective in eliciting copulas and auxiliary verbs ("Come and sit down"; "I am sitting down"; "Shut the door"; "It is shut").

Metalinguistic Procedures

Patterned Practice   Create a pattern and have the child follow it.

I'll Say:

(Past tense)
I see it today.   *You say:*   I saw it yesterday.
I know it today. *You say:*

(Auxiliary verbs in tag questions)
It's nice.   *You say:*   Isn't it.
That's not nice. *You say:*

(Possessive)
That cat belongs to Tom. *You say:*   That's Tom's cat.
That hat belongs to Ann. *You say:*

(Passives)
The horse ate the apple. *You say:*   The apple was eaten by the horse.
The wind broke the door. *You say:*

Sentence Imitation   Construct sets of sentences that present the structure in question in several forms and contexts. For example, Table 5–10 presents a

TABLE 5–10   Elicited Imitation for Auxiliaries

(is)	The boy is throwing the ball.
(are)	The kids are riding on the bus.
(am)	The girl said, "I am going home."
(were)	The dogs were swimming in the lake.
(was)	The baby was sleeping by the door.
(will)	The men will take away the trash.
(can)	We can sit on the steps.
(should)	The cook should wash his hands.
(has)	The lady has cut the grass.
(have)	We have eaten our breakfast.
(did)	We did like the new cereal.
(don't)	Cats don't like to get wet.
(doesn't)	He doesn't mind if we play here.
(2 aux.)	She will have gone home by now.
(2 aux.)	The men should have been on time.
(3 aux.)	He might have been sleeping when the girl called.

set of sentences for sampling auxiliary verbs. Ask the child to imitate the sentence.

REFERENCES

ANSFIELD, M., AND C. TUCKER. English Pluralization Rules of Six-Year-Old Children, *Child Development*, 38, 1967, 1201–17.

ANTINUCCI, F., AND R. MILLER. How Children Talk About What Happened, *Journal of Child Language*, 3, 1976, 167–89.

BAUGH, J. *Black Street Speech*. Austin, Tx.: University of Texas Press, 1983.

BAYLES, K., AND G. HARRIS. Evaluating Speech-Language Skills in Papago Indian Children, *Journal of American Indian Education*, 21, 1982, 11–20.

BELLAMY, M., AND S. BELLAMY. The Acquisition of Morphological Inflections by Children from Four to Ten. *Language Learning*, 20, 1970, 199–211.

BERKO, J. The Child's Learning of English Morphology, *Word*, 14, 1958, 50–77.

BLOOM, L., AND M. LAHEY. *Language Development and Language Disorders*. New York: John Wiley, 1978.

BLOOM, L., M. LIFTER, AND J. HAFITZ. Semantics of Verbs and the Development of Verb Inflection in Child Language, *Language*, 56, 1980, 386–412.

BRONCKART, J., AND H. SINCLAIR. Time, Tense, and Aspect, *Cognition*, 2, 1973, 107–30.

BROWN, R. *A First Language*. New York: Harvard University Press, 1973.

CHENG, L. *Assessing Asian Language Performance: Guidelines for Evaluating Limited-English-Proficient Students*. Rockville, Md.: Aspen Publishers, 1987.

CHRISTIAN, D., W. WOLFRAM, AND N. DUBE. *Variation and Change in Geographically Isolated Communities: Appalachian and Ozark English*. Final report, NSF Grant BNS 8208916, 1984.

COOPER, R. The Ability of Deaf and Hearing Children to Apply Morphological Rules, *Journal of Speech and Hearing Research*, 10, 1967, 77–86.

CRAGO, M. Development of Communicative Competence in Inuit Children: Implications for Speech-Language Pathology, *Journal of Childhood Communication Disorders*, 13, 1990, 73–83.

DEVER, R. A. Comparison of the Results of a Revised Version of Berko's Test of Morphology with the Free Speech of Mentally Retarded Children, *Journal of Speech and Hearing Research*, 15, 1972, 169–78.

DE VILLIERS, J., AND P. DE VILLIERS. A Cross-Sectional Study of the Acquisition of Grammatical Morphemes in Child Speech, *Journal of Psycholinguistic Research*, 2, 1973, 267–78.

DI PAOLO, M., AND C. SMITH. Cognitive and Linguistic Factors in the Acquisition of Grammatical Morphemes in Child Speech, *Journal of Psycholinguistic Research*, 2, 1978, 267–78.

DULAY, H., M. BURT, AND S. KRASHEN. *Language Two*. New York: Oxford University Press, 1982.

EMSLIE, H., AND R. STEVENSON. Pre-School Children's Use of the Articles in Definite and Indefinite Expressions, *Journal of Child Language*, 8, 1981, 313–28.

FLETCHER, P. The Development of the Verb Phrase,

in *Language Acquisition: Studies in First Language Development*, eds. P. Fletcher and M. Garman. New York: Cambridge University Press, 1979, pp. 261–85.

GEE, J., AND I. SAVASIR. On the Use of *Will* and *Gonna*: Toward a Description of Activity-Types for Child Language, *Discourse Processes*, 2, 1983, 143–75.

GITTERMAN, D., AND J. JOHNSTON. Talking About Comparisons: A Study of Young Children's Comparative Adjective Usage, *Journal of Child Language*, 10, 1983, 605–21.

GOODGLASS, H. Studies on the Grammar of Aphasics, in *Developments in Applied Psycholinguistic Research*, eds. S. Rosenberg and J. Koplin. New York: Macmillan, 1968, pp. 177–208.

GRAVES, M., AND S. KOZIOL. Noun Plural Development in Primary Grade Children, *Child Development*, 42, 1971, 1165–73.

HARNER, L. Children Talk About the Time and Aspect of Actions, *Child Development*, 52, 1981, 498–506.

HERRING, S. Tense Versus Aspect and Focus of Attention in the Development of Temporal Reference. Unpublished manuscript. Department of Linguistics, University of California, Berkeley, 1981.

HIRST, W., AND J. WEIL. Acquisition of Epistemic and Deontic Meaning of Modals, *Journal of Child Language*, 9, 1982, 659–66.

JOHNSON, C. The Emergence of Present Perfect Verb Forms: Semantic Influences on Selective Imitation, *Journal of Child Language*, 12, 1985, 325–52.

KAYSER, H. Speech and Language Assessment of Spanish-English Speaking Children, *Language, Speech, and Hearing Services in Schools*, 20, 1989, 226–44.

KEENEY, T., AND N. SMITH. Young Children's Imitation and Comprehension of Sentential Singularity and Plurality, *Language and Speech*, 14, 1971, 372–83.

KEENEY, T., AND J. WOLFE. The Acquisition of Agreement in English, *Journal of Verbal Learning and Verbal Behavior*, 11, 1972, 698–705.

KERNAN, K., AND B. BLOUNT. The Acquisition of Spanish Grammar by Mexican Children. *Anthropological Linguistics*, 8, 1966, 1–14.

KUCZAJ, S. The Acquisition of Regular and Irregular Tense Forms, *Journal of Verbal Learning and Verbal Behavior*, 16, 1977, 589–600.

KUCZAJ, S. Why Do Children Fail to Overgeneralize the Progressive Inflection? *Journal of Child Language*, 5, 1978, 167–71.

KUCZAJ, S., AND M. MARATSOS. What Children Can Say Before They Will, *Merrill Palmer Quarterly*, 21, 1975, 89–111.

KVAAL, J., N. SHIPSTEAD-COX, S. NEVITT, B. HODSON, AND P. LAUNER. The Acquisition of Ten Spanish Morphemes by Spanish-Speaking Children, *Language, Speech, and Hearing Services in Schools*, 9, 1988, 384–94.

LABOV, W., P. COHEN, C. ROBINS, AND J. LEWIS. *A Study of Non-Standard English of Negro and Puerto Rican Speakers in New York City.* USOE Final Report Project No. 3288, 1968.

LAYTON, T., AND S. STICK. Comprehension and Production of Comparatives and Superlatives, *Journal of Child Language*, 6, 1979, 511–27.

LINARES, N. Rules for Calculating Mean Length of Utterance in Morphemes for Spanish, in *Communication Assessment of the Bilingual Bicultural Child*, eds. J. Erickson and D. Omark. Baltimore: University Park Press, 1981.

MARATSOS, M. *The Use of Definite and Indefinite Reference in Young Children: An Experimental Study in Semantic Acquisition.* New York: Cambridge University Press, 1976.

MILLER, W., AND S. ERVIN. The Development of Grammar in Child Language, in *The Acquisition of Language*, eds. U. Bellugi and R. Brown. Monographs of the Society for Research in Child Development, 29, 1964, 929–34.

NATALICIO, D., AND L. NATALICIO. The Child's Learning of English Morphology Revisited, *Language Learning*, 19, 1969, 205–15.

NATALICIO, D., AND L. NATALICIO. A Comparative Study of English Pluralization by Native and Non-Native English Speakers, *Child Development*, 42, 1971, 1302–6.

NEWFIELD, M., AND B. SCHLANGER. The Acquisition of English Morphology by Normal and Educable Mentally Retarded Children, *Journal of Speech and Hearing Research*, 11, 1968, 693–706.

REICHENBACH, H. *Symbolic Logic.* Berkeley: University of California, 1947.

SACHS, J. Talking About the There and Then: The Sequence of Displaced Reference, in *Children's Language*, ed. K. E. Nelson. New York: Gardner Press, 1980.

SCARBOROUGH, H. Index of Productive Syntax. *Applied Psycholinguistics*, 11, 1990, 1–22.

SHULMAN, E. Speech and Language of the Limited English Proficient (LEP) Child. *Seminars in Speech and Language*, 9, 1988, 383–96.

SMITH, C. The Acquisition of Time Talk: Relations Between Child and Adult Grammars, *Journal of Child Language*, 7, 1980, 263–78.

WALES, R., AND R. CAMPBELL. On the Development of Comparison and the Comparison of Development, in *Advances in Psycholinguistics*, eds. G. B. Flores d'Arcais and W. J. J. Levelt. Amsterdam: Elsevier North-Holland, 1970.

WARDEN, D. The Influence of Context on Children's

Use of Identifying Expressions and References, *British Journal of Psychology*, 67, 1976, 101–12.

WEIST, R., H. WYSOCKA, K. WITKOWSKA-STADNIK, E. BUCZOWSKA, AND E. KONIECZNA. The Defective Tense Hypothesis: On the Emergence of Tense and Aspect in Child Polish, *Journal of Child Language*, 11, 1984, 347–74.

WOLFRAM, W. Language Variation in the United States, in *Nature of Communication Disorders in Culturally and Linguistically Diverse Populations*, ed. O. Taylor. San Diego, Calif.: College Hill Press, 1986.

WOLFRAM, W., AND D. CHRISTIAN. *Appalachian Speech*. Washington, D.C.: Center for Applied Linguistics, 1976.

WOLFRAM, W., AND R. FASOLD. *The Study of Social Dialects in American English*. Englewood Cliffs, N.J.: Prentice-Hall, 1974.

6

Syntax

In the last chapter, we discussed combining grammatical morphemes into words. In this chapter, we will be discussing *syntax,* which has to do with the structural regularities for combining words into larger meaningful units. Combining words involves combining ideas, and different kinds of ideas are communicated with distinctive syntactic structures. If we wish to indicate a specific entity (e.g., the pencil on the desk), we combine a noun that names the general class of the entity (*pencil*) with words that identify the specific object (e.g., *this, blue*). The structure of the resulting statement ("this blue pencil") is a noun phrase. If we wish to convey something about the pencil rather than simply identify it, we need a different syntactic structure—that is, we need a clause, such as "Hand me the pencil" or "The pencil fell on the floor." We have added a comment to the topic; or in syntactic terms, we have a clause consisting of a subject and a predicate. Noun phrases and clauses are the basic units that result from word combinations.

Syntax is closely related to pragmatics in that the specific syntactic structure of an utterance is determined by the intention behind the utterance and the context in which it is spoken. Asking a question is the most direct way to request information ("What is this?") or confirmation ("Is this yours?"). Less direct expression may be chosen because of the particular situation or conversational partner. A statement imparts information ("This is mine"), whereas an imperative conveys a command ("Give it to me"). The intent to reject ("I don't want it") or deny ("It's not true") is conveyed with negatives. Less direct expression may be chosen for any of these intentions because of the particular situation or conversational partner ("Do you suppose you could hand that to me?").

Awareness of listeners and their need for information is also reflected in syntactic structure. Along with elaborating noun phrases to aid the listener's identification of the topic ("that little blue box"), we can combine clauses to clarify referents for the listener ("I need the box that I gave you for your birthday"). We highlight new information for listeners by position in the clause ("The pencil is *blue*" vs. "The *blue* pencil is broken"). We tend to reduce redundancy that listeners do not need by use of elliptical structures ("What do you want to eat?" "*Clams*") and pronouns ("Give *it* to me").

Children obviously do not begin to use syntactic structures that are like adult syntax with their first combinations. Although it is relatively easy to recognize phrases and clauses, statements, imperatives, and the like in adult language and to describe their syntactic structure, word combinations in children's early speech often do not fall into these familiar categories. It thus becomes important to discern the regularities displayed in their combinations and to ascertain the communicative intent behind their utterances in order to know how their syntactic regularities function for them pragmatically.

We begin this chapter by discussing adult syntactic systems, since understanding these systems is helpful in describing regularities in children's productions as well as identifying children's deviations from adult grammar. Next, we will summarize syntactic development and then discuss doing structural analysis for syntactic regularities. Some other descriptions of English syntax that may be helpful can be found in Crystal, Fletcher, and Garman (1976), Quirk and others (1972), and Stockwell (1977).

We will not emphasize abstract syntax in our descriptions of syntactic structure; that is, you will not find a distinction made between deep and surface structure syntax in our discussions, although we do feel there is some evidence that the generative model developed by Chomsky has psychological reality for children and adults (see Chomsky, 1965). Our reason for not emphasizing abstract syntax is that we find its use as a clinical assessment approach to abnormal language impractical (see Crystal, Fletcher, and Garman, 1976, for a discussion).

SYNTACTIC SYSTEMS

Learning syntax involves organizing utterances on several different levels. Any one utterance can be analyzed for its conformance with the requirements of these different language organizing systems. The systems interrelate hierarchically. The most encompassing level of organization is the discourse structure, since the type of discourse will influence the syntax of sentences contained within it. Discourse will be discussed in Chapter 8. Sentence structure is the next level in the hierarchy. The sentence is composed of one or more clauses, each of which is organized with *clause structure* elements to include a subject and a predicate. The clause subjects and predicates are expressed with noun phrases and verb phrases, each of which have distinctive *phrase structure* organization. Finally, at the most molecular level, grammatical and lexical morphemes are organized to convey *morphological structure*, which we discussed in the last chapter.

This chapter is organized around the sentence structure, clause structure, and phrase structure rules that operate when words are combined to form multiword utterances. We begin lower in the hierarchy by discussing the organization of noun phrases and verb phrases, and then build to a higher level by relating these to the structure of simple clauses. This will lead us to analyzing the sentence organization involved in various types of multiple-clause sentences. We complete the discussion of syntactic systems by examining different *sentence types;* those which are usually used to ask questions, convey negative intent, or issue imperatives.

Phrase Structure

Noun Phrases   Nouns identify the entities that utterances are about—the people, objects, places, and mental operations, to name a few. While we sometimes use simple nouns to refer to those entities (e.g., "*Milk* is good for you"), we generally use modifiers to specify something about the entity or to identify the specific referent for our listener. Most frequently in English, modifiers precede the noun and with it comprise a noun phrase. We will refer back to those noun modifiers presented in Chapter 5 in describing noun phrase structure. Other modifiers follow the noun and involve more complex structure.

A *noun phrase* can consist of one or more modifiers preceding the noun. The order in which these elements can occur is restricted, and a sentence does not sound right if we deviate from this order. Most noun phrases begin with a *determiner*—an article, demonstrative, or qualifier. Determiners are mutually exclusive; that is, only one can occur in each phrase. (Utterances marked with an asterisk are ungrammatical in standard adult English.)

	a book		*my a book
WE CAN HAVE	my book	BUT NOT	*this either book
	this book		*my that book
	either book		*the any book

The only elements that can precede determiners are a special class of qualifiers that are called *initiators*. Thee include *all, both, half,* and *only,* along with limited forms of each, such as *not quite all* or *almost half.* Initiators also include many forms with *of,* such as *many of, several of,* and *either of.*

The *adjectivals* are the largest class of words that can occur before a noun, including descriptive adjectives (*big, old, red*), ordinals (*first, next, last*), and quantifiers (*two, several, many*). We also include in this class modifying nouns such as *college* student and *day care* center. A noun phrase may include several adjectivals which occur in a predictable order, with ordinals preceding quantifiers, quantifiers preceding descriptive adjectives, and modifying nouns immediately preceding the head noun. All of the adjectivals follow the determiner, so we can generate a string which contains all of these elements and know the order in which they would occur if spoken:

initiator—determiner—ordinal—quantifier—adjective—noun—noun
Only   the   first   two   little   boy   scouts

This phrase can be expanded further by including more adjectives:

Only the first two tired cold dirty hungry little boy scouts

Most adjectives seem to have a "right" place in a sequence; we say "big old house" and not "old big house." The usual sequence seems to be

characterizing adjective (size—age—color—composition) noun
e.g., Lovely big old red brick house

The ordering of prenominal adjectives has been described by Vendler (1968) and Martin (1968) as dependent on the "nounlike" qualities of the adjective, with the most nounlike adjective being closest to the noun in the phrase. Thus a composition adjective like *brick,* which can easily occur as a noun as well as an adjective, must come closer to the noun than a color adjective, which in turn is seen as more nounlike than size. For example, *red* can function as a noun in "Red is my favorite color" or "Give me some red" more readily than can *old* or *small* ("Old is my favorite age"; "Give me some small").

POST-NOUN MODIFIERS Nouns can also be modified by *prepositional phrases* that follow them and specify or describe the entity named by the noun; in this case the noun phrase contains two nouns. The relationship between adjectivals and post-noun prepositional phrases can be seen in the following examples:

The man *in the middle*   The middle man
The girl *with the blond hair*   The blond girl
A field *of corn*   The corn field

Finally, nouns can be modified by *relative clauses* that specify something about the entity they name. They are used either to help the listener identify the entity by conveying information that is presumed to be known, or to introduce new information. Additional information can be conveyed by the relative clause beyond that given with an adjective or prepositional phrase because it always contains a verb.

The man *who is standing in the middle*
The girl *who now has blond hair*
The field *where the corn is ripe*

MacWhinney (1984) distinguishes between *restricted relative clauses,* which convey what is presumed to be known information, and *nonrestricted relative clauses,* which introduce new information to fill the listener in on background for the main clause. For example, if a speaker says "The boy who is holding the bat is my cousin," the presumption is that the listener knows that a boy is holding a bat. On the other hand, "The boy, who is very good at baseball, will play with us," presumes the listener does not know about the boy's ability.

Verb Phrases The verb phrase of a sentence may be as simple as a single word (he *ran*) or may become extremely complex as the number of ideas and their refinement increases.

You *could have been the one chosen to give the speech.*

Analysis of the verb phrase involves the auxiliary system with main verbs and the relationship between the verb and the elements that follow it. Although we have introduced individual auxiliary verbs earlier, we will now look at how the auxiliary system works as a whole.

AUXILIARY SYSTEM The main verb of a clause may involve more than one auxiliary verb to convey increasingly subtle shades of meaning. These forms always involve a *have* or *be* auxiliary, or both, along with a modal auxiliary. The English auxiliary verb system has been described by Chomsky (1957) as

$$C + (M) + (have + en) + (be + ing) + verb$$

This specifies the order in which various auxiliaries can occur, with *M* representing modal verbs, *have + en* indicating the perfect form, and *be + ing* indicating the progressive form. The *C* indicates tense and number, which is expressed by the first occurring verb. The items in parentheses do not all have to be included before the main verb, but those present must occur in this order. To illustrate, consider the following sentences in which *C* represents present tense and singular number:

He runs	C + verb —no auxiliary verb —tense and number indicated by main verb
He is running	$C + be + ing$ + verb —tense and number indicated by *be* auxiliary —*ing* attached to next verb (*run*)
He has been running	$C + have + en + be + ing$ + verb —tense and number indicated by *have* auxiliary —*en* attached to next verb (*be*)
He may have been running	$C + M + have + en + be + ing$ + verb —tense and number indicated by modal

Clause Structure

The basic structure of a clause is a subject and a predicate. Subjects generally indicate the topic of the utterance, and predicates, which are always verb phrases, make some comment about the subject. The nature of the comment will determine the type of verb phrase used. Clauses are identified and classified by the verb; for every verb phrase in an utterance, there is a separate clause.

Clause Subjects Subjects may be simple nouns, noun phrases, names, pronouns, gerunds, and occasionally infinitives. Together they are referred to as *nominals*. Adverbs and adjectives can also be subjects with copulas. Subjects generally are the first element in the clause and precede the main verb.

Children play outside.	NOUN
The kids are all going.	NOUN PHRASE
That stinks.	PRONOUN
James went home.	NAME
Swimming is good exercise.	GERUND
Here is the one.	ADVERB
Blue is my favorite color.	ADJECTIVE
To finish is my goal.	INFINITIVE

Subjects can be identified by asking *to whom* or *to what* the verb refers:

The mayor of New York is speaking to the press.

WHO?

The mayor of New York

Subjects may be obvious from the context, so they are sometimes not included in the clause. We discuss clauses with implied subjects as *imperatives* later in the chapter. This include utterances such as "Look out" and "Hand me the salt."

Clause Predicates   We distinguish between clauses formed with copulas and those with lexical verbs because these two types of clauses convey different kinds of information, and we want to look at them separately. Clauses with copulas indicate characteristics about the subject, whereas lexical verb clauses focus on the subject's mental or physical activity. The distinction between these verb types was covered in Chapter 5, and we will review them only briefly here.

CLAUSES WITH COPULAS   Clauses with copulas have complements in their predicates following the verb. Copulas are forms of *be* (*be, been, am, are, is, was, were*) or other "linking" verbs that can be replaced by a *be* form (e.g., *feel, appear, taste*). These verbs create an identity between the subject and complement, which indicates some characteristic of the subject, such as its location, description, or identity. Complements may be be nominals and in addition, can be adjectives, adverbs, prepositional phrases, participles, or infinitives.

I'll be *the mother.*	NOUN PHRASE
He is *it.*	PRONOUN
I am *happy.*	ADJECTIVE
She is *here.*	ADVERB
He was *on time.*	PREPOSITIONAL PHRASE
She seems *interesting.*	PARTICIPLE
She was *to run.*	INFINITIVE

CLAUSES WITH LEXICAL VERBS   *Lexical verbs* add content to the sentence; they specify the action or state of subjects rather than referring to a characteristic of the subject. They cannot be omitted and still be implied, as copulas can, because each lexical verb conveys unique information. Lexical verbs can be divided into two types, depending on whether or not the verb is followed by an object. Verbs without objects, or *intransitive* verbs, express actions or states that do not need an object to be carried out.

Peggy *fell.*	INTRANSITIVE LEXICAL VERB
He *is sleeping.*	INTRANSITIVE LEXICAL VERB

Transitive verbs, on the other hand, express an action or a state that does need an object, person, or idea to be completed. These elements that complete the action of the verb are called *direct objects.*

Janet *broke* SOMETHING.	TRANSITIVE LEXICAL VERB
Harry *likes* SOMETHING.	TRANSITIVE LEXICAL VERB
The girl *saw* SOMETHING.	TRANSITIVE LEXICAL VERB

DIRECT OBJECTS   Direct objects are expressed with the same class of nominals as are subjects. They state the object, person, or activity needed to complete the action of the verb, and thus fill in the SOMETHING space in the last set of examples. They answer the question, "What does or did the SUBJECT VERB?"

What did Janet break?
Janet broke *her leg*.   NOUN PHRASE
Janet broke *it*.   PRONOUN

What does Harry like?
Harry likes *painting*.   GERUND
Harry likes *to eat*.   INFINITIVE

What did the girl see?
The girl saw *Casey*.   NAME
The girl saw *dandelions*.   NOUN

OBJECT COMPLEMENTS   A complement can follow an object (or another complement) when it indicates a characteristic of the direct object rather than the subject. It is as though there were a copula conjoining the object and its complement, and it implies a second underlying clause. Object complements may be nominals, adjectives, or participles.

I'd call him *a hero*.   NOUN COMPLEMENT
You get your fingers *dirty*.   ADJECTIVE COMPLEMENT
We made her *it*.   PRONOUN COMPLEMENT
She told Ed *to go home*.   INFINITIVE COMPLEMENT
There's a cat *sitting there*.   PARTICIPLE COMPLEMENT
I found the door *broken*.   PARTICIPLE COMPLEMENT

INDIRECT OBJECTS   Clauses may also contain elements that add other kinds of information. A subclass of transitive verbs can be used with elements which answer the question, "To or for whom is the action done?" This question will be answered with a name, noun, noun phrase, or pronoun, which is called the *indirect object*.

May gave *the dog* a bath.
He showed *her* the book.
She promised *him* to go home.

Since the indirect object is the recipient of the action, it must be a person, animal, or object that is referred to as though it were animate.

I gave *my plants* a drink.

The difference between the direct object and the indirect object in the above sentences can easily be seen by asking

What did May give?	A bath	DIRECT OBJECT
To or for whom?	The dog	INDIRECT OBJECT
What did he show?	The book	DIRECT OBJECT
To or for whom?	Her	INDIRECT OBJECT
What did she promise?	To go home	DIRECT OBJECT
To or for whom?	Him	INDIRECT OBJECT
What did I give?	A drink	DIRECT OBJECT
To or for whom?	My plants	INDIRECT OBJECT

Indirect objects may also look similar to object complements, but they should be distinguished since the complement type probably involves more complex syntactic rules and can be used as an indicator of more language competence.

Complements	*Indirect Objects*
I'd call him a *hero.*	I'd call *him* a taxi.
(He is a hero.)	(I'd call a taxi for him.)
She told me *to go home.*	She promised *me* to go home.
(I should go home.)	(For me, she promised she would go home.)

ADVERBIALS Clauses with either copulas or lexical verbs can also contain elements that answer the questions "Where?" "When," "How" "How many?" and "Why?" If these elements are single words, they will be *adverbs.*

Jeanne walks *home.*	WHERE
Jeanne walked *yesterday.*	WHEN
Jeanne walks *quickly.*	HOW
Jeanne walked *twice.*	HOW MANY

Prepositional phrases also serve to provide the same kinds of information.

Jeanne walks *to the bus.*	WHERE
Jeanne walks *with a cane.*	HOW
Jeanne walks *in the morning.*	WHEN
Jeanne walks *for her health.*	WHY

Both the simple adverbs and the prepositional phrases used in this way are called *adverbials.* A clause can have more than one adverbial.

Beth walks *quickly to the bus stop every day.*
Twice he hit the ball *over the fence yesterday.*

CONJUNCTIONS One last element that appears in clauses is the conjunction. The *coordinate conjunctions* may join single nominals, adjectives, or adverbials within the clause subject or verb phrase, creating compound structures. Coordinate conjunctions can also join independent clauses together forming a compound sentence.

Anita *and* Philip were elected.	NOMINALS
They were cold *and* hungry.	ADJECTIVES
She walked faster *and* faster.	ADVERBS

Subordinate conjunctions begin the clause and serve to connect it semantically to another clause. Unlike coordinate conjunctions, they cannot join subjects or objects within a clause.

Since you asked, I'll tell you.	SUBORDINATE
I'm going *because* it's late.	

Clauses with Displaced Elements The elements in basic simple clauses may at times be reordered for emphasis or direction of focus. The most common instance of this is the preposed adverb, most typically *here* and *there* at the beginning of the clause:

>*Here* it is.
>*There* he goes.

Sometimes clause objects are preposed before the subject, as in

>*Not now* I said.
>*A noise* I heard from that bird.
>*It was very wiggly* you know.

Appositives also present alteration of the clause structure by presenting two adjacent terms that refer to the same referent. Most typically, an appositive noun or noun phrase explains or describes the preceding noun.

>My sister, *June,* can't go.
>We got a new car, *a station wagon.*

In some dialects, it is acceptable to include an appositive pronoun which restates the subject:

>My sister, *she* can't go.

Box 6-1 summarizes the simple clauses described in this section.

BOX 6–1. *Summary of Simple Clauses*

```
  I. Subject + Copula + Complement
                       (nominal)
                       (adjective)
                       (adverbial)
     Subject + Copula + Complement + Complement
 II. Subject + Intransitive verb
III. Subject + Transitive verb + Object
                                 (nominal)
     Subject + Transitive verb + Object + Indirect object
                                          (noun)
                                          (pronoun)
     Subject + Transitive verb + Object + Complement
                                          (nominal)
                                          (adjective)
                                          (adverbial)
```

Any of these clauses may also be introduced by conjunctions and may have adverbial modifiers that indicate background information about the action or state, such as the time, place, or manner of execution. They may also have reordered elements or appositives.

Multiple-Clause Sentences

We can now identify the organizational structures of multiple-clause sentences. These utterances are used when a speaker wants to relate more than one event or state of affairs. We are guided in our identification of component clauses by locating verbs; for every verb there is a clause. We will identify several ways that clauses can be combined in one sentence, each of which serves a different function and has a different structure.

Compound Clauses *Compound clauses* are two or more simple clauses of any type joined together by a coordinate conjunction (*and, or, but*). Compound clauses often are structurally complete by themselves and could be stated as separate sentences.

> We could go to the movie *or* we could go home.
> I'd like to go *but* I can't.
> I went to the store *and* I spent all my money.

Some compound clauses are complete without a conjunction.

> These aren't shoes; they're clogs.

When the subject of both clauses is the same, it can be pronominalized or deleted in some cases. These are still considered compound clauses.

> Jack fell down and (he) skinned his knee.

As shown earlier, coordinate conjunctions also can join single nominals, adjectives, or adverbials within the clause subject or predicate, creating compound structures that we are not treating as a compound clause. In transformational grammars, these are seen as separate clauses with deleted elements, and in fact they do convey the same information as two clauses.

> Anita and Philip were elected.
> Anita was elected, and Philip was elected.

We are arbitrarily choosing to exclude these as compound clauses in order to be consistent with our protocol for analysis that specifies that the number of clauses in a sentence is determined by the number of verbs.

Subordinate Predicate Clauses Predicates can have more than one verb, in which case one verb will be associated with the main clause and the other with a subordinate clause. These subordinate clauses cannot stand apart from the main clause because they are a part of the structure of the main clause, as can be seen by parallels with single words.

I like *chocolate*.	SIMPLE OBJECT
I like *how you did that*.	OBJECT CLAUSE
That is *mine*.	SIMPLE COMPLEMENT
That is *for me to know*.	COMPLEMENT CLAUSE

The subordinate clause may be a complete simple clause that is the direct object of the verb in the first clause. These *object clauses* follow transitive verbs referring to states of thought such as *know, think, remember, wish. That* may be present as a connective following the cognitive verbs.

I hope (that) you are ready.
I knew (that) you were done.
I just remembered (that) you were coming.

These subordinate clauses may also convey incomplete or implied content and use a question word in its place. These *embedded questions* also can be objects of cognitive verbs or can be complements following copulas. In their full form, they are complete simple clauses following the interrogative connective.

I know *what she did.*
I wonder *who she called.*
That is *why I want to go.*

A different set of transitive verbs take indirect objects. These verbs can likewise take full object clauses or embedded questions.

He told *Mary*   (INDIRECT OBJECT)   *that Jane should go.*   (DIRECT OBJECT)
He told *Mary*   (INDIRECT OBJECT)   *why Jane should go.*   (DIRECT OBJECT)

The embedded questions can sometimes be reduced by eliminating the redundant subject and reducing the full verb to an infinitive.

I know *what I should do.*
I know *what to do.*
I told Mary *what she should do.*
I told Mary *what to do.*

We distinguish these from embedded questions that are complete clauses by referring to them as *reduced embedded questions.*
Some sentences have infinitives in the predicate clause without the question word. They may either be plain infinitives or *to* infinitives. We call these *infinitive clauses.* These generally are clauses with indirect objects, and in some cases the indirect object is expressed with *for.* The three forms of infinitive clauses are shown here.

I want *you to be there.*   *to* INFINITIVE
I need *you to go for me.*

I made *the car run.*   PLAIN INFINITIVE
I'll help *you do it.*

It is *for you to sit on.*   *for* + INFINITIVE
I would like *for you to be there.*

Typically when sentences have infinitives in the predicate clause, these infinitives have as their subject the noun immediately preceding them. The strategy involved in finding the subject for the infinitive has been called the *minimal distance principle* (Chomsky, 1969; Rosenbaum, 1967).

The minimal distance principle can be overgeneralized and applied in cases in which it is inappropriate because of the semantics of the main verb. The verbs *promise* and *ask* sometimes require the listener to suspend the minimal distance principle, and instead assign the subject of the main clause as the subject of the infinite clause (Rosenbaum, 1967). In the following two examples, this is the case, whereas in the third, the rule applies.

I promised Mary to do it.	*I* is subject of *to do*.
I asked Mary what to do.	*I* is subject of *to do*.
I asked Mary to do it.	*Mary* is subject of *to do*.

Subordinate Adverbial Clauses *Adverbial clauses* are also subordinate clauses; however, like simple adverbs, they are related semantically rather than structurally to the main clause. Rather than providing new information about a characteristic of the subject, as with a complement clause, or identifying the object of the verb, as with the object clause, they provide background information such as the time, place, or motivation for the action or state in the main clause. Adverbial clauses are complete simple clauses that begin with a subordinate conjunction.

She drank it *quickly*.	SIMPLE ADVERB
She drank it *like it was water*.	ADVERBIAL CLAUSE
Yesterday, I tried some.	SIMPLE ADVERB
After I washed them, I tried some.	ADVERBIAL CLAUSE

Subordinate Subject Clauses *Subject clauses* occur less commonly than do object or adverbial clauses. In these, subordinate clauses serve as the subject of the main clause.

It is obvious.	SIMPLE SUBJECT
That she is happy is obvious.	SUBJECT CLAUSE
A car is necessary.	SIMPLE SUBJECT
For me to have a car is necessary.	SUBJECT INFINITIVE CLAUSE

Relative Clauses *Relative clauses* were discussed in relationship to noun phrases because they serve to specify some information about an element named by a noun or pronoun. The nominal modified may be the subject, object, or complement of the main clause. Zubin (1979) finds that objects are most frequently modified by relative clauses, and hypothesizes that this is due to subjects generally referring to the topic that is already established. Objects, on the other hand, tend to present new information and are more likely to be elaborated. Relative clauses are generally introduced with relative pronouns (*that, who, which*). As with simple adjectives in a noun phrase, these clauses can be removed from a sentence without leaving it grammatically incomplete. They generally answer the question "Which one?"

The book *that I like* is gone.	WHICH BOOK? *that I like*
The book is gone.	

The book *I like* is gone.	WHICH BOOK?	(that) *I like*
The book is gone.		
That is the man *who fixed my bike.*	WHICH MAN?	*who fixed my bike*
That is the man.		

Compound, subordinate, and relative clauses may be combined in one utterance for a variety of multiple clause structures.

I went home *and* got the one *that I needed.*	COMPOUND WITH RELATIVE
I think I know *what you mean.*	EMBEDDED QUESTION WITHIN OBJECTIVE CLAUSE

See Box 6-2 for a listing of the types of multiple clauses described above.

Sentence Types

It is possible to use the clause, phrase, and sentence structures discussed so far for a variety of purposes other than to make the affirmative statements shown in the examples. To do so, however, involves different syntactic rules. We now turn to the formulation of the sentence types that are used to ask questions, negate assumptions, and give commands. These sentences are not the only way to express these intentions, so we distinguish between syntactic forms, which we identify as questions, negations, and imperatives; and intentions that may be expressed by these or other forms, such as requesting information, indicating disapproval, or directing others' behavior. In this section, we will discuss only the syntactic forms.

Questions   There are two types of questions that can be asked—those that call for a yes or no answer and those that require further content information. The latter are called *wh-* questions because they include a specific question word, most of which begin with *wh-* (*who, what, where, when, why, how*).

Yes–no questions can be asked in four ways, as follows:

1. *Intonation:* Rising intonation on the end of a word, phrase, or sentence conveys a questioning attitude:

   That's your dog?
   Milk?

2. *Inversion:* Beginning a sentence with an auxiliary verb or copula verb instead of the subject produces a yes–no question. This is referred to as inversion because the presumed underlying structure is a subject-verb-object statement that is transformed into a question by inverting the subject and verb. Notice that only the first auxiliary verb precedes the subject:

   Can I do it?
   Should I have been there?

3. *"Do" Insertion:* As mentioned in Chapter 5, the *dummy do* acts as an auxiliary but adds no meaning to the verb. It is used before the subject to ask yes–no questions where no other auxiliary verb is used. The *do* form used reflects the tense of the sentence:

   Do you want to go?
   Did you go?

BOX 6–2. *Summary of Multiple-Clause Sentences*

I. Complex verb phrases
   A. Object clauses
      I hope *that you are ready to go.*
      She told me *Amy was coming.*
   B. Embedded questions
      I wonder *who she called.*
      That is *what I want.*
   C. Reduced embedded questions
      I wonder *who to call.*
      She asked me *what to wear.*
   D. Infinitive clauses
      I want *you to be there.*
      It is *for you to sit on.*

II. Adverbial clauses
   A. Introductory adverbial clauses
      Since I can't go, Jo will bring the equipment.
      In order for you to win, you have to work harder.
   B. Noninitial adverbial clauses
      Jo will bring the equipment *since I can't go.*
      You will have to work harder *in order for you to win.*

III. Subject clauses
   A. *That* clauses
      That she is happy is obvious.
      That he is sick defies denial.
   B. Embedded questions
      Why she left is the real question.
      What the book said is beside the point.
   C. Infinitive clauses
      For me to be there would be a pleasure.
      To go slowly is safer.

IV. Relative clauses
   A. Subject modifiers
      The dog *that followed me home* is a setter.
      James *who has the new bike* gave me a ride.
   B. Object/complement modifiers
      I held the fish *that she caught.*
      That is the one *I like best.*

V. Compound clauses
   A. Complete clauses
      Harry called and then Jack showed up.
      I tried but I couldn't remember her name.
   B. Forward deletion and pronominalization clauses
      I tried but couldn't do it.
      Harry called and then he showed up.

4. *Tag Questions:* Tag questions involve making a statement that is presumed to be true and then requesting verification. The earliest forms of this, which might be called pretags, are the addition of "right?" "huh?" or "okay?" after a statement. True tags involve an auxiliary verb which is either negative or nonnegative to contrast with the main clause verb:

You will go, won't you?
You can't go, can you?
You saw it, didn't you? (dummy do)

Wh- questions involve a question word that specifies the kind of information being requested, such as location (*where*), time (*when*), and so on. These words usually are at the beginning of the sentence, but when we are asking for clarification or repetition of something previously said, they may occur in the position of the missing information. These are called *occasional questions* (Brown, 1968) and involve emphasis on the question word:

John will read *what?*
John will read *when?*

Some *wh-* questions occur along with a form of yes–no questions. These are one kind of embedded question (Brown, 1973):

Know where my games are?

Negatives   The basis of all syntactic negation is rejecting or denying an assumed or explicit affirmative statement. When we say "I'm not hungry," we are responding either to someone's suggestion that we are hungry, or to an assumption that we generally are hungry at this time of day. Volterra and Antinucci (1979) distinguish four types of negation, each with a different underlying assumption.

In type A, the speaker presupposes the listener is doing or about to do something that the speaker does not want the listener to do.

Don't drop it.

In type B, the speaker presupposes that the listener believes something that the speaker does not want the listener to believe.

It's not broken.

In type C, the speaker presupposes the listener wants the speaker to do something that the speaker does not want to do.

I don't want to go.

In type D, the speaker presupposes the listener wants confirmation or disconfirmation of a statement.

Q: Did you eat yet?
Speaker: No, I didn't.

In this last example, we see both a syntactic negative ("I didn't") and a nonsyntactic negative ("No"). The presence of a syntactic negative in a sentence does not in itself indicate which element of the statement is being negated.

> The man is not giving the award to the boy.

This sentence can be interpreted in a variety of ways, depending on which element we perceive as negated.

> Not the man, the woman
> Not giving it, selling it
> Not the award, the package
> Not to the boy, to the girl

Unless the meaning is clear from context, we generally stress the word to which the negative applies. Read the above sentences with stress on different words to see how the meaning seems to change. If the negative is stressed, the implication is that our presumption that the man is giving the award to the boy is false; but no other information is implied.

We have not mentioned the use of *no* as a single word utterance, generally in response to a question ("Do you want this?" "No"). These responses are of interest pragmatically because they demonstrate discourse cohesiveness and proposition sharing between the interactants, but they reveal nothing about the speaker's syntactic system. They are *nonsyntactic negatives* and are not included in an analysis of negation. Likewise, we exclude from our syntax analysis words that semantically convey negation, such as *none, nothing,* or *empty.* Syntactic negation includes *no* and *not,* and the contracted forms such as *can't* or *doesn't* when they are used to negate affirmative propositions.

MULTIPLE NEGATION   In standard English, the presence of more than one syntactic or semantic negative within a clause is not considered grammatical, and when two negatives occur across clauses, the sentence is considered to convey a positive rather than negative meaning ("There isn't much you can't do," meaning there is much you can do). The pattern of multiple negation is acceptable in many dialects, and it takes various forms. The following are common: (1) marking the negative in both the verb phrase and the indefinite forms that follow or precede the verb ("I can't do nothing for nobody"; "Nobody can't understand it"); (2) inversion of the negative auxiliary and negative subject pronoun ("Can't nobody find it"); and (3) multiple negatives across different clauses, which conveys an opposite meaning than that in standard English ("There isn't much you can't do," meaning there isn't much you can do).

Imperatives   There are a variety of ways that one person can verbally direct the behavior of someone else. The most direct way to do so is to use an imperative, such as "Sit down" or "Come here." Imperatives usually do not have expressed subjects, but because they are always directed to one or more specific people, "you" is the implied subject. These directives always have verbs that connote voluntary activities; other verbs cannot be used in imperatives as shown in these starred examples:

Get it for me.   *Want it for me.
Learn this.   *Think this.
Look at that.   *See that.

Imperatives should be distinguished from clauses that are incomplete because they have omitted subjects. The child who looks at his or her interactive partner and says "Wind up the car" as a request is using a complete correct clause structure. On the other hand, if a child points to someone who is winding up the car and means this as a comment rather than as a request, the obligatory subject identifying that person is missing, and the clause structure is incomplete.

SYNTACTIC DEVELOPMENT

Most of the research in child language from the mid-1960s through the early 1970s was directed to studying syntactic development of young children, and this continues to be an active research area. Thus there has been a vast amount of data collected and reported, and much is known about the patterns children display, at least up until about age five, which was the upper limit of many studies. There are still many unknowns, however, and several controversies exist about the nature of what children learn and how best to represent children's linguistic knowledge. In this section we summarize some of the observations that have been made about the development of children's understanding and production of syntax, with the goal of providing guidance in assessing children's regularities within the syntactic systems.

Stages of Syntactic Development

Many researchers have described syntactic development in terms of stages. The best known of these schemes is that of Roger Brown (1973). Brown's stages grew out of his observation that chronological age is not a good predictor of language development; he found that his three normally developing subjects, Adam, Eve, and Sarah, varied widely on the age at which they acquired specific linguistic features and in their general rate of language acquisition. In order to describe and compare the three children's language at the same level of language proficiency, he needed a measure other than age on which to match them. He found the average length of their utterances when measured in morphemes provided a satisfactory index for comparison between children and also a sensitive measure of a child's language development over time. Brown's guidelines for computing Mean Length of Utterance (MLU) are followed by most clinicians and researchers who use this measure. Rules for counting morphemes based on Brown's conventions are described in Box 6–3.

MLU has been widely used to describe the early stages of standard American English syntax development. It has also been applied to Spanish (Linares, 1983), British English (Wells, 1985), and Hebrew (Dromi and Berman, 1982). This measure has been found to correlate highly with a number of grammatical features including productive mastery of grammatical inflections (Brown, 1973; deVilliers and deVilliers, 1973), expression of semantic relations

---

BOX 6–3. *Computing Mean Length Utterance*

Exclude from Your Count

1. *Imitations* which immediately follow the model utterance and which give the impression that the child would not have said the utterance spontaneously.

2. *Elliptical answers* to questions which give the impression that the utterance would have been more complete if there had been no eliciting question (e.g., "Do you want this?" "Yes." "What do you have?" "My dolls").

3. *Partial utterances* which are interrupted by outside events or shifts in the child's focus (e.g., "That's my—oops").

4. *Unintelligible utterances* or utterances that contain unintelligible segments. If a major portion of a child's sample is unintelligible, a syllable count by utterance can be substituted for morpheme count.

5. *Rote passages* such as nursery rhymes, songs, or prose passages which have been memorized and which may not be fully processed linguistically by the child.

6. *False starts* and reformulations within utterances which may either be self-repetitions or changes in the original formulation (e.g., "I have one [just like] almost like that"; "[We] we can't").

7. *Noises* unless they are integrated into meaningful verbal material such as "He went xx"

8. Discourse markers such as *um, oh, you know*, not integrated into the meaning of the utterance (e.g., "(Well) it was (you know) (like) a party or something").

9. *Identical utterances* that the child says anywhere in the sample. Only one occurrence of each utterance is counted. If there is even a minor change, however, the second utterance is also counted.

10. Counting or other sequences of enumeration (e.g., "blue, green, yellow, red, purple").

11. Single word or phrase social responses such as "hi," "thank you," "here," "know what?"

Count as One Morpheme

1. Uninflected lexical morphemes (e.g., *run, fall*) and grammatical morphemes that are whole words (articles, auxiliary verbs, prepositions).

2. Contractions when individual segments do not occur elsewhere in the sample apart from the contraction. If either of the constituent parts of the contraction are found elsewhere, the contraction is counted as two rather than one morpheme (e.g., *I'll, it's, can't*).

3. Catenatives such as *wanna, gonna, hafta* and the infinitive modals that have the same meanings (e.g., *going to* go). This eliminates the problem of judging a morpheme count on the basis of child's pronunciation. Thus *am gonna* is counted as two morphemes.

4. Phrases, compound words, diminutives, reduplicated words which occur as inseparable linguistic units for the child or represent single items (e.g., *oh boy; all right; once upon a time; a lot of; let's; big wheel, horsie*).

5. Irregular past tense. The convention is to count these as single morphemes because children's first meanings for them seem to be distinct from the present tense counterpart (e.g., *did, was*).

6. Plurals which do not occur in singular form (e.g., *pants; clothes*), including plural pronouns (*us; them*).

7. Gerunds and participles that are not part of the verb phrase (*Swimming* is fun"; "He was *tired*"; "That is the *cooking* place").

continued

BOX 6–3. (continued)

Count as More Than One Morpheme

1. Inflected forms: regular and irregular plural nouns; possessive nouns; third person singular verb; present participle and past participle when part of the verb phrase; regular past tense verb; reflexive pronoun; comparative and superlative adverbs and adjectives.
2. Contractions when one or both of the individual segments occur separately anywhere in the child's sample (e.g., *it's* if *it* or *is* occurs elsewhere).

Computing MLU

1. Count the number of morphemes in each utterance.
2. Add total number of morphemes.
3. Divide the total number of morphemes by the total number of utterances. Use at least fifty utterances in determining MLU.

(Bloom, Lightbown, and Hood, 1975), number and diversity of grammatical categories such as verbs and articles (Newport and others, 1977; Shipley and others, 1969), interrogative and negative structures (Klima and Bellugi, 1966), and pragmatic and conversational abilities (Gerrard, 1990–1991).

The reliability and validity of MLU as a measure of syntax development have come under question (e.g., Klee and Fitzgerald, 1985; Crystal, 1979; Kramer, James, and Saxman, 1979), particularly when used with individuals at the higher MLU levels. Brown (1973) cautioned against using MLU as a measure of development beyond MLU 5.0. Subsequent validation studies using different measures of complexity (Rondal and others, 1987; Scarborough and others, 1991) demonstrate persuasively that MLU is a valid index of development until MLU of approximately 3.0 is reached. The association between length and grammatical complexity is weaker beyond that point. Scarborough and colleagues found this diminution of validity to be particularly notable with populations displaying delayed or atypical language development. They found that MLU above 3.0 overestimated the grammatical complexity of individuals with delayed language, Down syndrome, Fragile X syndrome, and autism, even more than for normal preschoolers. In light of these findings, we recommend that other measures of grammatical complexity be used beyond MLU 3.0.

Points on the MLU distribution at which the children were compared were taken to be indicators of stages, each named to characterize a facet of language learning that was new or exceptionally elaborate at that stage. Brown does not imply that stages are discrete, but rather that development is continuous, and his stages are arbitrary divisions to allow for comparison and characterization at different levels of language proficiency. Brown's stages are designated with Roman numerals, as follows:

Stage I	Semantic roles and syntactic relations	MLU 1.0–2.0
Stage II	Grammatical morphemes and modulation of meaning	MLU 2.0–2.5
Stage III	Modalities of simple sentences	MLU 2.5–3.25

Stage IV   Embedding   MLU 3.25–3.75
Stage V   Coordination   MLU 3.75–4.25

Brown found the stage in which the three children mastered each of the early grammatical morphemes and noted both the regularities and variations in order of appearance. Although Brown does not present his data as discrete or prescriptive stages, they have frequently been used in this manner by researchers and clinicians who use MLU to determine therapy goals.

Despite the findings by Brown and others that indicate a limited relationship between chronological age and MLU for normally developing children, there have been attempts to compare MLU to age as a measure of normalcy of language development. Miller and Chapman (1981), for example, found the average age at which their subjects displayed MLUs of 1.01 to 6.00; they also predict MLU from age (eighteen to sixty months).

Scarborough (1990) correlated age and MLU for a longitudinal sample of fifteen subjects between twenty-four and forty-eight months. His findings are similar to Miller and Chapman's cross-sectional data for children through forty-two months but diverge for children at forty-eight months, where he found MLUs to be lower than did Miller and Chapman. Miller (1981) presents the cross-sectional data with the warning that caution must be used in interpreting the relationship between MLU and age based on their norms since their relatively small sample was exclusively drawn from middle-class children who were engaged in conversation with their mothers. This caution seems to be well justified. The assumption that performance is deviant if it falls outside of the range of one standard deviation is questionable, as will be discussed further in Chapter 9. Also, as these investigators suggest with their guidelines for collecting samples, MLU is highly sensitive to event and exchange pattern differences. Samples gathered under different conditions should not be expected to be the same. MLU might better be seen as one tool for comparing the child's performance in different situations rather than as a stable characteristic of the child's language system.

Other authors have presented stages that are built on criteria other than MLU, with the stages being used to set goals for therapy. Crystal, Fletcher, and Garman (1976), in the LARSP procedure, use chronological age to identify seven stages. Stage I goes from nine months to eighteen months; the remaining stages are in six-month intervals, with stage VII having no specified upper limit (four and one-half years and older). Lee and Canter (1971), in DSS, describe eight stages that are based on specific forms identified in language samples of normally developing children. Eight stages of development are described for each of the following morphological and syntactic systems: indefinite pronouns, personal pronouns, verbs, secondary verbs (i.e., infinitives, gerunds, and participles), negatives, yes–no questions, *wh-* questions, and conjunctions. The various forms within a system that occur at a given stage are thought to correspond in normal development with forms in other systems at that stage (e.g., stage III negatives and stage III verbs). Miller (1981), in the ASS procedure, combines features of these approaches as he assigns stages based on MLU, age, and presence of specific forms. His stages correspond to Brown's stages.

We do not attempt to establish stages of syntactic development, as these and other authors have done, because it seems to lead to the erroneous assumption that language acquisition does in fact progress in stages and that children can be assigned to stages of development. There is little evidence that we can accurately predict for a given child the forms that will have been acquired in one system from knowing the forms acquired in another system. For example, knowing which question forms the child uses is not a particularly good predictor of his or her use of pronouns, at least not reliably enough for us to want to plan our therapy around this relationship.

There is another approach to stages that has been taken by researchers who attempt to identify natural stages children go through in the acquisition of a particular form or construct. Klima and Bellugi (1966), for example, found children had distinctive stages in their acquisition of questions. These stages may be identified as typically occurring at particular ages or MLU levels, but the boundaries of the stages are identified by observed changes in children's behavior rather than by arbitrary cutoff points (such as age or MLU). These stages are perceived as arising from different rules or mental constructs on the part of the child, with early rules giving way to later rules as the child moves to a new stage. Klima and Bellugi are not seeing development as simply adding new forms, as in the Lee and Canter stages.

We have taken this latter approach to stages of development. Thus, we have not tried to summarize all of the syntactic systems according to MLU or age, since the variability across children and across different conditions is too great to have confidence in generalizations. We do, however, report stages for specific structures when they are provided by the researchers of the studies to which we refer. Further, we will identify some general progression in the sequence of syntactic development.

Sequence of Syntactic Development

One-Word Syntax?   It has been argued that syntax begins at the one-word stage, with the word acting like a whole sentence. The term *holophrase* is often applied to convey this idea of single words that express ideas adults would say in a sentence. McNeill (1970) argues that children have something like a sentence in mind but use single words at the onset of speech because they are limited by memory and attention. Ingram (1971) feels that the limitation is lack of linguistic knowledge to translate the relatively complete ideas into sentences, so only single words are expressed. Bloom (1973) and Dore (1975) among others have argued against a holophrastic notion, pointing to the lack of evidence that children at this stage have any grammatical awareness. Interpreting children's utterances to mean the same as adult utterances and thus attributing adultlike meaning and categories to children has been called "rich" interpretation. Giving rich interpretation to single-word utterances to derive syntactic categories seems to lead us away from looking at the child's meaning for those words. Thus, at the beginnings of speech, when a child is producing mostly single-word utterances, we feel it is more appropriate to analyze these utterances pragmatically and semantically, and not syntactically.

Transition to Syntax   Toward the end of the single-word period some changes occur that appear to be indications that the child is moving toward word combinations. This might first be signaled by the child using the same word with different intonation patterns or accompanying gestures to express different intentions. This would indicate that the referent for the word is separate from the sought-after consequences of the utterance for the child. For example, the child may use "cup" both as a request for a cup and for an expression that the cup is not in its usual place, using different intonation and/or accompanying gestures with each expression. Leopold (1939) and Halliday (1975) among others report observations such as this during the first half of the second year. This separation of the referent (cup) from intention (request for cup; request for information about cup) seems to be a fundamental step to the use of syntax in expressions such as "want cup" or "where cup?"

Another indication of the transition to syntax is that multiple single words are thematically related. Prior to this, each single word typically refers to a different event. Bloom (1973) reports that near the end of her subject Allison's seventeenth month she began using successive single words that related to the same event. At first, the order of the words reflected the order of actions in the event, with as many as six separate single words referring to a sequence of actions. A short time later, the successive words referred to the entire event rather than to discrete parts or steps. Bloom describes these as holistic successive utterances. Scollon (1974) found a similar progression of single words referring first to unrelated events and then to the same event. He also presents evidence of a psychological difference for children when he finds that the phonetic representation of words in holistic successive utterances are often regressions of less mature forms as compared to the same words when unrelated to successive words. For example, he noted that a child omitted the final consonants from *tape* and *step* when they referred to her threat to step on the tape recorder but on the same day correctly included the final sounds when the words were said as isolated utterances. This would argue that the holistic successive utterances involve more effort on the part of the child, diverting concentration from another part of the system.

Two-Word Combinations Shortly after holistic successive utterances are observed, first true word combinations are common (Bloom, 1973; Leopold, 1949). The primary difference is intonation—that is, while successive single words each have separate intonation contours and sound separate even though spoken close together, word combinations are said together in a single intonation contour. While early combinations may have level stress on each word (Leopold, 1949), these combinations typically involve stress and pitch difference between the component words. Children are generally described as beginning to combine words around age eighteen months to twenty months, or when they have acquired a single-word vocabulary of about fifty words. There have been various characterizations of children's two-word combinations, each demonstrating that children display predictable regularities and not random combinations of words from their single-word vocabulary.

An early characterization of children's presentence utterances was to describe them as *telegraphic*. Brown and Bellugi (1964) described children's utterances as consisting of the content-carrying words—nouns, verbs, and adjectives—with omission of "functors," or low-information words, such as pronouns, articles, prepositions, and auxiliary verbs, along with inflectional morphemes. The analogy is drawn from the language used by adults when brevity is important, as in a telegram. The content words tend to correspond to stressed words in an utterance, which led to the speculation that differential stress is a factor in children's retention of content words. Telegraphic speech was used as a general description of presentence utterances that deviated from adult grammar, and not just two-word productions.

Several researchers in the 1960s independently described two word classes used by children in these early combinations (McNeill, 1970; Miller and Ervin, 1964; Braine, 1963). These word classes are most commonly described as *pivot* words and *open-class* words. Pivots are a small class of frequently used words, generally in combination with many other different words. Some pivots may always be used in the first position of a two-word combination by a particular child, for example:

> *allgone* milk
> *allgone* kitty
> *allgone* light

Other pivots may always be in the final position, as in

> me *down*
> kitty *down*
> shoe *down*

Some children will use a particular pivot word in the first position of two-word combinations, whereas other children may use the same word in the second position, but each pivot typically has its fixed position for a given child.

Open-class words consist of most words in the child's vocabulary and are the major additions as vocabulary grows. Whereas pivots rarely occur alone or with other pivots, open-class words can occur as single words, in combination with other open-class words, or with pivots. For example:

> milk   open
> more milk   pivot + open
> baby milk   open + open

The possible types of utterances that can be represented with pivot-open grammar can be summarized in the following manner:

1. P_1 + O (Pivot + Open)
2. O + P_2 (Open + Pivot)
3. O + O (Open + Open)
4. O (Open)

For example, if a child says

> shoe off
> blanket off
> light off

each of these utterances would be designated O + P$_2$, with *off* identified as a pivot by its combination with several open-class words, always in the second position.

It has been argued that pivot-open grammar is an inadequate description of these two-word utterances on two grounds. First, all children do not display these patterns in their two-word utterances but tend to show greater variety than that implied by pivot-open depictions (Bowerman, 1973). Second, the classification of all words as either pivots or opens obscures the variety of meanings children express. Bloom (1970), borrowing from case grammar depiction of adult language (Fillmore, 1968), proposed a description of two-word utterances to indicate the function that words serve in the presumed underlying sentence. She emphasized the importance of context to determine the sequence. In her most famous example, Kathryn, one of the children being studied, said "mommy sock" twice in one day—once when she picked up her mother's sock and again when her own sock was being put on her by her mother. Bloom describes the first utterance as *possessive,* and the second as *agent-object* on the assumption that the child is describing the agent of an action (*mommy*) and the object acted upon (*sock*). In a pivot-open grammar, both of these utterances would have been described simply as O + O. Brown proposed a similar and more extensive list of these grammatical function categories, referring to them as *semantic relations.* Bloom and Lahey (1978) have more recently enumerated twenty-one categories which they identify as semantic-syntactic relations, applying them to one-word and multiple-word utterances in addition to two-word combinations. (See Chapter 7 for further elaboration and critiques of these categories.)

It does not seem appropriate to analyze children's two-word utterances according to adult syntactic categories. Instead, our preference is to describe the structure of these word combinations in terms of the words or word classes the child combines. An example of this word class description is detailed in Crystal, Fletcher, and Garman (1976) who found children at the two-word stage who used primarily noun phrases, some with predominant patterns such as preposition + *here* or *there* (e.g., "in there"; "on here"); and other children with predominance of rudimentary clause structures with verbs expressed or implied (e.g., "carry it"; "sit here"). Examination of a child's two-word utterances may reveal these or other patterns.

The Two-Word Stage in Comprehension   There is also controversy about children's comprehension at this stage. Some reports suggest that they seem to single out two content words in the constructions they hear and form a relational meaning such as agent-action, action-object, possessor-possessed, or object-location (Miller, 1978; 1981). This would suggest that their comprehension is telegraphic and would benefit from telegraphic stimuli in which the selection of the words to be understood is already done for the children. For example, it seems they should do better in understanding "Mommy sock" than "Mommy will sock you." This has not been found to be true, however (Petretic and Tweney, 1977; Duchan and Erickson, 1976). Indeed, children who are at the one- and two-word stage in their production do more poorly in responding to commands that are telegraphic than to commands that contain function words (for an exception, see Shipley and others, 1969). Might it be that children benefit from the intonation contour offered by the full-formed utterance and that they disregard the sounds in the function words? This is apparently not the case. Duchan and Erickson (1976) found that when nonsense fillers were inserted to replace the function words, the children's comprehension was even worse than for the telegraphic forms. Thus, while children do seem to ignore the meaning of function words and some content words, they seem at the same time to notice that something is wrong when these words do not occur in an utterance. This suggests that they do not hear telegraphically, although they might be responding meaningfully to only two of the lexical items contained in the utterance.

Once we start examining descriptions of children's interpretations of two content words, we are met with the same difficulties that we find in the descriptions of two-word semantic relations in language production. That is, we are in danger of assuming too much knowledge, while instead the child may be working from a very limited or different sense of the relationship from adult language users. An example of this rich interpretation problem is revealed by a detailed longitudinal study of a child progressing from age one and one-half to two years by Miller and Weissenborn (1978). They found that early comprehension of locative commands (e.g., "Where is X?") was only in game contexts of pointing to pictures in books and body part identification and did not require that the child understand the idea of location as separate from the object being identified. While we may have assumed the child had the notion of location when she responded and pointed, saying "There" to "Where is your pacifier?" at age sixteen months, it was not until she was twenty-four months old that she answered "where" questions with place-naming answers. Extending the implications of this study to commands involving placing objects (N_1) in

$$(N_1) \qquad (N_2)$$

places (N_2), as in "Put the apple in the bathtub," we can see that the child could simply put both objects together without understanding that the command carried the idea of locative relation.

In an investigation of the comprehension of possessive relations Golinkoff and Markessini (1980) also raise questions about the degree of knowledge that can be attributed to young children. Using children in five MLU groups from 1.00 to 4 (mean ages one year, eight months to five years, five months), they sampled comprehension of several possessive relations—alienable ("girl's shoe"), "intrinsic" or body part ("mommy's face"), and reciprocal or reversible kinship relations of either a child–parent type ("baby's mommy") or parent–child type ("mommy's baby"). They also include anomalous relations of both alienable and intrinsic types ("shoe's boy"; "face's mommy"). Most of the children, excepting the youngest group, correctly interpreted the alienable possession items, but only the oldest group predictably used word order to interpret the reciprocal relations correctly. It is interesting to note that all children interpreted the parent–child relations correctly more frequently than the child–parent relations, indicating that children probably view parents as possessors of children more so than the reverse. Their performance on anomalous relations, in which children overwhelmingly chose the first noun ("Show me the face's mommy";

shows face), also shows their strong predilection to interpret utterances to be consistent with their knowledge of the world, at least until MLU 4 when the children began to interpret anomalous alienable phrases as adults do ("Show me the ball's mommy"; shows mommy).

A further problem with the conceptualization of the two-word semantic relations stage in language comprehension is that different relations require different kinds and levels of processing for deriving an answer that appears correct (Duchan and Erickson, 1976). That is, comprehension is not just deriving the meaning relationship between two words, but rather it involves recognizing that the words signal different grammatical relations. With the locative, for example, we require not only that the child understand that the first noun (N_1) is located in relation to the second (N_2), but we also require that the specific nature of the relation, expressed in English by a preposition occurring in a phrase with N_2 ("on the table," "in the attic," etc.) be understood. Prepositions are notably hard to learn (Slobin, 1973), thereby making locatives harder to comprehend than some other relations. In contrast, the possessive relation requires that the child respond by indicating only one of the nouns—the second one—and does not require the interpretation of a preposition. To get "mommy's hat" requires that the child hear and show a hat, not a mommy as well as a hat. Finally, other so-called semantic relations require understanding of action words, which are more difficult to understand and are acquired later than nouns (Miller, 1981). It is indeed the case, in keeping with predictions made from the preceding comments, that two-word locatives are relatively late to develop in language comprehension, following, in consecutive order, possessives, action-objects, and agent-action relations (Duchan and Erickson, 1976).

Finally, while we are describing here the child's linguistic knowledge, we cannot ignore context, although this is typically done. It is certainly the case, for instance, that comprehension of the relation of two content words will depend upon whether they occur in familiar contexts, whether one of the content words is known information or not, or whether it is within the perceptual saliency or attention of the child at the time the command is given; or whether a linguistic or nonlinguistic strategy is applicable to the sentence. Like the points made earlier, these pragmatic circumstances will affect the various semantic relations differently. This leads us to be suspicious of a conceptualization of a unified semantic relations stage in children's language comprehension.

Multiword Combinations   Longer utterances of three or more words typically begin to appear when children produce about equal numbers of one-word and two-word utterances (MLU 1.5). When children formulate clauses, we can begin to compare the structure of their utterances to adult grammar—they are beginning to use conventional means of word order and inflectional morphemes to convey information. Simple clauses become more expanded as articles, adjectives, adverbs, and other modifiers are added. Simple clauses also combine to form multiclause utterances. We can best describe the development of multiword utterances by tracing the development of clauses and other syntactic systems.

Clause Development

Simple Clauses Children seem to use simple clauses to express the same kinds of intentions and ideas they previously expressed with gestures, single words, and two-word combinations at successive points in time. What is added is the organization of content into conventional forms that approach adult structure. The earliest clauses, which lack morphological refinement, are typically of the forms

SVO	Eden make man
SVA	I sit chair
VO	Make a couch
VA	Sit daddy chair

Bloom, Lightbown, and Hood (1975) report from their study of four children that the first verbs to appear were simple action verbs, such as *eat, read, do,* and *fix;* followed later by verbs that indicate a change in location, such as *put, go,* and *sit;* and then by verbs indicating the state of the subject, such as *want, have,* and *know.* Copulas (*to be*) generally are not present at this stage, resulting in clauses with implied verbs.

I Eden

Demonstrative pronouns (e.g., *this, that, it*) may appear frequently as the subject of these sentences.

That a cow.
It my book.
There shoe.

As we indicated in Chapter 5, copulas appear to develop as grammatical morphemes rather than as lexical items, and their appearance is generally delayed until after other grammatical morphemes have emerged. We therefore consider the subject-complement utterance a clause when it occurs in a sample along with other clauses with explicit (lexical) verbs.

Comprehension of Simple Clauses

English-speaking children's comprehension of noun-verb-noun sequences have frequently been studied in the language acquisition literature, probably because they have been thought to represent the most basic sentence type, the simple active declarative sentence. Also, one of the most documented strategies used by children in their language comprehension is that of noun-verb-noun = subject-verb-object (NVN = SVO). Or if the orientation is a semantic one rather than one of grammatical relations, the strategy is described as NVN = agent-action-patient (NVN = AAP). The prevalence of this strategy perhaps reveals that children regard this as a basic sentence form which they use to interpret or misinterpret all NVN sentences.

While agent-action-patient is the most common semantic relation expressed in English with the NVN string, others are also possible, such as the first noun acting as instrument or the second acting as locative or dative. The agent and patient can even be in reverse order, as in "The apple is eaten by the cow"(NVN = PAA). The interpretation for an adult will depend upon the verb and what comes between the verb and the second noun. For children, these relations may be determined by the probabilities of events in the real world—that is, cows eat apples and apples do not eat cows. So, a sentence with these words in it would be interpreted by early language learners as *cow* = agent; *eat* = action; *apple* = patient, regardless of word order or other aspects of the sentence, thus overriding the NVN = AAP strategy. Sentences that have nouns that cannot be both agents and patients have been called *irreversible* or *probable sentences*. These sentences are the earliest to be understood because regardless of word order, the agent is always clear since the reverse is improbable, e.g., "The apple eats the cow."

Multiple Clauses   Sometime between two and three years of age, generally as length of utterance moves beyond MLU of 3, multiple-clause utterances appear. The earliest of these complex forms may have no connective but may consist of two parallel clauses:

> You take that one; I take that one.

or an object subordinate clause:

> I hope *I don't hurt it.*
> I don't want *you to read that book.*

Brown (1973) and Limber (1973) identify these object clauses as the most frequent complex form to appear first. Along with the absence of a conjunction, it can be noted that these subordinate clauses have the form of a simple sentence.

Brown (1970) observed that conjunctions begin to appear in early speech at about MLU 3.5. The earliest connective form expressed by virtually all children speaking English is *and*. Bloom and others (1980), in a comprehensive study of four children's acquisition of connectives up through age thirty-eight months, found all four used *and* productively between twenty-five and twenty-seven months of age, before the emergence of any other connectives. (By *productively* they mean the form is used at least five times in two successive observations.) The children used these early *ands* syntactically, and they also used them to chain an utterance to events occurring in the situation:

> (Eric picks up puppet, puts it in box with other puppets)
> E: *And* I close them.

Syntactically, *and* is used in two ways—to connect words within a phrase and to connect two clauses. When the connective is used within a phrase, it results in a compound element of a clause. Most typically, young children produce compound objects or complements:

> I want *this one and this one.*

Compound subject phrases are less common for young children:

Mommy and Becky drink coffee.

As we have noted, simple object subordinate clauses appear as early multiple-clause utterances. Connectives in subordinate clauses, along with more variety in their position in the main clause, appear somewhat later. There is less consistency in the order of age of acquisition of these connective forms than is found for *and*.

Bloom and her colleagues have studied the development of multiple-clause sentences of four children from two to three years of age. They first detailed the development of subordinate conjunctions (Bloom and others, 1980) and reported considerable variation in the age at which each child used these forms productively. An analysis of the children's development of modal-infinitive clauses expressing volition or intention (e.g., *want to; have to*) was reported in 1984 (Bloom, Takeff, and Lahey, 1984). More recently, Bloom and others (1989) present data on the children's acquisition of all other "complement-taking" verbs; that is, those that we identify as being followed by object clauses or embedded questions. These verbs, described as *epistemic* and *perception verbs*, were acquired later than the volition and intention verbs. They include *think, know, see,* and *look (at).*

Brown (1973) and Limber (1973) distinguish subordinate clauses introduced by *wh-* words (*what, where,* etc.) from those introduced by other subordinate conjunctions. They identify these former clauses as indirect or embedded questions and indicate that they develop first, with Dale (1976) reporting that clauses referring to location or time seem to emerge before other *wh-* clauses. For example,

I remember *where it is.*
When I get big, I can lift you up.

Bloom and others (1989), in contrast, found the acquisition of the various kinds of subordinate clauses to be lexically determined. Their findings suggest that rather than learn general rules for *wh-* complements and for object clauses beginning with subordinate conjunctions, children learn the structure for each main verb separately.

The earliest occurring subordinate clauses have the form of a simple sentence, as we have indicated. Simple sentence structure is modified as syntactic rules become more complex. The modification generally involves the infinitive form of the verb:

I don't want you *to read* that book.
It bothers me for you *to do* that.

We can identify general types of subordinate clauses that seem to correspond to levels of complexity and developmental sequence. Since it is unclear whether embedded questions or other subordinate conjunctions are simpler, we do not order them but do distinguish them from each other.

1. Object clause—simple complete sentence as object.
   e.g., "I want *you read that book.*"
2a. Embedded question—*wh-* word plus simple sentence.
   e.g., "Mommy know *what Roy do.*"
2b. Clause with other subordinate conjunction.
   e.g., "You can have it *if you want it.*"
3. Modifications of simple sentence structure.
   e.g., "I want *you to read that book.*"

Relative clauses appear slightly later than the early occurring subordinate clauses. *That* was the only relative pronoun found in the samples of children up to thirty-eight months of age by Bloom and others (1980) with *it* appearing after thirty-four months for all the children. The sequence of other relative pronouns and deleted pronouns is not clear. Relative clauses are first produced to modify objects or complements:

> That a box *that they put it in.*   COMPLEMENT
> I show you the place *we went.*   OBJECT

Menyuk (1977) reports that relative clauses referring to subjects develop after five years of age and are still relatively rare at age seven:

> The boy *who hit the girl* ran away.

More common would be expansion of the sentence object:

> I saw the boy *who hit the girl* and ran away.

Comprehension of Multiple-Clause Sentences

The NVN = AAP strategy, because it includes only one verb, does not always work for understanding utterances with more than one verb. Children may try to make it work, as can be evidenced by four-year-olds who act out sentences such as "The boy who hit the girl, hit the man" by having the girl hit the man, since the girl can be seen as the beginning of the NVN sequence. Relative clause sentences such as the previous ones require more and different kinds of linguistic knowledge. Bowerman (1979) describes the inadequacy of NVN = AAP as follows:

> Problems may arise because one clause interrupts another, because major constituents such as subject or object are replaced by pronouns or missing entirely in embedded and conjoined clauses, because the normal word orders of free-standing sentences are rearranged, and for a variety of other reasons. (Bowerman, 1979, p. 288)

The types of linguistic knowledge involved in interpretation of multiple-clause sentences require that the interpreter determine what propositions are expressed by the embedded or coordinated clauses and how the clauses work with one another. As we saw from the above misinterpretation of the hitting example, one of the difficulties with complex sentences is the determination of the grammatical relations for the various nouns and verbs within clauses and across clauses. Even when these determinations are made for the general case, the exceptions to these generalizations remain to be learned. Furthermore, certain complex sentences are difficult to learn because of their semantic or cognitive complexities. We will first discuss children's comprehension of compound sentences, then predicate clauses, relative clauses, and, finally, adverbial clauses.

Compound Sentences   Compound sentences, at first glance, should be the easiest of the multiple-clause sentences to understand, since the same word-order strategies should apply to them as to the simple sentences—just more than once. However, one of the characteristics of these sentences is that if there are overlapping ideas in the constituents, such as both having the same subject, the language allows for dropping out the duplication. So, if John both went to the store and bought some sardines, the apt speaker would not say "John went to the store and John bought some sardines" but rather would probably omit the second *John* and say "John went to the store and bought some sardines." Thus, ellipsis becomes a complicating factor in children's comprehension of compound sentences. The deletion can be one in which an element is mentioned and then, upon second mention, is omitted ("Mary sang and [Mary] played"); this has been called forward deletion. Or the deletion can be backward—it is made before the first mention of the duplicated element ("Mary [ran] and Jane ran").

Lust (1977) and Lust and Mervis (1980) found that two- and three-year-olds frequently use forward deletion, whereas backward reduction is rare to nonexistent. They also found that the children first acquired sentence coordination, often with redundancy (e.g., "That's a daddy and that's a daddy"), and then later acquired coordination within phrases (e.g., "The mommy and daddy"). This is consistent with some previous findings (Limber, 1973; Slobin and Welsh, 1973; Menyuk, 1969, 1971), but contradicts others. DeVilliers, Tager-Flusberg, and Hakuta (1977) found that there was no difference between children's comprehension of backward and forward deleted sentences. Further, their three- and four-year-olds were able to interpret full-sentence compound clauses and deletion within subject and verb phrases equally well.

Predicate Clauses   Tavakolian (1976, cited in Bowerman, 1979) found that three- and four-year-old children sometimes apply the compound strategy inappropriately. When presented with sentences that have infinitive clauses in the predicate, the children did not follow the minimal distance principle used by adults to locate the subject of the infinitive clauses but instead overgeneralized the compounding strategy. That is, they took the subject of the main clause and interpreted it to also be the subject of the infinitive clause as though the two clauses were compounds. Following this strategy, they correctly interpreted compound clauses such as

Donald told Bozo a story and lay down. Make him do it.

However, they incorrectly interpreted infinitive clauses such as

Donald told Bozo to lie down. Make him do it.

In this second case, the children incorrectly made Donald lie down, as though the sentence had been

Donald told Bozo (something) and lay down.

Older children generally interpret these correctly but may make the error of overgeneralizing the minimal distance strategy by not recognizing the situations in which it does not apply. In some cases, this is due to the semantics of the complement. Compare for example, "John is eager to see," which follows the minimal distance principle of assigning the immediately preceding noun (*John*) as the subject of the infinitive. In "John is easy to see," however, the strategy does not work, since *John* is being seen, not doing the seeing. Typical children come to understand these correctly between four and seven years (Fabian, 1977; Cromer, 1970). Somewhat more difficult are utterances with *ask* or *promise* as the verb of the main clause and an infinitive clause in the predicate.

Donald *asked* Bozo what to do.
Donald *promised* Bozo to do it.

Children as old as ten may overgeneralize the minimal distance principle and misinterpret these clauses (Kessel, 1970; Chomsky, 1969).

Relative Clauses   Tavakolian (1976) also found that her three- to five-year-old subjects used a compounding strategy in interpreting sentences with relative clauses; that is, they selected the first NP as the subject of both the main verb and the verb in the relative clause. This led to their systematic misinterpretation of sentences such as

The cat bit the dog that the rat chased.

The compounding strategy led them to have the cat bite the dog and the cat chase the rat.

DeVilliers and others (1977) found a different strategy was used by their three- to five-year-olds in interpreting relative clauses. These children elaborated on the NVN = AAP strategy and used the second noun both as object of the first clause and subject of the second. In the preceding example, the child with this

$$
NV \begin{Bmatrix} N \\ N \end{Bmatrix} VN = AA \begin{Bmatrix} P \\ A \end{Bmatrix} AP
$$

strategy would show the cat biting the dog and the dog chasing the rat.

The order of acquisition of different types of relative clause constructions depends, of course, on whether the children's strategy leads to a correct or incorrect interpretation. Thus, children who have a coordinated strategy would appear to learn center-embedded sentences first, such as "The boy who hit the girl ran away," while those with the complex

$$AA\begin{Bmatrix} P \\ A \end{Bmatrix} AP$$

strategy would correctly interpret sentences such as "The boy hit the man who kissed the doll" before other forms. Studies have combined children who are working with all these strategies, and thus the results are difficult to interpret and are in disagreement (see Bowerman, 1979, for a review).

Adverbial Clauses Understanding subordinate adverbial clauses is interesting because they require different interpretations depending on both the subordinate conjunction involved and its placement in the sentence. Clark (1971) found for *before* and *after* clauses that her three- and four-year-old subjects used a NVN = AAP interpretation for each clause and combined the two clauses with a semantic order-of-mention strategy; that is, they interpreted the first clause as happening first followed by the second. This would result in apparent correct interpretation of utterances that follow the order of events:

> Mary ran before Tom ran.
> After Mary ran, Tom ran.

Utterances that alter the order would be incorrectly interpreted.

> Before Mary ran, Tom ran.
> Mary ran after Tom ran.

Amidon and Carey (1972) found a different pattern. Their five- and six-year-old subjects responded only to the main clause, ignoring the adverbial clause. A possible resolution of the apparent contradiction in results is that the order-of-mention strategy occurs earlier than identification of the main clause.

Development of Questions

Children learning English begin to ask questions with single words by using rising intonation, so the first questions they ask are typically yes–no questions. Klima and Bellugi (1966) describe the development of questions in three periods that correspond to MLU. (Optional elements are enclosed in parentheses.)

Period 1:	Nucleus + intonation	See hole?
(MLU 1.75–2.25)		I ride train?
	What NP (*doing*)	What's that?
		What man doing?
	Where NP (*go*)	Where horse?
		Where horse go?

The *wh-* words are used only in a few routines that generally ask for names of objects, actions, or locations of previously present objects. At this stage, Klima and Bellugi found the children did not respond appropriately to *wh-* questions.

Period 2:	*What*		What book name?
(MLU 2.25–2.75)	*Where*	NP + (VP) + (NP)	Where my mitten?
	Why		Why you smiling?

In period 2, yes–no questions are still indicated only by intonation. *Wh-* questions are generally answered appropriately.

Period 3:	aux + NP + VP	Will you help me?
(MLU 2.75–3.5)	*do* + NP + VP	Does lions walk?
	wh- + NP + VP	Where the other Joe will drive?

At this stage, children are developing auxiliaries, beginning with the negatives *can't* and *don't* and then other *do* forms. They use them in the inverted order to ask yes–no questions but do not make this inversion in *wh-* questions when it is needed. We will add a final stage to describe this step in question formation as follows:

$$wh\text{-} + {}^{do}_{aux} + NP + VP \quad \text{What can the baby eat?}$$
Why don't you talk?

Tag questions and truncated questions (e.g., "Did he?") were found by Brown and Hanlon (1970) to occur later than other question forms, with truncated questions occurring after truncated answers (e.g., "He did," "He didn't") and before tag questions.

Evidence from the study of children acquiring languages other than English (for German: Wode, 1974; for Japanese: Okubo, 1967; for Korean: Clancy, 1989; and for Serbo-Croatian: Savic̀, 1975) indicates similarities in the order in which question words are acquired. Clancy (1989) suggests that differences are due to differences in interactive styles across caregivers and children, leading to different input frequencies of particular forms and individual children's selection of different forms to use.

Development of Negation

The acquisition of negation has extensively been studied in different languages (Japanese: McNeill and McNeill, 1968; Finnish, Samoan, and Luo: Bowerman, 1973; Korean and French: Choi, 1988). Attempts have been made to determine both the syntactic form and the sequence of acquisition of various types of negation. What we report here is based on children acquiring standard English.

The earliest negative to appear for most children is the nonsyntactic *no*. This has been reported in the single-word stage, below MLU 1.5, by both Bloom (1970) and Bowerman (1973). This early *no* suggests children have the concept of negation and use it to reject or deny someone else's statement or action.

Syntactic negation appears slightly later, when *no* or *not* are combined with other words, as in "no milk." Bellugi (1967) characterizes this stage of negation as

> neg + X, where X is the sentence nucleus

That is, the negative utterance is characterized as the same as a nonnegative utterance, with the addition of an initial negative. She found this form in children's samples from MLU 1.17 to 2.25. Bloom (1970) argues against this characterization of the negative outside of the sentence nucleus, since the nucleus in negative sentences tends to be less complex than that in nonnegative sentences. She also identifies some of these neg + X utterances as nonsyntactic *no* + affirmative statement in response to a previous statement or situation:

> D: Can Daddy do it?
> CHILD: No Mommy.

Bellugi did not find this kind of discourse tie with negation until between MLU 2.0 and 2.6.

Bellugi (1967) describes three periods of syntactic development of negatives. The first (MLU less than 2.25), as we mentioned, is

> neg + nucleus, where negatives are *no* and *not*

The contractions *can't* and *don't* along with *no* and *not* appear within clauses in period 2 (MLU 2.25 to 2.75):

> I can't catch you.
> He no bite you.
> Don't leave me.

The other auxiliary verb forms, besides *don't* and *can't*, and the copulas occur in period 3 (MLU 2.75 to 3.5), as well as the corresponding negative forms:

> I didn't do it.
> Donna won't let go.
> I am not a doctor.

ASSESSING SYNTAX

All children with language problems do not have syntax problems, and those who do may not need to have all syntactic systems analyzed. In this section we suggest some steps to guide you through syntactic analysis, beginning with looking for regularities in the use, misuse, and omission of forms in spontaneous productions. As you develop your familiarity with the elements to look for, it will become possible to choose those aspects of syntax that are most relevant for a particular child and to find shortcuts for carrying out the analysis. We generally are interested in the areas in which there are problems and would focus on those areas. A more comprehensive analysis might be desirable to show development of the language over time as new structures emerge or to find evidence of more complex structures than the child typically uses. In any case, the clinician will choose to analyze the aspects of syntax that are considered to be relevant. The steps we suggest for your initial analysis will work better with some children than with others; we can alert you to some common patterns, but children are infinitely creative in showing us new ones, and you must be prepared to adapt your transcription and analysis to fit those patterns.

The first step in doing syntactic analysis is to segment your sample into utterances. We follow the conventions presented in Box 6–4 to divide utterances. Since judgment about utterance boundaries sometimes depends on timing and intonation cues, these judgments must be made at the time the sample is transcribed rather than from a written account. The utterances are then listed and numbered, with separate number sequences for each interactant.

BOX 6–4. Guidelines for Segmenting Utterances

Judgment of utterance boundaries must be made at the time of transcription, using contextual and intonation cues. Once the words are written down, the information is lost. Indicate pauses with a slash (/).

1. The end of an utterance is indicated by a definite pause preceded by a drop in pitch or rise in pitch.
2. The end of a sentence is the end of the utterance. Two or more sentences may be said in one breath without a pause, but each one will be treated as a separate utterance for syntax analysis.
3. A group of words, such as a noun phrase, that can't be further divided without losing the essential meaning is an utterance, even though it may not be a sentence.
4. A sentence with two independent clauses joined by a coordinating conjunction is counted as one utterance. If the sentence contains more than two independent compound clauses, it is segmented so that the third clause, beginning with the conjunction, is a separate utterance.
5. Sentences with subordinate or relative clauses are counted as single multiclausal utterances.

Examples of Transcribed Sample

Well in school I always go to a a / kind of a / silly kind of school / (laugh) / well what we do is / with big pieces of papers / an we what we do is make make writing things like that with a *H* and *O* and all those kinds of homeworks//we make math homeworks on little little pieces of squares

Example of Segmented Sample

1. (Well in school) I always go to (a a) kind of a silly kind of school
2. (Well) what we do is with big pieces of papers (an we)
3. (Well) what we do is (make) make writing things like that with a *H* and *O* and all those kinds of homeworks
4. we make math homeworks on little little pieces of squares

Screening for Syntax

There are times when language samples need to be analyzed quickly to determine if two children or groups of children are comparable in development, or to get a general measure of a child's progress over time. As we indicated in the section on morphological analysis, a procedure such as that proposed by Scarborough (1990) is preferable to an unnaturalistic test sample. Scarborough presents fifty-six grammatical forms in four subscales. The two subscales that correspond most closely to the areas we have covered in this chapter are Questions/Negations and Sentence Structures. Each form is scored as 0, 1, or 2, depending on the number of times it is used in the sample. For some later developing forms, an earlier developing form might be credited even though it does not occur in the sample, since it is presumed to be in the child's repertoire. A sample of one hundred scorable utterances is recommended.

Analysis of Clause Structure Production

The particular utterances that will be used for a more complete analysis of syntax will depend on the type of analysis we are doing. If we suspect difficulty with sentence structure, we will make a listing transcript of only those utterances that reflect the child's clausal knowledge; that is, we will exclude those utterances that are excluded from MLU computation (see Box 6–3). Although they may be of interest in other types of analysis, they reveal nothing about the child's clause structure. In addition, we exclude questions from this analysis and treat them separately.

The remaining utterances are categorized by clause type, using worksheets such as those shown in Tables 6–1 and 6–2. Any utterance that has a grammatical error is indicated with an asterisk (*) to highlight where these errors are occurring. Once the utterances are categorized, the child's clause structure can be summarized by noting which clause types the child uses, which are used more frequently, and where errors occur. It may also be useful to look for regularities within and across clause types to determine which clause types are elaborated with adverbials and which have characteristic clause elements, such as always having pronouns as subjects.

Analysis of Clause Structure Comprehension

In the study of any phenomena, exceptions to the rule often offer the best test of that rule. If we postulate that children understand clause structures according to the strategies discussed, we would expect them to make mistakes interpreting sentences that are incompatible with those strategies. This is because they overgeneralize their rule to instances in which it does not apply. Assessment of their understanding of various clause structures can be done by presenting them with utterances to interpret in order to reveal inappropriate strategies if children are using them. Following are some strategies that children might be using, and some procedures that can be used to assess for those strategies. It is useful in this analysis to use neutral contexts and reversible sentences so that interpretation cannot be based on knowledge about the world rather than relying on linguistic knowledge.

TABLE 6-1 Worksheet for Simple Clauses

I. Clauses with copulas

Nominal	Copula	Complement	(Adverbial)
I	(a)m	so happy	today

II. Clauses with intransitive verbs

Nominal	Verb	(Adverbial)	
Mr. Finch	always yells	at me	
I	slept	on the couch	all day

III. Clauses with transitive verbs
Clauses with direct objects*

Nominal	Verb	Nominal	(Adverbial)
Janet	broke	her leg	this morning
Harry	really likes	to eat pie	

IV. Imperative clauses

	Verb Phrase	(Adverbial)
	Don't slam the door	
	Put the pan	on the stove

* Add columns for indirect objects and/or object complements if they occur in the sample.

Noun-Verb-Noun = Agent-Action-Patient   Present the child with objects to manipulate, and then ask him to use the objects to show actions such as the following. Adjust vocabulary and complexity for the child's level. If the child is using this strategy, the passive sentences (*) and those with subject relative clauses (**) will be interpreted incorrectly.

> The cat chases the squirrel.
> *The boy is hugged by the mother.
> **The boy who wanted to see his mother went home.
> The mother hugged the boy.
> *The truck was hit by the car.
> **The dog who chased the cat bit the mouse.

Compound Clause Strategy   Children can be asked to show actions with objects, or they can be asked to answer questions to reveal their interpretation of sentences such as the following. If the compounding strategy is being used inappropriately, the first set of utterances will be interpreted correctly, but the second set with object-relative clauses (**) will be misinterpreted. On the other hand, if the child is using the NVN strategy, the first set will be incorrectly interpreted, whereas the second set will be correct.

TABLE 6–2 Worksheet for Multiple-Clause Sentences

I. Predicate clauses
A. Object clauses

Nominal	Verb	(I.O.) Nominal	(that?)	Nominal	Verb Phrase/ Infinitive
I	told	you	that	I	already did it
She	said			she	didn't care
I	want			my dad	to come too

II. Adverbial clauses
A. Introductory adverbial clauses

Subordinate Conjunction	Nominal	Verb Phrase	Nominal	Verb Phrase
Because	I	(a)m only four	I	can't go
Like	I	told you	she	is too silly

B. Noninitial adverbial clauses

Nominal	Verb Phrase	Subordinate Conjunction	Nominal	Verb Phrase
I	hafta wash	because	I	(a)m all goopy
She	hasn't been here	since	I	was a baby

III. Relative clauses
A. Subject modifiers

Nominal	that/which who/whose	(Nominal)	Verb Phrase	Verb Phrase
The shoes	that	my mom	bought me	are tie ones
Dan the kid	who		lives next door	has his own TV

B. Object/complement modifiers

Nominal	Verb	Nominal	that/which/whom who/whose	(Nominal)	Verb Phrase
Strawberry	is	the flavor	that	I	like best
This	is	the only one	that		counts

IV. Compound clauses

Nominal	Verb Phrase	Coordinate Conjunction	(Nominal)	Verb Phrase
I	take him for walks	but	he	runs too fast
I	go home	or		go to my friend's

V. Other multiple clauses
That was the best part, I can tell you. (inverted object clause)
She told me a story that was real scary, and I couldn't go to sleep. (compound clauses with relative clause)
Why she did this is what I want to know. (subject clause)

The boy hugged the girl and kissed the baby. Who kissed the baby?
The boy patted the dog and sat down. Who sat down?
The baby who was kissed by the girl cried. Who cried?
The car was hit by the truck and turned over. What turned over?
The girl who hit the boy kissed the baby. Who kissed the baby?
**The dog chased the cat who ran away. Who ran away?
**The girl tickled the baby who cried. Who cried?
**The boy pushed the baby who fell down. Who fell down?
**The baby didn't like the boy who yelled. Who yelled?
**The girl hit the boy that kissed the baby. Who kissed the baby?

Order-of-Mention Strategy Children's comprehension of description of events in which the clauses referring to portions of the event correspond to or differ from the order of occurrence of those segments will assess the child's reliance on order of mention. Children who understand the semantics of adverbs will interpret the event description independently of the order of the clauses, whereas children interpreting according to the order of mention will misinterpret utterances in which the order of mention does not match the order of occurrence (*). Children can be asked to act out the events or asked "What happened first?" when presented with utterances such as the following. The descriptions should not include events that have a logical sequence ("First he got up and then he got dressed"), because they can be interpreted without relying on the linguistic indicators of order.

The bell rang before they ate.
After lunch they went to the park.
First he took a bath and then he ate a cookie.
*She ate a sandwich when the bell finished ringing.
*Before school, he drew a picture.
*They went to the store after they saw the dog.

Noun Phrase Analysis

When analyzing noun phrases, we are looking for two things. One, we want to determine the child's ability to elaborate on his or her descriptions or references to objects or people in order to provide the listener with the information needed to understand the message. Thus, we want to do an inventory of the amount and kind of referring expressions the child uses. Secondly, if the child has difficulty with the syntactic organization of noun phrases, we want to analyze the regularities within the error productions.

We begin by identifying the noun phrases in the running transcript. We eliminate those utterances that are stereotyped segments or direct imitations but include the elliptical utterances and questions that were excluded from clause analysis. Worksheets such as that shown in Table 6–3 can be used to identify the frequency and variety of modified nouns. Again, all error productions are indicated with an asterisk (*) to identify where the child is having problems with phrase structure.

TABLE 6–3   Worksheet for Noun Phrase Analysis

I. Two-element noun phrases

Modifier	Noun
My	name
Some	marbles

II. Three-element noun phrases

Modifier	Modifier	Noun
A	good	bet
The	blue	one

III. Four-element noun phrases

Modifier	Modifier	Modifier	Noun
A	little	tiny	mouse
Some	stinky	old	shoes

IV. Post-noun modifiers

Noun	Prepositional Phrase
Boy	in my class

Noun	Relative Clause
Chair	that got broken

Sentence Type Analysis

Question Analysis   All questions, including those formed with intonation, are identified in the running transcript. A worksheet such as that shown in Table 6–4 can be used to list and classify yes–no questions and *wh-* questions. Multiple-clause questions can be listed separately since they show more syntactic organization. All questions that have errors are indicated with an asterisk (*) to indicate where the child is having difficulty with question structure or meaning of question words. If the child does not use any questions or uses only one form, it should be noted.

Negation Analysis   If the child uses few instances of syntactic negation or if the forms used show deviations from adult structure, all syntactic negation forms should be listed. The worksheet in Table 6–5 separates correct and incorrect negations to allow for comparison between them.

Sample Analysis: Syntax

To illustrate the assessment steps, we will use the sample of Patty's language presented in Chapter 5 and analyze it for the syntactic structures that are present. An initial worksheet (Table 6–6) can be used to identify all of the

TABLE 6–4 Worksheet for Questions

YES–NO QUESTIONS

Intonation type:
You want to? ↑
That's yours? ↑

Auxiliary Inversion:
Can I help you?
Will you go?

Do Insertion
Do you like it?
Does it work?

Pretag
I can have it, okay? ↑
It's fixed, right? ↑

Tag
You'll do it, won't you?
It's not here, is it?

WH-QUESTIONS

*What you doing?	Missing auxiliary
*Why I can't?	No auxiliary inversion
What's that?	

MULTIPLE-CLAUSE QUESTIONS

*When my birthday come, you on a diet?	Missing auxiliary and verb

syntactic features and also to calculate MLU. Those portions that will be excluded from computing MLU are identified by closing them in parentheses. The notation can be more or less detailed than that shown, depending on the variety and complexity of the structures than that are used. For example, with this sample we have chosen to identify all verbs with *V* and distinguish copulas from lexical verbs by the complement that always follows them. Individual worksheets follow for each structure completed to organize the errors identified for analysis (Tables 6–7 to 6–11). Note that morphological errors are not considered when analyzing syntax. For example, "Me waiting for you" is considered to have correct clause structure, since it contains a subject and a verb even though the verb is not morphologically correct.

TABLE 6–5 Worksheet for Negation

Correct Negation	*Error Forms*
I can't	No want it
I don't know	

TABLE 6-6   Syntax Worksheet

Name: Patty C.
Event: Playing card game

Morphemes	Utterance	Clause Structure	Noun/Prep. Phrase	Negative/ Question
5	1. Me /waiting for you.	SVA	for you	
5	4. That's what you think.	Sub/Em ?		
2	6. This one.	—	this one	
3	12. Where is dat?			wh- ?
5	15. Me / do it better.	SVOA		
5	16. Me know where it is.	Sub/Em ?		
3	23. //Do/ it good?			yes–no ?
4	24. How much / me got?			wh- ?
6	25. Yeah / want / see how much you got.	Sub/Em ?		
6	26. Dis sure / better for me.	SVCA	for me	
2	27. One more.	—	one more	
6	31. Nothing fall/ down you drop/ it.	Compound		
3	32. You got it?			yes–no ?
7	36. Me do/ it before mommy go/ out.	Sub. Adv.		
3	40. Tomorrow's Friday.	SVC		
3	41. What day is /?			wh- ?
4	52. /Me do/ it good?			yes–no ?
—	59. (Yellow one)	—	yellow one	
5	62. Me like (/) come(/) over here.	SVOA	over here	
8	65. My brother / coming out / two more day/.	SVAA	my brother (in) two more day	
5	67. My Bobby / coming out.	SVA	my Bobby	
7	68. // Coming out / two more days.	VAA	(in) two more days	
5	69. [kʌp] call/ up last night.	SVA	last night	
8	70. He /go be home / two more days.	SVAA	(in) two more days	
4	72. You know me / lucky?	Sub./Obj.		
9	75. //All mixed up / got no room where you are.	Compound Sub./Adv.	no room	
6	76. Me got enough room this way.	SVOA	enough room this way	
4	77. Dis chair / real comfortable.	SVC	this chair	
3	78. Me like dat.	SVO		
1	79. / You?			yes–no ?
4	81. Me like dis chair.	SVO	this chair	
7	84. Look dere's a little one too.	SVCA	a little one	
4	85. That's real good.	SVC		
5	86. You know the big one.	SVO	the big one	

TABLE 6–6 Syntax Worksheet (*continued*)

Name: Patty C.
Event: Playing card game

Morphemes	Utterance	Clause Structure	Noun/Prep. Phrase	Negative/ Question
4	87. That's real small.	SVC		
5	92. / You eat that at home?			yes–no ?
7	93. Me eat carrot/ / home all / time now.	SVOAAA	(at) home all (the) time	
6	94. Me got one in my lunch.	SVOA	in my lunch	
6	95. Carrot and celery taste real good.	SVC		
4	98. How many / me got?			wh- ?
6	106. Watch your ring don't come off.	Sub./Obj.		do(es)n't
4	109. Better this way.	—	this way	
5	111. Me don't wanna kick you.	SVO		don't
6	123. How bout / do dis one too?		this one	wh- ?
8	127. Put that round / me / see that better.	Compound		
9	137. / Me tell you bout my brother coming up?		my brother	yes–no ?
4	140. Do dis one too.	VOA	this one	
4	141. Me like / see that	SVO		
4	142. Better for me.	—	for me	
7	143. See how much you got in here.	Sub./Em ?	in here	
6	145. Put all that stuff in here.	VOA	all that stuff in here	
6	146. See what you got in here.	Sub./Em ?	in here	
2	152. Stupid marble.	—	stupid marble	
7	155. /Me put all this away for you?		all this for you	yes–no ?
7	157. Me know that // suppose/ / have off tomorrow.	Sub./Obj.		
3	158. You funny you.	—	you funny you	
3	160. / Me turn it?			yes–no ?
280 =	Total morphemes			

Key to symbols:
  S = subject V = verb O = object C = complement A = adverbial
  Sub./Em? = subordinate clause with embedded question
  Sub./Obj = object subordinate clause
  Sub./Adv. = adverbial subordinate clause wh- ? = wh- question
  yes–no ? = yes–no question Compound = compound clauses

Mean Length of Utterance
  280 ÷ 56 = 5.0

TABLE 6–7 Worksheet for Simple Clauses

I. Clauses with copulas

Nominal	Copula	Complement	(Adverbial)
*26 This	/	sure better	for me
40 Tomorrow	's	Friday	
*77 This chair	/	real comfortable	
84 There	's	a little one	too
85 That	's	real good	
87 That	's	real small	
95 Carrot and celery	taste	real good	

II. Clauses with intransitive verbs

Nominal	Verb	(Adverbial)
1 Me	waiting	for you
65 My brother	coming	our (in) two more day
67 My Bobby	coming	out
*68 /	coming	out (in) two more days
69 [kʌp]	call up	last night
70 He	go be	home (in) two more days

III. Clauses with transitive verbs
Clauses with direct objects

Nominal	Verb	Nominal	(Adverbial)
15 Me	do	it	better
62 Me	like	(to) come	over here
76 Me	got	enough room	this way
78 Me	like	that	
81 Me	like	this chair	
86 You	know	the big one	
93 Me	eat	carrot	(at) home all the time now
94 Me	got	one	in my lunch
111 Me	don't wanna kick	you	
141 Me	like	(to) see that	

IV. Imperative clauses

	Verb Phrase	(Adverbial)
140	Do this one	too
145	Put all that stuff	in here

Summary: Patty successfully uses simple clauses with all three types of verbs; she occasionally omits the copula, but generally uses it correctly. In one instance, she omitted a required subject, but this was probably due to her use of the same subject in the immediately preceding utterance.

* = Error

TABLE 6–8 Worksheet for Multiple-Clause Sentences

I. Predicate clauses
A. Object and complement clauses

Nominal	Verb	(that?)	Nominal	Verb Phrase/ Infinitive
72 You	know		me	lucky
106	Watch		your ring	don't come off
*157 Me	know	that	(I)	suppose have off tomorrow

B. Embedded questions

Nominal	Transitive Verb/ Copula	(Nominal)	?	Nominal	Verb Phrase
4 That	's		what	you	think
16 Me	know		where	it	is
*25 (I)	want see		how much	you	got
143	See		how much	you	got in here
146	See		what	you	got in here

II. Adverbial clauses
A. Introductory adverbial clauses

Subordinate Conjunction	Nominal	Verb Phrase	Nominal	Verb Phrase
NONE				

B. Noninitial adverbial clauses

Nominal	Verb Phrase	Subordinate Conjunction	Nominal	Verb Phrase
36 Me	do it	before	Mommy	go out
*75 (you)	got no room	where	you	are

III. Relative clauses NONE

IV. Compound clauses

Nominal	Verb Phrase	Coordinate Conjunction	(Nominal)	Verb Phrase
31 Nothing	fall down		you	drop it
*75 (you)	(are) all mixed up	(and so)	(you)	got no room
*127	Put that round	(so)	me	see that better

V. Other multiple clauses NONE

Summary: Patty has more difficulty with multiple clauses than simple sentences but has several correct forms. She used several subordinate clauses correctly, most successfully where the object clause is a simple declarative sentence, with or without an introductory question word. Errors on these forms involved omission of required subjects of either the first or second clause, apparently when the same subject is intended for both clauses. She successfully used two subjects where the clause subjects were different. Patty used no coordinate conjunctions so she had difficulty expressing related ideas in compound clauses, although she attempted to do so. In two cases she attempted to express causal relationships.

* = Error

TABLE 6–9 Worksheet for Noun Phrase Analysis

I. Two-element noun phrases

	Modifier	Noun
6, 123, 140	this	one
76, 109	this	way
77, 81	this	chair
59	yellow	one
65	my	brother
*67	my	Bobby
94	my	lunch
69	last	night
75	no	room
76	enough	room
*93	all	time
155	all	this
152	stupid	marble

II. Three-element noun phrases

	Modifier	Modifier	Noun
65, 68, 70	two	more	day(s)
84	a	little	one
86	the	big	one
145	all	that	stuff

Summary: Patty uses a variety of two- and three-word noun phrases. Her errors appear to be due to overgeneralizing to idiosyncratic combinations, as when she uses the genitive article with a proper name ("my Bobby") and an initiator without an article ("all time"), which is appropriate before indefinite forms ("all this"; "all that stuff").

* = Error

TABLE 6–10 Worksheet for Prepositional Phrase Analysis

Correct		Error	
1,142	for you	65, 68, 70	(in) two more days
26,155	for me	94	(in) my lunch
143,145,146	in here		
62	over here	93	(at) home

Summary: Patty used few prepositions. She seems to have certain phrases that are used consistently correctly while the same or other prepositions tend to be omitted in obligatory contexts.

TABLE 6–11 Worksheet for Question Analysis

Yes–No Questions	
32	You got it?
92	You eat that at home?
*23	(Am I) Do(ing) it good?
*52	(Am) me do(ing) it good?
*79	(Do) you?
*137	(Did) me tell you bout my brother coming up?
*155	(Should/can) me put all this away for you?
*160	(Should/can) me turn it?

Wh- Questions	
12	Where is that?
*24	How much (do) me got?
*98	How many (do) me got?
*41	What day is (it)?
*123	How bout (we) do this one too

Summary: All yes–no questions are indicated by rising intonation; for those that do not require an auxiliary verb, this strategy produces acceptable structures, but others reflect her general lack of auxiliaries in all forms. The one *wh-* question has a copula verb, while two error forms are again missing auxiliaries. Nominals are missing in two forms, which may be idiosyncratic or may be due to increased complexity, as occurs with compound clauses.

* = Error

ELICITATION PROCEDURES FOR SYNTACTIC STRUCTURES

Eliciting Complements

1. *Introduce the unexpected.* Solicit comments from the child by offering material with characteristics that would not be expected. For example, milk with blue food coloring or shoes on the table are likely to prompt comments with complements ("It's blue"; "They're not supposed to be there").

2. *Description game.* "I'm thinking of something and it is . . ." (color, location, function, etc.).

3. *Verbal scenerios.* Give situation descriptions and have the child speak for a character. For example, Jane was sitting at the table. Her mother called her to come to the table for dinner. What would Jane say? ("I am at the table"; "I'm already here."). See Hughes and Till (1982) for more examples.

Eliciting Lexical Verb Clauses

1. *Improbable pictures.* Show the child pictures of incongruous actions and ask him or her to tell you what is wrong with the picture ("The man is holding a house"; "The zebra has an umbrella."). Suitable pictures are available commercially or can often be found in magazine advertisements.

2. *Description games.* The child is to tell a third person what the clinician is doing while the listener is to replicate the action ("She's putting the paper on the floor.").

Eliciting Multiple-Clause Sentences

1. *Description game.* A variation of the game mentioned above can have the clinician use coordinated actions. ("She put the cup in the bag and dropped it.") Use of objects that need to be distinguished for the listener can elicit relative clauses. ("She picked up the glass that is closest to the edge.")

2. *Story telling or retelling.* Narrative will generally elicit coordinate and subordinate clauses if the child has those structures. ("She couldn't go to the ball because she didn't have anything to wear"; "First she tasted the papa bear's porridge and it was too hot.")

Eliciting Question Forms

We have successfully used a messenger game for eliciting questions. In this game the child is asked by one person to find out some information from another. The "messenger" aspect of the game may have been experienced before by the child, thus giving it some realism. Table 6–12 illustrates the types of questions which can be elicited by this procedure.

Eliciting Negatives

1. *Create the need for objects that are not present.* If the child is asked to do something but not provided with the materials needed to do it, negation may be used to indicate the missing element (e.g., "I don't have"; "There isn't any"; "It's not on the . . .").

2. *Introduce the unexpected.* Negations are likely to be expressed if the child confronts unexpected difficulty or conditions of things not working. For example, given a jar with the lid on tightly, the child may express "I can't open it" or "It won't open." Broken or nonfunctioning objects may elicit comments such as "It doesn't have any wheels" or "She can't stand up."

TABLE 6–12   The Messenger Game—A Procedure for Eliciting Questions

This is a suggested procedure for eliciting questions from a child who does not readily ask them spontaneously. The method works best when three people are involved. The child acts as a messenger, carrying information from one person to another. It is also more realistic if the two people who are exchanging messages through the child are not within view of each other. A problem with the question formulation might be revealed if the child uses the request as a model for forming his or her own questions: e.g., Adult: "Ask her how she got to this school." Child: "How you got to this school?"

Message Carried by the Child	*Question Form Elicited*
1. Ask her where she lives.	Where + do
2. Ask her when her birthday is.	When
3. Ask her how she got to this school.	How + did
4. Ask her to tell you what this is for.	What + for
5. Ask her who she eats with.	Who + do
6. Ask her what time it is.	What
7. Ask her which one she wants—this one or that one?	Which
8. Ask her how many shoes she has on.	How many
9. Ask her when she is going home.	When
10. Ask her if she will eat out tonight.	Will
11. Ask her what color her hair is.	What
12. Ask her if she wants this.	Do
13. Ask her if she likes what she is doing.	Do (complex)
14. Ask her how she catches a ball.	How + do
15. Ask her when you can go to lunch.	When + can
16. Ask her why she isn't home now.	Why + aren't
17. Ask her if she can jump.	Can
18. Ask her if she will help you snap your fingers.	Will (complex)
19. Ask her why this won't work.	Why + won't
20. Ask her why this is dirty.	Why

3. *Patterned practice.* This puppet is bad; he always says no to his mother. If his mother says

| Come in here | he says | No, I won't |
| She is my friend | he says | No, she isn't |

REFERENCES

AMIDON, A., AND P. CAREY. Why Five-Year-Olds Cannot Understand Before and After, *Journal of Verbal Learning and Verbal Behavior*, 11, 1972, 417–23.

BELLUGI, U. The Acquisition of Negation. Ph.D. dissertation, Harvard University, 1967.

BLOOM, L. *Language Development: Form and Function in Emerging Grammars.* Cambridge, Mass.: M.I.T. Press, 1970.

BLOOM, L. *One Word at a Time.* The Hague: Mouton, 1973.

BLOOM, L., AND M. LAHEY. *Language Development and Language Disorders.* New York: John Wiley, 1978.

BLOOM, L., M. LAHEY, L. HOOD, K. LIFTER, AND K. FIESS. Complex Sentences: Acquisition of Syntactic Connectives and the Semantic Relations They Encode, *Journal of Child Language*, 7, 1980, 235–62.

BLOOM, L., P. LIGHTBOWN, AND L. HOOD. Structure and Variation in Child Language, *Monographs of The Society for Research in Child Development*, 40 (serial no. 160), 1975.

BLOOM, L., J. TAKEFF, AND M. LAHEY. Learning *to*

in Complement Constructions, *Journal of Child Language*, 11, 1984, 391–406.

BLOOM, L., M. RISPOLI, B. GARTNER, AND J. HAFITZ. Acquisition of Complementation, *Journal of Child Language*, 16, 1989, 101–20.

BOWERMAN, M. *Early Syntactic Development: A Cross-Linguistic Study with Special Reference to Finnish.* Cambridge, Mass.: Cambridge University Press, 1973.

BOWERMAN, M. Cross-Linguistic Similarities at Two Stages of Syntactic Development, in *Foundations of Language Development* (vol. 1), eds. E. H. Lenneberg and E. Lenneberg. New York: Academic Press, 1975.

BOWERMAN, M. The Acquisition of Complex Sentences, in *Language Acquisition,* eds. P. Fletcher and M. Garman. London: Cambridge University Press, 1979, pp. 285–306.

BRAINE, M. D. S. The Ontogeny of the English Phrase Structure, *Language*, 39, 1963, 1–13.

BRAINE, M. D. S. Children's First Word Combinations, *Monographs of The Society for Research in Child Development* (serial no. 164), 1976.

BROWN, R. The Development of *Wh-* Questions in Child Speech, *Journal of Verbal Learning and Verbal Behavior*, 7, 1968, 277–90.

BROWN, R. *Psycholinguistics.* New York: Free Press, 1970.

BROWN, R. *A First Language.* Cambridge, Mass.: Harvard University Press, 1973.

BROWN, R., AND U. BELLUGI. Three Processes in the Child's Acquisition of Syntax, *Harvard Educational Review*, 34, no. 2, 1964, 133–51.

BROWN, R., AND C. HANLON. Derivational Complexity and Order of Acquisition in Child Speech, in *Cognition and the Development of Language*, ed. John R. Hayes. New York: John Wiley, 1970, pp. 155–207.

CHOI, S. The Semantic Development of Negation: A Cross Linguistic Study, *Journal of Child Language*, 15, 1988, 517–531.

CHOMSKY, C. *The Acquisition of Syntax in Children from 5 to 10.* Cambridge, Mass.: M.I.T. Press, 1969.

CHOMSKY, N. *Syntactic Structures.* The Hague: Mouton, 1957.

CHOMSKY, N. *Aspects of the Theory of Syntax.* Cambridge, Mass.: M.I.T. Press, 1965.

CLANCY, P. M. Form and Function in the Acquisition of Korean *Wh-* Questions, *Journal of Child Language*, 16, 1989, 323–47.

CLARK, E. V. On the Acquisition of the Meaning of Before and After, *Journal of Verbal Learning and Verbal Behavior*, 10, 1971, 266–75.

CROMER, R. Children Are Nice to Understand: Surface Structure Cues for the Recovery of a Deep Structure, *British Journal of Psychology*, 61, 1970, 397–408.

CRYSTAL, D. *Working with LARSP.* New York: Elsevier, 1979.

CRYSTAL, D., P. FLETCHER, AND M. GARMAN. *The Grammatical Analysis of Language Disability.* New York: Elsevier North-Holland, 1976.

DALE, P. *Language Development: Structure and Function* (2nd ed.). New York: Holt, Rinehart & Winston, 1976.

DEVILLIERS, J., AND P. DEVILLIERS. A Cross-Sectional Study of the Acquisition of Grammatical Morphemes in Child Speech, *Journal of Psycholinguistic Research*, 2, 1973, 267–78.

DEVILLIERS, J., H. TAGER-FLUSBERG, AND K. HAKUTA. Deciding among Theories of Development of Coordination in Child Speech, *Papers and Reports on Child Language Development*, 13, 1977, 118–25.

DORE, J. Holophrases, Speech Acts, and Language Universals, *Journal of Child Language*, 2, 1975, 21–40.

DROMI, E., AND R. BERMAN. A Morphologic Measure of Early Language Development: Data from Modern Hebrew, *Journal of Child Language*, 9, 1982, 403–24.

DUCHAN, J., AND J. ERICKSON. Normal and Retarded Children's Understanding of Semantic Relations in Different Verbal Contexts, *Journal of Speech and Hearing Research*, 19, 1976, 767–76.

DUCHAN, J. F., AND N. J. LUND. Why Not Semantic Relations? *Journal of Child Language*, 6, 1979, 243–52.

FABIAN, V. When Are Children Hard to Understand? Paper presented at the Second Annual Boston University Conference on Language Development. Boston, Mass., 1977.

FILLMORE, C. The Case for Case, in *Universals in Linguistic Theory*, eds. E. Bach and R. Harms. New York: Holt, Rinehart & Winston, 1968.

GERRARD, K. A Guide for Assessing Young Children's Expressive Language Skills Through Language Sampling, *National Student Speech Language and Hearing Association Journal*, 18, 1990–1991, 87–95.

GOLINKOFF, R. M., AND J. MARKESSINI. Mommy Sock: The Child's Understanding of Possessing as Expressed in Two-Word Phrases, *Journal of Child Language*, 7, 1980, 119–35.

HALLIDAY, M. A. K. *Learning How to Mean: Explorations in the Development of Language.* London: Longman, 1975.

HOWE, C. The Meanings of Two-Word Utterances in the Speech of Young Children, *Journal of Child Language*, 3, 1976, 29–47.

HUGHES, D., AND J. TILL. A Comparison of Two Procedures to Elicit Verbal Auxiliary and Copula in Normal Kindergarten Children, *Journal of Speech and Hearing Disorders*, 47, 1982, 310–20.

INGRAM, D. Transitivity in Child Language, *Language*, 47, 1971, 888–910.

KESSEL, F. The Role of Syntax in Children's Comprehension from Ages Six to Twelve, *Society for Research in Child Development Monograph*, 35, 1970.

KLEE, T., AND M. D. FITZGERALD. The Relation Between Grammatical Development and Mean Length of Utterance in Morphemes, *Journal of Child Language,* 12, 1985, 251–69.

KLIMA, E., AND U. BELLUGI. Syntactic Regularities in the Speech of Children, in *Psycholinguistic Papers,* eds. J. Lyons and R. J. Wales. Edinburgh: Edinburgh University Press, 1966, 183–208.

KRAMER, C. A., S. L. JAMES, AND J. H. SAXMAN. A Comparison of Language Samples Elicited at Home and in the Clinic, *Journal of Speech and Hearing Disorders,* 44, 1979, 321–30.

LEE, L. L., AND S. M. CANTER. Developmental Sentence Scoring: A Clinical Procedure for Estimating Syntactic Development in Children's Spontaneous Speech, *Journal of Speech and Hearing Disorders,* 36, 1971, 315–38.

LEOPOLD, W. *Speech Development of a Bilingual Child: A Linguist's Record,* Vols. 1, 3. Evanston, Ill.: Northwestern University Press, 1939, 1949.

LIMBER, J. The Genesis of Complex Sentences, in *Cognitive Development and the Acquisition of Language,* ed. T. Moore. New York: Academic Press, 1973.

LINARES, N. Rules for Calculating Mean Length of Utterance in Morphemes for Spanish, in *The Bilingual Exceptional Child,* eds. D. R. Omark and J. G. Erickson. San Diego: College-Hill Press, 1983.

LORD, C. Variations in the Patterns of Acquisition of Negation, *Papers and Reports on Child Language Development,* No. 8. Department of Linguistics, Stanford University, Palo Alto, California, 1974.

LUST, B. Conjunction Reduction in Child Language, *Journal of Child Language,* 4, 1977, 257–88.

LUST, B., AND C. A. MERVIS. Development of Coordination in the Natural Speech of Young Children, *Journal of Child Language,* 7, 1980, 279–304.

MCNEILL, D. *The Acquisition of Language: The Study of Developmental Psycholinguistics.* New York: Harper & Row, 1970.

MCNEILL, D., AND N. MCNEILL. What Does a Child Mean When He Says "No?" in *Language and Language Behavior,* ed. E. Zale, New York: Appleton-Century-Croft, 1968.

MACWHINNEY, B. Grammatical Devices for Sharing Points, in *The Acquisition of Communicative Competence,* eds. R. Schiefelbusch and J. Pickar. Austin, Tex.: Pro-Ed, 1984, pp. 323–74.

MARTIN, J. E. A Study of the Determinants of Preferred Adjective Order in English. Ph.D. dissertation, University of Illinois, 1968.

MENYUK, P. *Sentences Children Use.* Cambridge, Mass.: M.I.T. Press, 1969.

MENYUK, P. *The Acquisition and Development of Language.* Englewood Cliffs, N.J.: Prentice-Hall, 1971.

MENYUK, P. *Language and Maturation.* Cambridge, Mass.: M.I.T. Press, 1977.

MILLER, J. Assessing Children's Language Behavior:

A Developmental Process Approach, in *Bases of Language Intervention,* ed. R. Schiefelbusch. Baltimore: University Park Press, 1978, pp. 269–318.

MILLER, J. Assessing Language Production in Children, Baltimore: University Park Press, 1981.

MILLER, J., AND R. CHAPMAN. The Relation Between Age and Mean Length of Utterance in Morphemes. *Journal of Speech and Hearing Research,* 24, 1981, 154–61.

MILLER, M., AND J. WEISSENBORN. Pragmatic Conditions on Learning How to Refer to Localities, *Papers and Reports on Child Language Development,* Stanford University, 15, 1978, 68–77.

MILLER, W., AND S. ERVIN. The Development of Grammar in Child Language. In U. Bellugi and R. Brown (eds.). *The Acquisition of Language,* Monograph #29. Chicago, Ill: Society for Research in Child Development, 1964.

MILLER, M., AND J. WEISSENBORN. Pragmatic Conditions on Learning How to Refer to Localities, *Papers and Reports on Child Language Development,* Stanford University, 15, 1978, 68–77.

NEWPORT, E. L., H. GLEITMAN, AND L. R. GLEITMAN. Mother, I'd Rather Do It Myself: Some Effects and Non-Effects of Maternal Speech Style, in *Talking to Children: Language Input and Acquisition,* eds. C. E. Snow and C. A. Ferguson. New York: C.U.P., 1977.

OKUBO, A. *Yooji Gengo no Hattatsu* (Children's Language Development). Tokyo: Tokyodoo, 1967.

PETRETIC, P., AND R. TWENEY. Does Comprehension Precede Production? *Journal of Child Language,* 4, 1977, 201–10.

QUIRK, R., S. GREENBAUM, G. LEECH, AND J. SVARTVIK. *A Grammar of Contemporary English.* London: Longman, 1972.

RONDAL, J. A., M. GHIOTTO, S. BREDART, AND J. BACHELET. Age-Relation, Reliability and Grammatical Validity of Measures of Utterance Length, *Journal of Child Language,* 14, 1987, 433–46.

ROSENBAUM, P. *The Grammar of English Predicate Construction.* Cambridge, Mass.: M.I.T. Press, 1967.

SAVIĆ, S. Aspects of Adult-Child Communication: The Problem of Question Acquisition, *Journal of Child Language,* 2, 1975, 251–60.

SCARBOROUGH, H. S. Index of Productive Syntax, *Applied Psycholinguistics,* 11, 1990, 1–22.

SCARBOROUGH, H. S., L. RESCORLA, H. TAGER-FLUSBERG, A. E. FOWLER, AND V. SUDHALTER. The Relation of Utterance Length to Grammatical Complexity in Normal and Language-Disordered Groups, *Applied Psycholinguistics,* 12, 1991, 23–45.

SCOLLON, R. One Child's Language from One to Two: The Origins of Construction. University of Hawaii: Working Papers in Linguistics, 6, no. 5, 1974.

SHIPLEY, E., C. SMITH, AND L. GLEITMAN. A Study in the Acquisition of Language: Free Responses to Commands, *Language,* 2, 1969, 45.

SLOBIN, D. I. Cognitive Prerequisites for the Acquisition of Grammar, in *Studies of Child Language Development,* eds. C. A. Ferguson and D. I. Slobin. New York: Holt, Rinehart & Winston, 1973.

SLOBIN, D. I., AND C. A. WELSH. Elicited Imitation as a Research Tool in Developmental Psycholinguistics, in *Studies of Child Language Development,* eds. C. A. Ferguson and D. I. Slobin. New York: Holt, Rinehart & Winston, 1973.

STOCKWELL, R. *Foundations of Syntactic Theory.* Englewood Cliffs, N.J.: Prentice-Hall, 1977.

TAVAKOLIAN, S. Children's Understanding of Pronominal Subjects and Missing Subjects in Complicated Sentences. Paper presented at the Winter Meetings of the Linguistic Society of America, 1976.

VENDLER, Z. *Adjectives and Nominalizations.* The Hague: Mouton, 1968.

VOLTERRA, V., AND F. ANTINUCCI. Negation in Child Language: A Pragmatic Study, in *Developmental Pragmatics,* eds. E. Ochs and B. Schieffelin. New York: Academic Press, 1979.

WELLS, G. *Language Development in the Pre-School Years.* Cambridge: Cambridge University Press, 1985.

WODE, H. Some Stages in the Acquisition of Questions by Monolingual Children, in *Child Language—1975,* ed. W. von Raffler-Engel. Special issue of *Word,* 27, 1974, 261–310.

ZUBIN, D. Discourse Function of Morphology: The Focus System in German, in *Syntax and Semantics, Vol. 12: Discourse and Syntax,* ed. T. Givon. New York: Academic Press, 1979.

7

Semantics

Semantics is the study of the meaning of words and word combinations. While we alluded to meaning in our discussions of morphology and syntax, the emphasis there was on the form rather than on the objects, events, and ideas being expressed with those forms. It is not easy to separate form and meaning, and it is probably making an artificial distinction to do so. As we discussed different word classes, we pointed out that each conveys distinct kinds of meaning, so choice of the morphemes to use and decisions about the syntactic structures in which to use them depends upon the meanings we want to convey.

The nature of meaning has long been debated (see Clark and Clark, 1977, for an introduction to theories of meaning). We will not go into these debates but will distinguish among several ways *meaning* is used and show how they relate to different aspects of semantics. The most familiar sense of *meaning* relates to the characteristics of the category to which a word applies. We call this *lexical meaning*. When we hear a new word and ask what it means, we are asking for its lexical meaning—that is, we are asking what class of beings, objects, events, or characteristics to which it applies. These are the referents for the word. Some words do not have identifiable referents, but rather express a relationship between beings, objects, and events. Words such as *and* or *in* have as their meaning particular relationships—they have what we call *abstract relational meaning*. Some words are described as having abstract relations to other words in a sentence as well as lexical meaning. A discussion of meaning must also take into account *nonliteral meaning,* or words' relation not to their usual referents but to some characteristic of those referents.

LEXICAL MEANING

Children's lexical meaning has been studied most extensively at the early stages of language development, with the focus on the meaning of children's first words and how they are represented in the child's *lexicon,* or mental dictionary.

We will first present some characteristics of adult lexical meaning and then discuss some ways child meaning differs from adult meaning.

Meaning as Prototypes

Rosch (1973) introduced the idea that a category or concept can be defined as its prototype or "best" example. Referents are included in the category based on their resemblance to the prototype, with some being very central because of their strong resemblance and others being more peripheral. Referents do not necessarily resemble each other and may in fact be quite different, but each shares some of the "family" characteristics with the prototype. This prototype view of category formation is in opposition to the more traditional "critical attribute" model, which defines members of a category in terms of one or several critical attributes that each must have in order to be included in that class. If we attempt to define the meaning of *dog,* for example, in terms of critical attributes, we would have difficulty explaining how we know a hairless, tailless, or nonbarking animal is in fact a dog, since having hair and a tail and barking would be considered part of the set of attributes that define *dog.* Using a prototype model, we could explain this inclusion in the category by noting the strong resemblance between the animal and our prototype dog, even though it lacks one or more of the features typical of a dog.

Adults seem to work from an abstract prototype that is composed of the most typical features of referents in a category. This can easily be demonstrated by having adults rate members of a class on how typical they are of that class. They will consistently find *robin* to be a "better" example of *bird* than *owl* or *stork,* for example. Some referents, such as *chicken* or *penguin,* will be very "poor" bird examples and may in fact lead to disagreements about whether they belong in the class. This demonstrates that although the features of the prototype are typical of the class, they are not necessary. Having few of the features accounts for some referents, such as penguins being at the periphery of the category. Referents that are most similar to the prototype are most similar to each other, whereas those nearing the boundaries may be quite dissimilar to each other and most susceptible to exclusion from the category under certain circumstances. For example, colors that are closely related to our prototype *red* all will be similar to each other, but those at different boundaries of the *red* category—those that approach purple or orange—will be perceived as very different from each other. Those at the boundaries are also more likely to be put into another category, depending, for example, on surrounding context of background color.

Some concepts, such as colors and shapes, have been described as natural categories (Palermo, 1978; Rosch, 1973) and have been demonstrated to have relatively stable prototypes across cultural and age groups (Mervis, Catlin, and Rosch, 1975; Rosch, 1973). Other categories appear to have the prototype determined more by experience. The concept of *clothing,* for example, would have a different prototype for individuals living in the arctic and the tropics. Children typically derive prototypes from the first referents they encounter (Rosch and Mervis, 1975). If their first experience with *bird* is the family canary, that will be their prototype against which the "birdness" of other objects is judged.

Meaning as Semantic Features

We have discussed the prototype in terms of the "features" of members of the class. By this we mean the perceptual and functional characteristics shared by some or all members of the class, such as, in the case of birds, feathers, wings, two legs, movement in a certain manner, and so on. Describing the lexical meaning in terms of semantic features involves portraying word meaning as a composite of such defining features. The meaning of *man,* for example, might be described as consisting of the features of *human, adult,* and *male.* The feature of *human* would contain such features as *animate* and *mammal.* The sense of different words can be described in terms of feature differences. Thus, the meaning of *woman* differs from *man* by including the feature of *female* rather than *male.* This feature conceptualization, unlike the prototype view, holds features to be critical attributes and thus necessarily present in each referent.

It appears that children's first referential words are based on dynamic functional features—that is, children are attentive to how objects act or can be acted on (Nelson, 1973). Later, the stable perceptual features such as shape and size appear to be more critical to the children's decisions on which referents will be included in the concept. Thus, *ball* may be an early word because the dynamic features of a ball make it interesting to the child—it can be picked up, thrown, bounced, rolled, and so on. It is likely to be the stable perceptual features, however, such as shape, that lead the child to identify a new referent as belonging to the ball category.

CHILDREN'S LEXICAL MEANINGS

There are some predictable patterns that children follow in the development of their semantic systems. There are other patterns that are less predictable because they are unique for a particular child. Through structural analysis, we look at the way children use words to try to determine the meaning they have at the time we are doing our assessment. Meanings change as children increase their experience with words, so we cannot take the semantic system to be stable. Some of the characteristics of children's early meanings will persist well beyond the development of complex syntax; others will be short-lived.

Overextension of Meaning

It has frequently been observed by investigators of child language that young children often use words to apply to a wider range of referents than adults do. An example of this is the child whose referents for *doggy* include cats, cows, sheep, and a variety of other four-legged animals. This type of confusion has been called *overextension* by Eve Clark (1973), and her hypothesis is that it results from children's creation of a category based on limited semantic features. In our example, it appears that the child's sense of *doggy* consists only of the features *animal* and *four-legged,* but not the other features that distinguish dogs from other animals (such as size, sound, way of moving, and so on). Clark (1973; 1974) gives examples of overextensions from many different children learning different languages and concludes that these overextensions are based on a selected perceptual property that the newly named object has in common with the original referent. Shape is the most frequently reported basis for overextensions, as, for example, in the use of *ball* for all round objects. In this case, it can be assumed that a ball was the original referent for the word *ball,* so other round objects are called *ball.* The properties of size, sound, movement, texture, and taste have also been reported to be relevant properties in over-extensions. Notably absent from this list is color—that is, children do not make errors such as calling all red objects *apple.* This leads us to speculate that certain perceptual properties are salient to children because they affect the way objects can be acted upon. Shape is salient because it determines whether the object can be rolled or stacked, for example. Size identifies objects that can be put in one's pocket or sat on. Color rarely makes a difference in the way an object acts or is acted upon until we get into activities such as card games, in which color is arbitrarily assigned significance.

In addition to those instances in which a child overextends on the basis of one or two critical properties, it has also been observed that children will use the same word for diverse new objects that share different properties with the original object. Bowerman (1976), for example, gives the illustration of Eva using *kick* in connection with (1) herself kicking a stationary object, (2) a picture of a cat with a ball near its paw, (3) a fluttering moth, (4) cartoon turtles on TV kicking their legs, (5) throwing an object, (6) bumping a ball with her trike wheel, and (7) pushing her chest against a sink. While these situations do not share a set of common features, all of them are characterized by one or more features of the original situation which involve waving a limb, sudden sharp contact, and an object propelled. Clark and Clark (1977) refer to this as *mixed overextension.* We could also say each of these referents bears a "family resemblance" to the original, or prototype.

Underextension of Meaning

Overextension can be seen as using a word for too wide a variety of reference; *underextension* (or *overrestriction*) refers to use of a word for only a subset of the referents in the adult category. Bloom (1973) provides the example of Allison at age nine months using *car* only for cars moving on the street below her window, not for cars standing still, pictured cars, or cars she rode in. While overextension can be explained as incomplete acquisition of semantic features, underextension can best be understood as children's prototypes derived from limited experience. As they learn that a word applies beyond the original referent, they may progress from underextension to overextension. For example, the child in our example may have learned *doggy* first in reference to the family pet, Jake. While the child used *doggy* exclusively for Jake, it was underextended. When the child began to apply *doggy* to other animals that shared some features with Jake, such as those having four legs, the word was overextended to include not only other dogs but nondogs as well.

Different Referent

Sometimes children's meanings are different from adults' because they pertain to another referent. Upon first hearing a word, a child may take it to refer to a different referent from that intended by the conversational partner. For example, Clark and Clark (1977, p. 486) relate these observations made by E. E. Maccoby:

> A mother said sternly to her child: "Young man, you did that on purpose." When asked later what *on purpose* meant, the child replied, "It means you're looking at me."
>
> A nursery school teacher divided her class into teams, spread a small blanket on the floor at one end of the room and said, "This team will start here," and then put another blanket at the other end of the room, saying "This team will start here." At home, later, a child put down a blanket and set her baby brother on it. He crawled off and the child complained to her mother: "He won't stay on my team!"

These examples clearly demonstrate the role that context plays in the acquisition of meaning.

Word Deficit

We frequently find evidence in children's language samples that they have the meaning of a word but *lack the adult phonological form* to match it. In these cases, they may invent their own form or create one out of known adult elements, such as referring to yesterday as "last day," probably as a parallel form to "last night." They may also rely heavily on *proforms*, such as the pronoun *it* or *those;* general descriptive terms, such as *this thing* or *the thingamajig*; or pro-verbs such as *do* or *make* in place of more specific verbs. Also common is the use of related words or descriptions to convey their meaning, such as "those things on your shirt" to refer to buttons. In some cases, it appears that the child simply has not learned the phonetic form of the word; in others, it seems the form has been temporarily forgotten. Both of these cases are referred to as having *word-finding difficulty*. If this is the case, the child may actively "search" for the word by trying several descriptions and will recognize the word immediately if it is offered (e.g., Q: "Do you mean buttons?" A: "Yes, that's it—buttons").

Understanding Lexical Meaning

Children's first understanding of single words for the most part is context bound in that the words are understood only if they pertain to present, familiar, and perceptually salient objects. Nonetheless, they do carry some of their own decontextualized meaning since children will occasionally switch their attention from what they are doing to the referent designated (Sachs and Truswell, 1978). Evidence for a one-word stage of comprehension is that found when children can be shown to ignore longer utterances (Shipley, Smith, and Gleitman, 1969); pick out one familiar word from a group of words and ignore the others (Benedict, 1979); or treat a group of words as though it were one word (Thomas, 1979).

Research on children's comprehension of linguistic forms usually assume that children's lexical knowledge is similar to adult knowledge; that is, that words have stable meanings with circumscribed adultlike boundaries. Typically in these studies children are asked to indicate the referent for adult words from choices that include an item that adults believe to be an exemplar of the named category. Young children often do not have fixed meanings for words; their word meanings fluctuate and are related to context. When their words do have fixed meanings, they often do not coincide with the adult sense of the word boundaries, so we may see overextension in comprehension as well as in expression, although there are some indications it is less frequent (Rescorla, 1980; Thomson and Chapman, 1977; Huttenlocher, 1974).

Clark (1983; 1987) has argued that children apply the *principle of contrast* when learning the meaning of new words; that is, they assume that words contrast in meaning and so look for the distinguishing features. This could explain how overextended meanings (e.g., *doggy* for all animals) are narrowed to correspond to adultlike meanings as children learn new words (*cat, sheep,* etc.). Tomasello, Mannle, and Werdenschlag (1988) investigated the role the principle of contrast plays in children learning new words by introducing two-year-olds to items that were either similar to or dissimilar from other items they had learned to name. The authors reasoned that the similar referents, unlike the dissimilar referents, would lend themselves to an easy contrast of features. They found that children learn a new word quicker when they are able to contrast its referent with that of a word they already know.

Definitional Meaning

The ability to define words is increasingly required and valued as children get older. Early investigations of children's ability to give definitions, as part of the development of IQ tests, revealed that there are qualitative changes with age in the kinds of information children include in their definitions (Binet and Simon, 1916). This has consistently been confirmed by subsequent studies (see Markowitz and Franz, 1988, for a review). Three stages of definitions have generally been identified. The earliest definitions offered by young children relate to sensory properties or functions ("A banana is to eat"). Around age seven, children begin to give categorical membership as a component of definitions ("A banana is a fruit"). Around age ten, children's definitions become adultlike in form and content and increasingly conform to the convention of including a superordinate and a restrictive complement ("A banana is a fruit that has a thick yellow skin when ripe") (Benelli, Arcuri, and Marchesini, 1988). Snow (1990) argues that children need to learn the adult forms for giving definitions as well as the logical information and that this lack of knowledge of adult forms accounts for some of the differences between more and less mature definitions. She presents evidence that children's performance on definitions is enhanced by practice giving definitions and, with bilingual children, demonstrates that ability to give definitions is related more closely to practice in giving definitions in a language than to overall exposure to or proficiency in that language.

ABSTRACT RELATIONAL MEANING

So far, we have been discussing how word meaning relates to the objects, events, or qualities that are the referents for that word. It is also possible to characterize the meaning of words as the relationship they express between referents. A word with constant lexical meaning can express several relational meanings, depending on the role it plays in a given utterance.

Case Grammar

The first systematic analysis of the relational meaning of words was done by Fillmore (1968), who describes the semantic role of *case* of nouns in relation to other elements in the sentence. His case grammar is based on descriptions of adult language, and identifies a set of "presumably innate" concepts expressed in all languages. Each noun is seen as expressing abstract relational meaning in addition to its lexical meaning. Fillmore's cases include

Agentive: The animate instigator of action, as in "*Sam* cut the bread."

Instrumental: The force or object causally involved in a state or action, as in "*The knife* cut the bread."

Dative: The animate being affected by the state or action, as in "Harry pushed *Joe.*"

Factitive: The object or being resulting from a state or action, as in "She baked *brownies.*"

Locative: The location or spatial orientation of a state or action, as in "I ate *at home.*"

Objective: The semantically most neutral case; any referent whose role depends on the meaning of the verb, as in "She hit *the ball.*"

Semantic Relations

Following Fillmore, several investigators of children's language have described the abstract relational meanings expressed in children's early word combinations (Brown, 1973; Schlesinger, 1971; Bloom, 1970). These taxonomies are not restricted to nouns but include other word classes that children frequently use as well. Brown (1973) found that a relatively short list of relational meanings accounted for 70 percent of the multiword utterances of his three subjects and of the early word combinations of children speaking other languages as well. The following taxonomy of Schlesinger (1971) illustrates the first descriptions of children's semantic relations.

agent + action	airplane go; daddy bye
action + object	see hat; throw ball
agent + object	mommy soup (mommy is making soup)
modifier + head	dirty soap; more milk
introducer + X	see book; there kitty
(X is any variable)	
X + dative	throw daddy (throw it to daddy)
(Dative is recipient or benefactor)	
X + locative	baby chair (baby is in the chair)

It can be observed that Schlesinger's noun categories do not exactly match Fillmore's categories. For example, *airplane* would not be an agent for Fillmore since it cannot instigate action; rather it would be an object or instrument. Also, *soup* as used above would be in the factitive case for Fillmore rather than being an object.

Semantic-Syntactic Relations

The most extensive taxonomy of children's abstract relational meanings is presented by Bloom and Lahey (1978). They refer to their twenty-one identified categories as semantic-syntactic relations in recognition of the interrelationship between the syntactic role that a particular word fills in the utterance, and its semantic role. That is, the same words can have different semantic relationships when they are in different syntactic arrangements. Also, some of the categories are identified by specific grammatical forms.

Bloom and Lahey (1978) include several kinds of meaning relationships in their list. Some of the categories represent a relationship between two referents. These include

> *Possession:* Refers to the relationship between people and the objects within their domain, such as "baby cap" or "my bed."
> *Locative action:* Indicates the relationship between locations and objects moving to or from that location, as when the child says "away block."
> *Locative state:* Indicates a relationship between a person or object and its location, such as "dolly up there."
> *Dative:* Indicates the relationship between an object or action and the recipient, such as "kiss for mommy."

Other categories identify ways in which events can be related to each other. These typically involve two clauses with an implied or explicit conjunction. These are discussed most fully in Bloom and others (1980).

> *Causality:* Indicates a dependency between two events or states with a cause-and-effect relationship. This may be expressed with *because* or *so,* or implied as in "Kiss it and make it better."
> *Coordination or additive:* Indicates that two events or states are independent of each other but are bound together in time or space, as in "I'll sit here and you sit there."
> *Antithesis or adversative:* Indicates that the dependency between two events or states is a contrast between them. This may be expressed with *but,* as in "I can go but you can't."
> *Temporal:* Indicates a temporal sequence or simultaneity between events or states, such as "Do this and then do that."

Several of the categories that are identified by Bloom and Lahey as semantic-syntactic relations appear to be performatives; that is, they have intentional meaning and are used to perform an activity rather than expressing a meaning relationship between words. These include some uses of negatives.

> *Rejection:* Indicates that the referent is present or is imminent, and is rejected or opposed by the child. This is performative because the child uses a negative (*no; don't*) to get rid of an unwanted object or to stop an action.

Nonexistence or disappearance: Indicates that the referent is not present. Nega
that express nonexistence or disappearance may be performatives when
function as a request for something (e.g., "no milk" while holding out an empty
cup). Alternatively, they may express an expected relationship between two
referents that does not exist (e.g., "no hood" when examining a jacket).

Denial: Indicates that the assertion made by someone else is not the case. Denial
statements are performatives in that they indicate disagreement or make corrections
(e.g., "I'm not tired" in response to "You're just tired").

Other semantic-syntactic relations which serve performative functions are:

Existence: Indicates that some object has the child's attention, and generally, that
the child is directing someone else's attention to the object. This may be done with
the object name, a demonstrative pronoun, or a routine question form ("What
that?")

Notice: Directs attention of the listener to a person, object, or event. These include
a verb of notice such as *see* or *lookit.*

Recurrence: Indicates multiple occurrences of an object or event, either sequentially
or simultaneously. Recurrence utterances are most commonly performatives in
that they are used to request continuation or repetition (e.g., "nother cookie";
"more jump"). The use of these utterances to indicate equivalent objects (e.g.,
"more kitty" when a second kitten appears) seems to come closer to expressing a
relationship.

Also included in Bloom and Lahey's relations are several categories that
appear to have specific words or word classes as their basis. These include:

Attribution: Refers to properties of objects, expressed by the child with adjectives.

Specifier: Indicates a specific person, object, or event by use of a demonstrative or
definite article (e.g., "that boy"). Object specification can also involve two clauses
which combine to describe an object (e.g., "It's round and you can roll it").

Action: Refers to movement, expressed with a verb, when the goal of the movement
is not a change in location (e.g., "I'm jumping").

State: Refers to states of affairs, which might be internal states (want, need);
external states (cold, dark); or temporary possession ("my seat").

Quantity: Designates number of objects or persons with a number or quantifier
such as *some.* Quantity can also be expressed morphologically with plural markers.

Epistemic: Indicates a state or event that is marked by certainty or uncertainty, as
is indicated by modals *may* and *will,* or with direct or embedded questions (e.g., "I
know what her name is").

Mood: Indicates the attitude of the speaker about the obligatory nature of the
event. This is indicated by the use of modal verbs such as *should* or *hafta.*

Time: This category relates to a single event, rather than the temporal relationships
between events. The concepts of tense and aspect are combined in one category.
Some references to time and aspect are made with grammatical morphemes (*-ed;
-ing*) or by modal verbs (*gonna; will*). These seem to be primarily syntactic relations.
Other utterances refer to time or aspect with adverbs such as *now* or *still;* these
seem to have a lexical basis.

Arguments against Semantic Relations

There have been a number of researchers who have argued against a semantic relations interpretation of children's productions. Braine (1976) found different patterns of development for structures that would be described as representing the same semantic relation, such as *other* + X, *big* + X, and *two* + X, which would all be considered in the category of modifier + X. On this basis, he argues that it is inappropriate to ascribe to children broad semantic relations categories. Howe (1976) also argued against a semantic relation interpretation of children's utterances, based on her judgment that children's cognitive capacities are not developed enough to understand the classifications attributed to them. Duchan and Lund (1979) found that children's responses to a task designed to elicit specific semantic relations could be explained more easily by looking to the children's interpretation of the situation rather than by postulating their expression of semantic relations. In this study, three-year-olds were asked a series of questions with the form "What do you (verb) with?" which predictably elicit responses from adults that could be classified as instrumental ("I cut with a knife"), accompanier ("I play with my friend."), or manner ("I drink with gusto"). The children tended to respond by indicating an object or location that was necessary in order for the action named by the verb to take place (e.g., "I eat with soup"; "I sit with a chair"). It thus seems that their responses reflected their sense of the event connoted by the verb rather than by their understanding of the relationship that potentially existed between elements within that event. This interpretation would argue against use of a priori semantic relations because they involve too rich an interpretation of children's productions.

Fillmore (1968) and other theoreticians assume that semantic relations are based on innate conceptual categories. Bowerman (1989) challenges that assumption. She notes differences in how languages categorize spatial relations and how they organize concepts underlying spatial words and takes these differences to be evidence against innate categories. She notes, for example, that Korean distinguishes between actions in which objects are brought into or out of a relationship of tight fit or attachment in contrast to those with loose or no attachment. Thus where English uses *in* to express both kinds of actions ("Put your hand in the glove"; "Put the apple in the bowl"), Korean could not express these relations with the same form nor would the Korean speaker see these as the same "semantic relation." Bowerman also points to differences in how languages deal with intransitive subjects as evidence that semantic categories differ. English, and other *nominative* languages, treats intransitive subjects like transitive subjects in that they occupy the same place in the clause and, if marked, are both marked as nominative case. In contrast, Eskimo and Samoan are *ergative* languages in that they treat intransitive subjects as they do clause objects in position and marking (Dixon, 1979). Using these and other examples, Bowerman (1989) argues for semantic categories being learned rather than being innate.

The implication for assessing and intervening in the area of semantic relations is to proceed with caution. If children do not have conceptual organization that corresponds to our semantic relations' categories, we cannot expect them to acquire or comprehend words to express those categories. We should be particularly careful with an ESL (English as a Second Language) child to determine the differences and correspondence in the relationships expressed in English and in the child's language.

Development of Semantic-Syntactic Relations

Among the earliest ideas which children develop are those about how animate objects and inanimate objects relate to one another. It has been assumed that the most basic action sequences, and the easiest to recognize by young children, are those involving an animate agent acting on an inanimate object (Slobin, 1981). Some hypothesize that one way for children to distinguish agents from recipients is to determine which objects in their environment are animate and which are inanimate, and then to assume that animate objects usually act as agents and inanimate ones as recipients.

Research on children's notions of animacy points to its development in the first months of life. Fitzgerald (1968), Stechler and Latz (1966), and Fantz (1963) found that infants younger than one month prefer social to nonsocial stimuli, suggesting that they are making some kind of distinction related to animacy. By two months of age, infants can differentiate between social and nonsocial objects (Gibson, 1969). Bell (1970) found that eight-and-one-half-month-old infants had more advanced notions of object permanence for people than for objects, indicating a developmental stage based on the ability of the child to distinguish animate from inanimate.

Golinkoff and Harding (1980, cited in Golinkoff, 1981) also found evidence for very young children making the animate-inanimate distinction. These authors created lifelike anomalous situations in which inanimate objects acted like animate ones. Sixty-four percent of the sixteen-month-old children and 84 percent of the two-year-olds they studied responded with surprise when a chair began moving as if on its own accord.

Knowing about animacy is not sufficient for determining agent from recipient because agents sometimes are inanimate ("*The sun* dried up the rain") and recipients can sometimes be animate ("The woman kissed *the boy*"). Robertson and Suci (1980) investigated normal children's acquisition of the difference between animate agents and animate recipients. They found that one-and-one-half-year-old children focused more on the agent when watching an animate agent act on an animate recipient. They showed the children a film of three people—an agent, a recipient, and a noninvolved participant. The film began with a three-second segment still of all three participants, then proceeded to a three-segment sequence in which the agent pushed the recipient, and ended with a three-second still of all three after the incident. To find out what the children were attending to, they covered each of the people for one-and-one-half seconds before, during, and after the action sequence. They tested the children's change in heart rate under the different hiding conditions. There was significantly more acceleration in heart rate when the agent was hidden from their view, indicating that one-and-one-half-year-olds assign higher salience to the agent in these sequences, thereby differentiating it from a passive recipient.

Golinkoff (1981) found additional support that one-and-one-half- to two-year-olds are able to tell the difference between agent and recipient when both were animate. She showed the children films of a puppet doing different things to a second puppet. After the children got used to the first puppet acting on the second, Golinkoff changed the event to one in which the second puppet became the agent, acting on the first. Some of the children (one-and-one-half-year-old girls and two-year-old boys) responded to the reversal in agent-recipient roles, indicating they had a concept of differences which was separable from the activity sequence.

Children's early language reflects their nonverbal understandings. They indicate in their first words things about animacy, about objects acting as recipients, and about how objects appear, reappear, and disappear. Bloom and Lahey (1978) have studied the order of ideas expressed in single words. Their children began talking by expressing existence (*this; here*), recurrence (*more*), and disappearance (*gone*). Brown (1973) identified these same three categories, which he called *nomination, recurrence,* and *nonexistence.* Many words in these categories are unusual in that they can express a wide variety of functions. They also are combinable with others words. Bloom and Lahey (1978) found that locative and action relations develop somewhat later, followed by modifiers such as attributive and possessive.

After children have learned to express basic semantic-syntactic relations, they begin expressing the relations between events which contain the basic relations. Bloom and others (1980) examine four children's development of connectives which the children use to express relations between events. Children's first expressions of these higher order relations were additive; that is, the children expressed two ideas strung together with the word *and.* All four of their subjects used additive *and* at twenty-six months. Other uses of *and* followed: temporal *and* at a mean age of twenty-eight months, and a causal *and* at thirty-one months. The use of *and* for object specification and adversative meaning was productive for two out of the four children prior to age three. Other developments, in order of acquisition, were

> *And then* and *when,* expressing a temporal relationship, both emerging about age thirty-one months.
>
> *Because* and *so,* expressing a causal relationship, emerging about thirty-two and thirty-three months of age, respectively.
>
> *What,* to express epistemic relationship and notice relationship. The epistemic meaning was noted about age thirty-two months, with notice appearing productively for two children about age thirty-five months.
>
> *Then,* expressing a temporal relationship emerged for two out of the four children about age thirty-three months.
>
> *If,* as an epistemic expression, was used productively by two children about age thirty-four months.
>
> *But* was used by all the children to express an adversative meaning; it appeared about age thirty-five months.
>
> *That,* as a relative pronoun to express object specification, appeared about age thirty-six months.

NONLITERAL MEANING

Forms of Nonliteral Meaning

When we say things such as "The lake is glass," "It's raining cats and dogs," and "Don't put all your eggs in one basket, " we are being nonliteral in our meaning. In a different context (e.g., "The bowl is glass"), the words have a literal meaning. The examples above illustrate several forms of nonliteral meaning. The first is a *metaphor,* in which one or more of a word's meaning features are changed. In this example, a feature of *lake*—that is, water—is changed to allow for the expansion of the meaning of *glass* to describe it. Literally, this statement is anomolous while non-literally it conveys meaning. The second example—"It's raining cats and dogs"—is an *idiom* in which the meaning, that is, a lot of rain is falling, cannot be derived from the meaning of the component words. Idioms are sometimes described as *dead metaphors* that are in the language and in the mental lexicon essentially as single words rather than as phrases composed of words with interpretable meanings (Chomsky, 1965; Katz, 1972).

Proverbs are a third form of nonliteral meaning. These "wise sayings" are meant to imply a meaning more general than the literal meaning of the component words. While we generally put "all our eggs in one basket" in a literal sense, we may try to avoid situations in which too much is at stake in a single unit or operation and thus follow this maxim in a nonliteral way.

Jokes and riddles are similar to idioms, metaphors, and proverbs in that they require us to suspend our usual literal meaning and appreciate the unexpected. These forms of humor often depend on an incongruity or a sudden shift of perspective.

The relationships between children's use and understanding of literal language and of nonliteral language is just beginning to be studied (e.g., Gibbs, 1987; Elbers, 1988). In contrast to the more traditional linguistic view that nonliteral meaning is not analyzable into units as is generative language (Chomsky, 1965), these more recent investigations see generativity as possible for nonliteral meanings. Elbers (1988) presents a framework for relating nonliteral metaphors and the more literal compound words as two mechanisms for creating new names from old words. Gibbs (1987) argues that idioms, and probably all nonliteral forms, are not in a separate domain from generative language but rather are extreme points on a grammatical continuum.

Development of Nonliteral Meaning

Metaphors Looking for evidence of nonliteral language in children's productions is confounded by possible alternative interpretations of what young children mean by what they say. When a three-year-old calls a chimney a "househat," as reported by Gardner and others (1978), or describes a bald man as having a "barefoot head" (Chukovsky, 1968), we might see these as metaphors. Alternatively, we can explain them as overextensions due to lack of awareness of restrictions on these words or due to making do with limited vocabulary.

Winner (1979) suggests that metaphors in early language can be identified by one of several criteria:

1. The child has also used the literal name for an object, demonstrating that it is not lack of knowledge of the conventional name that leads to the unusual word choice.
2. A familiar object is used in a novel way and is renamed accordingly (e.g., putting a basket on the foot and calling it "boot").
3. Familiarity with the literal name is assumed based on familiarity with the object and high probability of having frequently heard its name, even though it is not produced.
4. Utterances expressed in the form of similes (e.g., "This is like a moon").

Winner thus distinguished metaphors from anomalies, which she identifies as having no apparent overlap (e.g., calling the moon "piano"). She also distinguishes them from overextensions, which arise from the child's understanding that the objects in question belong to the same class and thus can be called by the same name.

Elbers (1988) adds the requirement that real and imagined worlds be simultaneously present in the child's mind, and thus does not consider as metaphors those renamings produced during pretend actions, such as calling a spoon "doll" while pretending it is a doll. These nonmetaphoric renamings are reported among children's early single-word utterances (Gardner and others, 1978).

At about two years of age children show the ability to hold more than one thing in their minds at a time (Sugarman, 1983), which is a prerequisite for true metaphor production. Elbers (1988) gives several examples of renamings produced by her subject Tim at age two years, three months, in which an object with a known literal label (e.g., *sock*) is described nonliterally ("Cheese!") to indicate the perceived similarities—in this case, the color. Winner (1979) examined the language samples of Adam, one of the children studied by Brown (1958), and found a few similar "nonpretend" renamings, primarily associated with action up to age four. After age four, children begin to explicitly formulate metaphoric comparisons such as "That pencil looks like a rocket ship" (Gardner and others, 1978). Winner suggests that this change reflects an increasing sensitivity to the needs of the listener as well as the metalinguistic awareness that language is being used in a somewhat special way. Several investigators indicate that after age four, children actually stop producing metaphors as they enter a *latent* stage that lasts until around age ten (Hakes, 1982; Gardner and Winner, 1979; Gardner and others, 1978). Elbers (1988), however, argues against such a literal stage. She presents examples of metaphors produced by four- to ten-year-olds and discusses possible functions they serve for speakers and listeners.

Investigations into children's understanding of metaphors has focused on words that have multiple meanings. Asch and Nerlove (1960) studied dual-function adjectives which refer to both physical and psychological properties. Children first learn adjectives such as *cold, sweet,* and *crooked* as descriptions of physical properties. They gradually begin to apply these terms to personal characteristics. Asch and Nerlove (1960) found that before age six, children understood these terms only in relation to objects or physical characteristics of people, such as

> The ice is cold.
> Her hands are cold.

Between seven and ten years of age, they may understand the use of these terms when applied to a personal characteristic but give two separate and totally distinct meanings to the same term, as in

> The ice is cold.
> She is a cold person.

It is not until children are between ten and twelve years old that they understand and verbally describe the relationship between application of the term to objects and to people. For example, "She is cold like ice means she isn't friendly."

In another study of this same class of adjectives used metaphorically, Winner, Rosenstiel, and Gardner (1976) asked six- to fourteen-year-olds to explain sentences such as

> After many years of working in the jail, the prison guard had become a hard rock that could not be moved.

Again, it was found that children under age ten could not appreciate the dual-function term (*hard*). While ten- and eleven-year-olds understood that a psychological trait was the topic (the guard's character in this example), only the adolescents could identify the mutual characteristics (e.g., the guard is stubborn, unyielding, stern, cruel, set in his ways).

Gardner, Winner, and their colleagues have also found that the complexity of the task affects children's understanding of metaphors. Children as young as eight years old can match the appropriate picture to a verbal metaphor, for example, the metaphor "He has a very heavy heart." Gardner (1974) found that preschoolers are able to match adjectives across modalities (e.g., *bright, soft, loud,* in relation to color or texture). He interpreted this as metaphoric matching. A nonmetaphoric interpretation would be that the literal meaning of these terms is more general for children, perhaps translating as degree of intensity and thus applicable across modalities.

Idioms The information we have on children's development of idioms is based on experimental studies of comprehension of these forms. In tasks that require subjects to point to two pictures that represent the meanings of a phrase (e.g., "He hit the sack"), children age six and above could identify most of the pictures corresponding to literal interpretation (e.g., beating a sack), while correct identification of the picture corresponding to a nonliteral interpretation (e.g., sleeping in bed) increased with age (Prinz, 1983; Lodge and Leach, 1975). Presenting the idioms within a supporting context increases understanding of the nonliteral meaning significantly for children as young as kindergarten (Gibbs, 1987) as well as for adolescents (Nippold and Martin, 1989); the facilitating effect of context has been found in Italian idioms as well as in English (Cacciari and Levorato, 1989). Gibbs (1987) has also analyzed the semantic characteristics of different idioms and concludes that children learn most easily those idioms which are *decomposable,* or analyzable, with the meaning of their parts contributing to their overall figurative meaning. Thus an idiom such as "lay down the law" is easier for children to understand than is "going against the grain," since "law" is semantically related to the intended meaning, that is, "rules," while *grain* is only metaphorically related to the implied meaning, that is, "resistance." The lack of control for inherent difficulty of the idioms in the various studies makes it unwise to compare their findings.

Proverbs It is also not until adolescence that proverbs are understood. This is not surprising, since these nonliteral forms are more abstract than metaphors because the domain that is the topic is not mentioned at all. While preadolescents may or may not be able to paraphrase proverbs, they have consistently been found unable to interpret them in any generalized sense (Billow, 1975; Richardson and Church, 1959; Piaget, 1926). Thus we might expect preadolescents to explain proverbs literally—for example, "Don't put all your eggs in one basket means you shouldn't put them all in one basket because you might drop it." We would not expect them to generalize this wisdom beyond eggs or even to other breakable objects.

Children's Humor Children often reveal interesting things about their semantic knowledge—and lack of knowledge—through the jokes and riddles they understand and tell. The source of humor in puns, jokes, and riddles is largely semantic, often involving multiple meanings and metaphor.

Jokes have been characterized in a variety of ways. Bever (1968, reported in McGhee, 1971a) distinguishes between deep structure and surface structure jokes, based on transformational theory. Surface structure jokes involve alternative segmenting of the words in the sentence:

Gladly, the cross-eyed bear (Gladly the cross I'd bear)

Deep structure jokes involve alternative interpretations of the same surface structure:

Q: What animal can jump higher than a house?
A: Any animal. Houses can't jump.

Shultz and Horibe (1974) elaborated on Bever's categories and added lexical jokes, involving ambiguity in a single word:

Q: What's black and white and red (read) all over?
A: A newspaper.

Metalinguistic jokes have been included in a categorization system of Fowles and Glanz (1977). These focus on the form of the language, rather than the meaning:

Q: What's at the end of everything?
A: The letter *g*.

Some jokes have no "trick" involved beyond creating an expectation for something other than the obvious:

Q: Why did the chicken cross the road?
A: To get to the other side.
Q: One horse was in the barn and another was in the pasture. Which one was singing "Don't fence me in"?
A: Neither one; horses can't sing.

Some jokes involve more than one technique to create ambiguity. They may also involve idioms or metaphorical meaning.

Q: Why did the little boy throw the watch out the window?
A: He wanted to see time fly.

Prior to about age six, children's "jokes" are largely nonlinguistic. Children may appreciate the incongruity in a picture or story, or find the pie-in-the-face episodes in cartoons funny, but they are not able to appreciate humor created with language alone. Certain topics or words may be funny in themselves for young children, but this is different from the humor that comes from the manipulation of language that is involved in linguistic humor.

The development of verbal humor may be tied to concrete operational thinking, as suggested by a series of studies by McGhee (1971a; 1971b; 1972; 1974). Other investigators (e.g., Brodzinsky, 1975; Prentice and Fathman, 1975; Shultz, 1974) also documented that six-year-olds, who are generally preoperational in their thinking, exhibit little appreciation for joke structure and enjoy jokes just as much when there is no incongruity or punch line. For example,

Q: What do giraffes have that no other animal has?
A: Long necks.

is appreciated just as much as when the answer is a twist on the expected:

Q: What do giraffes have than no other animal has?
A: Little giraffes. (Prentice and Fathman, 1975)

Our own observations indicate that children often acquire the frame for riddles and jokes before they have the semantic and metaphoric knowledge to understand them. It is not uncommon for young children to tell riddles or jokes that are formally correct but totally nonsensical from an adult perspective. We know of a six-year-old, for example, who loved to tell a "scary" story, complete with appropriate intonation, with a punch line that involved a mysterious noise made by "wrapping (rapping) paper." In his version, however, the culprit became "paper towels," which was just as funny to him as the original version. We also have observed older children who clearly have the format but not the sense (or nonsense) of riddles, as shown in their attempts to create novel riddles:

Q: What kind of animal likes to be picked up?
A: A cat. (John, age eight)

At this stage, children are likely to have "near misses" in retelling riddles they have heard:

Q: What's green and has wheels?
A: A garbage truck. (Steven, age seven)

Riddle buffs will recognize this as an attempt at "What has four wheels and flies?" Since Steven didn't appreciate the ambiguity of *flies* when he originally heard the joke, it became unnecessary in its retelling. At the same time, the form of the exchange is recognized as important in making a riddle, and children will often adhere rigidly to this frame, usually telling the riddle in exactly the same way (although not necessarily the "right" way). Children recognize that slight changes make a difference, even though they do not yet understand which changes make a difference and which do not. In the same joke-telling session, Steven retold a joke he had previously heard from someone who was not following joke-telling rules, but he did not recognize this since the frame was correct.

STEVE: What did the Chinese man say to the robber?
ADULT: What?
STEVE: I'm not going to tell you!
ADULT: Why not?
STEVE: That's it! That's the answer: I'm not going to tell you.

John also attempted a retelling of a joke, again a near miss, but revealing a possible reliance on phonological cues in recall:

Q: What kind of flower likes to be kissed?
A: A toilet. (instead of tulip; that is, two-lip)

Fowles and Glanz (1977) also found this stage wherein children understand the frame but not the linguistics of riddles in a study of six- to nine-year-olds. A prior stage that they identified was characterized by a vague, confused retelling of riddles with no evidence of the riddle frame. Explanation of riddles was confused and reflected no awareness of what made them funny. At the next stage (which is what we have been describing), children could coherently retell the riddle but changed the form, deleted portions necessary for a coherent interpretation, or added sections to make it informative rather than a riddle. Children's explanations at this level involve identifying something as funny in the riddle but not seeing that it is the language rather than the situation that makes it funny:

Q: How do you keep fish from smelling?
A: Cut off their noses.
EXPLANATION: [It's funny] because I don't think fish really have noses. (Fowles and Glanz, 1977)

At the third level, riddles are retold verbatim or nearly so. Explanations focus on the attributes of language rather than on the situation. In response to the above riddle, one child explained "It means smelling like sniffing instead of smelling like stinking." Prior to this third stage, children often attempt to answer the question, usually in a literal way, indicating they are still having difficulty recognizing the uniqueness of this speech event. They have not yet understood that the intent is not to exchange information, nor to attempt to answer a question. Fowles and Glanz also found that children's ability to recall and retell riddles was not necessarily predictive of their ability to explain them. Their findings did not indicate that level of competence with riddles was clearly related to age but did indicate some relation to reading ability. This would suggest that riddles might be useful for identifying children who are having difficulty dealing with language metalinguistically.

In a study of children aged eight, ten, and twelve years, Shultz and Horibe (1974) found children up to age nine to be most sensitive to jokes based on phonological structure. For example,

Q: What kind of flower likes to be kissed?
A: A tulip. (two-lip)

Between nine and twelve years of age, children also developed appreciation for jokes depending on dual interpretation of a single word:

Q: What has eighteen legs and catches *flies*?
A: A baseball team.

Not until after age twelve did children understand jokes that involved alternative deep-structure interpretation of the same surface structure:

Q: What makes people baldheaded?
A: Having no hair.

or jokes that involved alternative grouping of words in a sentence:

Q: What happened to the man who fell from a ten-story window?
A: Nothing. He was wearing a light fall suit.

ASSESSING SEMANTICS

It is possible when doing phonological, morphological, or syntactic analysis to work from a single spontaneous sample. In doing semantic analysis, however, there is rarely enough information in one sample to draw conclusions about the child's semantic knowledge. When we are attempting to determine what a child means by a given word, we must have multiple examples of the production of that word. When we investigate the lexical and relational meanings that the child can express, we must be aware that the situation and the topic have a great influence on the words and relations that are used, and thus we need to look across several sessions with the child to get a representative sampling. Initially, we may want to let the child take the lead in conversation to determine the natural mode of expressing ideas. Later, we will want to ask questions in our interactions with the child to encourage expression of particular meanings. We may also want to use more structured procedures to elicit specific semantic operations. We have previously described some procedures used by various researchers that can be adapted for clinical assessment and include here some other possible elicitation procedures.

Analysis of all aspects of semantics is generally not appropriate for a single child, so the clinician should not feel compelled to carry out unnecessary analysis in the name of being thorough. The child with limited expressive vocabulary would not be expected to display the later semantic relations or nonliteral language, for example. The older child who expresses a variety of ideas with rich vocabulary may appear to choose inappropriate words in some instances, calling for analysis of these errors. Clinicians must use some clinical judgment in deciding which kinds of assessment are most appropriate for a given child.

Assessment of Lexical Meaning

Working from Language Samples

1. Look through transcripts for instances in which the child uses a word or phrase differently than an adult would. Make a listing transcript of all such utterances, with context included. If a word occurs more than once, include all correct and incorrect instances to determine what the word means for the child. Look for evidence of overextension, underextension, or different referent for each word or phrase that is used in ways that seem inappropriate.
2. Look for evidence of word deficits, as revealed by a high proportion of indefinite or idiosyncratic terms. Make a listing transcript of all indefinite nouns, pronouns, descriptions, or gestures that replace specific words. Indicate what is meant where it is possible to do so. Determine whether word deficits fall within one or more classes of meaning (e.g., verbs of motion; superordinate terms).
3. Look for evidence of absence or restriction of any word class. It may be apparent in looking for indefinite terms that they largely replace words from a single word class, most likely nouns. In this case, list all definite nouns that appear in the sample and calculate the ratio of definite nouns to indefinite nominal terms. This ratio can be used to compare across samples collected in different situations and at different times.

Absence or restriction of word classes can also be revealed by making listing transcripts of each word class that is not readily apparent in the sample. Noun and verb deficits would most likely be revealed through analysis for indefinite terms, but absence of adverbials, noun modifiers, and conjunctions would not generally be detected in this way. Listing transcripts of these word classes should be examined to determine what meanings the child has for these forms.

Elicitation Procedures

ALTERNATIVE REFERENTS   When we find an apparent semantic error in the child's language sample, we sometimes can deep test by presenting the child alternative referents to determine the boundaries of the word used inappropriately. For example, if we find out that a child calls an orange "juice," we would want to determine what else is *juice* for that child. If we have present several other foods, or pictures of foods and juices, we may find that only the orange is *juice*. This would appear to be a case of using the wrong word for the referent; that is, *juice* means orange and not the adult *juice*. If *juice* applies only to a whole orange and not to one that is cut or sectioned, it appears to be underextension as well. If on the other hand, it applies not only to oranges but to other fruits, there may be overextension. Another possibility is that the child distinguishes between *juice* and *orange* when both are present.

DEFINITIONS One type of interview procedure is asking a child what a word means when it appears that the word is used inappropriately. We would not expect children under age six to give definitions and must adjust our expectations about the kind of definitions we will get according to the child's age.

GAMES Games can be designed that make it necessary for the child to use specific vocabulary if it is known. Variations of Simon Says, for example, can require the child to give directions that include verbs of motion and noun modifiers ("skip to the green chair"; "take three little steps"). Barrier games can be designed in which the child must use adverbials (*next to; toward*) and noun modifiers ("big cat"; "circle with the star in it") to direct someone how to position pictures or objects. Card games can likewise be used in which the child must name or request cards that have certain characteristics ("the one that hops"; "kangaroo").

SET UPS Situations can be planned to elicit the word class that seems to be missing or restricted. For example, if the child uses no adjectives in the sample, the clinician in the course of play could attempt to put on a doll shoe to elicit comments such as "baby shoe" or "little."

Assessment of Abstract Relational Meaning

Working from Language Samples Construct or review the listing transcripts of words and phrases that do not conform to adult usage, as previously described. Note which of these convey relational meaning—possession, location, dative relations, causality, coordination, antithesis, and temporal relations. Look particularly at the adverbials and conjunctions that tend to convey these relations. List together the error productions that express the same relationship, and then look through the transcript for instances in which the same relationship is expressed correctly. This gives an indication of how general or isolated the problem is. You may find, for example, that the child can express location with simple adverbials with no difficulty but has frequent problems with prepositional phrases used to indicate location. It would then seem to be the relational meaning of prepositions that is the problem rather than a problem with the concept of location.

Elicitation Procedures

FOLLOWING DIRECTIONS In the context of a game or activity, the child can be given directions to follow that require understanding of various relational meanings. Spatial prepositions, for example, lend themselves well to this technique to assess comprehension of locative relations. Possessive and dative relations can also be assessed in this way (e.g., "find the baby's cat" versus "find the baby cat"; "give the kitty the baby" versus "give the baby the kitty").

STORY RETELLING The child can be told a story that includes several kinds of relations between events, such as causal, temporal, coordinate, or adversative relations. When the child retells the story, the absense or presence of the necessary conjunctions is noted.

METALINGUISTIC EXERCISES Children's comprehension of some event relations can be assessed by presenting them with statements to interpret, such as the following:

> John will go and Henry will go. Who will go?
> John will go or Henry will go. Who will go?
> John will go so Henry will go. Who will go?
> John can go but Henry will go. Who will go?
> John can go because Henry will go. Who will go?

Assessment of Nonliteral Meaning

It is not necessarily significant if children do not show any spontaneous use of nonliteral meaning in their language samples. Our concern is primarily with the older child who uses such forms incorrectly or shows an inability to understand them.

Elicitation Procedures

METAPHORS Asch and Nerlove (1960) suggest an interview procedure to assess children's understanding of dual-function adjectives. After establishing that the child knows the literal meaning of *sweet, soft, cold, hard,* and *warm,* ask the child "Are people sweet? Do you know any sweet people? How do you know they're sweet?" Under age six, you would not expect the child to understand the psychological meanings. By nine or ten, children usually show awareness of connections between meanings. Another approach, used by Winner, Rosenstiel, and Gardner (1976), involves having the child explain sentences using these words metaphorically. You can create your own sentences that are adjusted in length and vocabulary to the child.

> She is a warm person and I like to visit her.

Elbers (1988) suggests we rely on our knowledge of the different functions of metaphors for children to design procedures to elicit metaphor production. She has found evidence that metaphors are used to suggest or connote attitudes, defend one's behavior or possessions, joke, and be precise in linguistically representing difficult ideas. Tasks where children are asked to explain difficult notions, describe sensations or feelings, or define concepts for which they do not yet know the appropriate superordinate category names would be likely candidates.

IDIOMS   Comprehension of idioms can be assessed using the picture-selection procedure of Lodge and Leach (1975) and Prinz (1983). Idioms are presented in a context that leads to either literal or nonliteral interpretation, and children are asked to find the picture that matches the meaning. Ezell and Goldstein (1991) presented twenty idiomatic phrases that they used to compare idiom comprehension of nine-year-olds with mental retardation and typical children matched for age or receptive vocabulary level.

PROVERBS   Asking older children to explain proverbs provides interesting insight into their ability to use language in a nonliteral way and to understand the implicatures of society's conventional sayings. Preadolescents may explain proverbs in a nonliteral fashion but typically cannot understand the implicatures. Some language tests designed for adolescents include proverb interpretation. Some examples of proverbs that may be used in elicitation follow:

Don't count your chickens before they're hatched.
The squeaky wheel gets the grease.
The grass is always greener on the other side of the fence.

JOKES   One of the most delightful ways to assess children's understanding of nonliteral meaning is through joke telling. Since children's appreciation of jokes does not always correspond to their understanding, you should ask the children to explain jokes they find amusing. Fowles and Glanz (1977) present a set of riddles they used in their research. You can also use any children's joke book to put together your own test items, choosing from a variety of types, some of which will be more difficult than others. Finding which jokes and riddles the child understands gives the clinician insight into that child's ability to deal with the ambiguities of the language.

REFERENCES

ASCH, E. S., AND H. NERLOVE.   The Development of Double Function Terms in Children, in *Perspectives in Psychological Theory*, eds. B. Kaplan and S. Wagner. New York: International Universities Press, 1960.

BANGS, T. E.   *Vocabulary Comprehension Scale*. Austin, Tex.: Learning Concepts, 1975.

BELL, S.   The Development of the Concept of Object as Related to Infant–Mother Attachment, *Child Development*, 41, 1970, 291–311.

BELLUGI, U., AND R. BROWN,   eds. The Acquisition of Language, *Monographs of The Society for Research in Child Development*, 29, 1964 (Serial no. 92).

BENEDICT, H.   Early Lexical Development: Comprehension and Production, *Journal of Child Language*, 6, 1979, 183–200.

BENELLI, B., L. ARCURI, AND G. MARCHESINI.   Cognitive and Linguistic Factors in the Development of Word Definitions, *Journal of Child Language*, 15, 1988, 619–36.

BILLOW, R. A.   Cognitive Developmental Study of Metaphor Comprehension, *Developmental Psychology*, 11, 1975, 415–23.

BINET, A., AND T. SIMON.   *The Development of Intelligence in Children*. Vineland, N.J.: Publications of the Training School, 1916.

BLOOM, L.   *Language Development: Form and Function in Emerging Grammars*. Cambridge, Mass.: M. I. T. Press, 1970.

BLOOM, L.   *One Word at a Time: The Use of Single Word Utterances Before Syntax*. The Hague: Mouton, 1973.

BLOOM, L., AND M. LAHEY.   *Language Development and Language Disorders*. New York: John Wiley, 1978.

BLOOM, L., M. LAHEY, L. HOOD, K. LIFTER, AND K. FIESS.   Complex Sentences: Acquisition of Syntactic Connectives and the Semantic Relations They Encode, *Journal of Child Language*, 7, 1980, 235–62.

BOWERMAN, M.   Semantic Factors in the Acquisition of Rules for Word Use and Sentence Construction, in *Normal and Deficient Child Language*, eds. D. M.

Morehead and A. E. Morehead. Baltimore: University Park Press, 1976.

BOWERMAN, M. What Shapes Children's Grammars? in *The Cross-Linguistic Study of Language Acquisition,* ed. D. I. Slobin. Hillsdale, N.J.: Lawrence Erlbaum, 1985.

BOWERMAN, M. Learning a Semantic System: What Role Do Cognitive Predispositions Play? in *The Teachability of Language,* eds. M. L. Rice and R. L. Schiefelbusch. Baltimore: Paul H. Brooks Publishing, 1989.

BRAINE, M. D. S. Children's First Word Combinations, *Monographs of the Society for Research in Child Development,* 1976 (serial no. 164).

BRODZINSKY, D. The Role of Conceptual Tempo and Stimulus Characteristics in Children's Humor Development, *Developmental Psychology,* 11, 1975, 843–50.

BROWN, R. *Words and Things.* New York: Free Press of Glencoe, 1958.

BROWN, R. *A First Language: The Early Stages.* Cambridge, Mass.: Harvard University Press, 1973.

CACCIARI, C., AND M. C. LEVORATO. How Children Understand Idioms in Discourse, *Journal of Child Language,* 16, 1989, 116–19.

CHOMSKY, N. *Aspects of the Theory of Syntax.* Cambridge, Mass: Cambridge University Press, 1965.

CHUKOVSKY, K. *From Two to Five.* Berkeley, Calif.: University of California Press, 1968.

CLARK, E. V. What's in a Word? On the Child's Acquisition of Semantics in His First Language, in *Cognitive Development and the Acquisition of Language,* ed. T. Moore. New York: Academic Press, 1973.

CLARK, E. V. Meanings and Concepts, in *Handbook of Child Psychology: Cognitive Development,* eds. J. Flavell and E. Markman. New York: John Wiley, 1983.

CLARK, E. V. The Principle of Contrast: A Constraint on Language Acquisition, in *Mechanisms of Language,* ed. B. MacWhinney. Hillsdale, N.J.: Lawrence Erlbaum, 1987.

CLARK, E. V., AND O. GARNICA. Is He Coming or Going? On the Acquisition of Deictic Verbs, *Journal of Verbal Learning and Verbal Behavior,* 13, 1974, 559–72.

CLARK, H. H., AND E. V. CLARK. *Psychology and Language,* New York: Harcourt Brace Jovanovich, 1977.

DIXON, R. Ergativity, *Language,* 55, 1979, 59–138.

DUCHAN, J. F., AND N. J. LUND. Why Not Semantic Relations? *Journal of Child Language,* 6, 1979, 243–52.

ELBERS, L. New Names from Old Words: Related Aspects of Children's Metaphors and Word Compounds, *Journal of Child Language,* 15, 1988, 591–618.

ELKIND, D. Piagetian and Psychometric Conceptions of Intelligence, *Harvard Educational Review,* 39, 1969, 319–37.

EZELL, H. K., AND H. GOLDSTEIN. Comprehension of Idiom Comprehension of Normal Children and Children with Mental Retardation, *Journal of Speech and Hearing Research,* 34, 1991, 812–19.

FANTZ, R. Pattern Vision in Newborn Infants, *Science,* 140, 1963, 296–97.

FILLMORE, C. J. The Case for Case, in *Universals in Linguistic Theory,* eds. E. Bach and R. T. Harms. New York: Holt, Rinehart & Winston, 1968.

FITZGERALD, H. Autonomic Pupillary Reflex Activity During Early Infancy and Its Relation to Social and Nonsocial Visual Stimuli, *Journal of Experimental Child Psychology,* 6, 1968, 470–82.

FLETCHER, P. The Development of the Verb Phrase, in *Language Acquisition: Studies in First Language Development,* eds. P. Fletcher and M. Garman. New York: Cambridge University Press, 1979, pp. 261–85.

FOWLES, G., AND M. E. GLANZ. Competence and Talent in Verbal Riddle Comprehension, *Journal of Child Language,* 4, 1977, 433–52.

GARDNER, H. Metaphors and Modalities: How Children Project Polar Adjectives into Diverse Domains, *Child Development,* 45, 1974, 84–91.

GARDNER, H., M. KIRCHER, E. WINNER, AND D. PERKINS. Children's Metaphoric Productions and Preferences, *Journal of Child Language,* 2, 1975, 125–41.

GARDNER, H., AND E. WINNER. The Development of Metaphoric Competence: Implications for Humanistic Disciplines, in *On Metaphor,* ed. S. Sacks. Chicago: University of Chicago, 1979.

GARDNER, H., E. WINNER, R. BECHHOFER, AND D. WOLF. Figurative Language, in *Children's Language,* Vol. I, ed. K. Nelson, New York: Gardner Press, 1978.

GIBBS, R. W. Linguistic Factors in Children's Understanding of Idioms, *Journal of Child Language,* 14, 1987, 569–86.

GIBSON, E. *Principles of Perceptual Learning and Development.* New York: Appleton, 1969.

GOLINKOFF, R. The Case for Semantic Relations, *Journal of Child Language,* 8, 1981, 413–37.

GOLINKOFF, R., AND C. HARDING. Directives in Preverbal Communication: Messages Mothers Can't Ignore. Southeastern Conference on Human Development. Baltimore: April 1980.

GOLINKOFF, R., AND L. KERR. Infants' Perceptions of Semantically Defined Action Role Changes in Filmed Events, *Merrill Palmer Quarterly,* 24, 1978, 53–61.

HAKES, D. T. The Development of Metalinguistic Abilities: What Develops? in *Language Development:*

Language, Thought and Culture, Vol. 2. Hillsdale, N.J.: Lawrence Erlbaum, 1982.

HILL, C. Linguistic Representation of Spatial and Temporal Orientation. Proceedings of the Berkeley Linguistics Society, 4, 1978, 524–39.

HOWE, C. The Meaning of Two-Word Utterances in the Speech of Young Children, *Journal of Child Language*, 3, 1976, 29–47.

HUTTENLOCHER, J. The Origins of Language Comprehension, in *Theories in Cognitive Psychology*, ed. R. L. Solso, Potomac, Md.: Lawrence Erlbaum, 1974.

JOHNSON, C. The Emergence of Present Perfect Verb Forms: Semantic Influences on Selective Imitation, *Journal of Child Language*, 12, 1985, 325–52.

KATZ, J. *Semantic Theory*. New York: Harper & Row, 1972.

LODGE, D. N., AND E. A. LEACH. Children's Acquisition of Idioms in the English Language, *Journal of Speech and Hearing Research*, 18, 1975, 521–29.

MCGHEE, P. E. Development of the Humor Response: A Review of the Literature, *Psychological Bulletin*, 76, 1971a, 328–48.

MCGHEE, P. E. The Role of Operational Thinking in Children's Comprehension and Appreciation of Humor, *Child Development*, 42, 1971b, 123–38.

MCGHEE, P. E. On the Cognitive Origins of Incongruity in Humor: Fantasy Assimilation Versus Reality Assimilation, in *The Psychology of Humor: Theoretical Perspectives and Empirical Issues*, eds. J. H. Goldstein and P. E. McGhee. New York: Academic Press, 1972.

MCGHEE, P. E. Cognitive Mastery and Children's Humor, *Psychological Bulletin*, 81, 1974, 721–30.

MARKOWITZ, J., AND S. FRANZ. The Development of Defining Style, *International Journal of Lexicography*, 1, 1988, 253–67.

MERVIS, C. B., J. CATLIN, AND E. ROSCH. Development of the Structure of Color Categories, *Developmental Psychology*, 11, 1975, 54–60.

NELSON, K. Structure and Strategy in Learning to Talk, *Monographs of The Society for Research in Child Development*, 38, 1973 (serial no. 149).

NIPPOLD, M. A., AND S. T. MARTIN. Idiom Interpretation in Isolation Versus Context: A Developmental Study with Adolescents, *Journal of Speech and Hearing Research*, 32, 1989, 59–66.

PALERMO, D. *Psychology of Language*. Glenview, Ill.: Scott, Foresman, 1978.

PIAGET, J. *The Language and Thought of the Child*. New York: Harcourt, Brace, 1926.

POLLIO, M., AND H. POLLIO. The Development of Figurative Language in Children, *Journal of Psycholinguistic Research*, 3, 1974, 185–201.

PRENTICE, N. M., AND R. E. FATHMAN. Joking Riddles: A Developmental Index of Children's

Humor, *Developmental Psychology*, 10, 1975, 210–16.

PRINZ, P. M. The Development of Idiomatic Meaning in Children, *Language and Speech*, 26, 1983, 263–72.

RESCORLA, L. Overextension in Early Language Development, *Journal of Child Language*, 7, 1980, 321–36.

RICHARDSON, C., AND J. A. CHURCH. A Developmental Analysis of Proverb Interpretations, *Journal of Genetic Psychology*, 94, 1959, 169–79.

ROBERTSON, S., AND G. SUCI. Event Perception by Children in the Early Stage of Language Production, *Child Development*, 51, 1980, 86–96.

ROCHESTER, S., AND J. MARTIN. The Art of Referring: The Speaker's Use of Noun Phrases to Instruct the Listener, in *Discourse Production and Comprehension*, ed. R. Freedle. Norwood, N.J.: Ablex Publishing, 1977.

ROSCH, E. On the Internal Structure of Perceptual and Semantic Categories, in *Cognitive Development and the Acquisition of Language*, ed. T. E. Moore. New York: Academic Press, 1973.

ROSCH, E., AND C. B. MERVIS. Family Resemblances: Studies in the Internal Structure of Categories, *Cognitive Psychology*, 7, 1975, 573–605.

SACHS, J., AND L. TRUSWELL. Comprehension of Two-Word Instructions by Children in the One-Word Stage, *Journal of Child Language*, 5, 1978, 17–24.

SCHLESINGER, I. Production of Utterances and Language Acquisition, in *The Ontogenesis of Grammar*, ed. D. I. Slobin. New York: Academic Press, 1971.

SAPIR, E. Grading: A Study in Semantics, *Philosophy of Science*, 11, 1944, 93–116.

SCHULTZ, T. R. Development of the Appreciation of Riddles, *Child Development*, 45, 1974, 100–105.

SCHULTZ, T. R., AND F. HORIBE. Development of the Appreciation of Verbal Jokes, *Developmental Psychology*, 10, 1974, 13–20.

SHIPLEY, E., C. SMITH, AND L. GLEITMAN. A Study of the Acquisition of Language: Free Responses to Commands, *Language*, 45, 1969, 322–42.

SLOBIN, D. The Origin of Grammatical Encoding of Events, in *The Child's Construction of Language*. ed. W. Deutsch. New York: Academic Press, 1981, pp. 185–99.

SNOW, C. E. The Development of Definitional Skill, *Journal of Child Language*, 17, 1990, 697–710.

STECHLER, G., AND E. LATZ. Some Observations on Attention on Arousal in the Human Infant, *Journal of the American Academy of Child Psychiatry*, 5, 1966, 517–25.

SUGARMAN, S. *Children's Early Thought*. Cambridge: Cambridge University Press, 1983.

THOMAS, E. It's All Routine: A Redefinition of Routines as a Central Factor in Language Acquisition. Paper presented at the Fourth Annual Boston University Conference on Language Development, Boston, Mass., 1979.

THOMSON, J., AND R. CHAPMAN. Who Is "Daddy" Revisited: The Status of Two-Year-Old's Overextended Words in Use and Comprehension, *Journal of Child Language*, 4, 1977, 359–75.

TOMASELLO, M., S. MANNLE, AND L. WERDENSCHLAG. The Effect of Previously Learned Words on the Child's Acquisition of Words for Similar Referents, *Journal of Child Language*, 15, 1988, 505–15.

WINNER, E. New Names for Old Things: The Emergence of Metaphoric Language, *Journal of Child Language*, 6, 1979, 469–91.

WINNER, E., A. ROSENSTIEL, AND H. GARDNER. The Development of Metaphoric Understanding, *Developmental Psychology*, 12, 1976, 289–97.

8

Discourse

This chapter is integrative, and that is why we needed to save it until after our discussion of various linguistic structures. It integrates information presented in earlier chapters in two ways: (1) it shows how various linguistic structures, previously described under separate parts of the language system (e.g., morphology, syntax, and semantics) function together in everyday communication, and (2) it offers an overall approach for studying ongoing language use in naturally occurring discourse.

We will follow the example of Hymes (1972) and Cazden (1979) and distinguish between two types of talk involving utterance sequences, which we will call *event talk* and *discourse*. (See Chapter 3 for discussion on this distinction.) Event talk occurs as events take place. Utterances in event talk are connected by virtue of being related to the ongoing happenings. Many communicative events involve talking, but the participants' sense of the event in event talking is that they are doing something rather than that they are just talking. Routinized events, for example, often involve talk which serves to carry out the event, such as those used during peek-a-boo: "Where's baby? There he is! Peek-a-boo." The event would not be peek-a-boo without the accompanying actions that are the focus during the routine. (See Chapter 3 for elaboration on event talk.)

Discourse has to do with how utterances are related. Discourse may be carried out by one person in monologue or between two in dialogue or among several people in a group situation. As with event talk, discourse comes in many varieties. The types have been called *genres*. Examples of those which require the participation of two or more people are conversations, arguments, class discussions, and negotiations. Stories, jokes, descriptions, reports, and lectures are usually monologues by one person to an audience of one or more listeners.

Discourse genres are distinguishable from one another in their overall structure as well as in their function. For example, stories begin with comments about the setting and characters; they have protaganists and contain episodes in which characters are often blocked from doing what they want to do. Stories function to entertain (Brewer and Lichtenstein, 1982). The structure and entertainment value of stories are not characteristic of other sorts of discourse, such as that involved in descriptions or in conversations.

Those engaged in discourse both understand and contribute to what is going on based on their general conceptualizations of the genre they are participating in. The general conceptualizations involve understanding the overall structure of typical examples of genres, what has been called its *global or macrostructure* (vanDijk and Kintsch, 1978). So, children telling a story do so by using a mental model of a story structure to guide them. Included in their mental model of a story might be information about what the child has found to be typical of stories—such as their having a beginning with a setting, an episode or two involving a troublesome event which a character must solve, followed by a resolution and story conclusion. Children (and adults) use their mental model of stories not only to create stories but also to understand and remember the stories they hear (Stein and Glenn, 1979).

Besides having a mental model of the global structure of discourse, children engaged in discourse must learn how to build the discourse structure, idea by idea, sentence by sentence. These elemental relations between subparts of discourse have been called the *local structure* of the discourse. The ways ideas are related has been referred to as *local discourse coherence*; the way the language is related has been called *discourse cohesion*.

In order to uncover what sorts of things are involved in the mental models children use to understand and produce discourse, we will first detail the global characteristics of different discourse genres. We will then proceed to local structuring, and discuss aspects of discourse coherence and discourse cohesion.

FIVE DISCOURSE GENRES

There has been a surge of research on discourse in the last few years, with the attempt being to find out its nature and how it is processed by speakers and listeners. Researchers' efforts have been to determine the structures underlying the following five types of discourse: stories, conversations, expositions, what we will be calling quizzes, and descriptions. The commonality across the discourse literature is that all these genres contain an underlying structure or *schema*. Speakers and listeners have a mental model or the appropriate schema to produce, understand, and remember the ideas contained in the particular unit of discourse (Brewer and Nakamura, 1984; Stein and Glenn, 1979; Rumelhart, 1975; Bartlett, 1932).

Stories

Story schemas have been studied by a number of investigators and have been found to contain the following: *setting*, in which the scene and characters are introduced; *episode*, which often conveys a protagonist's recognition and reaction to a blocked goal; and an *outcome* (Johnson and Mandler, 1980; Stein and Glenn, 1979). The higher order structures organize and give meaning to the individual sentences within the story, operating somewhat like a syntactic phrase in a sentence. Speakers and listeners follow the prescribed constituent structure as they produce and understand stories. The structure has been named *story grammar* to indicate that it is organized into hierarchical constituents just as sentences are.

Simple stories follow the story grammar, with one or two episodes, a single reaction, and a direct outcome.

> A boy was walking his dog.
> The dog got away.
> The boy chased him but couldn't catch up with him.
> He went home crying.
> When he got there, the dog was there to greet him.

Complex stories have more episodes, which may embed into one another; they may include more about a protagonist's thoughts and feelings, specify subordinate goals as well as overall goals, and have embedded outcomes. For example, "The Three Little Pigs" is a complex story, which Johnson (1983) has analyzed into five episodes containing subgoals as well as embedded outcomes.

Stories are used to entertain listeners. When adults create stories, they manipulate the component events so as to create effects such as surprise, suspense, or curiosity (Brewer, 1985). The entertaining components are built into the story when the speaker manipulates the event expectations of the listener—what Snyder (1984) has aptly called a "twist of events." Surprise occurs, for example, when a critical piece of information is omitted from the course of the event sequence and is revealed later, resulting in a new view on the event sequence. An example from Brewer and Lichtenstein (1982) is

> Charles got up from the chair. He walked slowly to the window. The window broke, and Charles fell dead. The sound of a shot echoed in the distance.

In the passage above, the storyteller omitted from early in the discourse the information that a sniper was outside the window.

Storytelling does not always occur under the same circumstances. Stories may be made up as they are being told. Or they may be recollected from others' tellings, from books, from picture cards, from television shows, or from real-life happenings. Children may be able to tell stories under some of these circumstances but not others. The first stories that most children are able to tell are those which they have heard repeatedly and which can be cued by pictures in a book. Although it may sound like a story because of the organization of the book, the children may have memorized what to say for each picture and thus not be thinking in terms of a story structure. Once the child begins to formulate narratives that contain an element of suspense or surprise and shows organization of constituents consistent with story schema, we have evidence that a child has a story schema.

Conversations

Conversations differ from stories in that they are not planned as much beforehand, they are not carried out just to entertain the listener, and they are not organized according to a story grammar structure. While it may be that stories occur during conversations and that a particular conversationalist sees his conversational role as an entertainer, good storytellers are not necessarily good conversationalists. To be a good conversationalist one needs to know how to do such things as (1) maintain an egalitarian interaction, (2) introduce topics or follow a partner's topic or intent, and (3) manage conversational turns and breakdowns.

Conversations between adults revolve around *topics*. Indeed, conversational topics are usually considered the most important part of conversations. When I tell you about a conversation I overheard, I am likely to emphasize what the people were talking about. A single conversation can contain a number of topics. Conversationalists can change topics abruptly by announcing a new topic or by asking permission to talk about something else. Topics also can change unobtrusively by fading into one another (Hurtig, 1977).

Sometimes speakers insert comments into conversations which serve to regulate how the conversation is carried out. *Conversational regulators* are needed to open or close the conversation (Schegloff and Sacks, 1973; Schegloff, 1968), to repair a conversational breakdown (Jefferson, 1972, 1973), or to invite new members into the ongoing conversation.

> Examples of conversational openings:
> Hi.
> Do you have a minute?
> What are you doing?

> Examples of closings:
> Well, I have to go now.
> Isn't your mother calling you?

> Examples of repairs:
> No, I meant . . .
> That one, not this one.
> I said that already.

> Invitations or disinvitations for new members:
> Would you excuse us?
> Hi, Jack, we were just talking about you.

Conversations, by definition, are verbal exchanges between two or more people. *Turn* is used to describe the time during which one speaker has the floor (e.g., "He had a long turn" or "He won't give up his turn"). The point at which one person stops talking and another begins is known as an *exchange*. Sometimes exchanges are made according to predetermined formats. For example, a question is followed by an answer, a greeting is followed by another greeting, and a request to end a conversation is followed by an end (or a refusal to end). Such familiar routinized exchange structures have been called *adjacency pairs* (Schegloff and Sacks, 1973).

Often turn exchanges occur when someone has finished making a conversational point. Speakers may indicate a willingness to give up a turn by stopping and then glancing at their partner. A more direct bid for the partner to take a turn is to ask a question ("What do you think about that?"). If a listener is not willing or interested in assuming a turn he might indicate so by nodding, looking away, or indicating verbally that the speaker still has the floor

("I see, and what then?"). A more active listener may comment on the speaker's latest point and then ask a question, giving away his recently earned turn. Active verbal returns which indicate that the listener should continue have been called conversational *turnabouts* (Kaye and Charney, 1981).

Expositions

Expository discourse is used to transfer information from one person to one or more others. These exchanges are common in classrooms or other settings where explicit reporting, teaching, or explaining is going on. The content of expositions is presented as "the truth"; that is, it is factual, impersonal, timeless, and nonfictional. Expository discourse presupposes that one participant, the "teacher," has some correct information that the other participant, the "student," does not.

There have been several attempts to describe the structural organization of written expository text with the apparent consensus that there are different logical relations expressed by different expositions (Meyer, 1987; Piccolo, 1987; Richgels and others, 1987; Horowitz, 1985a, 1985b). These authors have identified several types of logical relations found in expositions, including the following.

Comparison/contrast relations show how two things are the same and/or different.

The moon is much smaller than the earth.

Problem solving relations state a problem and offer a solution.

The problem with global warming can be addressed only through international cooperation.

Cause-effect relations give reasons why something happens.

Water runs downhill because of gravity.

Temporal relations are manifest in instructions for how to make or do something.

First shake the container well. Remove the red tab. Holding the container upright, press the black top firmly.

Descriptive relations indicate what something is.

A noun is the name of a person, place, or thing.

Enumerative relations give a list of things related to the topic.

When you go camping you need a tent, a sleeping bag, warm clothes, and insect repellent.

It is not known how these structures found in written expositories correspond to spoken expository exchanges. Snow (1983) argues that a relevant distinction in language learning is whether the language is contextualized or decontextualized, more so than if it is written or oral. Expositions fit her description of decontextualized language in that they often assume no knowledge on the part of the recipient, use precise lexical reference, control complex syntax necessary to integrate and explicate relations among bits of information, and maintain cohesion and coherence (Snow, 1987). This would support the parallel between written and spoken expository text.

Since expository text is intended to convey information the listener does not know, it is difficult for the listener to draw on previous knowledge to aid comprehension. It has consistently been found that students experience more difficulty understanding written expository passages than they do narrative passages (Spiro and Taylor, 1987; Dixon, 1979; Hall, Ribovich, and Ramig, 1979; Lapp and Flood, 1978). Narratives are read faster, are more absorbing, and are easier to comprehend and recall (Graesser and Goodman, 1985; Freedle and Hale, 1979). This suggests that spoken exposition would be more difficult for children to understand than would be spoken narratives.

Westby (1989) points out that narrative and expository texts differ in the types of content ideas and relationships between these ideas and thus require different kinds of knowledge to be understood. While narratives focus on goals and reasons for these goals, expositions have more physical state ideas that are related through consequences, attributes, and support for assertions. Understanding human motivation and goal-seeking behavior is critical for understanding narratives, while comprehending a variety of logical relationships is called on to understand expository texts.

Quizzes

Quizzes, like expositions, presume that one person, the teacher, knows some information. Unlike expositions, quizzes presume that the second participant, the student, also knows or should know the information. A discourse sequence qualifies as a quiz if (1) the person acting as teacher (the person might actually be a teacher, parent, or child) controls the content of the event and (2) the discourse is organized into a three-part exchange structure: initiation, reply, and evaluation (Mehan, 1979). The structure is initiated by a summons from the teacher such as a question or request; the student then responds with an answer or action, and the teacher evaluates the student's response.

The summons by the teacher is often in the form of a *test question*, which means that the teacher has an answer in mind and is using the question to test whether the student knows that answer. The evaluation portion of instructional talk involves accepting the answer ("That's right") or making corrections after the student gives what is judged to be an incorrect answer. The teacher may supply the correction directly or may soften the correction by accepting the answer and asking for a revision ("Yes, that's right, but what about . . . "). Rather than offer the correct answer, the teacher may ask the student to try again or may give a hint, in which case the student supplies the correction. In classroom lessons teachers often turn to another student and request the answer, indicating to the first that the answer was insufficient.

Event Descriptions

Speakers are often in the position of describing to their listeners something that happened. If the speaker creates suspense, curiosity, or surprise in the listener, the event description becomes more like a story. If instead they describe a set of occurrences that are ordered along the lines of an experienced or imagined event, the discourse becomes an event description (Duchan, 1986). For example:

> Yesterday my friend and I went to a Halloween party. We dressed up. I was an elephant. I had this big trunk made out of a vacuum cleaner hose. We had fun.

Research on event descriptions has come to the fore in recent years, ever since Schank and Abelson (1977) began to argue that in order to understand discourse, humans (or machine programs) need to know how events ordinarily take place. In order to understand a description of a restaurant scene, the listener needs to know about what ordinarily happens in restaurants. Schank and Abelson (1977) adopted the term *script* to refer to a type of schema which contains information about how frequent everyday events are ordinarily carried out. The script may include who the participants usually are, what activities they ordinarily carry out, and in what order they carry out their activities. Assume a computer is given the following information: "A man was very hungry. He went and got a telephone book." For the computer to give a sensible answer to the question, "What did the man do with the telephone book?" it must be programmed to know that phone books contain lists of restaurants and that restaurants are places where he can assuage his hunger.

Combining Genres

It is not uncommon for two or more genres to be combined in a single speech event. For example, school lessons may have both expository segments and quizzes, as when a child is given an explanation for something (expository) and then asked questions about it to check comprehension (quiz). Also, conversation may be punctuated with narrative segments or expository passages. If the embedded segment is a narrative, the listener usually willingly gives up his or her turns to be entertained with a story. In the case of an intrusive exposition, the listener may feel obligated to be lectured by someone in a more powerful position. In either case, the structure changes from an egalitarian interaction to a one-sided monologue.

The following segment from Pitcher and Prelinger (1963, p. 116) illustrates a speech event that combines narrative and expository genres. A five-year-old was asked to tell a story, but he is more inclined to provide information he knows about the planets. The utterances that seem like narrative are marked (*); the rest seem like expository.

1. When you pick up a piece of the moon and bounce it,
2. it goes down
3. and then it comes up.
4. Then it floats all around space

5. cause there isn't a single smidge of air.
6. On Jupiter you can live if you're in a space house.
*7. There's a little boy there
*8. and he cleans the space house.
*9. Once in a while he puts on his space suit
*10. and shoots off a piece of the moon.
11. Then there's rings all around Saturn.
*12. The boy looks at them
*13. and then he goes inside to look at them better.
*?14. But they're just clouds.
15. They're red hot pieces of rock
16. and when they come in earth's atmosphere they make a big hole.
17. Then Mercury is the hottest planet of all near the sun
19. and your blood would boil.
*20. The boy just stayed on Jupiter
*21. and looked at things
*22. and once in a while a meteor came down.
23. And Pluto has snow two hundred feet deep.

DEVELOPMENT OF DISCOURSE GENRES

While storytelling, conversations, expositions, quizzes, and event descriptions can be distinguished by their structural makeup, children do not seem to learn them separately. Rather, the discourse genres become embedded in one another, in that one unit such as an event description provides content and structure for a story or conversation (McCartney and Nelson, 1981; Nelson and Gruendel, 1981). The following stages in discourse acquisition are a rough chronology derived from the literature on normal standard English speaking children's discourse acquisition.

Preverbal Protoconversations

From birth children have been observed to communicate with others. The early communication exchanges exhibit turn taking between infants and caretakers. They may involve single action exchanges, in which the child does something (even so mundane as burping, moving, or crying), and the attending adult responds (Moore and Meltzoff, 1978; Snow, 1977; Trevarthan, 1977). The adult may respond by elaborating on the child's turn and providing an "interpretation." For example, when the baby burps, the caretaker may comment, "That feels better." The adult thereby provides both a model for conversational turn taking and a linguistic expression of what the infant presumably is experiencing. Exchanges involving imitation have been called *circular reactions* (Piaget, 1952). For example, the adult or child may issue a vocalization or gesture, and the conversational partner imitates it.

Another type of early appearing communication involves longer sequences of vocal or looking exchanges between caregivers and infants (Stern and others,

1977; Bateson, 1975). These exchanges occur after feeding, bathing, and dressing and are characterized by rhythmic sequences of vocal exchanges accompanied by changes in facial expression and mutual gaze. Bateson (1975) and Trevarthan (1977) call these *protoconversations* and find them occurring as early as three weeks after birth.

Beginning Verbal Exchanges

Once children reach the symbolic stage in which they use words to signify meanings, they enter a period of single conversational exchanges. The children's words are responded to by the adult, or the adult initiates and the child responds. Then the interaction either stops or goes on to another single sequence exchange. If we are to examine the single sequence exchanges in the context of the ongoing event, they may no longer seem to be a series of unrelated sequences but rather may cohere by virtue of being part of the speech event. Thus one finds adults and children engaged in labeling games, requesting activities, and question and answer exchanges. Examples of single exchanges between adults and children at this stage are:

CHILD: Single word request ("hat?")
ADULT: Granting the request ("here")

CHILD: Single word label ("book")
ADULT: Repetition, expansion, affirmation ("uh huh")

ADULT: *Wh-* question ("What's this?")
CHILD: Answer ("shoe")

ADULT: Command ("Come here.")
CHILD: Response ("no")

Beginning language learners can also engage in two-exchange sequences that involve three conversational turns. These exchanges may be child initiated, in which the child takes the first and third turn, or adult initiated, in which the child takes the second turn. Among the most interesting of these exchanges are those in which the stage is set in the initiation of the first turn. These stage setters may involve attention-getting initiations ("Y'know what?") or mutual referencing ("Is that your truck?"). Dore (1977) has called the stage setters *preparatory conditions*.

An example of a preparatory stage setter is the italicized segment in the following exchange:

CHILD: *What are you making?* (holds an animal in his hand)
PARTNER: A zoo.
CHILD: Can I put the animal in the zoo?

A second type of two-exchange sequence is begun by the child but not necessarily intentionally. That is, the child does not plan the third turn. Examples are *breakdown-repair sequences*, in which the adult asks the child to clarify in some way (Gallagher, 1977; Mishler, 1975); *expansions*, in which the partner elaborates on the child's initiation and the child repeats (Bellugi and Brown, 1964); or *prompts,* in which the child reports on a topic and the adult prompts for more information (Stoel-Gammon and Cabral, 1977).

An adult prompt or clarification request is italicized in the following exchange:

CHILD: Car.
ADULT: *What?*
CHILD: Car.

Scollon (1979) describes a third type of two-exchange sequence that he calls *vertical constructions* in which children express aspects of a proposition across several utterances. For example, the child may repeat a word until the adult responds, whereupon the child says a second word, completing a proposition. Vertical structures are italicized in the following exchange:

BRENDA: *Car.* (repeats four times)
ADULT: What?
BRENDA: *Go.*

Early Participation in Quizzes

Another common two-exchange sequence between adults and young children is the familiar initiation-response-evaluation exchange. Ninio and Bruner (1978) found this exchange type to be embedded in interactions involving picture and object naming. Cazden (1979) hypothesized that such labeling activities can be viewed as discourse training that will equip children for later participation in classroom quizzes.

MOTHER-TEACHER: What's this?
CHILD: Ball.
MOTHER-TEACHER: Yes, it's a big ball.

Early Event Descriptions

Children's early talk is of the here-and-now or of events that have just finished (Weist and others, 1984). The children use one-, two-, or three-word utterances to comment on what they notice is going on. (See Chapter 3 for how event talk develops.) By the time children are using three-word utterances, they know about everyday routines. They have experienced many meal and bath times and are becoming familiar with events outside the home such as birthday parties. Katherine Nelson and her colleagues (e.g., Nelson and Gruendel, 1981) have studied young children's non-here-and-now descriptions of such familiar events and found that children as young as three and one half are able to describe parts of familiar events in correct temporal order. The children's use of general pronouns (*you* or *we* rather than *I*) and tenseless verbs (*bake* rather than *baked*) indicates that they have a sense that these events are always conducted in this way; that is, they have a generalized sense. Nelson and Gruendel (1981) see these descriptions as generated by the children's *generalized event structures.* They found, in fact, that three-year-olds were more successful in describing how the events get carried out in general (e.g., what people usually do at birthday parties) than they were in describing particular instances of recurring events (e.g., what you did on your last birthday). Interestingly, when asked to give accounts of novel, nonrecurring events (what you did at the zoo on Sunday) the children were able to give long and vivid accounts. Apparently children's difficulty in recounting events is not related to the event specificity but to whether the children had a generalized representation of the specific event being asked about. It was when a specific event was part of a familiar type that the specific rendition of it became a problem. Nelson and Gruendel (1981) hypothesized that repeated experiences are fused together in the child's memory and that the individual instances comprising the fused accounts are then subsumed under the generalized representation, making individual recollections difficult. Since novel events do not have a generalized representation, they are easier to describe in a nongeneralized form.

Conversations Built on Event Reenactments

At about the same time children begin to describe events in specific and generalized ways, they begin to use their event knowledge to structure their conversations. Nelson and Gruendel (1979) offer the following example of a conversation between three-and-one-half-year-old girls as they enact a replay of a daily school routine:

CHILD 1:   Ok. Here's her house and she's sleeping right here. She's in here. Ok. Here comes. She's right next to the school. (Walks teacher to school) Right here. She doesn't have to walk too far.
CHILD 2:   (Rings bell) School's open.
CHILD 1:   Ding, ding. Go in.
CHILD 2:   Having snack.
CHILD 1:   (Rings bell)
CHILD 2:   Having snack. No, I want to ring the bell for snack. (Rings it)
CHILD 1:   Here here.
CHILD 2:   What's that?
CHILD 1:   In case she sits right there. (Puts people in chairs at tables)
CHILD 2:   Whoops. School is closed.
CHILD 1:   All the people out. (Moves them out) Out.
CHILD 2:   Walking home. Walking home.

Nelson and Gruendel (1979) conclude from their research on preschoolers' conversations that children under four need to have mutually shared event structures in order to carry out conversations in a coherent and directed way. Their counter example is a conversation between three-and-one-half-year-old boys which is not based on such event sharing:

CHILD 1:   I playing with this.
CHILD 2:   A what's a what's.
CHILD 1:   On nuts, Oh nuts.
CHILD 2:   Doodooodoo, round, round up in the sky. Do you like to ride in a helicopter?
CHILD 1:   Ok. I want to play in the sandbox.
CHILD 2:   Much fun. Do you want to ride in the helicopter?
CHILD 1:   I'm going outside.

Story Development

Stories differ from event descriptions in that something unexpected happens which differs from the usual course of events. Gruendel (1980) asked children to tell stories about making campfires, baking cookies, planting a garden, or having a birthday party. The children, instead of creating an unexpected sequence, described the event in question. Gruendel's eight-year-olds were able to create full-blown interesting stories. For example, they began with "once upon a time" and ended with "the end."

Gruendel's task in which she asked children to tell a story about a familiar event probably influenced her results. In these cases in which they knew about the event, they used generalized event descriptions to tell the story. Judging from the results of other researchers, it appears that on occasions when children are not offered a suggested event such as a birthday party to talk about, those under five years of age use other structuring devices upon which to hang their "story." For example, they may describe parts of a current visual scene such as a picture or storybook or may base their account on what they know about a main character (Westby, 1984; Applebee, 1978). The children at this age seem to be defining *story* as a lot of talk done by one person.

At around five, normal children can tell entertaining stories that contain most of the components specified in the story grammar (Westby, 1984; Applebee, 1978; Botvin and Sutton-Smith, 1977). They begin with a setting, build a problem to be solved, describe a goal and solution, and offer an ending. What is yet to be added by this developing five-year-old is identifying with the characters in the story and including statements about their thoughts and feelings (Botvin and Sutton-Smith, 1977). At six years of age the average storyteller begins to include how characters feel about what is going on and some solutions they might be thinking about. It is not until age eleven or so that children's invented stories contain multiple episodes or ones that are embedded into one another.

School Discourse

Meanwhile the growing child is also learning to participate in classroom discourse. While well versed in the exchange sequence of quizzes, the child has yet to learn the structure of most school events. School lessons often have recognizable openings, which allow certain interruptions; middles, which are less interruptable; and endings, which are again open to their initiations. Mehan (1979) in his often-cited study of primary grade children's participation in classrooms, found that the children learned during the course of the school year when their initiations would be noticed by the teacher. Their attempts to get the teacher's attention at the beginning of the year were successful only 10 percent of the time, whereas after a few months of "lesson training" they were successful in achieving responses to 50 percent of their bids.

School events usually have prescribed means for taking turns once the interaction is underway. Teachers may control turns by calling on the next speaker with or without waiting for children to raise their hands, or turn allocation may follow the seating arrangement. Children need to learn the signals that indicate when and how they should or may speak. The teacher will use *regulators* to remind them of the discourse "rules."

> Remember, Jose, only one person talks at a time.
> Pay attention, Mark.
> Hurry up, Joan; we can't wait all day.

Discourse learning for school performance in the upper grades requires that students learn the structures involved in expository text. Meyer (1981), for example, found educational materials organized into structures in which main ideas had supporting details, comparisons and contrasts were made, and problems were stated with solutions following.

DISCOURSE COHERENCE

While having a mental model of the global structure of a particular discourse genre is basic to carrying out discourse, that model is but a general schema, lacking in particulars. When a child tells about a significant event, he or she must be able to fill in the global schema with the particulars of the event being described, using linguistic expressions to convey who was involved and what happened. When conveying or understanding the discourse particulars, a child must learn how to read between the oral or written lines provided by the language; how the discourse conveys particular points of view; how specific concepts fit together in the mental model; and how to differentiate central ideas from those that are supportive. We will be discussing each of these aspects of discourse cohesion under the topics of inferencing, perspective taking, referencing, topic manipulation, and focusing.

Inferencing

Discourse inferencing is usually studied in relation to discourse comprehension. It involves going beyond the ideas conveyed by the language of the text in an effort to make sense of what is being said. This sensemaking involves combining information provided by the immediate sentence with that gleaned from previous sentences, adding what is known about the global structure of the discourse genre, and fitting these with background knowledge needed to make the text coherent. In order to understand the sentence "What big teeth you have," the child needs to understand the meaning of the words in the sentence; to put this into her working mental model, together with her expectations of how story lines unfold; and to fit it with the ongoing story. These tasks involve figuring out information about Red Riding Hood, her expectations, and her imminent danger due to the wolf's ulterior motives. That is to say, the child must read between the lines and infer how each line fits with the mental model in order to create story coherence.

Sometimes language devices in the discourse let the listeners know what kinds of relationships to infer between the newly presented information and the developing mental model. Conjunctions, for example, can signal the listener about the relationship between sentences or constituents within them as in the following: *and then* indicates an ordering and the final or turning point in a sequence, *while* marks event simultaneity, *because* implies the speaker's sense of causality, and *but* or *except* indicates a contrastive or exclusionary relationship.

I had been working at it for a while, *and then* I realized what was wrong.

Don't do that *while* I'm word processing.

He didn't want to do it *because* she said he had to.

He didn't want to do it *but* she said he had to.

Conjunctions do not always inform the listener as to the relationship between ideas in the discourse. The frequently used *and* simply indicates the units go together—the listener must infer the nature of the relationship from the language and background knowledge and from the current ongoing conceptual model.

The girl went to the store, *and* the boy stayed home.	TEMPORAL, SIMULTANEOUS
The boy went home *and* ate supper.	TEMPORAL, SEQUENTIAL
The rope was lowered, *and* the child grabbed hold.	ENABLEMENT
The man lost his keys *and* had to stay overnight.	CAUSAL

The logical relations between and among sentences sometimes call for a particular inference. Some examples of different logical types of inferences are listed below, along with some information about how and when children develop an ability to form the different inferences.

Whole-Part Inferencing   When carrying out this type of inferencing, a listener presumes that once an object or place is referred to, a part referred to later belongs to the first-mentioned whole:

The boy hit his friend in the face.

The bloody nose scared all who were present.

Inference: The nose is that of the boy who was hit.

Three-year-old children have been found to be able to engage in this sort of inference. Bennett-Kastor (1983) found that her three-year-old subjects used definite phrases for parts, once a whole scene or object had been identified. For example, they talked about *the* fireplace only after they had mentioned *a* house.

Inferring Presuppositions   Words or sentences can indirectly presuppose the existence or truthfulness of information. These presuppositions are apparent in questions such as "Have you stopped beating your wife?" which presupposes that you beat your wife.

Which cookie can I have?
Inference: I can have a cookie.

Judging from the naturalistic data obtained by Dore (1979) four-year-olds are able to infer information implied in the questions of their teachers. In the following example, one finds indications that the child is interpreting the question as containing a presupposition that he should have put something away, and his answer is an excuse for not having done so:

TEACHER: John, are you finished?
CHILD: They're out 'cause I'm sorting them.

Probable Event Inferencing Sentences are interpreted in terms of what would be expected under those circumstances. In some cases, this leads to misinterpretation:

ADULT: Put the man under the horse.
CHILD: (Puts the man on the horse)
Inference: Men go on horses, not under them.

A concrete demonstration of children's reliance on event knowledge is found in Lewis and Freedle's description (1973) of a thirteen-month-old child who, when given the two commands "Throw the apple" and "Eat the apple" responded differently depending upon context. She responded to both commands by eating the apple when she was in her high chair and throwing the apple when she was playing in the playpen.

Sachs and Truswell (1978) tried to control for such event influences in their testing of one-and-one-half- to two-year-olds' comprehension of usual and unusual two-word commands. The experimenters did not, for example, issue a command when the child was looking at or handling the object-referent named in the command. Nor did the researchers use gestures or routines in their presentations of the command. Under these more controlled circumstances, the young children could, on occasion, respond to unusual commands such as "kiss the flower" or "pat the bottle."

Despite Sachs and Truswell's findings (1978), it is apparent that comprehension under normal conditions is heavily influenced by the child's knowledge of what usually happens. Strohner and Nelson (1974) have called this the *probable event strategy*. They and others have found that two- and three-year-old normal children assign meanings to the utterances they hear on the basis of what they experienced as probable relationships between the referents designated by the utterance (Duchan, 1980; Duchan and Siegal, 1979; Strohner and Nelson, 1974; Bever, 1970). For example, when Strohner and Nelson (1974) asked their young subjects to interpret "The ball carries the wagon," the children responded by putting the ball in the wagon.

Spatial Inferencing Paris and Carter (1973) gave second- and fifth-grade children six sets of three related sentences. The sentences in each set were constructed to allow inferences, most of which were spatial inferences:

The bird is inside the cage.
The cage is under the table.
The bird is yellow.

Shortly thereafter, the researchers tested the children to see if they could tell whether a given sentence was among the original set. Among the test sentences were some with inferences that could be drawn from the original set (e.g., "The bird is under the table"). Both second and fifth graders consistently misidentified the inference sentences as being among those which they had actually heard, testifying to their ability to make spatial inferences.

Causal Inferencing   Brown (1975) studied the ability of five- and seven-year-olds to remember descriptions containing causal relationships and temporal relationships without a causal connection. She found that seven-year-olds remembered causal relations better than noncausal temporal ones, but that five-year-olds did not show this difference.

Motivational Inferencing   An interesting study by Omanson, Warren, and Trabasso (1978) with five- and eight-year-olds shows their use of goals and motivation in recalling propositions in a story. The authors used stories with two parts, a goal and a core. The core, which was presented to all of the children, consisted of actions that were unclear as to motives of people in the story. For example:

> Nancy saw what she wanted on the shelf. When the man came over, she pointed to it. She accidentally knocked over a lamp. The lamp fell with a crash. Nancy said she was sorry. The man said it was okay. He handed her the box. As she was walking out Nancy saw Fred. Nancy hid behind the door. (Omanson, Warren, and Trabasso, 1978, pp. 340–341)

Along with this core, some of the children were presented with a goal for the core (e.g., Nancy stole money from Fred to buy a skateboard for herself). The children were asked to recount the stories and to answer inference questions (e.g., Why did Nancy hide behind the door?). Children of all ages (five to eight) were better able to answer the inference questions when the goal was explicitly presented, suggesting they were able at this age to infer motivation.

Understanding Indirect Requests   Shatz (1975) in her study of children's responses to requests embedded in questions ("Can you find a truck?"), found that children as young as two years carry out the act rather than answer the question *yes* or *no*. Reeder (1980), Ervin-Tripp (1977), and Shatz (1975) doubt that children at this age are understanding the entire yes–no indirect request form, but rather that they are probably extracting the request nucleus ("find truck") and responding to it in accordance with their sense of the entire situational meaning. Some of Shatz's older children responded to yes–no questions with *yes* or *no* when the questions were in a context in which the adult was asking the child for information, but these older children also had a preference for carrying out the action rather than answering the question. Ervin-Tripp (1970) found that if the children were asked to do an impossible or unfeasible act ("Can you fly in the sky?"), they would answer *yes* or *no* rather than attempt to carry out the unlikely act. She also found three-year-olds were likely to respond to "Why don't you X?" with an answer rather than treating it as a request for action. This was related to their preference for answering *why* questions with "because + statement" responses.

Semantic Inferencing Brown (1976) found that children as young as four years were able to determine whether information presented in pictures was compatible with earlier information presented along with sequence pictures. The children were presented four pictures depicting stages in an unfolding event sequence. The experimenter told a story to accompany the four pictures which included information contained in pictures which they were not shown. Later, when shown six pictures, the children were unable to differentiate the two pictures which were compatible with the story from the ones they had seen. When shown pictures which were incompatible with the story theme, they were able to identify those as pictures which they had not seen. For example, from among a set of pictures showing stages of a boy sledding, the children indicated incorrectly that they had seen a picture of a boy sliding down a hill on a sled at the same time that they were able to correctly indicate that they had not seen a picture of the same boy located at the bottom of the hill with his sled at the top.

Markman's study (1979) gives an upper range to the acquisition of children's ability to semantically integrate incompatible information. She found that children up to twelve years were unable to detect inconsistent information in an expository paragraph. Markman's material required much more linguistic and cognitive knowledge for integration, as can be seen from the following example of her paragraphs:

> There is absolutely no light at the bottom of the ocean. Some fish that live at the bottom of the ocean know their food by its color. They will only eat red fungus.

Deictic Perspective Within Discourse

Most genres are cast within a particular perspective. The perspective includes, among other things, taking a speaker's or character's orientation to the time and place of what is being described. Usually the speaker's point of view is taken, especially in contexts of conversational discourse, event descriptions, and quizzes. The perspective taken for narratives is often that of a character in the story. Perspective in expository is more subtle, since expository texts tend not to be obviously grounded in a personal, spatial, or temporal perspective, but rather are cast as eternal truth, beyond particular viewpoints. However, as historians and scientists can attest, the language used can unintentionally betray a particular point of view.

> Columbus discovered America in 1492.

The consciousness verb *discover* in the above sentence displays a Eurocentric point of view, since it was the Europeans and not Native Americans who did not previously know about America.

Perspective in discourse can begin with the study of specific lexical items indicating person, time, and space orientations to what is being talked about. These are called *deictic terms*. The first- and second-person pronouns are examples of such terms. Reference with third-person pronouns or indefinite expressions can be disambiguated by looking to the broader linguistic or nonlinguistic context for their interpretation and are independent of the speaker. For example, when you hear "He's dirty" in the context of a muddy dog, you don't need to know who is saying this, or where he or she is located in order to interpret the utterance. The situation is different when first- and second-person pronouns are used, however, since they can be interpreted only by identifying the speaker (*I*, *my*) and the person addressed (*you*, *yours*). Thus these pronouns are deictic terms; the referent for *me* shifts depending on who is saying it, and the referent for *you* is whoever is being addressed. Likewise, terms such as *my mother* or *your son* involve *person deixis*.

Place deixis is involved in interpreting adverbs like *here* and *there*, pronouns like *this* and *that*, and verbs like *bring* and *take*. It can be seen that place deixis also involves person deixis, since the place or direction of motion referred to by these terms cannot be determined without knowing both the identity and the location of the speaker. That is, you would not know where to place an object with the direction "Put it here" without knowing both who is speaking and where the speaker is located.

Time deixis is involved in the use of terms such as *yesterday* and *next period* and the use of tense markers that depend upon the moment at which they are spoken for their meaning. *Today* is Monday, but in twenty-four hours *today* will be Tuesday and *yesterday* will be Monday. If you hear a two-week-old message "I'm going to the movies tonight. Want to join me?" on your telephone answering machine you must interpret the future tense as past in current time; that is, you have missed the movie. In contrast, nondeictic time reference would be to specific calendar or clock time (July 4, 1776; 3 P.M.) that can always be identified in the same manner.

In the past, the deictic terms have been regarded as lexical items, whose meaning comes from somewhere in the context. Within our mental models view of discourse analysis, we propose that the terms are not isolable, but rather that they derive from a particular perspective which speakers and listeners have as they engage in discourse. When someone says "Are you coming over tonight?" it will be interpreted as originating in the perspective of the speaker, with the *come* referring to where the speaker will be, and the *tonight* referring to the upcoming night related to the time when the sentence is spoken. The perspective assumed in the sentence above is referenced in the personal, temporal, and spatial here and now. That perspective can be said to having its origin in the current scene, which serves as the *deictic center* for the interpretation of terms relating to who, where, and when of the event being described (Bruder and others, 1986).

Deictic centers can be shifted to a different time and place, as is the case in the following taken from a story:

Charlotte said, "Are you coming over tonight?"

Charlotte is not the one telling the story. Rather, she is in the story. The time at which the addressee is to arrive is not the night following the telling of the story, but rather the night following Charlotte's invitation, the *come* is the place which Charlotte is thinking about, and the *tonight* is related to the evening of the day Charlotte said the sentence.

The deictic center of a segment of discourse is usually established through various language devices and, once established, is maintained until a shift is indicated. A frequently used means for establishing a center is to assert it directly. The segments which follow begin with statements which function to establish the who, where, and when of the upcoming discourse. The first segment is the beginning of a story, the second of an event description:

> Once there were three little pigs. They lived at home with their mother. One day they decided to go out on their own.

> Wait 'til you hear what happened to me yesterday. I was on my way home, and I ran into this familiar looking person, who stopped me and said, "Don't I know you?"

Opening segments such as these two usually contain several discourse devices identifying the main characters and the location and time in which the event took place. For stories, this segment of text has been identified as the story's *setting*. Setting sentences usually occur at the beginning of the story or event description, creating the deictic center for the mental model. They can also occur later in the discourse when there is a change in the deictic center, as in the following segment of a story told by a three-year-old in which he introduces new characters throughout the story:

> It's gonna ba a shark.
> Once a shark came
> and then it bite me
> and I was hiding behind its tail
> that's all
> then a friendly dolphin came
> that's all
> then mamma came
> and then there was a train track
> and the train runned me over
> the train was on this track
> and then it stopped
> then a "O" came
> and it made me around and around
> then a sharp thing cut me off
> then that's all (Sutton-Smith, 1981, p. 87)

The speaker has a variety of ways available in the language for use in establishing deictic centers and indicating a shift to a new center. Some language devices serve to indicate the character's point of view, others to indicate a spatial perspective for the text, and still others to indicate the text's temporal orientation (Bruder and others, 1986).

Establishing and Maintaining the* Who *of the Deictic Center In order to create a text which takes the point of view of a main character, the character must be introduced. This introduction is often made by asserting the character's existence directly through the use of a *there* indicator ("Once there was a boy") or by describing the character's arrival ("And then a monster came"). The existence descriptions usually occur at the beginning of a discourse segment, and the arrival descriptions occur after the action has begun and the setting has been established (Duchan, unpublished ms, 1991).

Introducing the character into the discourse does not automatically lead to an interpretation of the discourse from that character's point of view. Some characters are merely peripheral. Even central characters do not become the *who* of the discourse center unless there are indicators that the text is to be interpreted from that character's point of view. At the beginning of the story below, the baby lion is described in an objective way as crying because something was bothering him. The story then moves to the character's point of view, as is suggested by the sentence with the mental verb *knew* and by the adverb *outside* which takes the character's point of view from inside the house.

> Once some lions had a baby lion.
> And then at night-time the baby cried.
> Something was bothering the baby when he slept at night.
> And then he knew it was outside that you could hear it.
> It was a helicopter that was outside
> And the baby lion couldn't sleep.
> Now they had a new rule:
>   No helicopter can come at night.
> The end. (Five-year-old Jason from Paley, 1990, p. 54)

Discourse devices which signal a shift to a character's *subjective point of view* include mental state verbs indicating a character's perception or thought processes (see Wiebe, 1990, for more subtle indicators of subjectivity in discourse). Examples of mental state verbs serving as markers of deictic shifts into the subjective experience of a character are *knew, found, thought, saw, felt, guessed, wanted.*

Establishing and Maintaining the* Where *of the Deictic Center   Spatial indicators establishing the location in which the event of the discourse is centered are usually found at the beginning of the event description in the form of a place name (e.g., *home; castle*) or directional location indicated, for example in a prepositional phrase (*out west*). Sometimes the deictic location of the event being described is assumed and not explicitly indicated. For example, family stories told by children are presumed to take place in the children's home.

When the deictic location has been established, subsequent sentences assume it and need not restate it. For example, verbs indicating motion (*come; go; give; take; walk*) often are referenced against a centered location. When a character is described as *coming*, the listener can assume that she is approaching a known center.

Establishing and Maintaining the* When *of the Deictic Center   Just as for character perspective, the temporal center of deixis is often established by asserting at the outset when the event took place. Once the temporal center has been established, it is used as a reference point for indicators of time. So if the event being described took place three days prior to the time of speech, the term *yesterday* used in the event description would mean four days ago, and *tomorrow* would mean two days ago.

Sentences following the ones which establish a temporal center are usually taken to indicate the continuous progression of time. However, on occasion the time of the event jumps forward or backward, violating the norm of continuity. These temporal shifts can be indicated by using adverbial indicators of time such as the following: *earlier, the next morning, when he woke up, after the show*. The use of the term *then* also serves to signal a discontinuity either in the time or place or the ending of the event being described (Segal, Duchan, and Scott, 1991).

In the following event description, dictated to his teacher by a five-year-old, the time indicators are referenced against the time of an established deictic center.

1. Once upon a time there was a father and he had four boys.
2. One of them went out to see the woods and a lion killed him.
3. He didn't come back for four days
4. and then the father went out to find him.
5. The father broke his arm
6. and two of the sons carried him back.
7. They took the father to the hospital.
8. He couldn't come home for a year.
9. The last day he died.
10. The two boys went back to the forest
11. and a fairy said the other brother was still alive
12. because he was only resting
13. and he just looked dead.
14. So they all lived happily ever after. (from Paley, 1981, p. 36)

In the above example, several temporal shifts occur. The four-day interval in line 3 began just after the boy left home; the year in line 8 began after the father entered the hospital; the last day in line 9 being the last day of the year mentioned in line 8.

Box 8–1 includes linguistic indicators of deictic perspective in discourse.

BOX 8–1. Linguistic Indicators of Deictic Perspective in Discourse

WHO	WHERE	WHEN
phrases with *there* indicators	place names	time words (*date; day*)
mental state verbs to shift to subjective perspective of characters (e.g., *think; believe*)	prepositional phrases expressing location	temporal adverbials
	motion verbs (e.g., *come; go*)	

Development of Deixis Children's learning of deixis has been studied as part of semantics, where examinations have been made of their ability to understand and use specific deictic terms. Such terms have been found to be among children's first words, as for example, *da*, *this*, and *that* (e.g., Nelson, 1973; Leopold, 1939). Deictic terms are also reported to be common in early two-word utterances in a variety of languages (e.g., Bates, 1976; Braine, 1976; Bowerman, 1973; Bellugi and Brown, 1964). This early use of these terms does not, however, appear to be truly deictic, that is, recognizing speaker perspectives, but rather serves as attention-directing or quasi-referential (Atkinson, 1979; Lyons, 1975). Snyder (1914) observed that a child aged two years, five months who used *that* indicated the distinction between two objects by gesture rather than by appropriate use of deictic terms. Huxley (1970) found no deictic distinction between two children's use of *this* and *that* as late as age four years. Slobin (reported in Clark and Sengul, 1978) found children as old as four years, eight months used *there* equally as often to indicate a close object as a distant object.

It is more likely that *pronouns* are the first deictic terms used by children. Tanz (1980), in a study of several deictic forms with children from two years, seven months to five years, three months, found that the youngest children already knew the personal pronouns *I*, *you*, and *he*, while other forms were still unknown to most of them. It appears that the concept of speaker and listener is basic to all deictic systems and must develop first. Tanz offers some reasons why the personal pronoun system might be simpler to master than other deictic systems. She points out that boundaries between pronouns are all clearly defined. Speakers are always *I* and can never refer to self as *you* or *she* in direct discourse. It is never necessary to accompany *I* with a pointing gesture to clarify to whom it refers. Also, the contrast between persons is central to the meaning of pronouns unlike other deictic terms, such as *give* and *take* or *come* and *go*, which have meaning independent of person. These factors help to clarify the meaning of pronouns when used in context.

The other deictic systems seem to be less predictable in order or age of acquisition. Most studies have investigated contrasts within one deictic system, which makes comparison of the different systems difficult. In her investigation of children's comprehension of several contrasts, Tanz (1980) found general trends of development but much variation among children, except in the common development of personal pronouns. She found the spatial contrast between the prepositions *in front of* and *in back of* generally develop next (after personal pronouns), with the contrast being understood by most children around four years of age. Her four-year-olds also understood *at the side of*. These results are generally consistent with other investigations that report development of *in front of* and *in back of* around age four years (Kuczaj and Maratsos, 1974). Cox (1979) found that at four years of age children may understand one of these terms and be confused about the other but know they both refer to the same dimension in space.

It must be pointed out that *in front of*, *in back of*, and *at the side of* have nondeictic meanings if the object being referred to has an intrinsic front and back, as is the case with a person, chair, or television set, for example. With these "fronted" objects, the preposition relates to the named object and not to the position of the speaker—that is, "Put this behind your mother" has a "right" position regardless of where the speaker or the addressee are positioned.

Children learn the nondeictic meaning of *front*, *back*, and *side* with fronted objects before they understand them deictically (Tanz, 1980; Kuczaj and Maratsos, 1974). Tanz found, however, that there is generally not much of a lag before the deixis of these terms is learned, with both senses being learned during their fourth year.

Unlike pronouns, which have absolute boundaries, and unlike the deictic prepositions, which can be learned from concrete frontness-backness features of objects, the demonstratives *this* and *that* and the locative adverbs *here* and *there* indicate spatial relations that are relative and abstract. These terms relate to distance from the speaker, with *here* and *this* indicating proximity and *there* and *that* indicating distance. Distance is relative, however, and the boundary between close and far is not clearly defined, making it unclear in some situations whether *here* or *there* (or *this* or *that*) is the appropriate locater. As Fillmore (1971) points out, *here* can mean anything from "at this point" to "in this galaxy," and *there* can be as close as our own body as in "There's the spot that hurts." There are also no features of objects that make these distinctions easier—that is, there is no inherent *hereness* or *thereness* of objects in the same way there is *frontness* and *backness*.

As we have mentioned, these terms may appear among a child's first words as indications of notice or instruments for directing attention; it is not until considerably later that they are deictic. By three years of age, deVilliers and deVilliers (1974) found, children could comprehend *here*, *there*, *this*, *that*, *my*, *your*, *in front of*, and *behind* in a situation wherein the adult sat on one side of a low wall and gave instructions to a child on the other side (e.g., "The M & M is on *this* side of the wall"). Thus, perspectives of speaker and addressee were opposite, and the locative terms could have been interpreted like the pronouns (i.e., "on the side close to me" versus "the side close to you").

Understanding these terms as expressing relative distance from one point appears to be somewhat more complicated. Tanz investigated comprehension of *here*, *there*; *this*, *that*; and *close*, *far* and found that the proximal (closest to the reference point) member of each pair was most often correct across ages two years, six months to five years, three months. Her data suggest that children learn *close* before *far*, since five out of nine of the youngest children (mean age thirty-six months) knew *close*, while *far* was not known by over one half of the children until age sixty months. There is a strong tendency for children to learn the deictic *this* before *that*. There is less difference between the order of *here* and *there*, with children being equally likely to learn either first. Over one half of the children knew both *this* and *that* contrastively at age fifty-two months; understanding of contrast between *here* and *there* and *close* and *far* was shown by most of the five-year-olds. Tanz argues that only knowledge of both members of these pairs should be taken as evidence that the child knows the deictic contrast, since correct performance in response to one member of the pair does not demonstrate that the contrast is understood. Both Tanz and deVilliers and deVilliers found children tend to choose the option closest to themselves for point of reference. If the examiner makes this closest option the distance terms, as in the deVilliers and deVilliers study (*that* side and over *there* referred to the child's side), it appears they "know" the distance terms first. If this option is identified with the proximal terms (*this* one; *here*), the proximal terms appear to be "learned" first. Thus, it is only when children can demonstrate understanding of both members of a pair that we can be sure they understand either of them.

The verbs of motion; *bring*, *take* and *come*, *go*; involve direction of movement. The simplest deictic use of these terms relates to movement toward (*come*; *bring*) or away from the speaker (*take*; *go*):

> Bring it here.   Take it over there.
> Come here.   Go over there.

Interpretation becomes more complex when listener position must be considered. For example, "Come upstairs" and "Go outside" involve knowledge of where the listener as well as the speaker is located. A destination or reference point other than the speaker is possible. If these statements refer to past or ongoing events, they still generally indicate the speaker's perspective or "home base" at the time of occurrence.

> "She went to school," said her mother.
> "She came to school," said her teacher.

The verbs of transfer are similar to these verbs of motion in that they indicate both person and direction of action, but rather than involving overt movement, they describe a more subtle transaction. Gentner (1975) found the simplest of these verbs to be *give* and *take*, which were understood by children in this study by age three and one-half; *pay* and *trade* were mastered somewhat later; and *buy*, *spend*, and *sell* were still not understood consistently by most eight-year-olds.

In sum, it becomes apparent as we review studies of deixis that it clearly is not mastered all at once. There appears to be a strong tendency for children to acquire first the person deixis involved in pronouns. Spatial deixis of the prepositions *in back of* and *in front of* usually develops next, probably emerging from children's knowledge of the nondeictic *back* and *front*. Spatial deixis is also involved in *here*, *there*, and *this*, *that*, but in these cases acquisition is not aided by features of objects, which may account for the somewhat later emergence than the spatial prepositions. The verbs of motion can involve the spatial relationship between the speaker and addressee as well as the position of the object or destination in addition to direction of movement. Thus, mastery of these verbs is likely to extend over considerable time. The abstractness of the verbs of transfer account for the still later mastery of these forms.

Discourse Referencing

As we indicated in the last chapter, referencing is what speakers do when they designate to their listeners what they are referring to—what people, animals, or objects they are talking about; what places they are describing; or what event they are relating. Discourse referencing has to do with how speakers reference when they are engaged in various genres of discourse. How, for example, does a child let the listener know what is being referred to as the child tell stories, engages in conversations, transfers information, answers or asks questions, or describes events? Just as for event talk, misreferencing in discourse occurs when the speaker is not successful in selecting the intended referent. Problems occur in discourse referencing when the speaker does not take the listener's perspective into consideration. It is a problem with what we have been calling fine tuning.

Fine Tuning and Referencing   Discourse referencing, like discourse inferencing and perspective taking, can be influenced to different degrees by what the speaker takes to be the listener's current state of knowledge. Speakers who know their listener well and who are capable discourse users will select referring expressions based on what has been activated in their listener's mental model. Where needed, speakers will provide the listener with detailed information; where not needed, speakers will be brief. The first referring expression below is appropriate for a listener who already knows who is being talked about; the second is appropriate for placing a new character into the mental model of the listener:

> She never told me she had a sister.
> Mary, the girl who lives across the street, never told me she had a sister.

Successful referencing requires that the listener be able to understand what is being referred to by (1) retrieving the intended meaning from what is currently present in the context; (2) associating the referring expression with entities already activated in the mental model, (3) and adding new information to the emerging mental model. If, for example, the listener hears *that one* said with reference to an object that is currently present, he or she can interpret the expression directly as referring to that object. Halliday and Hasan (1976) called this type of referring *exophoric* in that the meaning is derived from what is present in the situation, not from information that is in the discourse.

Speakers often need to refer to nonpresent entities and to entities which are not yet in the listener's mental model. This type of referring occurs, for example, when speakers are first introducing the people, place, and time of an upcoming story or event description. In these cases, speakers often explicitly indicate their referent by naming or describing it. Expressions such as "a boy" or "a castle" can introduce referents into the listener's mental model and can be said to be *transparent* in that they are directly interpretable.

Once a referent is represented by the listener, it can be referred to through the use of pronouns or other nontransparent referring expressions. These expressions, which Halliday and Hasan (1976) have called *anaphoric* expressions, generally take their meaning from what is already present in the listener's mental model. In the following example, *she* and *it* are anaphoric expressions which are interpreted using the currently activated elements *Teri* and *class* in the mental model of the reader or listener.

> Teri ran to her class.
> She couldn't be late for it again.

Halliday and Hasan (1976) also have identified situations in which the referring expression indicates something yet to be mentioned in the discourse and not yet introduced into the listener's mental model. These forward-pointing phrases, called *cataphoric* expressions by Halliday and Hasan (1976), are exemplified in the following:

Wait until you hear *this*!

In some cases, referents are not explicit, but enough information is available from the mental model to allow listeners to infer the intended referent.

The professor will be furious with her.

The definite article *the* and the pronoun *her* in this example presents a dilemma in that they imply the existence of known, retrievable referents. If we see this statement as a continuation of the discourse about Teri above, we can use the activated elements in the mental model to infer *her* as Teri. There is not, however, an explicit referent for *the professor*, and we require further information for its interpretation. Listeners are likely to resolve this dilemma through inferencing. Listeners know that classes have professors and therefore infer that the specific referent is the professor for the class to which Teri ran.

In some cases, the speaker simply does not provide the listener with enough information to resolve the referencing problem. This may occur when the listener is provided with two or more plausible possibilities from which to choose a referent.

The man and the boy are running.
He looks tired.

In this case, *he* is ambiguous since it could refer either to the man or to the boy. Here the listener may use a strategy identified by Rochester and Martin (1977) as *disambiguation* and simply choose one of the two possibilities. The listener may then wait to see if subsequent information in the discourse confirms his or her choice.

In other cases in which the speaker leaves the listener with insufficient information to identify the referent, the listener may either suspend judgment and not make the effort to find the underlying referent, or acknowledge his or her failure to resolve the problem and ask for further information (e.g., The listener may ask, "Who looks tired?"). Referring expressions that are not interpreted at all or only with the help of additional information from the speaker we are calling *unresolved*.

She was at the theater last night.

Without supporting discourse or shared background knowledge, listeners are unable to identify who *she* is in the above example. Although clarification may come later, either with or without the listener's request, the ambiguity cannot be resolved at the time of the utterance.

BOX 8–2. *Types of Referring Expressions*

1. *Exophoric expressions*: The listener must identify the referent from the presenting situational contexts.
2. *Transparent expressions*: The listener can interpret the referent directly by interpreting the expression.
3. *Anaphoric expressions*: The listener has an active representation in a mental model of the referent which was previously presented in the text or inferred.
4. *Cataphoric expressions*: The referent is not yet in the listener's mental model but will be presented in upcoming text.
5. *Referring expressions requiring inferencing*: The listener must infer the referent from information already in the mental model or from background knowledge.
6. *Referring expressions requiring disambiguation*: The listener has more than one plausible interpretation for the referring expression.
7. *Referring expressions that are uninterpretable*: The listener does not have enough information to interpret the expression.

We can see, then, that speakers use referring expressions that obligate their listeners to use a variety of interpretation strategies. If the referent is clearly present in the preceding discourse or in the situation, this is an easy task. If it is not explicit, the listener must work harder to retrieve the referent. Box 8–2 summarizes the types of referring expressions a speaker may use when fine tuning to a listener.

Development of Discourse Referencing Children's first words are referring expressions. From the beginning of language they have been found to be able to refer unambiguously to what they mean, especially when what they mean is located in the here-and-now of the present situation. Peterson and Dodsworth (1991) have found in their study of two-year-olds, that one out of every five of the noun phrases used to introduce something new were ambiguous, and the remaining four new nouns were easily interpretable.

Bennett-Kastor (1983), in her study of children's use of noun phrases in discourse, found that children as young as two used transparent noun phrases with indefinite articles and adjectives at the beginning of their narratives to introduce referents. At three the children began to use phoric phrases, involving anaphoric referencing by way of inferencing. For instance, they talked about *the* cashier only after they had made mention of *a* store. At ages four and five the children employed transparent phrases using cultural implication such as the use of story archetypes to introduce characters such as "the witch" or "the wolf."

Children's sensitivity to the use of definite and indefinite expressions has also been studied by Karmiloff-Smith (1979). Unlike Bennett-Kastor, Karmiloff-Smith found that three-year-olds tended to use the indefinite *a* rather than the definite *the* to describe repeated events, indicating that they had not yet developed the use of the definite article to indicate previously referenced objects. At four years the children increased their use of definite articles, but the increase did not appear to be systematically related to previously identified referents. Rather, they seemed erratic and random. At five years, previous seeing as well as naming of a referent was associated with an increase in definite articles, and at six years, previous naming was the major determinant of article definiteness, rather than visual presentation. This was an indication that at six the children acquired notions of anaphora.

With regard to ambiguity in referencing, Klecan-Aker (1985) found that her sixth- and ninth-grade normal subjects were nonambiguous in their referencing 62 percent of the time. Klecan-Aker and Hedrick (1985), reporting further on the same data, found a greater incidence of ambiguity in pronoun referencing for normal sixth graders than for normal ninth graders.

Rochester and Martin (1977) have examined referencing in the discourse of normal adult speakers. They found that 80 to 90 percent of all noun phrases in the narratives of normal adult speakers had explicit referents. Most frequently, the referents were in the discourse, particularly when the task was telling stories. The use of exophoric referencing depended on the speaker's presumption that the listener could see what the speaker is talking about. No exophoric referents were used in recounting narratives in which there was no visible referent. In a task that involved discussion of cartoon pictures, the speakers used more personal pronouns when they presumed that the listener could see the pictures. This increase in exophoric referencing with shared knowledge was also found for seven- to ten-year-olds (Liles, 1985).

Topic Manipulation

Competent conversationalists are well aware that conversational etiquette requires that they keep to an established topic, unless they indicate to their partner that they are shifting topic. Conversationalists have available to them particular ways of initiating topics, maintaining them, and shifting to a new topic. The skills involved in such activities require background knowledge about the topic being discussed and linguistic and nonlinguistic knowledge about the pragmatics of how and when to initiate, maintain, and shift topics.

But what is a topic? Those involved in analyzing topics, especially topics in children's discourse have described the construct as elusive (Mentis and Prutting, 1991; Brinton and Fujiki, 1989; Brown and Yule, 1983). Perhaps part of its elusiveness is related to the lack of clear theorizing about the conceptual framework which underlies the everyday notion of topicalization. Some have proposed that topics are like titles; they are propositions or questions of concern which serve as a focal idea for the conversation (Mentis and Prutting, 1991; Brinton and Fujiki, 1984; Keenan and Schieffelin, 1976). Others have seen topics as formal elements or propositions which are common to adjacent utterances (Hurtig, 1977; Venneman, 1975). In this view, the topic of the following multiparty exchange is a proposition about whether coffee is good for you:

DAVID: Can I put a pot of coffee on?
JOAN: Sure.
DARLENE: No.

DAVID: You don't tell me.
DARLENE: Quiet. Too much coffee's bad for you.
JOAN: Too much coffee is bad for you though.
GARY: Why, who told you?
JOAN: It makes you nervous.
GARY: No it doesn't make you nervous. It makes you feel nice.
JOAN: Makes you jump all around.
GARY: Coffee's good for you. (from Hewitt, Duchan, Segal, 1993)

A richer notion of topic is provided by Brown and Yule (1983), who have argued against the propositional view of topics in favor of a schema theoretic view. Within the Brown and Yule (1983) model, topics are based on conceptual frames—frames used by conversationalists as a guide for possible elaboration. This topic framework notion is comparable to what we have been calling a mental model (see section on inferencing) in that it is a mental structure used by people to guide what they are saying and understanding. Like mental models formed by listeners to understand discourse, Brown and Yule see topics as originating in the speakers' mental models which grow and change when new information is added. The models contain not only new information but also a conceptual organization of information, both explicitly given and inferred, about what has already been talked about. In this mental models or topic framework view, the topic exists in the mind of the conversationalists and need not be explicitly indicated in the text.

Various researchers have found that the way topics are manipulated is shaped by the cultural community. Michaels and her colleagues (Michaels, 1986; Michaels and Cazden, 1986) have shown that African American preschool children organize their talk around subtopics, and that the children did not make explicit how their subtopics were related to an overall topic, unless they were asked directly (Michaels, 1986). When they related events during the "sharing time" period in their classroom, their contributions were often criticized by the classroom teacher. Below is an example of a teacher's response to a black child, Deena:

DEENA: I went to the beach Sunday
            and to McDonalds
            and to the park
            and I got this for my birthday (holds up purse)
            my mother bought it for me
            and I had two dollars for my birthday
            and I put it in here
            and I went to where my friend named Gigi
            I went over to my grandmother's house with her
            and she was on my back
            and I and we was walking around by my house
            and she was HEAVY
            she was in the sixth or seventh grade

TEACHER: OK I'm going to stop you
            I want you to talk about things that are
            really really very important
            that's important to you

but can you tell us things that are sort of
different
can you do that? (from Michaels and Cazden, 1986, p. 137)

The teacher in this case failed to detect indicators of subtopic shift and overall themes in the child's talk and therefore did not accept Deena's contribution as well formed. Michaels and Cazden (1986) found that the teachers expected the children to relate their sentences explicitly to an overall single theme rather than to express what the teachers saw as unrelated subtopics. Cazden (1988) took the contribution by Deena and read it to a group of black teachers and a group of white teachers, asking all of the teachers to evaluate the student based on the verbal sample of her talk. Cazden found

> In responding to the mimicked version of this story (by Deena), white adults were uniformly negative, with comments such as "terrible story, incoherent." . . . When asked to make a judgment about this child's probable academic standing, they without exception rated her below children who told topic-centered accounts. . . . The black adults reacted very differently, finding this story well formed, easy to understand, and interesting, "with lots of detail and description." . . . All but one of the black adults rated the child as highly verbal, very bright and/or successful in school. (Cazden, 1988, p. 18)

Topic Initiation   Topics are initiated at the beginning of conversations and in places where new topics are brought into conversations already in progress. Since both beginnings and shifts in conversations involve a change in discourse continuity, topic introductions often are accompanied by a verbal or nonverbal indicator that something unexpected is about to happen. These indicators may take a variety of forms.

PHRASES OF INTRODUCTION   The speaker may alert the listener to the new topic through the use of a sentence-initial phrase.

> *That reminds me;* I need a ride tonight.

In this example, the previous topic shared by these discussants may be related, but the introducing phrase "that reminds me" signals a topic shift. Keenan and Schieffelin (1976), MacWhinney (1984), and Brinton and Fujiki (1989) suggest some others:

> *Oh I forgot to tell you;* I already got it.
> *You know that* book you gave me? It's good.
> *Remember the* story you read? It was on TV.
> *There was a* big pile of books sitting there.

LEFT DISLOCATION   The new topic is sometimes introduced in the initial position of an utterance with a process called *left dislocation.*

John, I saw him yesterday at the zoo.

QUESTION FORMS Questions are often used in discourse to introduce new topics. Some examples show how these can be of various question types:

> Do you have any pets?
> Where's the pencil sharpener?
> You don't have any nickels, do you?
> Ya know what? I got a new sister.

REFERENT SPECIFICATION When modifiers are used it can be assumed by the listener that the modifier is indicating that the discourse focus is changing to include the modified information. Adjectives, relative clauses, and other modifying and identifying structures can indicate a shift in topic or focus.

> I ate some *green* apples, and got a stomachache.
> Watch for my car; it's an *old blue* Dodge.
> See my *shiny* shoes? They're new.

Topic Continuation Researchers have found that speakers have distinguishable ways of continuing a topic (Brown and Yule, 1983; Tracy and Moran, 1983; and Hewitt, Duchan, and Segal, 1993). One way is to relate to something in the most recent talk, and comment on it or add new information about it. This Brown and Yule call "speaking topically" (1983, p. 84).

Another structure for topic organization is to relate individual contributions to a general overriding issue. Brown and Yule refer to this second type as "speaking on a topic" (p. 85). When speaking on a topic, the contribution need not be related directly to the last utterance but can be related to it indirectly in that both can tie to an overarching concern, as is the case in the following passage. Here the kindergarten children offer their thoughts on the topic of what would happen if a tooth fairy were a tooth witch. The individual contributions do not necessarily relate to the last thing said, but the turns are all related to the general issue:

TEACHER: I wonder why people talk about a tooth fairy and not a tooth witch?
JILL: A tooth fairy comes through the wall and a witch has to knock on the door.
WALLY: If a witch came he might steal the child away.
EDDIE: Jill, I don't think a witch would knock—she'll break the door open. She could even steal a mother away.
JILL: The tooth fairy would leave a quarter and then the witch comes and steals the money. But then you wish for it again. (from Paley, 1981, p. 44)

Topic Shifting Topics continue along until they end naturally or until one of the conversational partners changes the topic. Topics also can end temporarily or permanently if they are interrupted. Participants in discourse sometimes indicate when they are ending, shifting, or interrupting a topic by using linguistic identifiers such as "and that's it" or "by the way" (Schiffrin, 1987; Grosz and Sidner, 1986; Jefferson, 1972). At other times the shifts are more gradual and thereby more difficult to identify. For example, Hurtig

(1977) has described *topic shading* as a gradual shift from one topic to another, with the boundaries of the two topics being difficult to identify, as in the following exchange from Brinton and Fujiki (1989) in which the topic shifts from taking off shoes to buying them:

SPEAKER 1: I was thinking of taking off my shoes and sitting on the floor.
SPEAKER 2: You should have. Oh, you should have. Oh, your shoes! I wish I could find some.
SPEAKER 1: I bought these on sale. They were a real bargain. (p. 53)

Since topics can be organized in a hierarchy, with general topics being continued through subtopics, some topic shifts may not be a shift away from the overriding issue, but rather a shift to another aspect or subtopic pertaining to the more general issue. Subtopics, too, are discontinuous, and seem abrupt unless they are introduced indicating that another aspect of the overall topic is about to be introduced. Indicators of shift used to move to a brand-new topic are the same as those which can be used to move to a new subtopic.

Topic and Functionality This discussion of topic manipulation leads to the conclusion that any aspect of a mental model would be appropriate as a discussion point for topic continuation. However, this open-ended view of topic maintenance does not account for the obvious inappropriateness of exchanges such as the following:

M: I gave a party last week. I was washing dishes afterward and I cut my hand. I had to go to the hospital.
D: I'm going to a party next week.

Although the idea of party has become part of D's mental model of what is being talked about, D has failed to comment on what must be M's main concern, the injury. Grosz and Sidner (1986) have formulated a theory of discourse which considers the importance of agenda in the organization of expository discourse. Tannen (1986) has argued that conversation often breaks down or seems unsatisfying to participants when their partner misinterprets their agenda. Indeed, it may seem to the participants that they are not connecting topically. In the following example, one participant is talking about going to her sister's house and the other about what to do in general.

SPEAKER 1: Do you want to go to my sister's?
(interp 1: WANTS TO GO, REQUEST)
(interp 2: ELICIT WHAT OTHER WANTS TO DO, SUGGESTION)
SPEAKER 2: Okay.
(response, acceptance)
SPEAKER 1: Do you really want to go?
(working under interp 2, confirming acceptance of the suggestion)
SPEAKER 2: You're driving me crazy! Why don't you make up your mind what you want?
(working under interp 1, first you hint then you renege, seen as reneging on request)

Children's Development of Topic Manipulation Several researchers have studied normally developing children's acquisition of the ability to continue topics which have been presented to them. The first indicators of children's ability to follow another's topic occur as early as one and one-half years, at which time the children can respond topically to an immediately preceding utterance.

Bloom, Rocissano, and Hood (1976) found that children from nineteen months responded to the topic of an adult's preceding utterance 56 percent of the time. This percentage increased with age to 76 percent by the time the children had reached thirty-eight months of age. Ervin-Tripp (1979) found that two-year-olds were able to respond to verbal summonses such as questions, commands, and offers. And Keenan and Klein (1975) found that the two-and-one-half-year-old twins they studied frequently repeated one another, which the researchers viewed as an early form of topic maintenance.

In their study of older children, Brinton and Fujiki (1984) found that five- and nine-year-olds introduced and changed topics more frequently than adults. Adults were more likely to continue topics and maintain them for longer periods of time than children. Finally, Brinton and Fujiki found that their adult subjects used topic shading significantly more than their child subjects. The authors also indicated considerable individual variation within the different subject groups.

Discourse Focus

A competent speaker fine tunes to the presumed knowledge of the listener, choosing the language that will best inform the listener about persons, objects, and events that are being referred to. Those referents take on relative importance depending upon what the speaker is emphasizing at that particular time in the discourse. The elements which are currently given attention or which are easily within conceptual reach make up what Grosz (1981) has called a *focus space*—a construct similar to what we have been calling the speaker and listener's mental model of the ongoing discourse. A particular element in a mental model or focus space becomes more or less central as the discourse progresses (Chafe, 1980). For example, *the dog* is introduced into the listener's mental model with a central focus in this next discourse segment in sentences 1 and 4, and is more peripheral in sentences 2 and 3.

1. One time my dog almost got hit by a car.
2. It was when my brother had a new bike.
3. He wasn't supposed to go out in the street, but he did.
4. And he, my dog, went chasing after him.

Determinants of Focus Two observers of the same event might well have a different *sense of the event*, and so are likely to bring into focus different aspects in their recounting of it. For example:

A. Well, this cat was sleeping on a chair, and a kid came over and started to pull on its tail and blow in its face, and the cat woke up and he was really scared, so he scratched him.

B. A little boy was just petting this cat, and when he put his face down close to it, he got scratched. He was really scared.

Observer A focuses on the cat, seeing the event as the cat being harassed by a child. Observer B focuses on the child, interpreting the same exchange as an attack on an innocent child by an unruly cat. The difference in focus is identifiable by seeing how easily the pronoun *he* is interpreted in each case. It refers to the cat, the element in focus in A, and the boy, the element in focus in B.

For the above descriptions, the speakers seem to have different *agendas*, each trying to sway the listener's sympathy for the chosen protaganist. If, instead, the agenda were to describe the series of actions that took place, or to refute someone's assumptions about what took place, the description might be constructed differently.

> A cat was lying on a chair with its eyes closed. A boy came up to it and ran his hand along its body and tail. The boy put his face close to the cat's face. The cat opened its eyes, pulled back, and hit the boy with its outstretched paw.

Not only does agenda play a role in creating a focus, but so does the speaker's need to *fine tune* to what the listener is thinking. The next example is cast under the speaker's assumption that the listener thinks the boy was at fault:

> The boy wasn't pulling the cat's tail or hurting it in any way; he was just petting it, and then he got scratched.

In the above examples, the boy and the cat are in the mental model of the listener, but each focuses on them differently, reflecting the speaker's sense of the event and agenda, and his or her fine tuning to what the listener might be thinking.

The Relation Between Focus and Topic Some researchers see focus and topic as being the names for the same thing (Sidner, 1983). Others separate them in intricate ways (Grosz and Sidner, 1986). Our reason for separating them is that it allows us to distinguish two different kinds of sensemaking, one emanating from children's understanding of how to organize the elements of the discourse, and the second from their understanding of overarching ideas governing the discourse. In each of the passages above, the topic, in our framework, would be the interaction between the boy and the cat, with the focus changing under the different renditions.

Linguistic Devices Indicating Focused Elements

FULL NOUN PHRASES Elements can be introduced directly into the mental model by a noun phrase (*Paul*; *the old woman*; *the one we saw yesterday*; *my first car*). Sometimes the noun phrases are directly interpretable and need no further explanation. We have called these *transparent* meanings when discussing referencing (see earlier). Other times the listener will not know enough about who or what is being referred to, as when a proper name is used with no other introduction. In these cases adult speakers will often insert a descriptive clause, describing the person (*Paul, my brother*), thereby focusing on the character and at the same time placing it into the mental model.

PRONOUNS   Once elements have been located either explicitly or implicitly in the focus space, they can be referred to by a pronoun. In fact, a test for whether an element is in a focus space is its interpretatibility under conditions of pronominalization.

DETERMINERS   Determiners such as *this*, *that*, or *those* are also used to indicate the importance of a referent when it is first introduced, thus placing it in focus in the mental model.

So I asked *this lady* to help me, and she did.
I like *those birds* that sing in the morning.

REFERENT SPECIFICATION   When modifiers are used the speaker may be indicating that the discourse focus is changing to include the modified information. Adjectives, relative clauses, and other modifying and identifying structures can indicate a shift in focus.

STRESS AND PROSODY   Suprasegmental indicators are sometimes used to mark focus in speech when the previously discussed conventions for indicating focus are violated or there is ambiguity for other reasons. When spoken with ordinary sentence stress, the following two statements appear to provide new information, the first about a characteristic and the second about an activity of the topic *Bridget*. This leads the listener to expect the information in the predicate to be in focus.

Bridget is good at math.
Bridget pushed her bike to school.

If we add extra stress to any one of the spoken words, however, this expectation changes. Stress usually implies a contrast with alternative or presumed assumptions. The focus of the sentence changes with the stress pattern. With stress on *Bridget*, the contrast is between Bridget and someone else, and the focus is thus on that comparison:

Bridget is good at math, but Ken isn't.

With stress on *is* or *good*, the contrast is with the assumption that she is not, and the focus on dispelling the presupposition:

Bridget *is* good at math, despite her poor grades.
Bridget is *good* at math, but she hates it.

When stress is put on "math," a contrast is implied with another skill, with the focus on features of Bridget:

Bridget is good at *math*, but not at art.

Beginnings of Focus Learning   Children's ability to distinguish central focal elements and to talk about them is evident from the time they utter their first words. When children begin talking in single word utterances, they do not arbitrarily name everything they are thinking about, but rather they indicate what is new and interesting among the items in their focus space.

Greenfield and Smith (1976) found that the two children they studied used their one-word utterances to indicate what was new or changing or uncertain in the current situation. When an object first appeared on the scene, the child was more likely to name it (e.g., *horsie*) than they would had the object been there for a while. When the object to be talked about is not present or has not been agreed upon by the participants, children at the one-word stage have been found to use what Scollon (1979) has called *vertical constructions*. The children identified what was in central focus, and then they commented on it. For example, Scollon's child focused on a fan, and then commented on it:

BRENDA:	Fan.
MOTHER:	Fan. Yeah.
BRENDA:	Cool.
MOTHER:	Cool yeah. Fan makes you cool.

Other examples of focusing for children this age occur when children indicate an action (*fall*) or feeling (*no*) about an action. The focus in these cases is not on a person or object but on some attribute or associated state.

At the two-word stage, children use word order and relative stress to indicate which of the two words is the given topic and which is elaborated information. Wieman (1976) found that in two-word utterances children usually indicated the focus by stressing the second word. Under certain circumstances, such as when the location of an object was known, the child placed the focus in first position, stressing it:

MOTHER:	What's in the street?
DAVID:	*Firetruck* street.

At four years of age children are able to use stress as a focusing mechanism in more complex utterances. Hornby and Haas (1970) asked four-year-olds to describe each of two pictures in which the second picture involved a change in agent, action, or patient. The children tended not to use contrastive stress when describing the first picture but did use it when describing the second picture. The stressing effect was much stronger when the second picture had a change in agent than for the action or patient changes.

In longer discourse, such as telling stories from a set of pictures, children under six years old have been found to violate conventions by changing the focus without indicating the change to their listeners (Karmiloff-Smith, 1981). For example, Karmiloff-Smith's young subjects produced sequences such as the following:

He's walking along (*he* = boy in the picture)
and *he* sees a balloon (*he* = boy)
and *he* gives him a green *one* (*he* = man; *one* = balloon)
and *he* walks off home (*he* = boy)

For children older than six, Karmiloff-Smith (1981) reports the following pattern, in which the speaker works hard to maintain *the boy* as a focus, revising the discourse in midstream to do so: (the asterisk indicates revisions)

The little boy is walking along.
He sees a balloon man.
* The balloon m . . . he asks for a balloon (*he* = boy)
and goes off happily.
* The balloo . . . he lets go of the balloon (*he* = boy)
and starts to cry.

DISCOURSE COHESION

While the relationship between words and phrases is clear from the study of syntax, the relationship between sentences is less obvious. Researchers have postulated that sentences cohere with one another not simply by inferencing, perspective taking, topic making, and focusing but also with various sorts of linguistic relationships which hold between text elements. This linguistic view is a closed text view and differs from the one assumed in the previous section.

Open Versus Closed Text View of Cohesion

Many scholars have studied discourse from a *closed text* point of view which presumes that the information needed to interpret the discourse is provided by the words and sentences in the text. We have been forwarding an *open text* point of view in which speakers and listeners understand discourse by going beyond the information provided in the text. They use inferencing to read between the lines, they place their own perspective on the words, and they often interpret the text using implicit topic structure.

An example of the closed text view is one used by Halliday and Hasan (1976) in their classic study of discourse cohesion. These authors define discourse *cohesion* as the "semantic ties between elements of a text." In this framework, an element can serve as a cohesive tie only if it relates to another element in the text. So, the following sentences provided by Halliday and Hasan form a text because the pronoun *them* forms a referencing tie to *six cooking apples*.

Wash and core six cooking apples.
Put them into a fireproof dish.

An open text view would allow for the two sentences to be related in that one can infer that both are from a recipe about how to bake apples. And, further, that the pronoun *them* refers not to the words *six cooking apples* but to the underlying conceptual representation of the apples which is located in the listener's mental model.

Halliday and Hasan have identified five types of cohesive ties found in discourse: reference, substitution, ellipsis, conjunction, and lexical cohesion.

We will describe each below and provide an alternative open text view following our description of Halliday and Hasan's linguistic-based approach.

Types and Indicators of Discourse Cohesion

Reference   Cohesion in reference occurs when a lexical item means the same thing as another in the text. There are different types of reference ties: (1) personal reference in which a referring expression identifies a person who is talked about elsewhere in the text, creating a tie between the two; (2) demonstrative reference in which a referring expression such as *this*, *that*, or *there* ties to another element in the text; and (3) comparative reference in which comparison terms such as *better* or *another* are used, which tie to an object of comparison.

Substitution   In substitution cohesion, an element is used which has the same structural function in the language as the element to which it ties. Substitutions may be nominal (*one*; *ones*; *the same*; *so*); verbal (*do*; *be*; *have*; *do the same*; *likewise*); or clausal (*so*; *not*). The following is a nominal substitution:

Yes, I was at a Wegman's grocery store last week.
I went to *the one in Rochester* the week before.

Ellipsis   An elliptical tie occurs when the speaker omits an element of a sentence and its meaning is understood from what was previously provided or is in the upcoming discourse. Halliday and Hasan distinguish nominal, verbal, and clausal ellipsis depending upon which element is omitted. The following is an example of nominal ellipsis:

Where is the car?
In the garage.

In this example *the car* is omitted in the second sentence but implied. Ellipsis occurs when nearby constituents have parallel linguistic functions (MacWhinney, 1984) as in the following example:

Bill knows why he is sick, but Sam doesn't.

The interpreter of the second clause supplies the ellipsed information "know why Bill is sick."

Conjunction   Conjunctions provide discourse cohesion when they occur between sentences (not within them). Common types of cohesive conjunctions are ones that indicate (1) additive relations (e.g., *and*; *further*); (2) temporal relations (e.g., *then*; *after*); (3) causal relations (*so*; *because*; *for this reason*); and (4) adversative or contrastive relations (*but*; *though*; *nonetheless*; *yet*).

Lexical Cohesion   Sometimes speakers repeat a word or use a synonym or related word, all of which fit what Halliday and Hasan call *lexical cohesion*. Rochester, Martin, and Thurston (1977) specify four types of lexical cohesion, besides exact lexical repetition: (1) use of the same root, (2) substitution of a synonym, (3) substitution of a superordinate term, and (4) substitution of a general term.

I'll be the baby.	REPETITION
The baby needs a hat.	
My shoe came untied.	SAME ROOT
Will you *tie* it again?	
Ed was really mad.	SYNONYM
He was so *angry* he spit.	
We've got a Ford.	SUPERORDINATE
It's the best *car*.	
I can carry the food in my basket.	GENERAL TERM
I put all the *things* in it.	

The above cohesion types relate elements found in the text. When reference is made to elements outside the text, such as using the word *there* to indicate an object in the situation, Halliday and Hasan do not consider it a cohesion device. This is because the closed text view assumes that cohesion depends upon the building of relationships between elements in the text.

The open text view assumes that texts themselves have no cohesion, but rather the interpreters of texts create mental models of the meanings conveyed by the text, and the elements in the mental model cohere because they make sense together (Brown and Yule, 1983). Under this perspective, what is important is not that words relate to one another with single ties, but that words have meaning and those meanings have multiple and intricate ties to one another. These ties are viewed to be in the mind of the participants, not in the structure of the text. Speakers do not leave out constituents through a process of ellipsis, but rather follow the principle that elements central in the mental model need not be mentioned again. Pronouns are not used to create cohesion, but rather to refer to entities already in the listener's mental model. Conjunctions do more than tie adjacent sentences together in the text: They also cue the listener about how to relate the new information to what is already known. Under the mental models framework the concern is how elements of the text make coherent sense to those experiencing them, rather than on text cohesion.

Discourse Disjuncture

The closed text method developed by Halliday and Hasan (1976) and expanded by others (Liles, 1985; Strong and Shaver, 1991) treat discourse as a woven fabric—tied together into a single piece through cohesion. What the notion of cohesion fails to convey is that discourse can consist of units which bear a loose tie to adjacent units. This is especially obvious in boundaries between large "chunks" of discourse. For example, conversations contain topic shifts, event descriptions contain deictic shifts, stories move from one episode to another. We suggest that these disjunctures between global units can provide more insight into a child's understanding of discourse than places which have a Halliday and Hasan-type cohesion relation.

One entre into the study of disjuncture in children's discourse is to examine it for linguistic indicators that the new thing being talked about is different from the previous utterance. Markers of discourse disjuncture have been found for various types of adult discourse. Schiffrin (1987) found, for example, that participants in arguments indicate their bottom line conclusion by using *so* and *then*. Goodenough and Weiner (1978) found adults use markers of *ok—all right* to signal a topic ending and turn exchange in conversation. Further, Grosz and Sidner (1986) found their speakers used markers such as *anyway* to indicate interruptions and return to main topics in conversations. And Young (1987) found terms such as *the point was* occur at the transitions between conversations and stories, and evaluative noises and concluding statements such as "tchew" and "that's the only thing about that" to occur at transition points where stories ended and conversation began.

Children's Development of Notions of Discourse Cohesion and Disjuncture

In their longitudinal study of cohesion of ten children over their second year of life, Peterson and Dodsworth (1991) were surprised to find that by age two the children were using most of Halliday and Hasan's cohesion types. The children used personal and demonstrative pronouns, verb and clause ellipsis, conjunctions, and lexical cohesion earlier, when their MLU was 2.5. By MLU 3.0 the children were using comparative references and nominal ellipsis, and by MLU 3.5 the children were indicating substitution-type cohesion. The children's use of personal and demonstrative pronouns increased significantly over an eighteen-month period, and their use of verbal and clausal ellipsis decreased significantly during that period. On the average children used two cohesion devices per utterance with an increase over the period they were studied. The most frequently used tie was lexical cohesion, comprising 42 percent of the total occurrences. This compares with 30 percent for normal adults (Rochester and Martin, 1979).

Bennett-Kastor (1983) found that as children got older they increased the number of times they repeat a noun phrase within a single discourse sequence. At two years, each noun phrase tended to recur an average of five times; at five years, the average had increased to fourteen. Further, there was an increase with age in the distance occurring between noun phrases and their reiteration. At two years, 81 percent of the reiterations were within one clause of the previous mention, and, at age five, only 59 percent were within a single clause away. By their fifth year the children had ten clauses between the reiteration of a noun phrase and its last mention.

In a study of school children five, seven, and nine years old, Fine (1978) found differences between the children in their social use of cohesion ties. With one exception, the devices were used by all the children more to tie together elements of their own utterances than to tie to previous utterances of the teacher. The exception was for five-year-olds who used more ellipsis when responding to the teacher (40 percent of their total use) than when continuing their own discourse (12 percent). The five-year-olds tended to use more conjunctions and anaphoric referencing to tie to the conversation of the teacher than did the older children.

Liles (1985), in her study of cohesion indicators used by both normal and language-disordered children older than six, found both groups able to use all of Halliday and Hasan's discourse cohesion types. In a second study of these same children, Liles (1987) found from her examination of discourse conjunctions that children in both groups were more facile using error-free conjunctions for marking cohesion within episodes than they were for marking disjuncture between episodes.

ASSESSING DISCOURSE

Children with language problems are likely to have difficulty participating in everyday discourse. The procedures described below assume that the discourse problem has to do with the child's knowledge of how discourse is organized, rather than with problems at other levels of language understanding and use (although both may be the case). The following questions could serve as a guide for deciding what sorts of analyses to carry out to determine whether a child has a discourse problem, and, if so, in what areas of discourse.

1. What sorts of everyday speech events does the child participate in?
2. Does the child seem more competent when participating in certain types of events than others?
3. What sorts of the events seem to be most difficult for the child, and how is the discourse of those events organized?
4. Which of the following applies to the child?
    a. The child does not seem to understand the organization of a particular genre or genres.
    b. The child seems to take other people literally and fails to infer meanings between the lines.
    c. It is difficult from the child's description to keep track of the characters as well as when and where the events take place.
    d. The child does not follow rules of topic introduction or maintenance.
    e. It is difficult to identify the boundaries of the discourse units used by the child.

Answers to each of the above questions can be found by analyzing how the child participates in everyday life speech events. The analyses can be designed to obtain particular information. Below are suggestions about approaches to the different areas of discourse knowledge which might account for a child's difficulties.

Analyzing Everyday Discourse

Ethnographers who have studied communication of children in different speech communities have found considerable differences among them (see Schieffelin and Eisenberg, 1984, for a review). One difference is what the children do or say as they participate in events in their daily life, and another is which people the children interact with. In order to determine the discourse requirements of life events for a particular child, it would be useful to follow that child around, taking field notes on the nature and structure of activities carried out at home and at school. The information from direct observation can be combined with interview information (see Chapter 2) to lead to conclusions such as those found by Eisenberg (1982) from her ethnography of Mexican-American children:

> . . . The majority of conversations involving adults and children were triadic rather than dyadic. Rather than asking questions to initiate conversations between themselves and young children, caregivers would help children initiate and maintain conversations with a third individual. Using the expression "dile" ("say to him/her/"), the adult would give the child a message to repeat to someone else. What the adults told the children to say reflected their beliefs concerning how different individuals should be addressed. When speaking to infants, children were taught to soothe and to get the infant's attention. When speaking to peers, they were taught to be assertive, to request politely, and to tease. Speech directed to adults emphasized politeness and the importance of responding to another person's utterances. (from Schieffelin and Eisenberg, 1984, p. 389)

Analyzing Discourse Genres

In order to determine whether children are able to use a variety of discourse genres, we begin our assessment procedure by eliciting a variety of discourse samples from a child. For example, we might elicit samples of the child telling stories, describing common events, explaining something, conversing, and performing during classroom lessons. The procedures used for eliciting each of these samples will depend upon the child's competence. A beginning storyteller may need the support of a familiar book and a familiar story for structuring his talk. A more advanced storyteller can be asked to make up a story about a picture, or to tell about something funny that happened to her. Similarly, a child who is just realizing how to describe events will require an elicitation procedure which offers support for the event descriptions, such as sequence pictures, videotaped scenarios, or guiding questions. The child will do best when asked to describe very familiar events which have generalized representations (Nelson and Gruendel, 1981). A more advanced child could respond to a task requiring a description of an infrequent and complex event, such as describing the steps to changing a tire. If the child's competencies are unknown at the outset, we recommend beginning with an easier discourse task and proceeding to those that are more difficult.

Eliciting discourse is best done naturally. For example, the clinician should first try to get a videotape of the child interacting with a parent. The interactions can be set up to elicit the different types of discourse. The pair could be asked to read a familiar storybook together, for example; or they may be asked to play together for a while, in order to see if event talk or conversations occur. A video- or audiotape of classroom interactions could provide the source of the sample of talk during lessons. Samples from several lessons might be needed to determine whether the participation problems are the result of not knowing about lessons or having problems with the lesson content.

If it is not feasible to get samples with familiar adults, the clinician may need to elicit the discourse more directly. The child may be asked to retell a story, to given an event description, to role play some conversation between toy characters, to explain the steps of a familiar task, or to pretend to be the teacher giving a quiz. Manipulation techniques can be used in which clinicians intentionally misorder an event description or story sequence or leave out an essential part. The presumption is that if children repair the ill-formed discourse, they have exhibited their knowledge of the discourse form.

Some suggestions for discourse manipulation are:

1. Tell the child a story and give the ending in the middle. Ask the child to retell the story and see if she reorganizes it, moving the end to its correct position.
2. Give the child a set of sequence pictures that depict only part of the story. Tell a story which is more inclusive. Ask the child later to pick the pictures which go with the story and see if he includes the compatible pictures which he had not seen originally.
3. Tell the child about how to do something he knows how to do, mixing up the order. See if the child corrects the order in the retelling or in carrying out the directions.

Once the samples are collected, they will need to be transcribed orthographically. We recommend a slight variant of the procedure for language sample transcription presented in other chapters in which the sentence or utterance is the basic unit. Here we suggest that the clause become the basic unit of analysis, and that each clause be given a separate line and number in the transcript. For discourse between two or more people, we recommend that each participant be given a column in the transcript, and each clause spoken by any of the speakers be numbered consecutively.

Upon completion of the transcription the analysis of discourse can proceed. If there is some doubt as to the discourse type or whether the particular discourse segment has the needed ingredients to qualify for a particular type, an analysis of the characteristics of the segment should be done. The following guidelines can be followed.

Stories To qualify as a well-formed story the discourse should contain an introduction of characters, a setting, an episode indicating a problem and a solution, and a conclusion. Thus the analysis would involve identifying which aspects of the discourse would qualify under each of the parts and then examining which parts are systematically omitted across stories (see Johnston, 1982; Graybeal, 1981; Dennis, 1980).

Conversations A conversation involves the participants' cooperation in sustaining topics, taking turns, and repairing breakdowns. One type of analysis for conversations would be to indicate when, how, and by whom new topics are introduced and how well they are maintained. If there is evidence of talking overlap, interruptions, or conversational breakdowns, analysis should be directed to the places where the problems occur and ways the participants may be attempting to repair the problems.

Quizzes Analyzing the child's ability to perform according to the discourse rules involved in classroom quizzes would require examining the child's ability to adhere to the teacher's agenda and to the preestablished rules of turn taking and interruption. Wilkinson (1984) recommends that discourse effectiveness during classroom interactions be measured by examining what percentage of the initiations made by a learner are received by the teacher and how this compares with the classmates. A detailed analysis of when and under what conditions teachers allow for interruptions would provide direction for training a child to bid for the teacher's attention (Eder, 1982; Green and Wallat, 1981).

Expositions Children's ability to produce and understand expository discourse will depend upon their abilities to create and interpret the different kinds of logical structures found in different expositions. Discussions about factual information might occur naturally at school during academic subjects, such as during a science or history lesson. Analysis of children's participation during these sessions can reveal their ability to handle different logical relations found in expositions. The analysis of children's understanding of expositions can be combined with the analysis of their understanding of logical inferences in genres other than expository, since it is likely that if children understand causal relations in expository contexts, they will also understand them in other contexts, such as narrative and event descriptions.

Event Descriptions To qualify as an event description the discourse should follow a chronology in keeping with the event being described and should highlight the important aspects of the event and minimize the incidentals. Analysis of event descriptions would involve segmenting the transcript into subparts of the event such as the actions which go together to accomplish the same goal (washing dishes) or subgoals (washing: fill sink with soap and water, wash glasses first, then plates, then silverware, then pots and pans) and evaluating whether the steps are clear enough and well-enough organized to give the listener a good idea of what the event is about, and how it progresses.

Analyzing Inferencing

An important aspect of understanding discourse involves being able to read between the lines. This inferencing ability may require particular sorts of knowledge, such as part-whole, probable event, spatial, temporal, and causal. These are only a few of the perhaps infinite types of knowledge which can be drawn upon to understand discourse. It is recommended, therefore, that assessment of inferencing be approached generally in answer to the question of whether the child draws on needed background knowledge when interpreting text. If the child has difficulty, then it might be worthwhile to assess particular subtypes of inferencing knowledge. What follows are some suggested approaches for assessing inferencing in older children, drawn from the literature on inferencing in normal children and adults.

1. Tell the child a story about a set of sequence pictures. Then show the original pictures along with two types of foils, ones that are compatible with the original story and ones that are inconsistent with it. Ask the child which pictures were seen before. Good comprehenders will think they have seen the compatible pictures and that they have not seen the incompatible ones (adapted from Brown, 1976).

ORIGINAL PICTURES
1. Girl gets canvas and easel.
2. She paints.
3. She frames her completed painting.
4. She hangs up the framed painting.

COMPATIBLE FOIL   Girl admires the completed painting.
INCOMPATIBLE FOIL   Girl hangs up partially completed painting.

2. Read or allow the child to read a paragraph describing how to do something. In one case tell the child what you are describing, and in the other case don't tell what you are describing. After each description, ask the child to tell you what he or she remembers to see if the child's recall improves when he or she knows what the paragraph is about. If it does not, it would indicate that the child does not make inferences based upon knowing the topic (adapted from Bransford and Johnson, 1972). The following paragraph has to do with removing dishes from a dishwasher:

> When it stops open it up. Roll out the top. Collect all the similar objects and put them away with the others. Keep doing this until there are no more left. Push it back in and roll out the bottom. Do the same with the bottom as you did with the top. Save the basket for last. Push the bottom back in and close it up.

3. Have the child make up or remember what comes before or after a specified event (from Brown and French, 1976).
4. Give the child two paragraphs to read or listen to. For the first give questions beforehand to show what is important. Ask questions afterward and then check to see whether the child did better when given questions before the paragraphs (from Goelman, 1982).
5. Have children recall stories which are distorted in various ways. For example, mix up the temporal or logical order, or relate two stories together. See if the children reorder or separate the stories when they retell them (from Nelson and Gruendel, 1981).

> A little girl and her mother were in the kitchen.
> They decided to do something.
> So they put the pan in the oven.
> They got out the flour and sugar.
> They stirred in the chocolate chips.
> They spooned the dough into the pan.
> They beat the dough until it was all mixed.
> Then they took it out
> and ate them all up.

6. Read a story aloud to the child and then ask two types of questions—factual ones in which the answers are in the presented story and inference ones in which the answers must be inferred (from Crais and Chapman, 1987).

Analyzing Discourse Deixis

Tanz (1980) has studied children's understanding of deictic terms by creating scenarios and asking children questions about them. She studied their understanding of deictic verbs by having children choose one of several dolls to be the speaker and another to be the addressee of imperatives containing these verbs. She used the child's ability to identify the speaker as the criterion for understanding the deictic meaning. An example of her task would be

> The pig says, "Can I come/go into the barn?"
> Which animal is he talking to?
> (Child is presented with a lion in the barn and a monkey in the barnyard.)

When analyzing discourse for its deictic organization, one needs to determine whether the discourse contains a deictic center—a coherent organizational structure placing the events within the perspective of a person, place, and time. To do so, one can examine text for linguistic indicators of deixis. The following two passages from Nelson and Gruendel (1981) are from two children describing a birthday party. As can be seen from the use of deictic terms, the descriptions differ in their deictic orientation, with the first being from the perspective of the host (told by a child age four years, nine months) and the second from that of the guest.

Host Perspective

1a. and then all the people come you've asked
2a. and then they give you some presents
3a. and then you play with them
4a. and then that's the end
5a. and then they go home
6a. and they do what they wanta (p. 135).

Guest Perspective

1b. then you go to the birthday party
2b. then usually they always want to open one of the presents
3b. then they have the birthday cake
4b. then sometimes they open up the other presents
5b. or they could open them all at once
6b. after that they like to play some more games
7b. and then maybe your parents come to pick you up
8b. and then you go home (p. 135).

The *you* in the above examples is a general term functioning to mean a general person such as *one*. In the host segment the *you* is taken to mean the host (3a) and in the second it is the guest (8b). Both children use *they* to refer to the other characters, those who are not centered. In the host segment the *they* refers to the guests (5a), and in the guest segment the *they* refers to the hosts (2b). The motion verbs *come* and *go* are also reflective of the host–guest difference, with the host perspective describing guests as coming to the party (1a) and the guest perspective having them go to the party (1b).

When assessing a child's ability to manage conceptual and linguistic devices related to deictic centering, the first step would be to see if the discourse of the child seems confusing in that it is difficult to keep track of what is going on. In the following example, told by a five-year-old, the characters seem to be outside as indicated by their living in the forest and the boy waiting in the rain (lines 1 and 2), yet the motion verb *come* and spatial adverb *inside* in lines 2 and 3 require that the characters be inside. This conflict results in deictic incoherence.

1. Once there was a little boy who lived in the forest with his mother and father and his pet water beetle.
2. He waited in the rain for his water beetle to come inside.
3. He said, "Come inside, water beetle!"
4. "No, I'm supposed to like the rain.
5. That's why they call me the water beetle." (Paley, 1981, p. 159)

While this particular story suggests that the child has some difficulty with the expression of discourse deixis, this is not bourne out when examining nineteen of his other stories. In order for a child to be diagnosed as having a problem with discourse deixis, multiple examples of the difficulty must be evident.

Analyzing Referencing Abilities

Since all discourse involves the use of referring expressions, the child's ability to reference clearly and unambiguously can be done by analyzing the same transcripts that are used for the discourse genre analysis. If the child seems to have special problems with referencing, a special elicitation procedure might be designed which focuses on the child's referencing abilities. A procedure that is commonly used in the literature on referencing is a communication game in which the child is asked to describe a scene to a listener sitting behind a barrier. The listener's job is to find (or draw) the picture being described or move objects in specified ways, without being able to see the reference items (Creaghead and Tattershall, 1985; Glucksberg and Krauss, 1967). The task is a good one for assessing the child's referencing abilities, since the listener has only the child's referring expressions to go on and cannot rely on background knowledge or situational knowledge for guessing which object or location the child is trying to identify. The task can be made more or less difficult by altering the codability (ability to be named) of the picture items being described and by altering the contrasting items from which the described picture must be selected. For example, a task which involves the description of a nonsense design would be more difficult than one with a known object; and one involving pictures which are very different from the one being described would be easier than having to distinguish between pictures which are nearly identical (Asher and Parke, 1975).

After eliciting and transcribing the discourse segment, it can be analyzed to determine the percentage of expressions which are ambiguous. It can also be analyzed to determine whether the attending listener can make good guesses as to the intended referent and whether the child revises the referring expression when the listener indicates confusion. The idea is that the degree of difficulty in referencing will be indicated by the number of uninterpretable referring expressions. The more expressions whose referents cannot be determined, the greater the referencing problem.

We recommend use of a coding procedure to determine the percentage of referring expressions which are uninterpretable or ambiguous in a sample of discourse. The procedure is an adaptation of one developed by Earle, Duchan, and Weitzner-Lin (1984) and Earle (1983) and involves coding a transcript of discourse as follows:

1. Underline all nominals.
2. Identify expressions which are ambiguous and code with *amb*.
3. Identify expressions which are uninterpretible and code as *un*.
4. Count *amb* and *un* and divide by total number of noun phrases to determine the percentage of unclear out of the total noun phrases produced.

If the percentage is relatively high (40 percent as a base using Klecan-Aker, 1985), then an assessment needs to be done to examine the reasons underlying the referencing problem. For example, it may be one in which the child is unable (1) to make comparisons among the possible referents, (2) to take the listener's perspective, or (3) to find or pronounce the words needed for unambiguous referencing.

BOX 8–3. Sample Analysis: Referencing

Patty	Clinician
1. <u>Me</u> waiting for <u>you</u>.	1. <u>You</u> ready?
2. ok.	2. <u>You</u> want to go first?
3. ok.	3. <u>I'm</u> going to win today.
4. <u>That's</u> what <u>you</u> think.	
	4. <u>Patty</u>
5. Huh?	5. <u>Patty</u>, take <u>a</u> <u>card</u>.
6. <u>This one</u>.	
(Patty picks up card.)	
	6. Do you need <u>it</u>.
7. Yea.	
	7. Take <u>the</u> <u>next</u> <u>one</u>.
8. Oh boy.	
9. Now?	8. Go ahead.
10. Oh boy.	
11. Oh boy.	9. Can you lay <u>some</u> down.
12. Where is *<u>that</u>?	10. What?
13. Where is *<u>that</u>?	
	11. <u>I</u> guess <u>it's</u> <u>my</u> <u>turn</u>.
14. Go.	12. <u>I'm</u> not doing so well.
15. <u>Me</u> do ?<u>it</u> better.	
16. <u>Me</u> know where *<u>it</u> is.	
	13. <u>Patty</u>, hold <u>your</u> <u>cards</u> right.

Sample Analysis: Referencing A portion of the transcript presented in Chapter 3 (Box 3–4) is analyzed below according to the four-step procedure to identify any referencing difficulties Patty is having (Box 8–3).

SUMMARY Patty shows some difficulty in identifying her referents in the brief sample given in Box 8–3. A total of one third of the nominals that she used were unclear. They are starred to indicate their problem status. (Note: Sample analysis would not be carried out clinically on a sample this short.)

There are a total of eleven instances of nominals used by Patty in the above sample (the underlined segments). Of those, three are not readily interpretable (the starred items) and one, marked with a question mark, is ambiguous (the *it* in utterance 15). The ambiguous plus unresolved count is 4, and when divided by 11 the result is 36 percent. This is close to the 40 percent identified by Klecan-Aker (1985) as a normative base, suggesting that Patty should be further evaluated with a longer sample to determine whether she has particular difficulty with referencing, and if so, what the source of that difficulty is.

Analyzing for Topic Maintenance

Children who have trouble initiating or maintaining topics may be seen as reticent talkers or may appear rude or abrupt. An analysis of their conversations can reveal their source of difficulty in everyday conversational actions.

First, one needs several samples of conversation on different topics, preferably with familiar and nondominant interactants. It is best to include topics that are both familiar and unfamiliar to the child being evaluated. A conversation on a favorite topic can be compared to one on a neutral topic, and conversations with topics initiated by the child can be compared with those initiated by the partner. An even more important comparison to be made is between the child's ability to maintain a topic about an event or information when the listener is familiar with the circumstances surrounding the event (shared information) versus one which the listener knows little about. (See Liles, 1987, for comparisons between shared and unshared knowledge effects on conversation.) If the child does not converse readily, the elicitation can be done in a loosely structured play context.

The analysis of transcripts could involve clauses which introduce a new topic or subtopic (I), maintain the topic (M), shade the topic (S), or reintroduce an old topic (R). (Brinton and Fujiki, 1984, 1989, present a similar but more detailed coding scheme.)

Some topic shifts are appropriate, such as those that occur in contexts in which a topic has just been completed. Others are indicators of trouble in the conversation, such as those which occur when one speaker has asked a question, and the second changes the topic instead of responding to the question. Analysis for inappropriate topic shifts can be fruitful for identifying a problem conversationalist. The analysis would involve separating out those contexts which would quality as shifts—that is, the categories of reintroductions (R) or new topic introductions (I). Once the reintroductions and shifts are identified, the context preceding them should be coded into one of two types: ones that allow for a topic continuation (C), and ones that allow for a new topic, a noncontinuation context (NC). That is, if a speaker finishes a topic (NC context), the shift is appropriate. If, on the other hand, the speaker asks a question or offers the child an opportunity for comment on a topic, the context requires a contingent response.

For example, in the exchange in Box 8–4, taken from Sonnenmeier (1991), B shows evidence of topic shift in contexts of both continuation and noncontinuation. B's topic shift in utterance 7 is not inappropriate, since R's previous turn requires continuation of the topic (indicated with NC) because of question intonation. The turn he takes here, however, seems incomplete and calls for continuation (C), which he does not provide in utterance 8, instead reintroducing the topic of school colors. An interesting interpretation of *South* in utterance 7 is that B is attempting to bring his own school, South High School, into the discussion. If we could determine that this were in fact the case, we would code utterance 7 as M (topic maintained) and C (continuation required).

When the coding is complete, patterns can be identified. A logical first step would be to identify the number of topic shifts and reintroductions in continuation contexts, in contrast to those that occur in noncontinuation contexts where the shift is appropriate. If there are several examples of new topics being introduced in continuation contexts, it suggests that the child is having difficulty

---

BOX 8–4. Sample Analysis: Topic

1. I	B:	*What color are the jackets at UB here?*
2. M	R:	I don't know.
3. M	R:	I think they might be blue.
4. M	B:	*What color blue?*
5. M	R:	I don't know.
6. M-NC	R:	Maybe navy blue?
7. S-C	B:	*South.*
8. RI	B:	*Buffalo State is black and orange.*
9. M	R:	Is it?
10. S	R:	Is it because they're the Buffalo State Bengals?
11. M	B:	*Yes.*
12. M	R:	Uhhuh.
13. M	B:	*The UB what?*
14. M	R:	Uh bulls?
15. M	R:	Is that right?
16. RI	B:	*What color?*
17. S	B:	*What are they what material are they made of?*
18. M	R:	They are probably like that nylon stuff.
19. M	B:	*And corduroy.*
20. M	R:	You think so?
21. M	B:	*Yep.*
22. M	B:	*And wool.*

maintaining topics. However, before drawing a conclusion that there is a problem, we recommend examining the shifts for whether there are identifiable extenuating circumstances causing the shifting. For example, Blank, Rose, and Berlin's analysis (1978) of children's responses to teacher's questions would suggest that topic contingency will depend upon whether the child understands what is said to him. Upon further analysis one might find that the child tends to continue some topics that he or she initiates, but not those of others, as was found for a child studied by Tomblin and Liljegreen (1985). Or one might find that what seemed to be topic shifts for a listener who does not know the child were judged as topic continuations by the listener who could fill in between the lines (see Johnston, 1982). Finally, one might find that the adult or peer who is talking with the child also fails to follow topic, indicating that rather than the problem being in the language-impaired child it may be due to a lack of fine tuning between partners.

Analyzing for Discourse Continuity and Discontinuity

Discourse genres are likely to differ in how they are organized, but they are all likely to be comprised of units which have meaning continuity within them, and discontinuity between them. Indicators of discontinuity are the same as we have discussed before in relation to topic shift, deictic shifts, and episode shifts—content shifts in topic, location, character, or time, along with discourse markers indicating such shifts. An analysis of discourse discontinuity would thus coincide with an analysis of the boundaries between the global units of genres, and with topic and deictic shifts. In the following story there are three discontinuities: (1) between the setting and the first episode, (2) between the two episodes, and (3) between the last episode and the closing statement.

Setting

1. Once there was a man and a mother and two sisters and a brother.

Episode 1

2. First the oldest sister ran away.
3. Then the second sister decided to stay home with the father
4. but he ran away too.
5. So the little brother and the sister were left.
6. And she learned how to cook.

Episode 2

7. One day a lion came because she wished for a lion
8. And also they lived in the jungle.
9. He said "Can I be your pet?"
10. She said, "I was just wishing for a lion pet.
11. You can carry us wherever you want."

Closing Statement

12. So they lived happily ever after. (from Paley, 1981, p. 12)

The segmentation of global units was accomplished by responding to shifts in discourse content, as well as the discontinuity indicators (*first*; *one day*; *so*). The content shifts occurred in temporality when (1) moving from the timelessness of the setting statement to the real time of the first episode; (2) when a new character arrives on the scene in episode 2; and (3) at the end of the second episode, when the shift occurs from the action time to the timelessness of the ever after.

Once a stretch of discourse has been analyzed for its discontinuity boundaries, the global units can be studied to determine the nature of their internal continuity. What is it that ties the utterances together? This analysis may call on the procedures used for topic maintenance in conversation; for deictic centering if the segments are maintained within a specified deictic center; for analysis of a character's goals and related actions if it is part of a story episode. The aim of the continuity analysis is thus different from that of a cohesion analysis such as that proposed by Halliday and Hasan (1976). Continuity analysis is done to answer how ideas lead to coherence rather than how grammatical or lexical elements tie to one another in the creation of semantic cohesion.

REFERENCES

APPLEBEE, A. *The Child's Concept of Story.* Chicago: University of Chicago Press, 1978.

ASHER, S., AND R. PARKE. Influence of Sampling and Comparison Processes on the Development of Communication Effectiveness, *Journal of Educational Psychology*, 67, 1975, 64–75.

ATKINSON, M. Prerequisites for Reference, in *Developmental Pragmatics*, eds. E. Ochs and B. Schieffelin. New York: Academic Press, 1979.

BARTLETT, F. *Remembering.* London: Cambridge University Press, 1932.

BATES, E. *Language and Context: The Acquisition of Pragmatics.* New York: Academic Press, 1976.

BATESON, M. Mother–Infant Exchanges: The Epigenesis of Conversational Interaction, in *Developmental Psycholinguistics and Communication Disorders*, eds. D. Aaronson and R. Rieber. Annuals of the New York Academy of Sciences, Vol. 263, 1975.

BELLUGI, U., AND R. BROWN, eds. The Acquisition of Language, *Monographs of The Society for Research in Child Development*, 29, 1964 (serial no. 92).

BENNETT-KASTOR, T. Noun Phrases and Coherence in Child Narratives, *Journal of Child Language*, 10, 1983, 135–49.

BEVER, T. The Cognitive Basis for Linguistics, in *Cognition and the Development of Language*, ed. J. Hayes. New York: John Wiley, 1970.

BLANK, M., S. ROSE, AND L. BERLIN. *The Language of Learning: The Preschool Years.* New York: Grune and Stratton, 1978.

BLOOM, L., L. ROCISSANO, AND L. HOOD. Adult–Child Discourse: Developmental Interaction Between Information Processing and Linguistic Knowledge, *Cognitive Psychology*, 8, 1976, 521–52.

BOTVIN, G., AND B. SUTTON-SMITH. The Development of Structural Complexity in Children's Fantasy Narratives, *Developmental Psychology*, 13, 1977, 377–88.

BOWERMAN, M. *Early Syntactic Development: A Cross-Linguistic Study with Special Reference to Finnish.* Cambridge, Mass.: Cambridge University Press, 1973.

BRAINE, M. D. S. Children's First Word Combinations, *Monographs of The Society for Research in Child Development*, 1976 (serial no. 164).

BRANSFORD, J., AND M. JOHNSON. Contextual Prerequisites for Understanding Some Investigations of Comprehension and Recall, *Journal of Verbal Learning and Verbal Behavior*, 11, 1972, 717–26.

BREWER, W. The Story Schema: Universal and Culture-Specific Properties, in *Literacy, Language and Learning*, eds. D. Olson, N. Torrance, and A. Hildyard. Cambridge: Cambridge University Press, 1985.

BREWER, W., AND E. LICHTENSTEIN. Stories Are to Entertain: A Structural-Affect Theory of Stories, *Journal of Pragmatics*, 1982, 6, 473–86.

BREWER, W., AND G. NAKAMURA. The Nature and Functions of Schemas, in *Handbook of Social Conditions*, eds. R. Wyer and T. Srull. Hillsdale, N.J.: Lawrence Erlbaum, 1984.

BRINTON, B., AND M. FUJIKI. Development of Topic Manipulation Skills in Discourse, *Journal of Speech and Hearing Research*, 27, 1984, 350–58.

BRINTON, B., AND M. FUJIKI. *Conversational Management with Language-Impaired Children.* Rockville, Md.: Aspen Publishers, 1989.

BROWN, A. Recognition, Reconstruction, and Recall of Narrative Sequences by Preoperational Children, *Child Development*, 46, 1975, 156–66.

BROWN, A. Semantic Integration in Children's Reconstruction of Narrative Sequences, *Cognitive Psychology*, 8, 1976, 247–62.

BROWN, A., AND L. FRENCH. Construction and Regeneration of Logical Sequences Using Causes or Consequences as the Point of Departure, *Child Development*, 47, 1976, 930–40.

BROWN, G., AND YULE, G. *Discourse Analysis.* New York: Cambridge University Press, 1983.

BRUDER, G., J. DUCHAN, W. RAPAPORT, E. SEGAL, S. SHAPIRO, AND D. ZUBIN. Deictic Centers in Narrative: An Interdisciplinary Cognitive Science Project. *Technical Report 86-20.* Buffalo, N.Y.: SUNY at Buffalo, Department of Computer Science, 1986.

CAZDEN, C. Peek-a-boo as an Instructional Model: Discourse Development at Home and at School, *Papers and Reports on Child Language Development*, 17, 1979, 1–29.

CAZDEN, C. *Classroom Discourse.* Portsmouth, N.H.: Heinemann, 1988.

CHAFE, W. The Deployment of Consciousness in the Production of a Narrative, in *The Pear Stories*, ed. W. Chafe. Norwood, N.J.: Ablex Publishing, 1980, pp. 9–50.

CLARK, E. V., AND C. J. SENGUL. Strategies in the Acquisition of Deixis, *Journal of Child Language*, 5, 1978, 457–75.

CLARK, H. Space, Time, Semantics, and the Child, in *Cognitive Development and the Acquisition of Language*, ed. T. Moore. New York: Academic Press, 1973.

CLARK, H., AND W. CHASE. On the Process of Comparing Sentences Against Pictures, *Cognitive Psychology*, 3, 1973, 472–517.

CLARK, H., AND W. CHASE. Perceptual Coding Strategies in the Formation and Verification of Descriptions, *Memory and Cognition*, 2, 1974, 101–11.

CLARK, H., AND S. HAVILAND. Comprehension of the Given-New Contract, in *Discourse Production and Comprehension*, ed. R. Freedle. Norwood, N.J.: Ablex Publishing, 1977, p. 1040.

COULTHARD, M. *An Introduction to Discourse Analysis.* New York: Longman, 1977.

COX, M. V. Young Children's Understanding of In Front of and Behind in the Placement of Objects, *Journal of Child Language*, 6, 1979, 371–74.

CRAIS, E., AND R. CHAPMAN. Story Recall and Inferencing Skills Language/Learning Disabled and Nondisabled Children, *Journal of Speech and Hearing Disorders*, 52, 1987, 50–55.

CREAGHEAD, N., AND S. TATTERSHALL. Observation and Assessment of Classroom Pragmatics Skills, in *Communicative Skills and Classroom Success: Assessment of Language-Learning Disabled Students*, ed. C. Simon. San Diego, Calif.: College Hill Press, 1985, pp. 105–31.

DENNIS, M. Strokes in Childhood, I: Communicative Intent, Expression, and Comprehension after Left Hemisphere Arteriopathy in a Right Handed Nine-Year-Old, in *Language Development and Aphasia in Children*, ed. R. Rieber. New York: Academic Press, 1980, pp. 45–67.

DEVILLIERS, P., AND J. DEVILLIERS. On This, That, and the Other: Nonegocentrism in Very Young Children, *Journal of Experimental Child Psychology*, 18, 1974, 438–47.

DIXON, C. Text Type and Children's Recall, in *Reading Research: Studies and Applications*, eds. M. Kamil and A. Moe. Clemson, S.C.: National Reading Conference, 1979.

DORE, J. "Oh Them Sheriff": A Pragmatic Analysis of Children's Responses to Questions, in *Child Discourse*, eds. S. Ervin-Tripp and C. Mitchell-Kernan. New York: Academic Press, 1977, pp. 139–64.

DORE, J. Conversation and Preschool Language Development, in *Language Acquisition: Studies in First Language Development*, eds. P. Fletcher and M. Garman. New York: Cambridge University Press, 1979, pp. 337–61.

DUCHAN, J. The Effect of Cognitive Bias on Children's Early Interpretations of Locative Commands, *Language Sciences*, 2, 1980, 246–59.

DUCHAN, J. Learning to Describe Events, *Topics in Language Disorders*, 6, 1986, 27–36.

DUCHAN, J. Preschool Children's Introduction of Characters into Their Oral Stories: Evidence for Deictic Organization of First Narratives. Unpublished ms, 1991.

DUCHAN, J., AND L. SIEGEL. Incorrect Responses to Locative Commands: A Case Study. *Language Speech and Hearing Services in the Schools*, 10, 1979, 99–103.

EARLE, C. Confusion Resulting from Misreferencing: A Case Study of a Language/Learning Disabled Adult. Unpublished Master's Thesis. SUNY Buffalo, 1983.

EARLE, C., J. DUCHAN, AND B. WEITZNER-LIN. Coding Reference Errors in Discourse of Older Language Disordered Speakers. Paper presented at the New York State Speech, Language, and Hearing Association, Monticello, New York, 1984.

EDER, D. Differences in Communicative Styles Across Ability Groups, in *Communicating in the Classroom*, ed. L. Wilkinson. New York: Academic Press, 1982.

EISENBERG, A. Language Development in Cultural Perspective: Talk in Three Mexicano Homes. Unpublished Ph.D. dissertation, Dept. of Psychology, University of California, Berkeley, 1982.

ERVIN-TRIPP, S. Discourse Agreement: How Children Answer Questions, in *Cognition and the Development of Language*, ed. J. Hayes. New York: John Wiley, 1970.

ERVIN-TRIPP, S. Wait for Me Roller Skate, in *Child Discourse*, eds. S. Ervin-Tripp and C. Mitchell-Kernan. New York: Academic Press, 1977.

ERVIN-TRIPP, S. Children's Verbal Turn Taking, in *Developmental Pragmatics*, eds. E. Ochs and B. Schieffelin. New York: Academic Press, 1979.

FILLMORE, C. Space. Unpublished manuscript, 1971.

FINE, J. Conversation, Cohesive and Thematic Patterning in Children's Dialogues, *Discourse Processes*, 1, 1978, 247–66.

FREEDLE, R., AND G. HALE. Acquisition of New Comprehension Schemata for Expository Prose by Transfer of a Narrative Schema. In *New Directions in Discourse Processing*, ed. R. Freedle. Norwood, N.J.: Ablex, 1979, 121–135.

GALLAGHER, T. Revision Behaviors in the Speech of Normal Children Developing Language, *Journal of Speech and Hearing Research*, 2, 1977, 303–18.

GENTNER, D. Validation of a Related-Component Model of Verb Meaning, *Papers and Reports on Child Development*, No. 10. Stanford University, September 1975.

GLUCKSBERG, S., AND R. KRAUSS. What Do People Say After They Have Learned How to Talk? *Merrill Palmer Quarterly*, 13, 1967, 309–16.

GOELMAN, H. Selective Attention in Language Comprehension: Children's Processing of Expository and Narrative Discourse, *Discourse Processes*, 5, 1982, 53–72.

GOODENOUGH, D., AND S. WEINER. The Role of Conversational Passing Moves in the Management of Topical Transitions. *Discourse Processes*, 1, 1978, 395–404.

GRAESER, A., AND S. GOODMAN. Implicit Knowledge, Question Answering and the Representation of Expository Text. In *Understanding Expository Text*, eds. B. Britton and J. Black. Hillsdale, N.J.: Erlbaum, 1985.

GRAYBEAL, C. Memory for Stories in Language-Impaired Children, *Applied Psycholinguistics*, 2, 1981, 269–83.

GREEN, J., AND C. WALLAT. *Ethnography and Language in Educational Settings*. Norwood, N.J.: Ablex Publishing, 1981.

GREENFIELD, P., AND J. SMITH. *The Structure of Communication in Early Language Development*. New York: Academic Press, 1976.

GROSZ, B. Focusing and Description in Natural Language Dialogues, in *Elements of Discourse Understanding*, eds. A. Joshi, B. Webber, and I. Sag. New York: Cambridge University Press, 1981, pp. 84–105.

GROSZ, B., AND C. SIDNER. Attention, Intentions, and the Structure of Discourse, *Computational Linguistics*, 12, 1986, 175–204.

GRUENDEL, J. Scripts and Stories: A Study of Children's Event Narratives. Doctoral dissertation, Yale University, 1980.

HALL, M., J. RIBOVICH, AND C. RAMIG. *Reading and the Elementary School Child*. New York: Van Nostrand, 1979.

HALLIDAY, M., AND R. HASAN. *Cohesion in English*. London: Longman, 1976.

HEWITT, L., J. DUCHAN, AND E. SEGAL. Structure and Function of Verbal Conflicts Among Mentally Retarded Adults, *Discourse Processes*, in press.

HORNBY, P., AND W. HASS. Use of Contrastive Stress by Preschool Children, *Journal of Speech and Hearing Research*, 13, 1970, 395–99.

HOROWITZ, R. Text Patterns: Part I, *Journal of Reading*, 28, 1985a, 448–54.

HOROWITZ, R. Text Patterns: Part II, *Journal of Reading*, 28, 1985b, 534–41.

HURTIG, R. Toward a Functional Theory of Discourse, in *Discourse Production and Comprehension*, ed. R. Freedle. Norwood, N.J.: Albex Publishing, 1977.

HUTTENLOCHER, J., K. EISENBERG, AND S. STRAUSS. Relation Between Perceived Actor and Logical Subject, *Journal of Verbal Learning and Verbal Behavior*, 7, 1968, 527–30.

HUTTENLOCHER, J., AND E. HIGGINS. Adjectives, Comparatives, and Syllogisms, *Psychological Review*, 78, 1971, 487–504.

HUXLEY, R. The Development of the Correct Use of Subject Personal Pronouns in Two Children, in *Advances in Psycholinguistics*, eds. G. D'Arcais and W. Levelt. New York: American Elsevier Publishing Co., 1970.

HYMES, D. Models of the Interaction of Language and Social Life, in *Directions in Sociolinguistics: The Ethnography of Communication*, eds. J. Gumperz and D. Hymes. New York: Holt, Rinehart & Winston, 1972.

JEFFERSON, G. Side Sequences, in *Studies in Social Interaction*, ed. D. Sudnow, New York: Free Press, 1972.

JEFFERSON, G. Error Correction as an Interactional Resource, *Language in Society*, 2, 1973.

JOHNSON, N. What Do You Do if You Can't Tell the Whole Story?: The Development of Summarization Skills, in *Children's Language*, Vol. 4, ed. K. Nelson. Hillsdale, N.J.: Lawrence Erlbaum, 1983.

JOHNSON, N., AND J. MANDLER. A Tale of Two Structures: Underlying and Surface Forms in Stories, *Poetics*, 1980, 9, 51–86.

JOHNSTON, J. Narratives: A New Look at Communication Problems in Older Language-Disordered Children, *Language, Speech, and Hearing Services in the Schools*, 13, 1982, 144–55.

KARMILOFF-SMITH, A. *A Functional Approach to Child Language*. Cambridge: Cambridge University Press, 1979.

KARMILOFF-SMITH, A. The Grammatical Marking of Thematic Structure in the Development of Language Production, in *The Child's Construction of Language*, ed. W. Deutsch. New York: Academic Press, 1981, pp. 121–147.

KAYE, K., AND R. CHARNEY. Conversational Asymmetry Between Mothers and Children, *Journal of Child Language*, 8, 1981, 35–50.

KEENAN, E., AND E. KLEIN. Coherency in Children's Discourse, *Journal of Psycholinguistic Research*, 4, 1975, 365–80.

KEENAN, E., AND B. SCHIEFFELIN. Foregrounding Referents: A Reconsideration of Left-Dislocation in Discourse. Proceedings of the Second Annual Meeting of the Berkeley Linguistics Society, University of California, Berkeley, 1976.

KLECAN-AKER, J. Syntactic Abilities in Normal and Language-Deficient Middle School Children, *Topics in Language Disorders*, 5, 1985, 46–54.

KLECAN-AKER, J., AND D. HEDRICK. A Study of the Syntactic Language Skills of Normal School-Age Children, *Language Speech and Hearing Services in Schools*, 16, 1985, 187–98.

KUCZAJ, S., AND M. MARATSOS. Front, Back, Side: Stages of Acquisition. *Papers and Reports on Child Language and Development*, 8, 1974, 111–28.

LAPP, D., AND J. FLOOD. *Teaching Reading to Every Child*. New York: Macmillan, 1978.

LEOPOLD, W. *Speech Development of a Bilingual Child* (4 vols.). Evanston, Ill.: Northwestern University Press, 1939.

LEWIS, M., AND R. FREEDLE. Mother–Infant Dyad: The Cradle of Meaning, in *Communication and Affect: Language and Thought*, eds. P. Pliner, L. Krames, and T. Alloway. New York: Academic Press, 1973.

LILES, B. Cohesion in the Narratives of Normal and Language-Disordered Children, *Journal of Speech and Hearing Research*, 28, 1985, 123–33.

LILES, B. Episode Organization and Cohesive Conjunctives in Narratives of Children with and without Language Disorders, *Journal of Speech and Hearing Research*, 30, 1987, 185–96.

LYONS, J. Deixis as the Source of Reference, in *Formal Semantics of Natural Language*, ed. E. L. Keenan. Cambridge, England: Cambridge University Press, 1975.

MCCARTNEY, K., AND K. NELSON. Children's Use of Scripts in Story Recall, *Discourse Processes*, 4, 1981, 59–70.

MACWHINNEY, B. Starting Points, *Language*, 53, 1977, 152–68.

MACWHINNEY, B. Grammatical Devices for Sharing Points, in *The Acquisition of Communicative Competence*, eds. R. Schiefelbusch and J. Pikar. Baltimore: University Park Press, 1984, pp. 325–74.

MARKMAN, E. Realizing That You Don't Understand: Elementary School Children's Awareness of Inconsistencies. *Child Development*, 50, 1979, 643–55.

MEHAN, H. *Learning Lessons: Social Organization in the Classroom*. Cambridge, Mass.: Harvard University Press, 1979.

MENTIS, M., AND C. PRUTTING. Analysis of Topic as Illustrated in a Head-Injured and Normal Adult, *Journal of Speech and Hearing Research*, 34, 1991, 583–95.

MEYER, B. *Prose Analysis: Procedures, Purposes and Problems*. Prose Learning Series, Research Report Number 11. Tempe, Arizona: Arizona State University, 1981.

MEYER, B. Following the Author's Top-Level Organization: An Important Skill for Reading Comprehension, in *Understanding Readers' Understanding*, eds. R. Tierney, P. Anders, and J. Mitchell. Hillsdale, N.J.: Lawrence Erlbaum, 1987.

MICHAELS, S. Narrative Presentations: An Oral Preparation for Literacy with First Graders. In *The Social Construction of Literacy*, ed. J. Cook-Gumperz. New York: Cambridge University Press, 1986, 94–116.

MICHAELS, S., AND C. CAZDEN. Teacher/Child Collaboration as Oral Preparation for Literacy, in *The Acquisition of Literacy: Ethnographic Perspectives*, eds. B. Schieffelin and P. Gilmore. Norwood, N.J.: Apex Publishing, 1986.

MICHAELS, S., AND J. COOK-GUMPERZ. A Study of Sharing Time with First Grade Students: Discourse Narratives in the Classroom. Proceedings of the Fifth Annual Berkeley Linguistics Society, 1979.

MISHLER, E. Studies in Dialogue and Discourse: An Exponential Law of Successive Questioning, *Language in Society*, 4, 1975, 31–51.

MOORE, K., AND A. MELTZOFF. Object Permanence, Imitation, and Language Development in Infants: Toward a Neo-Piagetian Perspective on Communicative and Cognitive Development, in *Communicative and Cognitive Abilities: Early Behavioral Assessment*, eds. F. Minifie and L. Lloyd. Baltimore: University Park Press, 1978, pp. 151–84.

NELSON, K. Structure and Strategy in Learning to Talk, *Monographs of The Society for Research in Child Development*, 38, 1973 (serial no. 149).

NELSON, K., AND J. GRUENDEL. At Morning It's Lunchtime: A Scriptal View of Children's Dialogues, *Discourse Processes*, 2, 1979, 73–94.

NELSON, K., AND J. GRUENDEL. Generalized Event Representations: Basic Building Blocks of Cognitive Development, in *Advances in Developmental Psychology*, eds. A. Brown and M. Lamb. Hillsdale, N.J.: Lawrence Erlbaum, 1981, pp. 131–58.

NINIO, A., AND J. BRUNER. The Achievement and Antecedents of Labeling, *Journal of Child Language*, 5, 1978, 1–15.

OMANSON, R., W. WARREN, AND T. TRABASSO. Goals, Inferential Comprehension and Recall of Stories by Children, *Discourse Processes*, 1, 1978, 68–77.

PALEY, V. *Wally's Stories: Conversations in the Kindergarten*. Cambridge, Mass.: Harvard University Press, 1981.

PALEY V. *The Boy Who Would Be a Helicopter.* Cambridge, Mass.: Harvard University Press, 1990.

PARIS, S., AND A. CARTER. Semantic and Constructive Aspects of Sentence Memory in Children, *Developmental Psychology,* 9, 1973, 109–13.

PETERSON, C., AND P. DODSWORTH. A Longitudinal Analysis of Young Children's Cohesion and Noun Specification in Narratives, *Journal of Child Language,* 18, 1991, 397–415.

PIAGET, J. *The Origins of Intelligence in Children.* New York: International Universities Press, 1952.

PICCOLO, J. Expository Text Structure: Teaching and Learning Strategies, *The Reading Teacher,* 40, 1987, 838–47.

PITCHER, E., AND E. PRELINGER. *Children Tell Stories.* New York: International Universities Press, 1963.

REEDER, K. The Emergence of Illocutionary Skills, *Journal of Child Language,* 7, 1980, 29–40.

RICHGELS, D., L. MCGEE, R. LOMAX, AND C. SHEARD. Awareness of Four Text Structures: Effects on Recall of Expository Text, *Reading Research Quarterly,* 22, 1987, 177–97.

RIPICH, D., AND F. SPINELLI. *School Discourse Problems,* San Diego, Calif.: College Hill Press, 1985.

ROCHESTER, S., AND J. MARTIN. The Art of Referring: The Speaker's Use of Noun Phrases to Instruct the Listener, in *Discourse Production and Comprehension,* ed. R. Freedle. Norwood, N.J.: Ablex Publishing, 1977.

ROCHESTER, S., AND J. MARTIN. *Crazy Talk: A Study of the Discourse of Schizophrenic Speakers.* New York: Plenum, 1979.

ROCHESTER, S., J. MARTIN, AND S. THURSTON. Thought-Process Disorder in Schizophrenia: The Listener's Task, *Brain and Language,* 4, 1977, 95–114.

RUMELHART, D. Notes on Schemas for Stories, in *Representation and Understanding,* eds. D. Bobrow and A. Collins. New York: Academic Press, 1975.

SACHS, J., AND L. TRUSWELL. Comprehension of Two-Word Instructions by Children in the One-Word Stage, *Journal of Child Language,* 5, 1978, 17–24.

SCHANK, R., AND R. ABELSON. *Scripts, Plans, Goals and Understanding.* Hillsdale, N.J.: Lawrence Erlbaum, 1977.

SCHEGLOFF, E. Sequencing in Conversational Openings, *American Anthropologist,* 70, 1968, 75–95.

SCHEGLOFF, E., AND H. SACKS. Opening Up Closings, *Semiotica,* 8, 1973, 289–327.

SCHIEFFELIN, B., AND A. EISENBERG. Cultural Variations in Children's Conversations. In *The Acquisition of Communicative Competence,* ed. R. Schiefelbusch and J. Pikar. Baltimore, Md.: University Park Press, 1984, 379–420.

SCHIFFRIN, D. *Discourse Markers.* New York: Cambridge University Press, 1987.

SCOLLON, R. A Real Early Stage: An Unzippered Condensation of a Dissertation on Child Language, in *Developmental Pragmatics,* eds. E. Ochs and B. Schieffelin. New York: Academic Press, 1979.

SEGAL, E., J. DUCHAN, AND P. SCOTT. The Role of Interclausal Connectives in Narrative Structuring: Evidence from Adults' Interpretations of Simple Stories, *Discourse Processes,* 14, 1991, 27–54.

SHATZ, M. How Young Children Respond to Language: Procedures for Answering, *Papers and Reports in Child Language Development,* 10, 1975, 97–110.

SIDNER, C. Focusing and Discourse, *Discourse Processes,* 6, 1983, 107–30.

SNOW, C. Mothers' Speech Research: From Input to Interaction, in *Talking to Children,* eds. C. Ferguson and C. Snow. Cambridge: Cambridge University Press, 1977.

SNOW, C. Literacy and Language: Relationships During the Preschool Years, *Harvard Educational Review,* 53, 1983, 165–89.

SNOW, C. Beyond Conversation: Second Language Learners' Acquisition of Description and Explanation, in *Research in Second Language Learning: Focus on the Classroom,* eds. J. Lantolf and A. Labarca. Norwood, N.J.: Ablex Publishing, 1987.

SNYDER, A. Notes on the Talk of a Two-and-a-half Year Old Boy, *Pedagogical Seminar,* 21, 1914, 412–24.

SNYDER, L. Developmental Language Disorders: Elementary School Age, in *Language Disorders in Children,* ed. A. Holland. San Diego, Calif.: College Hill Press, 1984, pp. 129–58.

SONNENMEIER, R. Topic Manipulation Skills of an Autistic Speaker. Unpublished manuscript, 1991.

SPIRO, R., AND B. TAYLOR. On Investigating Children's Transitions from Narrative to Expository Discourse: The Multidimensional Nature of Psychological Text Classification, in *Understanding Readers' Understanding,* eds. R. Tierney, P. Anders, and J. Mitchell. Hillsdale, N.J.: Lawrence Erlbaum, 1987.

STEIN, N., AND C. GLENN. An Analysis of Story Comprehension in Elementary School Children, in *New Directions in Discourse Processing,* Vol. 2, ed. R. Freedle. Norwood, N.J.: Ablex Publishing, 1979.

STERN, D., B. BEEBE, J. JAFFE, AND S. BENNETT. The Infant's Stimulus World During Social Interactions, in *Studies of Mother–Infant Interactions,* ed. H. Schaffer. New York: Academic Press, 1977.

STOEL-GAMMON, C., AND L. CABRAL. Learning How to Tell It Like It Is: The Development of the Reportative Function in Children's Speech, *Papers and Reports on Child Language Development,* 13, 1977, 64–71.

STROHNER, H., AND K. NELSON. The Young Child's Development of Sentence Comprehension: Influence of Event Probability, Nonverbal Context, Syntactic Form and Strategies, *Child Development,* 45, 1974, 567–76.

STRONG, C., AND J. SHAVER. Stability of Cohesion in the Spoken Narratives of Language-Impaired and Normally Developing School-Aged Children, *Journal of Speech and Hearing Research*, 34, 1991, 95–111.

SUTTON-SMITH, B. *The Folkstories of Children.* Philadelphia, Pa.: University of Pennsylvania Press, 1981.

TANNEN, D. *That's Not What I Meant.* New York: William Morrow, 1986.

TANZ, C. *Studies in the Acquisition of Deictic Terms.* Cambridge, England: Cambridge University Press, 1980.

TOMBLIN, J., AND S. LILJEGREEN. The Identification of Socially Significant Communication Needs in Older Language-Impaired Children: A Case Example, in *School Discourse Problems*, eds. D. Ripich and F. Spinelli. San Diego, Calif.: University Park Press, 1985, pp. 219–30.

TRACY, K., AND J. MORAN. Conversational Relevance in Multiple-Goal Settings, in *Conversational Coherence: Form, Structure and Strategy*, eds. R. Craig and K. Tracy. Beverly Hills, Calif.: Sage, 1983, pp. 116–35.

TREVARTHAN, C. Descriptive Analyses of Infant Communicative Behavior, in *Studies in Mother–Infant Interaction*, ed. H. Schaffer. New York: Academic Press, 1977.

VAN DIJK, T., AND W. KINTSCH. Cognitive Psychology and Discourse, in *Current Trends in Textlinguistics*, ed. W. Dressler. New York: Walter de Druyter, 1978, pp. 61–80.

VENNEMAN, T. Topic, Sentence Accent, and Ellipsis: A Proposal for Their Formal Treatment, in *Formal Semantics of Natural Language*, ed. E. Keenan. New York: Cambridge University Press, 1975.

WEIST, D., H. WYSOCKA, K. WITKOWSKA-STADNICK, E. BUCZOWSKA, AND E. KONIECZNA. The Defective Tense Hypothesis: On the Emergence of Tense and Aspect in Child Polish, *Journal of Child Language*, 11, 1984, 347–74.

WESTBY, C. Development of Narrative Language Abilities, in *Language Learning Disabilities in School-Age Children*, eds. G. Wallach and K. Butler. Baltimore: Williams and Wilkins, 1984, pp. 103–27.

WESTBY, C. Assessing and Remediating Text Comprehension Problems, in *Reading Disabilities: A Developmental Language Perspective*, eds. A. Kamhi and H. Catts. Boston: Little, Brown, 1989.

WIEBE, J. Recognizing Subjective Sentences: A Computational Investigation of Narrative Text, *Technical Report 90-03*. Buffalo, N.Y.: SUNY at Buffalo, Department of Computer Science, 1990.

WIEMAN, L. Stress Patterns of Early Child Language, *Journal of Child Language*, 3, 1976, 283–86.

WILKINSON, L. Research Currents: Peer Group Talk in Elementary School, *Language Arts*, 61, 1984, 164–69.

YOUNG, K. *Talewords and Storyrealms.* Boston, Mass.: Martinus Nijhoff Publishers, 1987.

9

Tools of Assessment

The structural model we have presented emphasizes assessment in naturalistic contexts in order to find the patterns that emerge when the child is part of a communicative interaction. Formal tests have not been included in our assessment procedures because tests by their very nature and purpose present language removed from ordinary intentionality. When taking tests, children do not respond to a test item to share information or make requests. Rather, these items entail specialized demands that do not typically occur in real situations. Part of the unnaturalness of tests comes from the removal of contextual clues in order to assure the child "knows" the answer only from the language forms given. As we have attempted to demonstrate, this is an artificial separation, since language typically depends on context for interpretation. Not only is the intention and the context artificial in test situations, the language itself is often characteristically different from language in everyday communicative exchanges. We ask children to label objects, fill in missing words, or imitate words or sentences that elicit different structures from those they would ordinarily use. We have previously discussed some of the problems in assessing phonology with one-word responses or syntax with imitation. These caveats should be applied to most tests.

Arguments against the use of formal tests to assess language have been repeatedly and persuasively made (e.g., Muma, Lubinski, and Pierce, 1982; Duchan, 1982; Siegel and Broen, 1976). We obviously agree with the others that tests cannot be substitutes for structural analysis in finding regularities in children's performance. Tests can be helpful, however, if we understand their limitations. We include this chapter to discuss how tests and other formalized procedures relate to the questions asked in language assessment. We will introduce various concepts that we consider to be relevant to the use and interpretation of tests and relate these to some commonly used language tests. Our intent is not to provide the clinician with a comprehensive list of tests, since such a list is rapidly outdated and other authors have compiled extensive and useful descriptions of commercial language tests (e.g., Wiig and Semel,

1980; Darley, 1979). Rather, our intent is to provide a framework for evaluating these and other tests to determine their role in addressing the assessment questions we posed in Chapter 1.

PURPOSE OF A TEST

The general purpose of any test is to provide a sample of behavior for analysis, and the type of sample desired depends upon the specific purpose of the test. Tests are generally designed to accomplish one or both of the following goals.

Rank Individuals   Tests that are designed to determine relative ranking of individuals who take the test are described as *norm referenced.* In using these tests, we compare the score of a given child with the scores of other children who have taken the test and determine where our child's score falls within the distribution of scores. The population of children our child is compared to is taken to be representative of the general population and thus the "norm." Norm-referenced tests are typically used to make decisions about whether or not the child should be considered as having a language disorder.

Tests that are designed to determine a child's ranking in an area (language or otherwise) will be constructed from selected items that should be representative of that area, without attempting to be comprehensive in its coverage. For example, school achievement tests and intelligence tests do not attempt to include every skill that would indicate achievement or intelligence but rather are constructed to be a sample of such skills. Some norm-referenced language tests sample several kinds of language behavior, with the intent being to give a ranking of general language skill. Other tests are restricted to one or a few specific areas of language and thus are used to assess ranking within those areas only.

The ranking obtained with norm-referenced tests can help us to answer the first assessment question: Does the child have a language problem? If the child's rank is comparable to other children of the same age and cultural background, we judge that there is no problem within the area tested; if the rank is very low, we have found evidence that a problem exists—if we have confidence that the child's performance on the test is representative of nontest abilities. These tests may also help us identify areas of deficit and thus address the third assessment question—the child's areas of deficit. If a test primarily covers one area of language and a child ranks low on that test, we have evidence of one area of deficit; it may not be the only or the most handicapping area of deficit. If a test covers several areas in some depth, we may find that the child shows deficits in one or more areas and not in others.

Describe Regularities of Performance   Tests designed to meet this second purpose of testing sample multiple instances of a specified type of behavior, with the goal of identifying the specific behaviors the child does or does not possess. If, for example, a teacher wants to determine if a child knows the multiplication tables, a test would be chosen or constructed that includes all numbers from one to nine as the multiplicand to assess this. The teacher's interest in this case is not how the child ranks relative to a group of children, so this test does not have to be norm referenced. Rather, the question is whether or not the child knows the specific objectives that the teacher has chosen to be important to know. This type of test has been called *criterion referenced.* Some of these instruments are described as rating scales or checklists where particular behaviors or abilities are listed and the assessor either uses a subjective scale to judge adequacy or indicates presence or absence of the behavior or skill. Some commercial tests of this type have been norm referenced so it is possible to use them to rank children, but ranking is not the primary purpose. Since the intent of these tests is identification of specific kinds of knowledge that the child has or lacks, it is appropriate to teach the items that are missed; on the other hand, this is inappropriate with tests designed to rank individuals, in which items should be representative but not inclusive of knowledge being sampled.

Criterion-referenced language tests of this type are designed to answer the fourth assessment question: What are the regularities in this child's language? When they are used to supplement structural analysis of spontaneous language, they are helpful in identifying goals for intervention.

MEASUREMENT ISSUES

When choosing a test to rank an individual or to describe regularities of performance, there are two relevant issues the clinician needs to consider. First, how comprehensively does the test cover the area it purports to test? If, for example, it is designed to test prepositions, how inclusive or representative is the set of prepositions presented? This is particularly critical when we are testing for regularities of performance, since we want to make sure we have sampled enough to make generalizations about the child's patterns. A second question concerns the appropriateness of this test for a given child. A clinician would generally not give a test unless there were some indications in the child's behavior that there might be a problem in the area of language covered by the test. A clinician's wholesale use of tests simply because they are available is the mark of one who is insecure in making any clinical judgments; this clinician has the mistaken assumption that finding the right test or battery of tests is the answer to all assessment questions.

Use of tests designed to determine ranking raises some other measurement issues that come from the need for confidence in the scores when we are making decisions based on an individual's rank relative to others. We will briefly discuss types of scores, reliability, validity, and standardization population. More detailed explanations can be found in texts on testing, such as Cronbach (1970) or Salvia and Ysseldyke (1978).

Types of Scores

An individual's rank on a test can be derived from comparison to the original sample of people taking the test in two ways, resulting in age-equivalent scores or scores of relative standing.

Age-Equivalent Scores The individual's score can be compared to all age groups in the original sample to determine which group he or she scores most like. If, for example, a child's score is the same as the average (mean) score for six-year-olds, his or her age-equivalent score would be 6 years. Scores falling between means for adjacent age groups are interpolated or estimated to yield an intermediate age equivalent, such as 6.2 (six years, two months). These scores might be identified in various ways, such as language age, mental age, or receptive vocabulary age. Age-equivalent scores can be converted to *developmental quotients* by comparison to the child's chronological age.

$$\text{Developmental quotient} = \frac{\text{age equivalent}}{\text{chronological age}} \times 100$$

There are several problems with age-equivalent scores and developmental quotients. First, they provide no way of knowing the amount of significance to attach to a discrepancy between the child's chronological age and the derived age-equivalent score. Some behaviors may be most typical of one age group but may still be exhibited by a significant proportion of normal children at an older age. It becomes impossible to interpret age-equivalent scores on a single test or to compare them between two different tests unless the amount of variability shown by normal children from the same cultural group is known. Some clinicians follow the guideline that if the child earns an age-equivalent score that is eighteen months or two years below chronological age, he or she can be considered to have a language problem. One problem with this approach is that it assumes a two-year gap is equally significant across the age-range of childhood, whereas it is obvious that the proportional discrepancy would be greater the younger the child. Using the developmental quotient has similar problems, since the variance of age scores within the chronological age groups is different, and thus the same quotient means different things at different ages.

Another problem with these scores is that they assume that equal scores indicate equal performance. The six-year-old who achieves a score equal to the mean score for four-year-olds may not in fact have performed at all like a four-year-old. The approach to items as well as the specific items missed may be different. Further, this age-equivalent score tends to foster the false assumption that there are "average" four-year-olds to whom our child is being compared, when this is merely the mean of four-year-olds' scores.

As we have already mentioned, scores that fall between the means of each age group in the original sample are interpolated on the assumption that increase in knowledge is linear and even. Thus, if the mean score for four-year-olds is 20, and the mean score for five-year-olds is 30, a score of 25 will be assigned the age equivalence of 4.6 (four years, six months) even though it has not been demonstrated that this is the average score for children who are four years, six months old. Likewise, scores are sometimes extrapolated or estimated for ages younger and older than the children in the original sample. This presents another obvious weakness of these scores. In general, we do not recommend using age-equivalent scores due to the problems of interpretation.

Scores of Relative Standing   The second way a child's score can be interpreted is by comparing it to others of the same age group in order to determine the child's standing relative to his or her peers. One type of comparison is based on the statistical concept of the normal curve, or "normal" distribution of test scores. The mean score for each group, which is the average obtained by adding up all scores of each member of the group and dividing by the number in the group, is in the middle of the distribution. To get an idea of how far away an individual's score is from the mean, we must know the standard deviation for the group. This is a measure of the range of scores that were obtained by a certain proportion of the group. One standard deviation above the mean and one standard deviation below the mean (± 1 S.D.) give us the score range of 68 percent of the group; ± 2 S.D. account for 95 percent, and ± 3 S.D. give us the score range for 99 percent, or almost the entire group. To give an example, on the *Test of Auditory Comprehension—Revised* (1985), the mean score ($\overline{X}$) for the 60- to 65-month age group is 76.10, with S.D. = 16.69. So we know:

> 68 percent of this group scores between 59.4 and 92.79 ($\overline{X} \pm 1$ S.D.)
> 95 percent scored between 42.7 and 109.48 ($\overline{X} \pm 2$ S.D.)
> 99 percent scored between 26.03 and 126.17 ($\overline{X} \pm 3$ S.D.)

The decision as to what constitutes the "normal range" is an arbitrary one. Most people would certainly accept that at least 68 percent of the population must be considered "normal," so we would not see any score falling between ± 1 S.D. as deviant. It is common for makers of test classification schemes to take ± 2 S.D. as the division between normal and deviant, on the assumption that 95 percent of the sampled population should be considered normal. With this guideline, a five-year-old taking the TACL—R would have a score below 43 before we would consider his or her performance to be outside of normal limits.

Some tests use *standard scores,* which are derived by assigning the mean an arbitrary number and using a constant value to indicate 1 standard deviation. Intelligence tests, for example, typically assign 100 to the mean and 15 for 1 S.D. Standard scores make it possible to compare groups with different means and degrees of variability with each other. A child's score can be converted to a standard score to indicate in standard deviation units how much the given scores deviates from the mean of the group. This can be computed as a *z-score* in the following manner:

$$z = \frac{\text{child's score (X)} - \text{mean } (\overline{X})}{\text{standard deviation (S.D.)}}$$

For example, your child scores 45 on a test; you find in the test manual that the mean for the child's age group is 55 and standard deviation is 7.00. To find the child's z-score, we follow the formula

$$z = \frac{45 - 55}{7} = \frac{-10}{7} = -1.42$$

We can now see that this child's score is within -2 S.D. of the mean and not in the deviant range. This is a simple and useful means of comparing ranking on different tests as well.

Another way a child's score can be compared to his or her age peers is by using *percentile ranks*. These norms are established by arranging the scores of everyone within the sample age group from high to low and computing the percentage of individuals at and below each score. If 10 percent of the group score at and below 28 on a given test, then a child who receives a score of 28 is in the tenth percentile. It should be emphasized that this is not a measure of the percent correct for a given child, but rather an indication of relative standing in comparison to peers.

Stanines are closely related to percentile ranks. Stanines are derived by dividing the distribution into nine parts, rather than into 100 parts as is done to arrive at percentiles. Scores are reported according to the stanine within which they fall, with the fifth stanine being the midpoint of the distribution. Since a range of scores occurs within each stanine, this is a somewhat less precise indicator of relative ranking, but one that is less vulnerable to variations in scores based on incidental factors.

Percentile and stanine ranks are not based on a normal distribution as are standard scores. When stanines or percentiles are used with a normally distributed population, we can note a relationship between them and deviation scores. The sixteenth percentile and the third stanine correspond to approximately -1 S.D. The second percentile and the first stanine are closest to -2 S.D., which might lead us to interpret performance below the third percentile or in the first stanine as deviance from normal to be consistent with -2 S.D. as the cut off. More often, test makers recommend the tenth percentile be used as an indication that further assessment is warranted.

Tests designed for ranking individuals can have the following types of scores:

1. *Age-equivalent scores,* which compare a child to children at all ages sampled, and assign an age-equivalent score corresponding to the age group the child scores like. These can be converted to developmental quotients, but either method of reporting has intrinsic problems of interpretation.
2. *Relative ranking scores,* which compare a child to children of the same age, with the score indicating how the child ranks relative to peers. There are two basic ways of doing this:
   a. *Standard scores,* which can be used to compare a child's score to a presumed normal distribution of scores to determine the degree of deviation from the mean of the age group. Scores within -2 S.D. of the mean are generally considered to be in the normal range.
   b. *Percentile ranks,* which indicate the percentage of peers who score below a given child's score. Related to percentiles is division of the range into *stanines* (ninths).

Reliability

The reliability of a test is a measure of the stability or consistency of test results and indicates the amount of confidence one can have in the score. If children's performance on a test is dependent primarily on their knowledge of the material being tested rather than extraneous factors, reliability should be high. Several kinds of reliability are generally reported.

Interexaminer reliability refers to the consistency of scores when the test is administered by more than one examiner. *Test-retest reliability* is derived by administering the test to the same children twice within a short period of time to determine the stability of scores. Tests that have *alternate forms* (two or more versions of the same test) will report reliability coefficients between the forms to show how comparable they are. To measure the internal consistency of the test, *split-half* or *odd-even* reliability is derived by comparing the score on one half of the items to the score on the other half. If all items are testing the same general ability, this should be high.

Reliability can be adversely affected by factors other than the test items. If test directions are unclear or complicated, individual testers or children being tested may then interpret them differently, thus changing the nature of the test. Test makers generally indicate the kind of training examiners should have prior to administering the test, in order to achieve reliable results.

Reliability is a minimal requirement for any test, and most tests on the market report reasonable reliability when directions for administration are followed.

Validity

The validity of a test is an indication of how well it measures what it purports to measure. A test can be highly reliable but have little validity, as would be the case, for example, if we took shoe size as an indicator of language ability. It would be easy to demonstrate that shoe size is stable, and therefore reliable, but that does not make it a reasonable way to measure language skill. Demonstrating validity is more difficult than showing reliability, particularly in the area of language, since the ability or disability being measured is usually ambiguously defined.

There are various ways of reporting validity, and type as well as degree of validity should be a major concern of a clinician choosing a test. One common measure of validity is showing a correlation with other standardized tests that are presumed to measure the same skill. The questions that are then relevant are whether or not that skill is what you intend to measure and how well the validity of the comparison test has been demonstrated. Being highly correlated with an intelligence test does not necessarily indicate a language test is valid, unless we make the assumption that language ability is a direct reflection of intelligence or that the intelligence test measures primarily language ability, which violates the assumptions of most such tests. Another common way to describe validity is to report the correlation between test scores and age; that is, to show that older children get more items correct than younger children. This correlation should be high, since this would be the trend on almost any measure, including shoe size. It is at best a weak argument for the validity of the test. A more meaningful measure of validity is whether the test identifies those children who have language problems and whether the test scores are correlated with severity of the problem. The best reference criterion is probably the clinical judgment of experienced clinicians as to whether the test predicts nontest language behavior, since ultimately the diagnosis of language disorder must be based on the child's nontest performance. Most language tests do not report impressive validity data, if any at all, so usually the clinician must make judgments about the appropriateness of individual items. This is known as content validity and is the responsibility of the test user. The model of language on which the test is developed becomes an important question in this judgment, since that will determine the type of items that are seen as relevant to measuring language. If clinicians do not understand or accept the model of the test maker, it is not a valid test for their purposes, i.e., to identify the children who have language problems.

Standardization Population

The norms on a test are derived from administering the test to a number of individuals and then using their scores as representative of the population at large. Since those tested are not usually selected at random from the general population, it is relevant to determine the particular characteristics of this standardization population. If they differ in some significant way from the individual child we are testing, it may be inappropriate to compare our child's score to this group. Just as we would not compare the performance of a child speaking French to the norms for English speakers, we cannot use the performance of a dissimilar geographic or social group to judge the normalcy of a child. The standardization populations generally do not include individuals who deviate from the "typical" in any way. Thus, in order to compare an atypical child to this group, we must assume that his or her pattern of language development is the same as the normally developing child but perhaps at a slower rate. It is not clear that this is an acceptable assumption to make. If the clinician is seeking a test to determine ranking for a particular child, it is important to choose one which was standardized with a population similar in cultural background to that child.

Another question that needs to be raised about the standardization population is its size. Since the performance of this group is assumed to represent the general population, it should be large enough to make this a reasonable assumption. The total size of the sample is not as informative as the number of individuals in each age group sampled, since the norms to which a child is compared are derived within these subgroups. If there are 100 individuals in a subgroup, each person represents 1 percent, so that the lowest scoring person's score would identify the first percentile, and so on. Since by definition 2.27 percent fall below -2 S.D., there would be fewer than three people in the standardization group in that range. Most normalizing populations have considerably fewer than 100 persons in each age group, so norms are often extrapolated or inferred from data on a few individuals, particularly at the extremes of the distribution.

When evaluating the usefulness of tests to rank individual children, the clinician should determine that the test is

1. *Reliable*—that is, results can be assumed to be stable and repeatable. We can have most confidence in the reliability of tests with high reliability coefficients, which should be reported in the test manual.
2. *Valid*—validity measures, when reported by test makers, may or may not be of significance to the clinician, depending on the type of validity that is reported.

Predictive or content validity are probably the most meaningful for making clinical decisions; these are rarely demonstrated.

3. *Standardized* on a population to which the individual child can reasonably be considered similar in background.

Cultural Bias of Formal Tests

The development of formal tests have grown out of a cultural milieu which was middle-class, Western, and literate (McShane, 1991; Sears, 1975). Test makers presume, from their cultural experience, that test takers will be willing to take tests. Those making tests, for instance, assume that test takers will be willing to answer questions which are tests of their knowledge rather than sincere questions requesting unknown information. The makers further assume the takers will try to respond even when the tasks do not make obvious sense. It has been noted, for example, that the items of tests are unrelated to one another, appearing as discrete elements rather than integrated (Oller, 1979).

Test makers and givers also assume that those taking the test will follow what Grice (1975) has called the *cooperative principle*—that is, it is assumed that test takers will want to perform to their best ability and will try to provide relevant and concise answers. Furthermore, test makers and test givers take for granted that the methods involved in administering the test will be transparent to the test taker. Children are assumed to be able to understand the discourse and conceptual requirements of tasks involving matching, multiple choice, and fill-ins. Lastly, it is assumed that the test takers will have been exposed to information which will lead them to the right answer on the test. That is, the test is of knowledge that should have been learned, and if not, that the child may have a "learning problem." Children taking an English version of the Peabody Picture Vocabulary Test are assumed to know that a picture of a hotdog is the answer to "Show me wiener."

However, it is often not valid to assume that the test taker will accept or want to follow the cooperative principle, should understand the task requirements, or will have had exposure to the information needed to answer the questions correctly. By making such assumptions, the test giver is demonstrating a lack of knowledge about children with non-middle-class or non-Anglo backgrounds. For example, Navajo children are raised in a culture in which events begin with silence, especially unfamiliar events (Saville-Troike, 1986). This silence convention conflicts with the cooperative principle expectations of the test giver which requires children to answer when asked questions. Further, Navajo children have been found to understand tests as unusual events, rather than as events which lead to evaluations of their competence (Deyhle, 1987). So, for Navajo children, it is inappropriate for the test giver to assume that the children understand the relevance of tests. Finally, Navajo children who speak Navajo and are raised in the Navajo tradition have different world views than their English-speaking Anglo counterparts. For example, they have different conceptual schemas for colors, shapes, and animals (Saville-Troike, 1986). A test which counts their responses as incorrect because they do not fit the test maker's category system is one that is culturally biased and invalid for determining whether a Navajo child or any child from a non-standard background has a language problem.

The above considerations lead to the conclusion that children's communication cannot be properly evaluated with tests that are likely to misrepresent their abilities. A viable and preferred alternative to evaluation using formal tests is to use informal assessment methods such as those presented in the various chapters of this book (see also, Kayser, 1989; Leonard and Weiss, 1983). This alternative is especially relevant for answering questions about what the child's language is like. It is less effective when answering the question about whether the child has a language learning problem, since for that question to be answered, the child needs to be compared with other children of the same age, culture, and language learning background. Informal assessment methods which are not based on norms do not provide direct information about whether or not the child is developing language normally. Besides answering the normative questions, there are other reasons why clinicians might need to resort to using standardized tests with children from diverse cultures. The clinician may be working within a context in which tests are required. For example, institutions such as school boards or state education departments sometimes require that children be given formal tests in order for them to qualify for special education services. Under these circumstances, the clinician may need to design nontraditional ways to obtain standardized scores in order to counteract some of the cultural bias inherent in traditional approaches.

There have been a variety of approaches presented in the literature for when formal tests should be used to evaluate the communication abilities of children from diverse cultures (for reviews see Hamayan and Damico, 1991; Vaughn-Cooke, 1986, 1983; Evard and Sabers, 1979). Among the approaches forwarded to minimize cultural bias of formal tests are the following seven: (1) design new tests appropriate for the culture; (2) do not use existing tests with groups for whom the tests have been found to be culturally biased; (3) translate existing tests into the child's first language; (4) alter the way existing standardized tests are administered; (5) rescore previously administered standardized tests; (6) collect your own norms for existing tests; and (7) include disclaimers and cautions about the validity of formal tests' results when writing diagnostic reports.

Counteracting Cultural Bias

DESIGN NEW TESTS APPROPRIATE FOR THE CULTURE   Some researchers and clinicians have developed instruments which can serve to answer whether or not particular children in an underrepresented culture have language problems in their first language or their home dialect. The emphasis has been on developing tests that evaluate the children's phonology and syntax rather than semantics or pragmatics (Vaughn-Cooke, 1986). For example, the Del Rio Language Screening Test (Toronto and others, 1975) is designed to measure the language competence of Spanish-speaking Mexican-Americans whose dominant language is either Spanish or English. The test measures their receptive vocabulary and their ability to repeat sentences differing in length and complexity, to follow oral commands, and to understand stories.

While this approach of designing new tests can overcome the bias resulting from using one culture's standard language to evaluate members of another culture, it does not resolve the bias emanating from the test-taking procedure itself. For example, children who have not had experience with test questions will still have problems with taking formal tests, even those given in their own language that are based on their own life experiences. A second problem with this approach is that it assumes that a test normed on one community that speaks a given language will be appropriate for members of other communities that speak that same language. Mexican Spanish is different from Venezuelan Spanish, and so will be the children's responses to test items that reflect these differences. The same is true for bias toward speakers of different dialects of English.

DO NOT USE EXISTING TESTS WITH GROUPS FOR WHOM THEY HAVE BEEN FOUND TO BE BIASED   Certain tests have obvious or documented bias toward certain cultural groups. Examples that have been identified in the literature can be found in Box 9–1.

TRANSLATE AND RENORM EXISTING TESTS INTO CHILD'S FIRST LANGUAGE   A number of tests have been translated into different languages and renormed to fit different cultural groups. For example, the Northwestern Syntax Screening Test (NSST) has been translated into Spanish, renamed "Screening Test of Spanish Grammar," and administered to 192 Hispanic children, both Mexican-American and Puerto Rican children from poor urban neighborhoods in Chicago (Toronto, 1973).

The receptive portion of the NSST has also been translated into Igbo, a Nigerian language, with adaptation of some pictures and appropriate consideration for the special syntactical and morphological features of Igbo (Ogbalu

---

BOX 9–1. *Existing Tests with Documented Bias Against Particular Cultural Groups*

Test	Bias Against What Groups?	Source
Arizona Articulation Proficiency Scale	Low socioeconomic, Black English speakers	Cole and Taylor, 1990
Grammatic Closure Subtest of the Illinois Test of Psycholinguistic Abilities	Black English speakers	Arnold and Reed, 1976 Duchan and Baskervill, 1977 Wolfram, 1983
Peabody Picture Vocabulary Test	Black English speakers	Kreschek and Nicolosi, 1973
Photo Articulation Test	Low socioeconomic, Black English speakers	Cole and Taylor, 1990
Templin-Darley Tests of Articulation (second edition)	Low socioeconomic, Black English speakers	Cole and Taylor, 1990
Test for Auditory Comprehension of Language	Low socioeconomic, Black English speakers	Musselwhite, 1983
Test of Language Development	Black English speakers	Weiner, Lewnau, and Erway, 1983

and Lund, 1976). It was administered as part of a longitudinal study to ninety urban and rural first, second, and third graders in Nigeria (Ogbalu, 1990).

The NSST is but one of many of the translated tests; others are listed in Box 9–2, and further elaborated in Appendix A of Hamayan and Damico (1991) and in Deal and Rodriges (1987). Translated tests do not solve all problems of test administration to Limited English Proficient (LEP) children. Indeed, they solve only the problems which relate to the child's inability to understand the surface features of English. Other problems remain. First, the test context itself may be alienating and unfamiliar to children from particular cultures. Second, a simple translation does not alter the cultural bias of particular test items. Pictures of stores rather than marketplaces, of Westerners rather than Asians, of houses rather than apartment buildings are culturally biased for those unfamiliar with the pictured items. Third, translated tests cannot be given by the monolingual test giver since children may respond in their own language with an appropriate yet unexpected response, and be scored as wrong by someone who is only casually acquainted with the child's language and culture. Finally, direct translations of tests are bound to reflect the selection bias of the original test maker. Erickson and Iglesias (1986) offer an example of this type of bias where the original test in English measures noun-verb agreement, a grammatical rule judged important to English, while it will not likely include a gender-agreement item even though gender agreement is important for the language into which it is translated.

In some cases clinicians have attempted to translate a particular test into the child's language, and then to use the test's original standardized norms to score the child's responses. This is not a valid procedure, even for vocabulary tests which involve one-word translations, since lexical items, inflectional morphemes, and syntax in one language are processed and learned differently in a second language. *Jurisprudence* in English is a difficult notion and is a late and difficult item which occurs on the Peabody Picture Vocabulary Test. There may be no direct translation of *jurisprudence* into the child's language. If the translator translates the English word into another word which in the child's language includes the concept of judge, it could be a much easier idea for the

---

BOX 9–2. *Tests Originally Developed in English Which Have Been Translated into Other Languages*

Boehm Test of Basic Concepts (Spanish, Igbo)

Compton Speech and Language Screening Evaluation (Spanish)

Expressive One-Word Picture Vocabulary Test (Spanish)

Northwestern Syntax Screening Test (Spanish, Igbo)

Peabody Picture Vocabulary Test (Spanish)

Preschool Language Assessment Instrument (Spanish)

Preschool Language Scale (Spanish)

Receptive One-Word Picture Vocabulary Test (Spanish)

Test for Auditory Comprehension of Language (Spanish)

Test of Early Language Development (Spanish)

child to grasp—the child simply points to the picture of the judge without having to rely on his or her understanding of the notion of righteous judging.

ALTER THE WAY STANDARDIZED TESTS ARE ADMINISTERED For children who have limited English proficiency, but who are given tests in English, it has been recommended that the test be given in different ways to compensate for the bias inherent in the English version. Below is a list of various suggested types of alterations (elaborated from Toliver-Weddington and Erickson, 1991; Erickson and Iglesias, 1986).

1. *In order to insure that the child understands the task and is familiar with the procedures:* Give instructions in his or her other language if the child seems confused by English instructions; rephrase confusing instructions when necessary; provide additional demonstration examples if needed.

2. *In order to allow the child needed time to process information:* Give the child more time to respond, and repeat items if not responded to initially.

3. *In order to prevent nonacceptance of legitimate responses from children:* Keep track of the child's "incorrect" responses, and give credit if they are appropriate within the child's frame of reference. (For example, Kovarksy determined that Native American children responded *snake* in answer to what season it was because members of their culture called autumn the season of the snake—personal communication.) If children's answers are not interpretable in your frame of reference, ask them for clarification or explanation, or ask a member of their community about why the child may have responded as he or she did.

4. *In order to keep the child from being discouraged and feeling failure:* Omit items or subtests which you know from previous experience or research to be biased against your child's cultural group. For example, we know that the Grammatic Closure subtest of ITPA is particularly biased against Black English speakers (Wolfram, 1983; Duchan and Baskervill, 1977) and therefore that test should not be used when giving the ITPA to Black English-speaking children.

5. *If the child has difficulty understanding your dialect of English:* Ask someone who speaks the child's dialect to administer the test in that dialect.

RESCORE PREVIOUSLY ADMINISTERED STANDARDIZED TESTS Some researchers and clinicians have gathered typical English answers provided by normal children of different cultural groups as alternatives to what can be counted as correct for various standardized tests. For example, Hemingway, Montague, and Bradley (1981) have offered a set of responses from first-grade children who speak Black English, as allowable alternative responses on the Carrow Elicited Language Imitation test; Duchan & Baskervill (1977) and Wolfram (1983) have offered acceptable responses for Black English speakers to the Grammatic Closure subtest of the ITPA; Weiner and others (1983) have offered a list of typical responses from Black English-speaking children to the sentence imitation subtest of the TOLD; and Cole and Taylor (1990) have provided dialect sensitive scores for Black English speakers on several tests of articulation.

In order to rescore tests which have been already administered, the clinician will need to know what the child's responses were. If known, the clinician can credit the child with responses that conform to what is known about the features of the child's dialect. Thus, the clinician will need to determine the features of English which are altered due to the influence from the child's first language in order to distinguish errors from differences due to interference from the child's first language. (See chapters on phonology, morphology, and syntax for descriptions of features which are commonly used by speakers of various nonstandard forms of English.)

COLLECT YOUR OWN NORMS FOR EXISTING TESTS Some researchers and clinicians have advocated renorming existing tests using scores of children from targeted cultures as the new standard against which particular children can be compared (Musselwhite, 1983; Evard and Sabers, 1979; Mercer, 1979, 1984). While this method, called *pluralistic assessment* by Mercer (1984), provides children from different cultural and language groups with a fairer comparison group, it has its problems. DeAvila and Havassy (1974) note potential misuses of this cultural norm technique. The new norms do not eliminate the major problem of tests: that they are biased against children from diverse cultures. When ESL or dialect-speaking children do not perform as well as standard English speakers, the lower norms are taken as evidence that the whole group, as well as individuals within the group, are inferior on that skill.

INCLUDE DISCLAIMERS AND CAUTIONS ABOUT VALIDITY OF FORMAL TESTS' RESULTS WHEN WRITING UP EVALUATION REPORTS If any of the above departures from typical test administration are followed, they need to be described in the diagnostic report of the child being evaluated. When the traditional procedures are slightly changed (e.g., the items are repeated, in violation of the instructions), the changes can be justified, described, and the score reported. In those cases where the items are scored twice, once where the child's cultural background is discounted, and the second where it is counted, an account of discrepant scores needs to be included.

In those cases where the child's responses to formal tests are very limited and it is suspected that the performance is due to the child's lack of exposure to formal test situations or suspected cultural alienation from the testing context, it is recommended that the poor performance not be reported as a score. Rather the possible cultural reasons for the child's inability to respond should be indicated, and alternative ways of evaluating the child's communication in a more culturally congenial context should be undertaken.

TYPES OF TESTS

While recognizing that any classification system can lead to artificial distinctions, we have chosen to discuss some of the existing language tests according to our perception of the purpose and scope of the instruments. Our impression of these attributes does not always correspond with that of the test maker but reflects our own examination of test items. We begin again with our two broad categories of tests—those to determine an individual's rank and those for finding regularities in performance.

We now return to the assessment questions posed in Chapter 1 and discuss the usefulness and limitations of tests in answering those questions. The norm-referenced tests for ranking can all be used to address the question of whether the child has a language problem, with the judgment of normalcy being based on the child's performance relative to a larger "normal" population from his or her cultural group. It must be kept in mind, however, that the determination of which ranks are normal and which are deviant is arbitrary. Data from these tests are useful only to document administrative decisions; they are not useful for planning remediation.

Some ranking tests or combinations of tests are helpful in determining relative areas of strength and deficit, thus addressing another assessment question. However, that there are no tests covering all potential deficit areas, so tests cannot be relied on to get a complete profile of language ability. Further, these tests can be used only to suggest general areas of deficit—they do not sample any specific area in enough detail to find regularities.

Tests of regularities, on the other hand, are always confined to specific areas, since the intent is to determine patterns of performance within an area. Analysis of items that are right and wrong is the essence of scoring these tests, rather than quantifying results. Our goal here is to analyze the child's responses so we can understand what led to them.

Some available tests are clearly of the ranking type and others are for revealing regularities. Several tests attempt to do some of both. We will discuss examples of each type. Table 9–1 shows how some of these tests can be categorized according to their purpose and the areas they address.

Ranking Tests

Developmental Scales   All developmental scales are based on a normative model of assessment and are designed to rank children. They are characterized by having ages attached to specific behaviors and scores which are reported as age-equivalent curves. Typically, there are several behaviors reported to be normal at each age level, so an individual child is observed or directed to perform these behaviors and then scored according to the age group his or her score is closest to. There are some variations on this scoring system with the individual scales, as well as differences in the number and range of behaviors sampled.

Following are some examples of popular developmental scales. Some are broad and cover other areas as well as language skills. Others are addressed primarily to a level of general language functioning. None offer a coherent picture of the child's language competency nor identify areas of deficit.

The *Preschool Language Scale—Revised* (Zimmerman, Steiner, and Evatt, 1979) has separate sections for evaluating comprehension and expression of language. Each section has four behaviors at each six-month interval from age eighteen months to seven years. Receptive vocabulary, concept acquisition, and understanding of commands are sampled on the comprehension scale. The expressive section (verbal ability) samples some labeling, expression of concepts, memory span for digits, limited syntax and morphology, and articulation. Age equivalence is derived for each of the two sections by adding together the number of behaviors displayed and counting each as one-and-one-half months of development (a method of calculation which actually violates the assumptions of a norm-referenced measure).

The directions for administering and evaluating each of the items on the *Preschool Language Scale* are very clear and explicit. A picture book is included for use with some of the items. A Spanish (Mexican-American) version of the

TABLE 9–1 Representative Language Tests by Type and Purpose

Test	Purpose		Areas of Emphasis				Mode	
	Ranking	Regularity	Morph.	Syn.	Sem./Vocab.	Pragmatics	Recep.	Express.
Developmental Scales (Age Equivalence)								
Preschool Language Scale	X							
Sequenced Inventory of Communication Development	X							
Communicative Evaluation Chart	X							
Denver Developmental Screening Test	X							
Survey Tests (Pass/Fail)								
DIAL: Developmental Indicators of Assessment Learning	X							
Screening Test of Adolescent Language	X							
Test of Early Language Development	X							
Compton Speech and Language Screening Evaluation	X		X	X	X			
Area of Deficit Tests								
Bankson Language Screening Test	X		X	X	X			X
Test for Auditory Comprehension of Language	X		X	X	X		X	
Tests of Language Development	X		X	X	X		X	X
Test of Adolescent Lanaguage	X			X	X		X	X
Clinical Evaluation of Language Functions	X			X	X		X	X
Northwestern Syntax Screening Test	X		X	X			X	X
Miller-Yoder Language Comprehension Test	X		X	X			X	
Peabody Picture Vocabulary Test	X				X		X	
Expressive One-Word Picture Vocabulary Test	X				X			X
Receptive One-Word Picture Vocabulary Test	X				X		X	
Test of Word Finding	X	X			X		X	X
Illinois Test of Psycholinguistic Abilities	X		X		X		X	X
Tests for Determining Regularities								
Carrow Elicited Language Inventory	(X)[a]	X	X	X				X
Oral Language Sentence Imitation Screening/Diagnostic Tests		X	X	X				X
Boehm Test of Basic Concepts	(X)	X			X		X	
Communications Development Inventory		X			X			X
Vocabulary Comprehension Scale		X			X		X	
McCarthy Scales of Children's Ability	(X)	X			X		X	X
Environmental Language Inventory		X			X			
Assessment of Children's Language Comprehension		X		(X)	X		X	X
Multilevel Informal Language Inventory		X		X	X			X
Evaluating Communicative Competence		X				X	X	X
Interpersonal Language Skills Assessment		X				X		X
Communication and Symbolic Behavior		X				X	X	X
Test of Pragmatic Skill		X				X	X	X
Communicative Development Inventory		X			X			X

[a] (X) indicates information is available to use the test for this purpose, but we consider it secondary.

scale is included in the manual, and Spanish scoring forms are available. The authors do not view this as a test but rather as an instrument to isolate areas of strength and deficiency in language. It is scored, however, as a standardized test.

The *Sequenced Inventory of Communication Development—Revised* (Hedrick, Prather, and Tobin, 1984) is also divided into receptive and expressive language behaviors, with an age range of from four months to four years. Rather than assigning each behavior to a given age, the authors indicate the ages at which 25, 50, 75, and 90 percent of their standardization population accomplish each behavior, which is useful information on normal development. A nonstandardized Spanish (Cuban) translation is included along with guides for assessing other populations. Receptive and expressive communication age-equivalent scores can be computed. Items on each scale are arranged developmentally, with receptive items ranging from awareness of sound to speech sound discrimination. Expressive items include motor and vocal imitation as well as answers to questions and a spontaneous sample. Play behaviors and prelinguistic responses are sampled, along with viewing language as part of a social system. Receptive and expressive profiles organize the items into semantic, syntactic, pragmatic, phonological, and perceptual categories, which offer some information about deficit areas.

The *Communicative Evaluation Chart* (Anderson, Miles, and Matheny, 1963), for infants from three months to five years old, presents receptive and expressive language behaviors along with items to assess motor coordination and visual-motor perceptual skills at each age level. No normative data are available, and there are no directions or suggestions for how to elicit each behavior.

The *Denver Developmental Screening Test* (Frankenburg and others, 1975) is divided into four areas: personal-social, fine motor, language, and gross motor. An age range for each item is shown by giving the age at which 25, 50, 75, and 90 percent of children pass that item. Language behaviors sampled are very limited but include some items that assess structure as well as vocabulary. Detailed directions are given for each test item. This scale was standardized in Denver using 1,036 normal children aged two weeks to six years, four months.

Survey Tests   Survey tests are designed to provide a sampling of relatively broad-based behavior in a brief period of time for the purpose of selecting children who need further language evaluation or for identifying areas of deficit in which further assessment is indicated. They are often identified as "screening" tests, but since this label is applied to such a wide variety of standardized and informal assessment procedures, we choose not to use it here. Survey tests are norm referenced, but unlike the developmental scales, they do not yield age-equivalent scores. Instead, they have established criteria for what is considered adequate performance at a given age. If a child fails to meet this criteria, he or she is considered a candidate for more extensive testing or observation to determine the nature and severity of the language disorder. The survey tests are ranking tests because they match the child's performance to a normal sample in several language areas, as well as in some nonlanguage areas.

The *Developmental Indicators of Assessment and Learning* (*DIAL*) (Mardell and Goldenberg, 1975) was developed to assess the needs of large numbers of prekindergarten children for support services in motor or language abilities. It is designed to have each child observed individually by a team of four examiners in the areas of gross motor skills, fine motor skills, concepts, and communication. Points are given for each task, and scores are computed for each of the four areas tested. The need for follow-up intervention or further assessment is determined by comparing the child's score in each area with the cutoff score specified by chronological age, with the tenth percentile of the standardization population being used as the criterion for arriving at cutoff scores. Items were selected from a battery of norm-referenced tests and developmental scales. The concepts and communication subtests cover a variety of receptive and expressive language skills, including articulation, vocabulary use and recognition, following directions, and formulating original sentences in response to questions and story pictures (parts of speech and length of longest sentence are scored). There is no breakdown of performance into areas of language, and individual items should not be interpreted as identifying areas of deficit.

The authors of the DIAL indicate that the examiners need only limited training to administer the test. We suspect that the reliability of scoring, particularly of the communications portion, would be heavily dependent upon the examiner's training or experience. The DIAL kit includes most of the materials needed for the survey, except for a Polaroid camera and film for photographing each child. The DIAL is intended for use with children from age two years, six months to five years, five months. It takes approximately twenty-five to thirty minutes for a typical child to complete the four subtests. It could be administered to an individual child by one examiner, but its uniqueness is that it provides a format which facilitates surveying a large number of children at a time. It would not be useful as a language test for a child who is already suspected to have a language impairment, since it provides little additional information.

The *Screening Test of Adolescent Language* (*STAL*) (Prather and others, 1980) provides a quick indication of the expressive and receptive language abilities of junior and senior high school students in order to identify those who are in need of further assessment. It provides synonyms to assess vocabulary comprehension and sentence imitation to evaluate syntax. The ability to deal with abstract and nonliteral language is sampled through proverb interpretation and identification of verbal absurdities. The brief administration time (approximately seven minutes) and the explicit guidelines for scoring make this an attractive aid in surveying this age group.

The *Test of Early Language Development* (*TELD*) (Hresko, Reid, and Hammill, 1981) is a thirty-eight item screening test designed to determine whether three- to eight-year-olds have difficulty with receptive or expressive language. The test items have a linguistic focus, where children are asked questions to elicit responses in the areas of phonology, syntax, and semantics.

The *Compton Speech and Language Screening Evaluation* (Compton, 1978) is another example of a survey test designed to be given quickly to large numbers of children to identify those children who should have in-depth speech and language evaluation. It is intended to screen three- to six-year-olds in the areas of articulation, vocabulary, memory span, morphology, syntax, fluency, and voice quality. Standards for passing each subtest are established for each age level.

> ***Tests for Determining Areas of Deficit*** These tests differ from the survey tests in that they are designed to determine the child's ranking in a specific area or to compare more than one area, rather than to determine a general, overall age equivalent or adequacy.

The *Bankson Language Screening Test* (*BLST*) (Bankson, 1977) consists of a battery of seventeen subtests covering semantics, morphology, syntax, and auditory and visual perception. It focuses on expression rather than reception. The semantics subtests range from concrete vocabulary items to more abstract generalizations, such as functions and opposites. Most of the early grammatical morphemes are covered in various subtests, with syntax getting less emphasis. The auditory perception subtests include memory for words and sentences, following commands, story sequencing, and phonemic discrimination. The visual perception subtests are included on the rationale that children with oral language deficits often will also have difficulty with reading and that this test can serve as a tool for early detection of such problems.

Items on the BLST are scored as right or wrong. Total raw score can then be converted to percentile rank, with the author recommending further language evaluation for children with scores at or below the thirtieth percentile, with a strong therapy recommendation for those below the sixteenth percentile. The validity of these criteria points has not been demonstrated, and clinicians may find other cutoff points more useful when using this test to identify children for further evaluation. It is also possible to score each subtest separately, for comparison with means and standard deviations presented by age group. This would be more helpful than overall percentile rank in identifying areas of deficit. The BLST was norm referenced on 637 children between the ages of four years, one month and eight years. It takes approximately twenty-five minutes to administer. A shorter version is possible by administering thirty-eight items identified as being the most discriminating. There are no norms available for this version, however. A preferable means of shortening the test would be to eliminate the subtests on visual and auditory perception that are less directly relevant to identifying language areas of deficit. Norms for the remaining subtests could still be used, but of course the total score would not be converted to an overall percentile rank.

The *Test for Auditory Comprehension of Language—Revised* (*TACL–R*) (Carrow-Woolfolk, 1985) seeks to identify children who have difficulty with receptive language and to help the clinician discover specific areas of grammar that need additional testing. The test is divided into three sections, each of which is scored separately. Section I is identified as word classes and relations and is made up primarily of single words, including nouns, verbs, adjectives, and adverbs. Several word combinations are also presented in this section, including some noun phrases (*a large blue ball*) and verb phrases (*riding a little bicycle*), which are designed to assess various semantic relations. Section II assesses comprehension of grammatical morphemes, pronouns, prepositions, and derivational suffixes and presents these forms within short simple sentences. Section III presents a set of elaborated sentences, including a variety of question forms, negatives, and passives, as well as coordinate, subordinate, and relative clauses.

Items within each section are arranged by graduated difficulty, and beginning points for different ages are suggested to allow older children to skip the easier sections. Basal and ceiling levels are established for each section, which reduces administration time relative to the earlier version of the TACL. Norms are provided for ages three years to nine years, eleven months. The raw score for each section or for the total test can be converted to a percentile rank for either the child's chronological age or grade, which in turn can be used to derive several standard scores. Age-equivalent scores can also be derived for each section. The extensive manual provides a description of the standardization sample and the process of test development and standardization. A review of research on earlier versions of the TACL, including validation studies and application to special populations, is also included. There is a Spanish version of the TACL, which yields different results, depending upon the Spanish group to which it is administered (Wilcox and Aasby, 1988; Linares-Orama and Sanders, 1977; Rueda and Perozzi, 1977). When Musselwhite (1983) used the TACL to evaluate the language of African American children in a Head Start program in North Carolina, she found it biased against children of low socioeconomic status.

The *Tests of Language Development* (*TOLD*) (Newcomer and Hammill, 1982) now come in two versions: the TOLD-Primary for children four to nine years, which is essentially the same as the original version (1977), and the TOLD-Intermediate for children eight years, six months, through thirteen. The test is developed on a linguistic model, including subtests that assess facets of semantics, syntax, and phonology both expressively and receptively. The semantic subtests are limited to identifying named pictures and giving definitions. Comprehension of morphology and syntax is tested through identification of pictures described with sentences. Along with comprehension of a variety of grammatical forms (e.g., negatives, plurals, subordinate clauses), several specific vocabulary items are assessed by the subtest (e.g., *different, middle*), making it difficult to isolate comprehension of grammatical forms. Expressive syntax and morphology are assessed through imitation of thirty sentences, and morphology is also sampled through sentence completion. Phonology is assessed through single-word responses to pictures. A word discrimination subtest is also included. Scores for each subtest are computed separately and can be converted to age-equivalent, percentile, and standard scores. Computer scoring systems are also available. This test has been found to be particularly biased against speakers of Black English (Weiner, Lewnau, and Erway, 1983). The Prueba del Desarrollo Inicial del Lenguaje (Hresko, Reid, and Hammill, 1982) is a Spanish test modeled after the English version of the TOLD-Primary.

Hammill and his colleagues have also developed a test that is designed for populations of older subjects. The *Test of Adolescent Language* (*TOAL*) (Hammill and others, 1980) is intended for students in grades six through twelve, and norms are presented for ages eleven through eighteen years, five months. Subtests assess vocabulary and grammar through reading and writing as well as with oral language.

The *Clinical Evaluation of Language Functions (CELF)* (Semel and Wiig, 1980) was developed by Semel and Wiig to determine areas of deficit in the language of school-age children from kindergarten through grade twelve. The authors describe the test as testing for deficits in linguistic knowledge in the areas of phonology, syntax, and semantics. The test also is designed to determine whether children have problems in language processing. The test battery is composed of six subtests identified as processing subtests. They include tasks where children must select which picture goes with a given verbal item (e.g., "The lamp is behind the chair") and where children are read short paragraphs and are asked questions about them. Besides the six processing subtests, which all emphasize language comprehension, there is a set of four production subtests, in which children are asked to rapidly give the days of the week and months of the year, to name colors and shapes when presented with pictures, to list from memory as many animals and foods they can think of, to imitate complex sentences, and to formulate a sentence that includes a particular word (e.g., *after*). The battery also contains two supplemental tests for testing phonological competence.

The *Northwestern Syntax Screening Test (NSST)* (Lee, 1971) was also developed on a linguistic model and consists of items to sample receptive and expressive morphology and syntax. It was designed to identify children significantly impaired in these skills (defined as those scoring more than 2 standard deviations below the mean), as well as those who need further testing to establish the existence of a clinically significant language delay (as evidenced by scores below the tenth percentile). Separate scores are derived for expressive and receptive portions, and each can be compared to percentile ranks by age group.

The inappropriateness of using this test as a diagnostic tool for children who have already been identified as language-impaired has been emphasized by Lee (1977) as well as by others who have found a lack of consistency on particular structures between test performance on the NSST and spontaneous language (Prutting, Gallagher, and Mulac, 1975). The standardization sample consisted of children from middle- to upper-middle-class suburban communities in the Midwest, with fewer than fifty children in some of the age groups. Subsequent studies have shown that the norms are not appropriate for children from other populations (Larson and Summers, 1976). Lee emphasizes that the NSST is applicable only to children learning the standard English dialect. The age range of the test is given as three to eight years, but it is apparent from looking at the norms that the test is not sensitive to differences beyond the six year, eleven month age level. Even below this age, the statistical support of reliability and validity is meager.

Toronto (1973) has developed a Spanish version of the NSST, *Screening Test of Spanish Grammar*, which has been normed on 192 Mexican-American and Puerto Rican children in Chicago. Ogbalu and Lund (1976) developed the *Igbo Syntax Screening Test*, based on the NSST and normed on Nigerian school children.

The *Miller-Yoder Language Comprehension Test (MY)* (Miller and Yoder, 1984) assesses comprehension of essentially the same ten grammatical contrasts addressed by the NSST. The forty-two test plates can be given either in random order or in order of difficulty. Each item is identified by the age at which 60 percent and 90 percent of the standardization sample passed it. The score form is coded for a number of variables, including two age levels for the item, picture location, and grammatical form being assessed, which makes it somewhat confusing to use until the administrator is familiar with it. Interpretation of results is also problematic. An approximate age equivalent can be derived from the total score, but there is no direct comparison to same-age peers. The authors stress the importance of clinical judgment in interpreting the scores.

The *Peabody Picture Vocabulary Test—Revised (PPVT—R)* (Dunn and Dunn, 1981) of receptive vocabulary evolved out of a normative orientation to language, with the words chosen for their frequency of occurrence rather than semantic content. Raw scores can be converted to age equivalents, standard scores, stanines, or percentiles with an age range of two years, six months to forty years, eleven months. Two forms are included (L and M) to provide for retesting. Scores on forms A and B of the original PPVT (1965) cannot be compared directly to scores on the new forms, but means of comparing between the two versions are detailed in the revised manual.

The PPVT—R is one of the best standardized language tests available, but it should also be emphasized that it can only identify a deficit in the area of receptive vocabulary and should not be used as a measure of general language functioning. The PPVT is available in a Spanish version from the developers of the test.

The *Expressive One-Word Picture Vocabulary Test* (Gardner, 1979) presents individually a series of 110 pictures to be named with single words. This test is purported to be a measure of verbal intelligence and a screening test for speech or learning disorders as well as a means of sampling expressive vocabulary. Scores derived include percentiles, mental age equivalents, and deviation IQs. Caution is advised in interpretation of the latter two scores. The test is standardized for children from ages two to twelve years. A version for children from twelve to sixteen years is also available, which is designated as the Upper Extension. Both versions, along with a companion assessment of receptive vocabulary (*Receptive One-Word Picture Vocabulary Test,* Gardner 1985) are available in Spanish. Since there are regional dialects of Spanish, it is generally necessary to adapt the translation to correspond to local useage.

The *Test of Word Finding* (German, 1986) attempts to distinguish between vocabulary deficits and problems with word retrieval. It samples the child's skill in finding the appropriate nouns, verbs, and category words through picture naming, sentence completion, and descriptions and then assesses the child's comprehension of target words that are not used correctly. Both response time and accuracy of response are evaluated. Standard scores and percentile ranks are computed, and additional informal analysis is encouraged. The test is designed for children in first through sixth grades.

The *Illinois Test of Psycholinguistic Abilities (ITPA)* (Kirk, McCarthy, and Kirk, 1968) has evolved into a self-defining view of language. Designed for children from two to ten years of age, it consists of twelve subtests, each intended to identify a potential area of deficit. It could be argued that some of the subtests, such as auditory sequential memory, are also used to identify a possible cause of a language problem, depending on the clinician's view of the nature of language disorders—that is, poor auditory memory may be seen as either a symptom or a cause of a language problem. The raw score for each subtest is converted to a scaled score to allow for comparison across subtests. An age-equivalent score ("psycholinguistic age") is calculated for the entire test.

The ITPA was standardized on predominately middle-class Illinois and Wisconsin children, all of whom demonstrated average intellectual functioning, academic achievement, adjustment, and sensorimotor integrity, which severely limits the population of which the norms are representative. Test-retest reliabilities are relatively low, ranging from .12 to .86. Validity as a test of language function has not been demonstrated, but it correlates highly with chronological age (Salvia and Ysseldyke, 1978) and intelligence tests (Huizinga, 1973).

The subtests of the ITPA follow:

Comprehension Subtests

Auditory reception: This subtest includes fifty questions of the type "Do dogs eat?" "Do dials yawn?" with vocabulary becoming increasingly more difficult.

Visual reception: This subtest includes fifty items, each consisting of a stimulus picture and four response pictures from which the child is to choose the one conceptually similar to the stimulus picture.

Expressive Subtests

Verbal expression: An object is presented and the child is asked "Tell me all about this." The score is the number of discrete, relevant, factual concepts expressed. The manner or structure of expression is not regarded, thus making this a vocabulary test or test of conceptual attribution.

Manual expression: The child is shown fifteen pictures of common objects and asked to pantomime the appropriate action of each.

Association Subtests

Auditory association: The child is presented with sixty-two verbal analogies of the form "I cut with a saw; I pound with a _____?" with items of increasing difficulty.

Visual association: This subtest has two parts. On the first, the child is to choose one of four pictures that "goes with" the stimulus picture. On the second part, visual analogies are presented (e.g., tennis ball, tennis racket; baseball, _____).

Grammatic closure: The child is given thirty-three orally presented items accompanied by pictures and is to complete the second statement through use of automatic habits acquired through redundancies of the language. Items are of the form "Here is a bed; here are two _____?"

Visual closure: This subtest consists of four scenes, each containing fourteen or fifteen common objects concealed in varying degrees. The child is to identify them from incomplete visual representations.

Auditory sequential memory: This tests ability to recall sequences of digits increasing in length from two to eight.

Visual sequential memory: The child is asked to reproduce a sequence of nonmeaningful figures from memory.

Auditory closure (optional): Thirty words with sounds omitted are said to the child, who is to identify and repeat the word, filling in the missing sounds.

Sound blending (optional): The sounds of a word are spoken singly at half-second intervals, and the child is asked to synthesize the word and say it correctly.

The Grammatic Closure Subtest of the ITPA has been found particularly inappropriate for second language learners and dialect speakers of English (Duchan and Baskervill, 1977). Some authors have provided an alternate scoring system for Black English dialect speakers (Arnold and Reed, 1976).

Other Ranking Tests   Three other types of tests have been devised for ranking children's behavior. They are more informal than the others we have been discussing in that they do not rely on norms, but rather depend upon the clinical judgment of the ranker. They fall into three types: rating scales, checklists, and performance profiles.

Rating Scales   A number of tests have been designed to determine and contrast a child's level of proficiency in various areas of performance. Prutting and Kirchner (1983; 1987) developed a protocol, consisting of thirty parameters to assess the "pragmatic aspects" of language. They include conversational items such as topic initiation and maintenance, vocal and fluency items, and nonverbal aspects such as eye gaze and facial expression. Subjects' performance is judged to be appropriate or inappropriate on each parameter.

Many rating scales have been designed for bilingual or multilingual children to determine their relative proficiency in the different languages. These language proficiency rating scales require that the evaluator judge a child's performance along a scale ranging from poor to outstanding performance. Box 9–3 lists some language proficiency scales available and a brief description of each. These scales can be useful for determining which is the child's best language so that decisions can be made about what language to use for assessing language abilities and providing therapy.

Checklists   Measures of proficiency have been designed to evaluate children's performance in areas of language which are highly context dependent and which do not lend themselves well to standardized procedures and obtaining scores. These have taken the form of checklists, in which the evaluator checks which of a list of designated skills the child can or cannot carry out successfully. For example, Bedrosian (1985) designed a checklist of various discourse areas including topic initiation, maintenance, and turn taking as a gross indicator of a child's discourse proficiency. Cheng (1987) has designed two checklists for evaluating the communicative proficiency of Asian children. One she calls a *Functional Communication Checklist.* It includes a list of thirty-four different speech acts and discourse competencies (e.g., asks questions, pleads, gives off-topic responses). A second is an *Assessment of Nonverbal Behavior,* and it includes an itemized list of behaviors involving head movements, facial expressions, hand movements, gazing, and body movements. Both instruments involve determining if the child exhibits the behavior (yes or no) and how frequently (frequent or infrequent).

Performance Profiles   Comparing a child's relative strengths and weaknesses on a variety of language measures yields a *profile* of performance. A profile

BOX 9–3. Rating Scales for Determining Language Dominance

Assessment Instrument for Multicultural Clients (Adler, 1991): This instrument involves five point ratings of five dimensions of the language used by speakers of nonstandard dialects or speakers of more than one language. The dimensions include pragmatic usage, language structure, suprasegmentals and body language, voice and fluency, and auditory acuity and comprehension.

Bilingual Syntax Measure (Burt, Dulay, and Hernandez-Chavez, 1976): This test assesses syntactic ability in Spanish, English, Tagalog, Italian, and Chinese. There are two levels, one for grades kindergarten to two, and the second from grades three to twelve. The test consists of twenty questions about a series of seven cartoon pictures designed to elicit specific grammatical structures. Total raw score for each language places the child at one of five levels of proficiency for that language.

James Language Dominance Test (James, 1975): This test elicits single words in Spanish and English. It is designed for children in kindergarten and first grade. The examiner presents forty pictures in conjunction with the questions: "What is this?" (expressive) and "Where is the ____?" (receptive). Students are also scored on three questions to determine home language use. Scores are used to place the child into one of five categories of language proficiency.

Language Assessment Scales (DeAvila and Duncan, 1981): The Spanish version of this battery of tests was standardized on Mexican-American, Latin American, and Puerto Rican children. The English version was standardized on English-speaking children in the southwestern United States. The test was standardized on children grades kindergarten through twelve. The subtests include sound discrimination, phoneme production, vocabulary usage, sentence comprehension, and storytelling. The child is placed at one of five levels of proficiency.

Oral Language Proficiency Measure (El Paso Public Schools): This measure was designed to determine proficiency of English- and Spanish-speaking fourth to sixth graders. Students are asked a series of questions about three stimulus pictures. Scores are based on number of words and number of grammatical responses. The test places students in one of five levels of English and Spanish usage.

Spanish/English Language Performance Test (Southwest Educational Development Laboratory): This test is designed to place four- and five-year-old students in one of six language levels in English and Spanish. It involves a fifteen-minute controlled interview in which the student is required to answer questions, name objects, follow directions, describe objects, and describe pictures. The child is placed in a language category based on the number of responses in each part of the test and the language in which the majority of responses are made.

Spotting Language Problems (Damico and Oller, 1985): This is a pragmatic language screening measure geared to children five years and older. It can be used to determine proficiency in Spanish, Zuni, French, German, and Vietnamese. The evaluator observes students and comments on student's effectiveness along seven dimensions of oral-dialogic language usage. The seven dimensions are nonfluencies, revisions, inordinate delays, nonspecific referential terms, inappropriate responses, poor topic maintenance, and need for multiple repetitions.

System of Multicultural Pluralistic Assessment (SOMPA) (Mercer, 1979): This system assesses cognitive and sensorimotor abilities and adaptive behavior of children age five to eleven years. It includes parent interviews, which can be conducted in English or Spanish, student assessment materials, and the *Adaptive Behavior Inventory for Children (ABIC)*, which also can be used independently. Normative data for black, Hispanic, and white children are included.

can provide a broad picture of the child's abilities and allow for an informed selection of intervention goals.

One approach for profiling a child's competencies is to *determine a level of development for different areas of performance,* and then to compare across levels. This is the basis of Miller's Assigning Structural Stage procedure (1981), which is designed to arrive at a structural stage for the child's performance in the areas of morphology, syntax, and semantics. Miller's approach involves doing a detailed analysis of the child's language in each area so that the child can be compared with the developmental norms established in the research literature on normally developing children. Relative strengths and deficits can then be determined.

Another profiling approach is to *subjectively rate the child's performance in different areas* using a preestablished checklist of performance areas. This procedure is especially prevalent in the area of pragmatics (e.g., Prutting and Kirchner, 1987; Bedrosian, 1985; Roth and Spekman, 1984; Gerber and Geller, 1982). For example, Prutting and Kirchner (1987), using their list of thirty parameters, develop pragmatic profiles by indicating which parameters are appropriate or inappropriate. They identified distinct profiles for different diagnostic groups. One of the procedure's aims is to compare a person's profile across different communicative contexts. For example, Mentis and Prutting (1991) have reported on an adult with a head injury, who was rated as inappropriate on the same pragmatic dimensions across conversational conditions.

Tests for Determining Regularities

Unlike the ranking tests, the assessment tools discussed here are designed to identify specific problems a child has with language rather than simply determining whether or not, or to what degree, a problem exists. It thus is appropriate to look at each item individually and to compare it with other items to determine what regularities are present in the child's performance. These measures are all restricted to specific areas of deficit rather than representative of general language function. As we have mentioned, some of them have been norm referenced and so can be used to arrive at a level of functioning on a specific task, but this is not their primary purpose. These norms do make it possible, however, to quantify children's performance and thus report scores when they are desired. Many of these tools have not been adequately standardized to use as measures of relative rank. This is not a serious criticism of them as long as they are not used for that purpose. In any event, scores are of little value for the purposes of describing language and planning therapy, so clinicians must analyze performance on each item. Again, we have not attempted to be comprehensive in our coverage, but rather we give examples of various types of descriptive tools. We have organized this discussion according to the area of deficit being investigated. An important criterion for the usefulness of these measures is the adequacy of the sample obtained for indicating regularities in performance.

Phonology Assessment There are numerous articulation tests available that sample expressive phonology, usually by having the child say the name of pictured objects or read test sentences. The *Goldman-Fristoe Test of Articulation* (Goldman and Fristoe, 1972) and the *Fisher-Logemann Test of Articulation Competence* (Fisher and Logemann, 1971) are popular examples of this type; both provide normative data for comparison. With these tests, each phoneme is sampled in one to three words. If a child consistently produces one or more of the phonemes in an atypical manner, these tests will provide an adequate sample for describing that difference. If, however, the child's phonological rules are atypical, samples obtained will not be comprehensive enough to identify the regularities that exist. Limitations of the traditional articulation tests for assessing phonology are discussed in Chapter 4. We will comment here on only a few tests that offer some unique features.

There are no tests of receptive phonology that we take to be descriptive of that area of deficit. Despite the fact that the authors of some discrimination or perception tests have described their instruments as useful in describing or identifying the cause of language (or learning) problems, the relationship of the skills tested to understanding language has not been demonstrated.

A *Deep Test of Articulation* (McDonald, 1964) assesses error phenomes in multiple-phonetic contexts, thus making it possible to observe the degree of variability in the child's production. Words are produced in combinations, which more closely approximates phonological sequences involved in formal discourse than does production in single words, even though the combinations are semantically unlikely.

The *Test of Articulation Performance (TAP)* (Bryant and Bryant, 1983) has both a diagnostic and a screening version. The diagnostic tool assesses each consonant several times in both initial and final positions of words, and thus provides more data for discovering consistency of patterns than is typical of these tests. The data can be used to do a place, manner, and voicing analysis. The percentage of correct production is computed as a measure of deviance. The screening version is based on judgment of whether each test word is correct or incorrect rather than assessing production of individual sounds. It thus can be administered by nonprofessionals.

The *Arizona Articulation Proficiency Scale—Revised* (Fudala, 1974) assigns a value to each consonant and vowel sampled, and the total points that a child accumulates by saying phonemes correctly is compared to a standard score for his or her age. The child's articulation is then indicated as normal, moderately deviant, or severely deviant based on this comparison. Values accumulated are also related to intelligibility. This tool may be attractive to clinicians who need to document that children's phonology is severely delayed in order to provide them with intervention.

The *Kahn-Lewis Phonological Analysis* (1986) utilizes the stimulus words presented in the *Goldman-Fristoe Test of Articulation* and details the phonological processes that are evidenced in various error productions of each stimulus word. Like the original scoring procedure for this test, the Kahn-Lewis adaptation handles only error productions that are substitutions for correct forms. It goes beyond merely identifying the substitution, however, and aides the clinician in identifying error patterns. The test form provides guidelines for evaluating the severity of a child's phonological deviation.

Hodson (1980) has developed a procedure for analyzing children's phonological processes from their single-word productions. The children are asked to name fifty-five common objects. The objects are used as an elicitation procedure to assess all English consonants in prevocalic and postvocalic positions. From their errors, Hodson determines which of forty-two processes the children may be exhibiting. Hodson's processes are divided into subcategories:

1. Nine basic processes, indicating those commonly used by normally developing children
2. Twelve miscellaneous processes, involving less commonly occurring place, manner, and voicing errors
3. Thirteen sonorant deviations, including errors of vowel, glide, nasal, and liquid sounds
4. Five assimilations
5. Four articulatory shifts involving types of lisping and f and v substitutions for interdental fricatives

Hodson's scoring procedure involves indicating in a table when a particular word is said incorrectly. Checks are made in a column that best characterizes the error. For example, if the child says /tar/ for /star/, a check is made in the column labeled *cluster reduction of obstruents*. Hodson's use of phonological process to characterize errors implies that the term *process* is synonymous with deviation.

Weiner's *Phonological Process Analysis (PPA)* (Weiner, 1979), like Hodson's scoring procedures, departs from traditional articulation tests in that it focuses on discovering rule-ordered articulatory patterns rather than listing specific sound errors. Stimuli were selected to detect particular phonological rules rather than to sample all standard sounds. Test words are elicited both in isolation and in phrases through delayed imitation. The phonological processes identified by Weiner are indicated in Table 9–2 under the PPA column.

Natural Process Analysis (NPA) (Shriberg and Kwiatkowski, 1980) also focuses on rule-ordered deviations. It is a further departure from traditional articulation testing in that it utilizes a sample of continuous speech for phonological analysis rather than a test-generated sample. Eight phenomena are identified as natural processes that frequently occur in the samples of speech-impaired preschoolers and school-age children. Five processes are identical to those identified by Weiner. These are final consonant deletion, stopping, cluster reduction, unstressed syllable deletion, and liquid simplification (gliding). Weiner's "fronting" category is divided into velar fronting (/tæt/ for *cat*) and palatal fronting (/si/ for *she*) in NPA. Also distinguished in NPA (but counted as one process) are regressive assimilation (/gɔg/ for *dog*) and progressive assimilation (/dɔd/ for *dog*).

Other deviations are noted but not included in the analysis. Detailed guidelines are provided for sampling and transcribing connected speech and for interpreting observed process deviations from standard productions. Analysis includes attention to syllable configuration and contextual influence. Measures of reliability are provided, and a discussion of construct and predictive validity is included. The authors find that experienced clinicians can transcribe a 200-word sample in approximately 50 minutes, with another 50 minutes spent

TABLE 9–2 Patterns Identified for Phonological Analysis with Four Different Systems*

Lund & Duchan	PPA† (Weiner)	NPA† (Shriberg & Kwiatkowski)	Ingram
Substitutions	Feature Contrasts		
Place features			
fronting	fronting	velar fronting	velar fronting
		palatal fronting	palatal fronting
backing			
alveolarizing			
etc.	glottal		apicalization
	replacement		
Manner features			
stopping	stopping	stopping	stopping
			initial fricatives
			initial affricates
frication			
nasalization	denasalization		denasalization
affrication	affrication		deaffrication
gliding	gliding	liquid	liquid gliding
		simplification	
vocalization	vocalization		vocalization
Voicing features			
voicing			
devoicing			
Position + feature			
Context Sensitive	Harmony		
Assimilation	Assimilation	Assimilation	Assimilation
perseverative	velar	progressive	velar
anticipatory	labial	regressive	labial
bidirectional	alveolar		prevocalic
	prevocalic voice		devoicing final C
	final C. devoice		
	manner harmony		
Coalescence			
Syllable Structure			
Weak syl. delet.	Weak syl. delet.	Unstressed syl. delet.	Unstressed syl. delet.
Reduplication	Syllable harmony		Reduplication
Restricted syllable			
CV structure			reduction of disyllab.
final C. deletion	final C. deletion	final C. deletion	final C. deletion
Cluster reduction	Cluster reduction	Cluster reduction	Cluster reduction
Syllable addition			
Transposition			
			Homonymy

* See text for description of systems.
† PPA, Phonological Process Analysis; NPA, Natural Process Analysis.

completing analysis. This seems to be fairly efficient for the amount of information that is obtained from the sample.

Ingram (1981) has recently extended his original list of phonological processes identified in normal phonological development (Ingram, 1976; see our Chapter 4) to include procedures for analysis of deviant phonology. Sampling is either through use of an articulation test or a language sample. The entire elicited lexicon is then listed in alphabetical order and transcribed phonetically to show variations in production of the same word. From this list, the child's repertoire of sounds and syllable configurations is summarized. The analysis also includes identifying the phonological processes accounting for deviations from adult forms. Ingram lists twenty-seven types of phonological processes. In general, these are the same processes described by Weiner and by Shriberg and Kwiatkowski, but with more detailed distinctions. For example, Ingram divides *deletion of final consonants* into consonant type, including separate processes for deletion of nasals, voiced stops, voiceless stops, voiced fricative, and voiceless fricatives. Table 9–2 is a comparison of the processes analyzed by Ingram with *Phonological Process Analysis* (Weiner, 1979), *Natural Process Analysis* (Shriberg and Kwiatkowski, 1980), and the processes described in Chapter 4 of this book. A unique feature of Ingram's system is analysis of homonymy. He defines a homonymous form as a phonetic form of the child's that represents two or more lexical types (Ingram, 1981, p. 45). For example, a child's homonymous form /dɔ/ may mean *dog, call,* or *talk.* This analysis leads the clinician to determine the extent of homonymy in a child's language.

Syntax-Morphology Assessment   Children's ability to use syntactic rules to produce word combinations can be meaningfully described only through analyzing their connected speech. The two most common approaches to getting such a sample are through *elicited imitation* and *spontaneous discourse.* There are advantages and limitations to both sampling techniques.

ELICITED IMITATION FOR ASSESSMENT OF SYNTAX   Elicited imitation refers to a sampling procedure in which the child is instructed to imitate a model, as distinct from analysis of child-initiated imitation. The assumption behind using elicited imitation to assess expressive language is that it is an efficient and valid means for sampling the child's grammatical performance. It is efficient because sentences can be formulated to contain all grammatical structures of interest to the examiner, including those that may occur only infrequently in spontaneous discourse. The assumption of validity is based on research findings of Menyuk (1963) and Ervin (1964), among others, that a child's imitations of sentences will closely resemble the manner in which the child would spontaneously produce those sentences—that is, in general, children cannot imitate structures in sentences that they would not ordinarily use, but instead reformulate the sentences to fit their grammatical capabilities. The primary limitation of elicited imitation tasks for syntax assessment lies in the exceptions to this generalization. Some children can imitate accurately certain grammatical structures that they cannot use spontaneously, particularly if the model sentence is short or if the child is inclined to echo adult utterances. There are also children who are unable to imitate utterances which they are capable of producing spontaneously. This could be described as due to difficulty with auditory processing (Weiner, 1972), but it also demonstrates that the speech act of imitation is different from speaking spontaneously. Slobin and Welsh (1973) describe a child's inability to imitate her own spontaneously produced utterance at a later point in time when the situation is no longer appropriate for the utterance. Thus, while imitation tasks can provide an efficient way to sample many structures, they may overestimate or underestimate some children's grammatical capabilities.

When results are interpreted with some caution, sentence imitation tasks can be useful for describing many children's syntactic production. They can also provide some indication of comprehension deficit, since children cannot maintain the meaning of a sentence in their reformulation if they do not understand it. For example, if in response to the model "The girl is pushed by the boy" the child responds "Girl push boy," it appears that the passive form of the verb is not understood. Of course, we cannot be sure how the child is conceptualizing the actual event related to "Girl push boy" (i.e., who is pushing whom), but it gives a clue to possible misunderstanding of the syntactic construction presented.

While there are some sets of sentences available that are widely used for elicited imitation, such as those presented by Menyuk (1963) and Carrow (1974, see the following), it is possible to design sentence lists to meet particular assessment needs. Since the primary purpose of such assessment is to describe a child's regularities, it is best to sample each structure more than once. Several structures can be sampled in each sentence to keep the number of sentences to a minimum. Vocabulary, of course, should be well within the range of the child being assessed to eliminate confusion on those grounds. These criteria of completeness, multiple occurrence of structures and simplicity of vocabulary can also be used to evaluate published sentence imitation tests.

The *Carrow Elicited Language Inventory (CELI)* (Carrow, 1974) consists of one phrase and fifty-one sentences, ranging in length from two to ten words. It samples primarily simple clause structures; a few subordinate clauses are included, but there are no coordinate or relative clauses. Negatives, *wh*-questions, imperatives, pronouns, prepositions, and various types of noun phrases are sampled. Plural (but not possessive) noun inflection is included, and verb inflections are extensively covered. Uninflected adjectives and adverbs are included.

An elaborate scoring procedure is presented in the CELI manual, along with a training guide and tape to facilitate accuracy of scoring. If the test is to be scored for normative purposes, it is necessary to undergo this training because of the unique categorization and scoring conventions used, some of which seem of questionable accuracy. When it is used to describe regularities of production, clinicians can derive their own categories for reporting results.

The *Oral Language Sentence Imitation Screening Test (OLSIST)* and the *Oral Language Sentence Imitation Diagnostic Inventory (OLSIDI)*, both developed by Zachman and others (1977a; 1977b) are two complementary tests that use imitation for assessment of syntax. Although the goal of the screening version as described is to ascertain normalcy of function, it is not norm referenced and should not be used for this purpose. It is useful, however, in identifying particular structures that are difficult for the child. It consists of twenty sentences that include multiple occurrences of eighteen to twenty-three different morphological and syntactic forms, depending upon the language level of the child. The diagnostic test is designed as a deep test for those structures missed on the screening version. It is composed of twenty-seven individual sentence imitation tests, each with ten sentences containing a particular structure.

SPONTANEOUS DISCOURSE FOR SYNTAX ASSESSMENT   Spontaneous discourse refers to utterances that occur naturally in everyday conversations. It excludes performance on tests or elicited imitation. Assessing children's discourse has come into favor in recent years because of its ecological validity. The disadvantage of relying on discourse for assessment of syntax lies in the amount of time required for all structures to emerge spontaneously. Also, the skill and experience of the adult interacting with the child have a great influence on the richness of the sample obtained. We have discussed some approaches to eliciting discourse in Chapter 2. Here we will comment briefly on some systems for describing syntax of spontaneous discourse. The specific structures assessed by each system, including the structural categories outlined in this book, are compared in Table 9–3.

The *Language Assessment, Remediation, and Screening Procedure (LARSP)* described by Crystal, Fletcher, and Garman (1976) is based on a structural linguistic model of syntax which is thoroughly described and is in many ways similar to our description of syntactic structures. They identify seven stages of syntactic development corresponding to chronological age (nine months to four years, six months) and describe the syntactic characteristics of each stage. Analysis of structures present and absent at the child's age level leads to remediation goals. Assignment of particular features to the various levels is based on the literature in developmental psycholinguistics and apparently the authors' experience with this assessment procedure. Several "patterns" of language disabilities are discussed that correspond to profiles obtained from the *LARSP,* but no normative data are presented, since the emphasis is on describing individual children's regularities.

The *Language Sampling, Analysis, and Training (LSAT)* procedure described by Tyack and Gottsleben (1974) relies on a 100-sentence sample of spontaneous speech. The child is assigned a "linguistic level" based on a ratio of mean number of words to mean number of morphemes per sentence. For each level, there is an inventory of grammatical features that according to the authors should be expected for children at or above that level. The data for this assignment of grammatical features to various levels come from a study of fifteen normal and fifteen language-deviant children (Morehead and Ingram, 1973) and should not be interpreted as a standardized measure. Various types of clause structures are included in analysis, as well as negatives, questions, pronouns, prepositions, and conjunctions. Noun and verb inflections are thoroughly covered. As the title implies, the analysis portion of this procedure is designed to lead directly to identification of therapy goals and training, which is touched upon in the manual.

The *Developmental Sentence Types (DST)*, described by Lee (1966; 1974) and followed by *Developmental Sentence Scoring (DSS)* (Lee, 1974; Lee and Canter, 1971), was the first widely used approach to analysis of spontaneous discourse.

TABLE 9–3 Comparison of Grammatical Structures Analyzed Using Different Language Sample Analysis Procedures

Structure	LARSP	LSAT	DSS	L&D
Noun Phrase Structure				
Articles	+	+	−	+
Demonstratives	+	+	+	+
Possessives	−	+	−	+
Adjectives	+	+	−	+
Qualifiers	G	G	+	+
Quantifiers	G	+	+	+
Ordinals	G	G	+	+
Initiators		G	−	+
Pronouns		+	+	+
Subject	G	G	+	+
Object	G	G	+	+
Possessive	G	G	+	+
Reflexive	G	G	+	+
Indefinite	G	G	+	+
Verb Phrase Structure				
Verb	+	+	+	+
Copula	+	+	+	+
Auxiliaries	+	+	+	+
Modals	+	+	+	+
Particles	+	+	−	+
Irregular past tense	+	+	+	+
Regular past tense	+	+	+	+
Present participle	+	+	+	+
Past participle	+	+	+	+
Third person singular indicative	+	+	+	+
Passive	+	−	+	+
Questions	+	+	+	+
Rising intonation	−	G	−	+
Auxiliary inversion	+	G	+	+
Do insertion	−	G	+	+
Tags	+	G	+	+
Wh- questions	+	G	+	+
Negatives	+	+	+	+
Simple Clause Structure	+	+	−	+
Complex Clauses				
Compound	+	+	+	+
Subordinate	+	+	+	+
Relative	+	+	−	+
Other	+	+	G	G
Other Parts of Speech				
Prepositions	−	+	−	+
Adverbs	+	+	−	+
Gerunds, infinitives	−	+	+	+

LARSP = Language Assessment, Remediation, and Screening Procedure
LSAT = Language Sampling, Analysis, and Training
DSS = Developmental Sentence Scoring
L&D = Lund and Duchan
+ means system analyzes this feature
− means system does not analyze this feature
G means system does not specify this feature but covers general area

DST is based on 100 utterances and is used primarily to classify *presentence* utterances according to the grammatical relationship between the words produced. It distinguishes between noun phrases, clauses with lexical verbs, clauses with implied copulas, and *fragments* that have no subject or verb, such as prepositional phrases. Morphological inflections and some syntactic features are noted as elaborations and modifications of basic sentence types. Since this is intended to be a descriptive measure rather than normative, Lee encourages clinicians "to modify, enlarge, or simplify the DST procedure in any way that is appropriate to their needs" (Lee, 1974, p. 131).

The DSS analysis is based on fifty consecutive utterances that contain a subject and verb, thus qualifying them as sentences. Scores are assigned for each pronoun, verb, negative, question, and conjunction used, with the size of the score depending on the identified developmental sequence within each category. Many morphological and syntactic forms are thus not scored. The total score can be compared to norms presented or compared on subsequent analysis to assess progress over time. In view of the considerable time and training involved in using this procedure, analysis beyond derived scores would be warranted. DSS uses standard dialect for the criterion for correctness of production, and Lee cautions against using this analysis with children who come from other language backgrounds. There is an unpublished version of a scoring procedure based on DSS categories to be used with Black English dialect speakers (Nelson, 1983). Toronto (1973) has published a version of DSS for Spanish speakers.

The *Index of Productive Syntax* (*IPSyn*) developed by Scarborough (1990) is based on four subscales of Miller's ASS procedure: noun phrase, verb phrase, questions and negatives, and sentence structure. Items were eliminated that were very infrequent or did not distinguish between ages. A scoring system assigns points for different structures used, and credit is given for developmentally earlier items if more mature forms are used. A scoresheet lists fifty-six grammatical forms, with items arranged for difficulty within each subscale. Items of comparable difficulty are arranged at same height on the page for ready comparison. Each item is scored 0, 1, or 2 depending on frequency; only the first two occurrences of each structure are tallied and written down. The IPSyn is reliable and age sensitive from twenty-four to forty-eight months. The recommendation is to use at least one hundred utterances whenever possible, but Scarborough provides a conversion table to estimate score with as few as fifty utterances. No norms are available as the IPSyn has not been used yet with large samples. Scarborough (1990) suggests generating local norms and adapting the Index to meet specific needs. It appears to be most suitable for comparing or matching groups of subjects and research groups with respect to overall syntactic complexity.

COMPUTER-ASSISTED SAMPLE ANALYSIS The last decade has seen increasing emphasis on the development of computer software to assist with analysis of spontaneous speech and language samples (e.g., see Hubbell, 1988; Lahey, 1988; Klee, 1985; and Schwartz, 1985, for reviews). Computer versions of some existing analysis systems have been developed (e.g., *CALARSP*). Two of the most sophisticated and widely used programs for language analysis are the *Systematic Analysis of Language Transcripts* (*SALT*) (Miller and Chapman, 1985), and the *Child Language Analysis Program (CLAN)* (MacWhinney, 1988). CLAN was developed primarily as a research tool as part of the *Child Language Data Exchange System (CHILDES)* (MacWhinney and Snow, 1985). By providing conventions for transcribing spontaneous samples, this system promotes access and efficiency for researchers who wish to share their data. With a large data base that can be accessed by microcomputer, CHILDES provides participants with cross-linguistic language samples, with data for analyzing particular structures. CLAN programs generate several analyses including MLU, frequency distribution of word and utterance length, frequency count on individual words and morphemes, distributional analysis of all forms in the sample, and number of topic initiations and continuations. It has the capability for multilevel coding and analysis, so the relationship between different linguistic systems can be investigated, such as the syntactic structure of utterances serving to initiate topics.

SALT was developed as a clinical tool as well as for research applications. Users can either carry out analysis using a number of preset programs or design their own analyses. The preset programs include distribution of complete, unintelligible, and nonverbal responses; MLU; type-token ratio; Brown's linguistic stage; and alphabetic listing and frequency of individual words and morphemes, with separate lists for question words, negatives, conjunctions, auxiliaries, and pronouns. The user-designed analyses allow great flexibility in the clinical and research questions that can be addressed, including the relationship between adjacent utterances or across speakers (Sonnenmeier, 1991). Weitzner-Lin, Lund, and Lin (1989) developed a procedure for creating a data base using SALT that allows for comparison across children. Weston, Shriberg, and Miller (1989) present a protocol for transcribing samples for use with both the SALT procedure and for phonological analysis using Shriberg's *PEPPER: Programs to Examine Phonetic and Phonologic Evaluation Records* (1986).

Semantics Assessment

SPECIFIC VOCABULARY ASSESSMENT   These tests may be identified as "conceptual domain" tests, since the vocabulary assessed is associated with specific conceptual categories. The tests are not intended to provide a measure of general vocabulary functioning, and although they present some normative data for comparison, they are more useful for identifying specific problems than for answering questions about normalcy. Thus their general deficiency in meeting standardization criteria is not a problem.

The *Boehm Test of Basic Concepts* (Boehm, 1971) includes fifty vocabulary items in the categories of space, quantity, and time, along with a miscellaneous category, that are typically used in work materials for kindergarten children. Comprehension of individual words is tested by having the child choose from a set of pictures with items arranged developmentally. Each item is tested only once, so clinicians will want to follow up this test with deep testing of items missed. Although the manual identifies the items as useful for a population of kindergarten to second-grade children, many of the items would be appropriate for use with preschoolers. There are two equivalent forms of the Boehm and also Spanish directions for each form available. Two equivalent forms of an Igbo version of the Boehm were developed (Ogbalu, Osuagwu, Oruchalu, and

Lund, 1976) and administered to Nigerian first through third graders (Ezikeoha, 1981) as part of a longitudinal study and in a comparison with the English version with bilingual fourth graders (Osuagwu, 1978).

Several researchers have developed lists of words that are likely to be understood or used by children during their second year. These lists are given to parents who are asked to indicate which words they have heard their child use. The methodology has an advantage over diary methods, where parents are asked to record their child's productions, in that they provide the parents prompts for words they might otherwise forget or overlook. Also, they group the words into semantic categories which helps parents organize their observations. The most researched of these checklists is the *Communication Development Inventory (CDI) WORDS* developed by Elizabeth Bates and her colleagues (Bates, Bretherton, and Snyder 1987; Bretherton and others, 1983; Snyder, Bates, and Bretherton, 1981). Reasonable correlations have been found between the CDI WORDS and different comprehension tasks (Reznick, 1982) and between CDI WORDS and the Bayley Scales (Dale and others, 1989). Reznick and Goldsmith (1989) divided the 615 words on the CDI WORDS into five nonoverlapping 123-word lists. The authors suggest use of the shorter lists when the child's vocabulary is being monitored longitudinally or when time or parental cooperation are limited.

A later version of the CDI WORDS, the *MacArthur Communicative Development Inventory: Toddlers (CDI Toddlers)* (outlined in Dale, 1991), combines parent information on vocabulary with parents' reports on level of syntactic development. Dale (1991) found high correlations between parent reports and a variety of structured and naturalistic assessment procedures. He further notes that parents generally enjoy the experience of completing a questionnaire, an observation previously made by Rescorla (1989).

The *Vocabulary Comprehension Scale* (Bangs 1975) has the unique feature of assessing vocabulary comprehension through use of toy objects (which are included) rather than pictures. The vocabulary items test for the concepts of spatial relations, size, quantity, and quality, and also for personal pronouns. As with the Boehm, there is only one item for testing each word, so follow-up assessment would be necessary for items.

The *McCarthy Scales of Children's Ability (MSCA)* (McCarthy, 1970) has several subtests in its verbal scale that can be useful in assessing children's semantic knowledge. In particular, there are the following:

> *Word knowledge:* In part I of this subtest, children point to five common objects and name four pictured objects. In part 2, they define words.
>
> *Verbal memory:* Part 2 of this subtest has children relate the highlights of a paragraph read to them and thus demonstrate awareness of theme as well as semantics.
>
> *Verbal fluency:* Children must name words that fall into each of four different categories within a time limit.
>
> *Opposite analogies:* Children provide opposites in an analogy form.

The MSCA is designed for children from two and one-half to eight and one-half years of age. It is norm referenced if the entire scale is used, but no norms are available for individual subtests, which is not a problem when used to assess regularities.

SEMANTIC-SYNTACTIC RELATIONS   Bloom and Lahey (1978) present an extensive discussion of semantic-syntactic relations along with an assessment approach that coordinates semantic relations with syntactic structure. This approach, which is designed for analysis of spontaneous discourse, identifies twenty-one relations that have frequently been reported in the speech of children up to three years of age. The emergence of syntactic structures to express the various relations is tied to eight developmental phases, which are based on MLU (phases 1–5) and successive samples of three children (phases 6–8). Assessment involves comparing the syntactic forms used by a child to express various relations with the description of the forms expected at the various phases. For example, attribution is described as occurring at successive phases with the following forms:

PHASE 1	single word	hot
PHASE 2	adjective + noun	dirty pants
PHASE 3	combined with existence relation	That's a yellow one.
PHASE 4	combined with action relation	Make a big tree.
PHASE 5	combined with state relation	I got a new pair.
PHASE 6	combined with locative action relation	Here goes a green wheel.

The child's failure to express particular relations can also be noted. The intent of assessment is not to determine normalcy, but rather to lead to an appropriate sequence of therapy goals.

The *Environmental Language Inventory* (*ELI*) (MacDonald, 1978) was the first test designed to assess regularities in children's use of semantic relations. It evaluates multiword utterances according to the presumed semantic roles. Eight semantic grammatical rules, based on Schlesinger's (1971) position rules and Brown's (1973) early sentence types, are assessed.

1. agent + action
2. action + object
3. agent + object
4. agent or object + location
5. action + location
6. negation + X
7. modifier + head (attribution)
                                       (possession)
                                       (recurrence)
8. introducer + X

Description of these rules is included in the manual. The child's expression of each semantic relation is sampled three times for a total of twenty-four items. Each item consists of a nonlinguistic cue (object or event), a conversational cue (e.g., "What did I do?"), and an imitation cue (e.g., "Say, 'Kick big ball'"). The child is presented the conversation cue twice for each item, before and after the imitation cue. This manner of presentation is to provide the clinician with information regarding the child's stimulability through imitation. For diagnostic purposes, the imitation and second conversational cue are included only if the child does not respond to the first conversational cue with an expression of the intended rule. A sample of speech in free play is also recorded and scored for semantic relations expressed as well as several measures of utterance length and intelligibility. Analysis of assessment results leads to determining goals for intervention, with suggested training procedures following a behavioral model of stimulus-response-consequence and the stimuli being the same nonlinguistic, conversational, and imitative cues used in assessment.

The ELI model of assessment and training focuses entirely on production. It is most appropriate for use with individuals with good receptive skills and expression limited to two- and three-word utterances. Before using this test, the examiner should be thoroughly familiar with semantic relations categories in order to understand the categories.

The *Assessment of Children's Language Comprehension (ACLC)* (Foster, Giddan, and Stark, 1973) was not formulated on a semantic relations model, but it can be interpreted within this framework. It was designed to assess children's comprehension of different word classes in various combinations of length and complexity. Although these word classes are identified as *critical elements,* they could be analyzed according to their semantic roles of agents, actions, objects, locations, and attributes. The test is organized into four sections. Part A is a fifty-item vocabulary test that serves as a pretest to assure that the child is familiar with the vocabulary used in the remaining sections. The remainder of the test presents combinations of two (part B), three (part C), and four (part D) critical elements for the child to interpret by choosing the right picture from several foils. Parts B, C, and D each have ten items representing several semantic relations in each. Combinations appear to be selected somewhat arbitrarily and are sometimes agrammatical ("Show me 'on table'"). Performance can be evaluated either according to the length of the stimulus by comparing scores on each part or by analyzing patterns of error on each part.

The *Multilevel Informal Language Inventory (MILI)* (Goldsworthy and Secord, 1983) assesses children's use of syntactic structures and semantic relations and the correspondence between them. Three levels of elicitation are provided: presentation of action pictures for the child to describe so as to elicit a brief spontaneous language sample; pictured stories that the child listens to and then retells to elicit more circumscribed structures; finally, single pictures to elicit specific structures. Several specific probes within each of the following categories are included: verbs, nominals, modification, adverbs, prepositions, negation, interrogatives, and conjunctions. The specific items that assess these syntactic structures are chosen to correspond roughly to the MLU level and age at which they would be expected to appear. This tool is not norm referenced, however, and is not intended to give relative rankings of individuals. The semantic relations assessed are based on Kretchmer and Kretchmer (1978) and include items taken from several taxonomies.

Pragmatics Assessment Developing formal assessment tools in the area of pragmatics presents a special set of difficulties. Since evaluating a child's pragmatic competencies involves recognition of the contextual and interactional influences, it is not possible to have a "context-stripped" assessment tool, as might be developed to assess structural components of language where attempts are made to present test items under carefully controlled conditions. Evaluating aspects of pragmatics involves comparing the child's performance under a variety of conditions, with the expectation that situational differences will lead to differing performance. The aspect of pragmatics that is generally addressed using standardized assessments is functionality; that is, identification of the intents that the child expresses in one or more situations. The pragmatics tests generally attempt to simulate a "natural" situation, such as having the child play a game or attempt to accomplish a task, while the examiner, working from a list of possible intents, indicates which ones the child exhibits. As we discussed in Chapter 3, there are problems involved in using a priori categories of intents; the tendency is to make the child's responses fit into categories that may not actually reflect what the child is intending to express. It is probably best to view these tests as screening measures, with individualized assessment being used as a follow-up when potential problems are indicated. It is likely that numerous new tests of this variety will be developed as clinicians begin to recognize the importance of pragmatic considerations in assessment. They may be helpful in stimulating the child to use a variety of speech acts, but like other tests, they should not be used to replace individually designed informal assessment when it is indicated.

Although the attempt to devise controlled, standardized procedures for measuring a child's abilities in pragmatics is doomed to failure, researchers have begun developing modified standardized procedures for evaluating pragmatic competencies. For example Simon (1984a; 1984b) in her test *Evaluating Communicative Competence* (Simon, 1984a) has compiled a set of procedures for evaluating expressive and receptive pragmatic competencies in learning-disabled children with an average word sentence length of 4.5. The receptive and expressive elicitation tasks are drawn from formal tests (for example, subtests of the ITPA) and from informal procedures. The informal procedures include asking the adolescent to give identifying information (such as birthdate and phone number), to determine absurdities in sentences and paragraphs, to play both listener and speaker in the barrier game (see Chapter 8 for a description of the barrier game), and to tell a story from a set of sequence pictures. Simon invites the clinician to analyze the information gained for syntactic and morphological forms, discourse coherence, and language functions (using Halliday's categories—see Chapter 3). Simon's taxonomy involves an unusual mixture of information, reflecting an eclectic approach. For example, she includes processing evaluations (e.g., response to rate of presentation) with analogies and the ability to follow directions.

Another pragmatics "test" has been developed by Blagden and McConnell (1983). Their *Interpersonal Language Skills Assessment* uses a standardized procedure of having a student (aged eight to fourteen years) play a table game with friends. The student's comments are tallied on a score sheet and classified into the functional categories of advising, predicting, commanding, criticizing, informing, justifying, requesting, and supporting. The utterances are also classified into errors and "nonerrored" comments. The errors are then analyzed for such things as production efficiency, grammatical accuracy, and degree of completion. While the language sampled is in only one event, it is a naturalistic situation, and the functional categories are ones likely to be important in the communicative interactions of children approaching adolescence.

Wetherby and Prizant (1990) have developed a pragmatics evaluation instrument for use with children whose functional communication abilities range from prelinguistic intentional communication to first multiword utterances. They named the test *Communication and Symbolic Behavior*. The test, normed on children from eight months to two years, is a rating instrument for abilities in seven areas of communication and symbol formation: communicative functions, communicative means (gestural and vocal), reciprocity, social/affective signaling, verbal symbolic behavior, and nonverbal symbolic behavior. The children's behaviors are elicited using naturalistic tasks such as book sharing and play. The outcome measures yield a profile of performance across areas.

Shulman (1985) designed a test of pragmatics for children slightly more advanced than those targeted by Wetherby and Prizant. Shulman's test, the *Test of Pragmatic Skills,* was normed on children from three to eight years. It focuses on determining what conventional intents children use and includes the following nine intent categories: requesting information, requesting action, rejection/denial, answering/responding, informing, reasoning, summoning/calling, greeting, and closing conversation. The intents are elicited under four contexts: a conversation between puppets, a drawing task, a telephone conversation, and a block construction task. The child's response to the tester's probe questions are ranked from 0 (no response) to 5 (contextually appropriate response with elaboration). (For a detailed description and review of this test, see King, 1989.)

Assessment of Other Areas

There are several areas of interest to speech-language pathologists that do not fall into the deficit areas we have previously elaborated. We group these together here, although they address different aspects of communication. The first two measures assess regularities in the performance of children who are prelinguistic or at the beginning stage of verbal communication. We consider these to assess precursors to language from different perspectives. The third assessment tool discussed focuses on the role of perceptual complexity and abstraction in exchanges with children.

In *Assessment in Infancy* (1975), Uzgiris and Hunt present six assessment scales based on Piaget's descriptions of the sensorimotor period of development. Each scale tests for a certain area of sensorimotor performance by eliciting specific behaviors that demonstrate cognitive functioning in that area. For example, in the scale entitled "Visual Pursuit and the Permanence of Objects," a beginning task is to observe the child's reaction to a moving object. Low-ranking performance on this task is for the child not to follow the object; high-ranking performance is to follow it visually through its 180-degree arc. This particular scale progresses from this primitive task to the advanced level of finding an object which has been seen hidden several times. Good performance on the hidden-object task is to search for it in the reverse order of the hiding sequence (i.e., looking in the last place the object was hidden, then the next to last, and so on).

The six scales are

SCALE 1:	Visual Pursuit and the Permanence of Objects
SCALE 2:	Means for Obtaining Desired Environmental Events
SCALE 3a:	Vocal Imitation
SCALE 3b:	Gestural Imitation
SCALE 4:	Operational Causality
SCALE 5:	Construction of Object Relations in Space
SCALE 6:	The Development of Schemes Relating to Objects

The scales are not scored, but behaviors are arranged developmentally within each. Use of these scales can help the clinician to structure observation of the nonverbal child; and, while it has not been demonstrated that a given level of cognitive development is necessary for the acquisition of language, some of the scales have been found to be particularly useful in predicting readiness for language (e.g., Bates, 1976; Chapman and Miller, 1980).

Translation of the findings on these scales into clinical goals and procedures is the intent of Dunst (1980) in a clinical manual developed for use with the Uzgiris and Hunt scales. Scoring sheets are included that facilitate interpretation of results, along with directions for administering and scoring the tasks.

The *Environmental Pre-Language Battery* (*EPB*) (Horstmeier and Mac-Donald, 1978) has a verbal and a nonverbal section and is intended for individuals with language skills at or below the one-word level. Prior to administration of this battery, the authors recommended completion of the *Oliver: Parent-Administered Communication Inventory* (MacDonald, 1978). With this, the parent provides comprehensive information about communication behaviors and typical activities at home. Based on this background information and initial observation, a beginning level of assessment is selected. The nonverbal section of the EPB includes a brief history of sound production and observation of "preliminary skills" (attention, sitting, object permanence, gestures), along with tests of functional play with objects, motor imitation, identifying objects, understanding action verbs, identifying pictures, and following directions. Each of these tests has four items. If response to any item is not correct, the adult first models and then physically assists the child to perform it correctly, and then the child repeats the item without assistance. This is to assess response to this training procedure. Points are assigned for each item and totaled to give a pass, not pass, or "emerging" designation for each test. Tests are supposedly arranged developmentally so that if two consecutive tests are not passed, testing is discontinued on the assumption that subsequent tests would also not be passed. Tests in the verbal section are likewise constructed and scored and include sound, single-word, and two-word phrase imitation and spontaneous production. Scores on the EPB are designed to indicate the level at which to begin intervention or to evaluate change over time. They are not normative scores.

The *Preschool Language Assessment Instrument* (*PLAI*) (Blank, Rose, and Berlin, 1978) is designed to present the child with four categories of demands, identified as (1) matching perception, (2) selective analysis of perception, (3) reordering perception, and (4) reasoning about perception. These are seen as different levels of difficulty as abstraction increases and the perceptual task becomes more complex; in the test, levels of difficulty are interwoven so that the child must be able to shift from one level to another. For each item, there are criteria given for assessing a response as fully adequate (which is worth 3 points), acceptable (2 points), ambiguous (1 point) or inadequate (0 points). Data are presented on the scores of the experimental population of three- to five-year-olds, but there are no norms for judging normalcy. Differences were found between middle-class and lower-class children. The motivation for this test was the observation that children are often confronted with demands that exceed their conceptual capacities in the course of preschool activities. Our preference would be to assess the difficulties within those contexts rather than with an instrument that decontextualizes the demands. Our observation is that children have difficulty with many of the items on this test that they might be able to do if the demands were made within the context of an ongoing event.

• • •

We have presented a chapter on formal assessment approaches with trepidation. The controlled contexts of formal texts work against our preference for naturalistic approaches, and the notion that tests can reveal information that is relevant for children's nontest communication is suspect. However, speech-language pathologists working in today's world live in a culture of formal tests and are likely to be at a disadvantage unless acquainted with the types of tools discussed here. In recent years there has been an increase in the number of assessment instruments that are less controlled in their use, such as those based on natural language sample analysis. We hope for the day that clinicians design their own structural analytic approaches to fit the needs of particular children and for when assessment to determine what the child is thinking and saying is emphasized more than assessment carried out to answer normative questions.

REFERENCES

ADLER, S. Assessment of Language Proficiency of Limited English Proficient Speakers: Implications for the Speech-Language Specialist, *Language, Speech, and Hearing Services in Schools*, 22, 1991, 12–17.

ANDERSON, R., M. MILES, AND P. MATHENY. *Communicative Evaluation Chart*. Golden, Colo.: Business Forms, 1963.

ARNOLD, K., AND L. REED. The Grammatic Closure Subtest of the ITPA: A Comparative Study of Black and White Children, *Journal of Speech and Hearing Disorders*, 41, 1976, 477–85.

BANGS, T. *Vocabulary Comprehension Scale*. Boston, Mass.: Teaching Resources Corporation, 1975.

BANKSON, N. *Bankson Language Screening Test*. Baltimore: University Park Press, 1977.

BATES, E. *Language and Context: The Acquisition of Pragmatics*. New York: Academic Press, 1976.

BATES, E., I. BRETHERTON, AND L. SNYDER. *From First Words to Grammar: Individual Differences and Dissociable Mechanisms*. New York: C.U.P., 1987.

BEDROSIAN, J. An Approach to Developing Conver-
sation Competence, in *School Discourse Problems*, eds. D. Ripich and F. Spinelli. San Diego, Calif.: College Hill Press, 1985.

BLAGDEN, C., AND N. MCCONNELL. *Interpersonal Language Skills Assessment*. Moline, Ill.: LinguiSystems. 1983.

BLANK, M., S. ROSE, AND L. BERLIN. *Preschool Language Assessment Instrument*. New York: Grune and Stratton, 1978.

BLOOM, L., AND M. LAHEY. *Language Development and Language Disorders*. New York: John Wiley, 1978.

BOEHM, A. *Boehm Test of Basic Concepts*. New York: The Psychological Corporation, 1971.

BRETHERTON, I., S. MCNEW, L. SNYDER, AND E. BATES. Individual Differences at 20 Months: Analytic and Holistic Strategies in Language Acquisition, *Journal of Child Language*, 10, 1983, 293–320.

BROWN, R. *A First Language: The Early Stages*. Cambridge, Mass.: Harvard University Press, 1973.

BRYANT, B., AND D. BRYANT. *Test of Articulatory Performance*. Austin, Tex.: Pro-Ed, 1983.

BURT, M., H. DULAY, AND E. HERNANDEZ-CHAVEZ. *Bilingual Syntax Measure.* New York: Harcourt Brace Jovanovich, 1976.

CARROW, E. *Carrow Elicited Language Inventory.* Austin, Tex.: Learning Concepts, 1974.

CARROW-WOOLFOLK, E. *Test of Auditory Comprehension of Language–Revised.* Allen, Tex.: DLM Teaching Resources, 1985.

CHAPMAN, R., AND J. MILLER. Analyzing Language and Communication in the Child, in *Nonspeech Language Intervention*, ed. R. Schiefelbusch. Baltimore: University Park Press, 1980.

CHENG, L. *Assessing Asian Language Performance: Guidelines for Evaluating Limited English Proficient Students.* Rockville, Md.: Aspen, 1987.

COLE, L. AND O. TAYLOR. Performance of Working Class African-American Children on Three Tests of Articulation. *Language Speech and Hearing Services in Schools*, 21, 1990, 171–176.

COMPTON, A. *Compton Speech and Language Screening Evaluation.* San Francisco: Carousel House. 1978.

CRONBACH, L. *Essentials of Psychological Testing.* New York: Harper & Row, 1970.

CRYSTAL, D., P. FLETCHER, AND M. GARMAN. *The Grammatical Analysis of Language Disability: A Procedure for Assessment and Remediation.* London: Edward Arnold, 1976.

DALE, P. S. Validity of a Parent Report Measure of Vocabulary and Syntax at 24 Months, *Journal of Speech and Hearing Research*, 34, 1991, 565–71.

DALE, P. S., E. BATES, J. S. REZNICK, AND C. MORISSET. The Validity of a Parent Report Instrument of Child Language at 20 Months, *Journal of Child Language*, 16, 1989, 239–50.

DAMICO, J., AND J. OLLER. *Spotting Language Problems.* San Diego, Calif.: Los Amigos Research Associates, 1985.

DARLEY, F. *Evaluation of Appraisal Techniques in Speech and Language Pathology.* Reading, Mass.: Addison-Wesley, 1979.

DEAL, V. AND V. RODRIGES. Resource Guide to Multicultural Tests and Materials in Communicative Disorders. Rockville, Md.: American Speech-Language-Hearing Association, 1987.

DEAVILA, E., AND S. DUNCAN. *Language Assessment Scales.* San Rafael, Calif.: Linguametrics Group, 1981.

DEAVILA, E., AND B. HAVASSY. The Testing of Minority Children–A Neo-Pigetian Approach, *Today's Education*, 63, 1974, 72–77.

DEYHLE, D. Learning Failure: Tests as Gatekeepers and the Culturally Different Child, in *Success or Failure?* ed. H. Treuba. Rawley, Mass.: Newbury House, 1987, pp. 85–108.

DUCHAN, J. The Elephant Is Soft and Mushy: Problems in Assessing Children's Language, in *Speech, Language and Hearing*, eds. N. Lass, L. McReynolds, J. Northern, and D. Yoder. Philadelphia: W. B. Saunders, 1982.

DUCHAN, J., AND D. BASKERVILL. Responses of Black and White Children to the Grammatic Closure Subtest of the ITPA, *Language, Speech, and Hearing Services in Schools*, 8, 1977, 126–32.

DUNN, L. AND L. DUNN. *Peabody Picture Vocabulary Test-Revised (PPVT-R).* Circle Pines, Minn.: American Guidance Service, 1981.

DUNST, C. *A Clinical and Educational Manual for Use with the Uzgiris and Hunt Scales of Infant Psychological Development.* Austin, Tex.: Pro-Ed, 1980.

ERICKSON, J., AND A. IGLESIAS. Assessment of Communication Disorders in Non-English Proficient Children, in *Nature of Communication Disorders in Culturally and Linguistically Diverse Populations*, ed. O. Taylor. San Diego, Calif.: College Hill Press, 1986, pp. 181–218.

ERVIN, S. Imitation and Structural Change in Children's Language, in *New Directions in the Study of Language*, ed. E. Lenneberg. Cambridge, Mass.: M.I.T. Press, 1964.

EVARD, B., AND D. SABERS. Speech and Language Testing with Distinct Ethnic-Racial Groups: A Survey of Procedures for Improving Validity, *Journal of Speech and Hearing Disorders*, 44, 1979, 271–81.

EZIKEOHA, N. B. A Comparative Study of Basic Concepts Acquired in Igbo by Lower Grades in Primary School in Imo State of Nigeria. Unpublished thesis, State University of New York at Buffalo, 1981.

FISHER, H., AND J. LOGEMANN. *The Fisher-Logemann Test of Articulation Competence.* Boston, Mass.: Houghton Mifflin, 1971.

FOSTER, R., J. GIDDAN, AND J. STARK. *Assessment of Children's Language Comprehension.* Austin, Tex.: Learning Concepts, 1973.

FRANKENBURG, W., J. DODDS, A. FANDAL, E. KAZUK, M. COHRS. *Denver Developmental Screening Test.* Denver, Colo.: LADOCA Project and Publishers Foundation, 1975.

FUDALA, J. *Arizona Articulation Proficiency Scale—Revised.* Los Angeles: Western Psychological Services. 1974.

GARDNER, M. *Expressive One-Word Picture Vocabulary Test.* Novato, Calif.: Academic Therapy Publications, 1979.

GARDNER, M. *Receptive One-Word Picture Vocabulary Test.* Novato, Calif.: Academic Therapy Publications, 1985.

GERBER, S., AND E. GELLER. Methods of Assessing Pragmatic Abilities, in *The Role of Pragmatics in Language Development*, ed. J. Erwin. Calif.: Fox Point Publishing, 1982.

GERMAN, D. *Test of Word Finding.* Allen, Tex.: DLM Teaching Resources, 1986.

GOLDMAN, R., AND M. FRISTOE. *Goldman-Fristoe Test of Articulation.* Circle Pines, Minn.: American Guidance Service, 1972.

GOLDSWORTHY, C., AND W. SECORD. *Multilevel Infor-*

mal Language Inventory. Columbus, Ohio: Chas. E. Merrill, 1983.

GRICE, H. Logic and Conversation, in *Syntax and Semantics 3: Speech Acts*, eds. P. Cole and J. Morgan. New York: Academic Press, 1975, pp. 41–58.

HAMAYAN, E. AND J. DAMICO. (eds.). *Limiting Bias in the Assessment of Bilingual Students*. Austin, Tex.: Pro Ed, 1991.

HAMMILL, D., V. BROWN, S. LARSEN, AND J. L. WIEDERHOLT. *Test of Adolescent Language*. Austin, Tex.: Pro Ed, 1980.

HEDRICK, D., E. PRATHER, AND A. TOBIN. *Sequenced Inventory of Communication Development—Revised*. Seattle, Wash.: University of Washington Press, 1984.

HEMINGWAY, B., J. MONTAGUE, AND R. BRADLEY. Preliminary Data of Revision of a Sentence Repetition Test for Language Screening with Black First Grade Children, *Language, Speech, and Hearing Services in Schools*, 12, 1981, 153–59.

HODSON, B. *The Assessment of Phonological Processes*. Danville, Ill.: Interstate Printers and Publishers, 1980.

HORSTMEIER, D., AND J. MACDONALD. *Environmental Pre-Language Battery*. Columbus, Ohio: Chas. E. Merrill, 1978.

HRESKO, W., D. K. REID, AND D. HAMMILL. *Test of Early Language*. Austin, Tex.: Pro Ed., 1981.

HRESKO, W., D. REID, AND D. HAMMILL. *Prueba del Desarrollo Inicial del Lenguaje*. Austin, Tex.: Pro Ed, 1982.

HUBBELL, R. *A Handbook of English Grammar and Language Sampling*. Englewood Cliffs, N.J.: Prentice-Hall, 1988.

HUIZINGA, R. The Relationship of the ITPA to the Stanford-Binet Form L-M and the WISC, *Journal of Learning Disabilities*, 6, 1973, 53–58.

INGRAM, D. *Phonological Disabilities in Children*. New York: Elsevier, 1976.

INGRAM, D. *Procedures for the Phonological Analysis of Children's Language*. Baltimore: University Park Press, 1981.

JAMES, P. *James Language Dominance Text*. Austin, Tex.: Learning Concepts, 1975.

KAHN, L., AND N. LEWIS. *Kahn-Lewis Phonological Analysis*. Circle Pines, Minn.: American Guidance Services, 1986.

KAYSER, H. Speech and Language Assessment of Spanish-English Speaking Children, *Language, Speech, and Hearing Services in Schools*, 20, 1989, 226–44.

KING, F. Assessment of Pragmatic Skills, *Child Language Teaching and Therapy*, 5, 1989, 191–201.

KIRK, S., J. MCCARTHY, AND W. KIRK. *The Illinois Test of Psycholinguistic Abilities* (rev. ed.). Urbana, Ill.: University of Illinois Press, 1968.

KLEE, T. Clinical Language Sampling: Analyzing the Analysis, *Child Language Teaching and Therapy*, 1, 1985, 182–98.

KRESCHEK, J., AND L. NICOLOSI. A Comparison of Black and White Children's Scores on the Peabody Picture Vocabulary Test, *Language, Speech, and Hearing Services in Schools*, 4, 1973, 37–40.

KRETCHMER, R., AND L. KRETCHMER. *Language Development and Intervention with the Hearing Impaired*. Baltimore: University Park Press, 1978.

LAHEY, M. *Language Disorders and Language Development*. New York: Macmillan, 1988.

LARSON, G. W., AND P. A. SUMMERS. Response Patterns of Pre-School-Age Children to the Northwestern Syntax Screening Test, *Journal of Speech and Hearing Disorders*, 41, 1976, 486–97.

LEE, L. Developmental Sentence Types: A Method for Comparing Normal and Deviant Syntactic Development, *Journal of Speech and Hearing Disorders*, 31, 1966, 311–30.

LEE, L. *Northwestern Syntax Screening Test*. Evanston, Ill.: Northwestern University Press, 1971.

LEE, L. *Developmental Sentence Analysis*. Evanston, Ill.: Northwestern University Press, 1974.

LEE, L. Reply to Arndt and Bryne, *Journal of Speech and Hearing Disorders*, 42, 1977, 323–27.

LEE, L., AND S. CANTER. Developmental Sentence Scoring: A Clinical Procedure for Estimating Syntactic Development in Children's Spontaneous Speech, *Journal of Speech and Hearing Disorders*, 36, 1971, 315–41.

LEONARD, L., AND A. WEISS. Application of Nonstandardized Assessment Procedures to Diverse Linguistic Populations, *Topics in Language Disorders*, 3, 1983, 35–45.

LINARES-ORAMA, N., AND L. SANDERS. Evaluation of Syntax in Three-Year-Old Spanish Speaking Puerto Rican Children, *Journal of Speech and Hearing Research*, 20, 1977, 350–57.

MCCARTHY, D. *McCarthy Scales of Children's Abilities*. New York: Psychological Corporation, 1970.

MCDONALD, E. *A Deep Test of Articulation*. Pittsburgh, Pa.: Stanwix House, 1964.

MCSHANE, J. *Cognitive Development: An Information Processing Approach*. Cambridge, Mass.: Basil Blackwell, 1991.

MACDONALD, J. D. *The Environmental Language Inventory*. Columbus, Ohio: Chas. E. Merrill, 1978.

MACWHINNEY, B. *CLAN: Child Language Analysis: Manual for the CLAN Programs of the Child Language Data Exchange System*. Pittsburgh, Pa.: Carnegie Mellon University, 1988.

MACWHINNEY, B., AND C. SNOW. The Child Language Data Exchange System, *Journal of Child Language*, 1985, 12, 271–96.

MARDELL, D., AND D. GOLDENBERG. *DIAL: Developmental Indicators for Assessment of Learning*. Highland Park, Ill.: DIAL, Inc., 1975.

MENTIS, M., AND C. PRUTTING. Analysis of Topic as Illustrated in a Head-Injured and a Normal Adult, *Journal of Speech and Hearing Research*, 34, 1991, 583–95.

MENYUK, P. A Preliminary Evaluation of Grammatical Capacity in Children, *Journal of Verbal Learning and Verbal Behavior*, 2, 1963, 429–39.

MERCER, J. *SOMPA: System of Multicultural Pluralistic Assessment.* New York: Psychological Corporation, 1979.

MERCER, J. What Is a Racially and Culturally Non-discriminatory Test? A Sociological and Pluralistic Perspective, in *Perspectives on Bias in Mental Testing*, eds. C. Reynolds and R. Brown. New York: Plenum Press, 1984, pp. 293–356.

MILLER, J. *Assessing Language Production in Children.* Baltimore: University Park Press, 1981.

MILLER, J., AND R. CHAPMAN. *Systematic Analysis of Language Transcripts: User's Manual.* Madison: University of Wisconsin, 1985.

MILLER, J., AND D. YODER. *Miller-Yoder Language Comprehension Test.* Baltimore: University Park Press, 1984.

MOREHEAD, D., AND D. INGRAM. The Development of Base Syntax in Normal and Linguistically Deviant Children, *Journal of Speech and Hearing Research*, 16, 1973, 330–52.

MUMA, J., R. LUBINSKI, AND S. PIERCE. A New Era in Language Assessment: Data or Evidence, in *Speech and Language: Advances in Basic Research and Practice* (Vol. 7), ed. N. Lass. New York: Academic Press, 1982.

MUSSELWHITE, C. Pluralistic Assessment in Speech-Language Pathology: Use of Dual Norms in the Placement Process, *Language Speech and Hearing Services in Schools*, 14, 1983, 29–37.

NELSON, N. Black English Sentence Scoring: A Tool for Nonbiased Assessment. A paper presented at the American Speech-Language-Hearing Association Convention, Cincinnati, Ohio, 1983.

NEWCOMER, P., AND D. HAMMILL. *The Test of Language Development.* Austin, Tex.: Empire Press, 1982.

OGBALU, F. C. Comprehension of Igbo Syntax and Morphology by First through Third Graders in Igbo Schools. Unpublished thesis, State University of New York at Buffalo, 1990.

OGBALU, F. C., AND N. J. LUND. *Igbo Syntax Screening Test.* Unpublished manuscript. Owerri, Nigeria: Alvan Ikoku College of Education, 1976.

OGBALU, F. C., B. I. N. OSUAGWU, O. ORUCHALU, AND N. J. LUND. *Igbo Test of Basic Concepts.* Unpublished manuscript. Owerri, Nigeria: Alvan Ikoku College of Education, 1976.

OLLER, J. *Language Tests at School.* London: Longman, 1979.

OSUAGWU, B. I. N. Comparison of Basic Concepts Acquired in Igbo and English by fourth Graders in Imo State. Unpublished thesis, State University of New York at Buffalo, 1978.

PRATHER, E., S. BREECHER, M. STAFFORD, AND M. WALLACE. *Screening Test of Adolescent Language.* Seattle, Wash.: University of Washington Press, 1980.

PRUTTING, C., T. GALLAGHER, AND A. MULAC. The Expressive Portion of the N.S.S.T. Compared to a Spontaneous Language Sample, *Journal of Speech and Hearing Disorders*, 40, 1975, 40–48.

PRUTTING, C., AND D. KIRCHNER. Applied Pragmatics, in *Pragmatic Assessment and Intervention Issues in Language*, eds. T. Gallagher and C. Prutting. San Diego, Calif.: College Hill Press, 1983, pp. 29–64.

PRUTTING, C., AND D. KIRCHNER. A Clinical Appraisal of the Pragmatic Aspects of Language, *Journal of Speech and Hearing Disorders*, 52, 1987, 105–19.

RESCORLA, L. The Language Development Survey: A Screening Tool for Delayed Language in Toddlers. *Journal of Speech and Hearing Disorders*, 54, 1989, 587–599.

REZNICK, J. S. The Development of Perceptual and Lexical Categories in the Human Infant. Unpublished doctoral dissertation, University of Colorado, Boulder, 1982. Cited in J. S. Reznick and L. Goldsmith, A Multiple Form Word Production Checklist for Assessing Early Language, *Journal of Child Language*, 16, 1989, 91–100.

REZNICK, J. S., AND L. GOLDSMITH. A Multiple Form Word Production Checklist for Assessing Early Language, *Journal of Child Language*, 16, 1989, 91–100.

ROTH, F., AND N. SPEKMAN. Assessing the Pragmatic Abilities of Children: Part 1. Organizational Framework and Assessment Parameters, *Journal of Speech and Hearing Disorders*, 49, 1984, 2–11.

RUEDA, R., AND J. PEROZZI. A Comparison of Two Spanish Tests of Receptive Language, *Journal of Speech and Hearing Disorders*, 42, 1977, 210–15.

SALVIA, J., AND J. YSSELDYKE. *Assessment in Special and Remedial Education.* Boston: Houghton Mifflin, 1978.

SAVILLE-TROIKE, M. Anthropological Considerations in the Study of Communication, in *Nature of Communication Disorders in Culturally and Linguistically Diverse Populations*, ed. O. Taylor. San Diego, Calif.: College Hill Press, 1986, Chap. 3, pp. 47–72.

SCARBOROUGH, H. S. Index of Productive Syntax, *Applied Psycholinguistics*, 11, 1990, 1–22.

SCHLESINGER, I. Production of Utterances and Language Acquisition, in *The Ontogenesis of Grammar*, ed. D. Slobin. New York: Academic Press, 1971.

SCHWARTZ, A. Microcomputer-Assisted Assessment of Linguistic and Phonological Processes, *Topics in Language Disorders*, 6, 1985, 26–40.

SEARS, R. Your Ancients Revisited: A History of Child Development, in *Review of Child Development Research* (Vol. 5.) ed. E. Hetherington. Chicago: University of Chicago Press, 1975.

SEMEL, E., AND E. WIIG. *Clinical Evaluation of Language Functions.* Columbus, Ohio: Chas. E. Merrill, 1980.

SHRIBERG, L. *PEPPER: Programs to Examine Phonetic and Phonologic Evaluation Records.* Madison: Software Development and Distribution Center, University of Wisconsin, 1986.

SHRIBERG, L., AND J. KWIATKOWSKI. *Natural Process Analysis: A Procedure for Phonological Analysis of Continuous Speech Samples.* New York: John Wiley, 1980.

SHULMAN, B. *Test of Pragmatic Skills.* Tucson, Ariz.: Communication Skill Builders, 1985.

SIEGEL, G., AND P. BROEN. Language Assessment, in *Communication Assessment and Intervention Strategies,* ed. L. Lloyd. Baltimore: University Park Press, 1976.

SIMON, C. *Evaluating Communicative Competence: A Functional-Pragmatic Procedure.* Tucson, Ariz.: Communication Skill Builders, 1984a.

SIMON, C. Functional-Pragmatic Evaluation of Communication Skills in School-Aged Children, *Language, Speech, and Hearing Services in Schools,* 15, 1984b, 83–97.

SLOBIN, D., AND C. WELSH. Elicited Imitation as a Research Tool in Developmental Psycholinguistics, in *Studies in Child Language Development,* eds. C. Ferguson and D. Slobin. New York: Holt, Rinehart & Winston, 1973.

SNYDER, L., E. BATES, AND I. BRETHERTON. Content and Context in Early Lexical Development, *Journal of Child Language,* 8, 1981, 565–82.

SONNENMEIER, R. New Approaches to Language Sampling: Application of Computer Analysis Programs. New York State Speech-Language Hearing Convention, 1991.

TOLIVER-WEDDINGTON, G., AND J. ERICKSON. Suggestions for Using Standardized Tests with Minority Children, in *Multicultural Literacy in Communication Disorders: A Manual for Teaching Cultural Diversity Within the Professional Education Curriculum,* ed. L. Cole. Washington, D. C.: ASHA, 1991.

TORONTO, A. *Screening Test of Spanish Grammar.* Evanston, Ill.: Northwestern University Press, 1973.

TORONTO, A., D. LEVERMAN, C. HANNA, P. ROSENZWEIG, AND A. MALDONADO. *Del Rio Language Screening Test.* Austin, Tex.: National Educational Laboratory Publishers, Inc., 1975.

TYACK, D., AND R. GOTTSLEBEN. *Language Sampling, Analysis and Training: A Handbook for Teachers and Clinicians.* Palo Alto, Calif.: Consulting Psychologists Press, 1974.

UZGIRIS, I., AND J. McV. HUNT. *Assessment in Infancy.* Urbana, Ill.: University of Illinois Press, 1975.

VAUGHN-COOKE, F. Improving Language Assessment in Minority Children, *ASHA,* 25, 1983, 29–34.

VAUGHN-COOKE, F. The Challenge of Assessing the Language of Nonmainstream Speakers, in *Treatment of Communication Disorders in Culturally and Linguistically Diverse Populations,* ed. O. Taylor. San Diego, Calif.: Little, Brown, 1986, Chap. 2, pp. 23–48.

WEINER, F. *Phonological Process Analysis.* Baltimore: University Park Press, 1979.

WEINER, F., E. LEWNAU, AND E. ERWAY. Measuring Language Competency in Speakers of Black American English, *Journal of Speech and Hearing Disorders,* 48, 1983, 76–84.

WEINER, P. The Perceptual Level Functioning of Dysphasic Children: A Follow Up Study, *Journal of Speech and Hearing Research,* 15, 1972, 423–38.

WEITZNER-LIN, B., N. J. LUND, AND W. LIN. Computer Assisted Language Assessment: Creating a Database. New York State Speech Language Hearing Convention, 1989.

WESTON, A., L. SHRIBERG, AND J. MILLER. Analysis of Language-Speech Samples with SALT and PEPPER, *Journal of Speech and Hearing Research,* 32, 1989, 755–66.

WETHERBY, A., AND B. PRIZANT. *Communication and Symbolic Behavior Scales—Research Edition.* Chicago, Ill.: Riverside Publishing, 1990.

WIIG, E., AND E. SEMEL. *Language Assessment and Intervention for the Learning Disabled.* Columbus, Ohio: Chas. E. Merrill, 1980.

WILCOX, K., AND S. AASBY. The Performance of Monolingual and Bilingual Mexican Children on the TACL, *Language, Speech, and Hearing Services in Schools,* 19, 1988, 34–40.

WOLFRAM, W. Test Interpretation and Sociolinguistic Differences. *Topics in Language Disorders,* 3, 1983, 8–20.

ZACHMAN, L., R. HUISINGH, C. JORGENSEN, AND M. BARRETT. *The Oral Language Sentence Diagnostic Inventory.* Moline, Ill.: Linguisystems, 1977a.

ZACHMAN, L., R. HUISINGH, C. JORGENSEN, AND M. BARRETT. *The Oral Language Sentence Imitation Screening Test.* Moline, Ill.: Linguisystems, 1977b.

ZIMMERMAN, I., V. STEINER, AND R. EVATT. *Preschool Language Scale.* Columbus, Ohio: Chas. E. Merrill, 1979.

Index

AUTHOR INDEX

NOTE: Page numbers in italics are References entries.

371

Welsh, C., 218, *240*, 354, *369*
Werdenschlag, L., 246, *266*
Werner, H., 67, *108*
West, C., 80, *108*
Westby, C., 7, *15*, 24, 27, *53*, 272, 278, *323*
Weston, A., 358, *369*
Wetherby, A., 36, *53*, 89, 90, 95, *108*, 363, *369*
Wexler, K., *108*
White, R., 73, 79–80, *108*
White, S., 73, 79–80, *108*
Wiebe, J., 286, *323*

Wiederholt, L., *367*
Wieman, L., 302, *323*
Wiig, E., 324, 344, *369*
Wilcox, K., 343, *369*
Wilkinson, L., 309, *320*
Winkler, E., *106*
Winner, E., 254, 255, 262, *264*, *266*
Witkowska-Stadnir, K., *323*
Wode, H., 221, *240*
Wolfe, J., 167, *186*
Wolfram, W., 132, 171, *185*, *187*, 334, 336, *369*
Wollner, S., 89, *108*
Woodcock, R., 3, *14*

Wright Cassidy, K., *106*
Wysocka, H., *323*

Yoder, D., 339, 344, *368*
Yoder, P., 74, 81, *108*
Yonclas, D., 90, 95, *108*
Young, K., 306, *323*
Ysseldyke, J., 326, 346, *368*
Yule, G., 294, 295, 297, 305, *319*

Zachman, L., 354, *369*
Zaslow, M., 69, *106*
Zimmerman, I., 338, *369*
Zubin, D., 199, *240*, *319*

SUBJECT INDEX